T0386752

A HOUSE BY THE RIVER

A HOUSE BY THE RIVER

West Indian Wealth in West Devon: Money, Sex and Power over Three Centuries

Malcolm Cross

Signal Books

First published in 2022 by
Signal Books Limited
36 Minster Road
Oxford OX4 1LY
www.signalbooks.co.uk

© Malcolm Cross, 2022

The right of Malcolm Cross to be identified as the author of this work has been asserted by him in accordance with the Copyright, Design and Patents Act, 1988.

All rights reserved. The whole of this work, including all text and illustrations, is protected by copyright. No parts of this work may be loaded, stored, manipulated, reproduced or transmitted in any form or by any means, electronic or mechanical, including photocopying and recording, or by any information, storage and retrieval system without prior written permission from the publisher, on behalf of the copyright owner.

A catalogue record for this book is available from the British Library

ISBN 978-1-8384630-07 Cloth

Cover Design: Tora Kelly
Typesetting: Tora Kelly
Cover Images: 'Maristow, Seat of Sir Manasseh Lopes, Bart', FWL Stockdale, 1826 (Rostron & Edwards); sugar cane, Jamaica, 1891 (Valentine & Sons)
Printed in India by Imprint Press

Contents

Acknowledgments

This book is a product of Wilde's aphorism that 'I never put off till tomorrow what I can possibly do – the day after'. It has, however been an enjoyable journey even if from time to time I cannot recall why I started out on it. Perhaps it was the beguiling setting of Maristow House; what the seventeenth-century antiquarian, Tristram Risdon, is reputed to have called 'the genius of the scene'.

Along the way I have accumulated an extraordinary number of debts for kindness and assistance. Chief among them are those owing to numerous archivists of county collections, most notably the Plymouth and West Devon Record Office now successfully deported from their improbable home on an industrial estate to the luxury of a corner in The Box, tacked on to the old museum and art gallery in the city centre. In a welcome age of rehousing the past, the same gratitude should be recorded for the staff of the Cornwall Records Office, now freed from their dilapidated temporary home in Truro to the splendour of their newly converted brewery in Redruth (Kresen Kernow/Cornwall Centre). Among other archives whose help is gratefully acknowledged are the Bodleian Library, the National Archives, Norfolk Records Office, Westminster Abbey Library and West Sussex Records Office.

The last third of this book would have been much less well informed without the assistance offered from the Hon George Lopes, brother of Henry, the late 3rd Baron Roborough, whose enthusiasm for his family's history was infectious. It is a pleasure too to thank Jeanette Corniffe for research assistance in Jamaica. Others who went above and beyond to offer information and advice include Barbara Chaworth-Musters, Kristen Costa (Newport Restoration Foundation), Fiona Eastman, Elizabeth Frankish, James Gelly, Professor Hilary J. Grainger, Clare Greener, Tony Harding, Susan Hardy, John Harbord-Hamond, Joe Hess (Maristow Estate),

Julian Land, Fiona Megeary, Kit Martin, Dr Martin Myrone (Tate Gallery), Helen Pegg, Alan Pereira, Rev. Hazel Robinson, David Rymill (Highclere Estate), Dr Annette Schlagenhauff (Indianapolis Museum of Art), Professor Michael Silber, Geoffrey Todd, Dame Gillian Wagner and Joe Weber (American Jewish Archives).

My wife, Jette Johst, made many helpful suggestions for improving the text as did James Ferguson, prime mover of Signal Books, who, unusually, appears to read the books he publishes. Brenda Stones dealt admirably with indexing and with identifying some inconsistencies in the text, and sincere thanks to Tora Kelly for her first rate design and layout skills. Sadly, only I can be held responsible for what errors and absurdities remain but for all four a reminder of Mark Twain's lament: 'I would have written a shorter book, but I did not have the time'.

MC

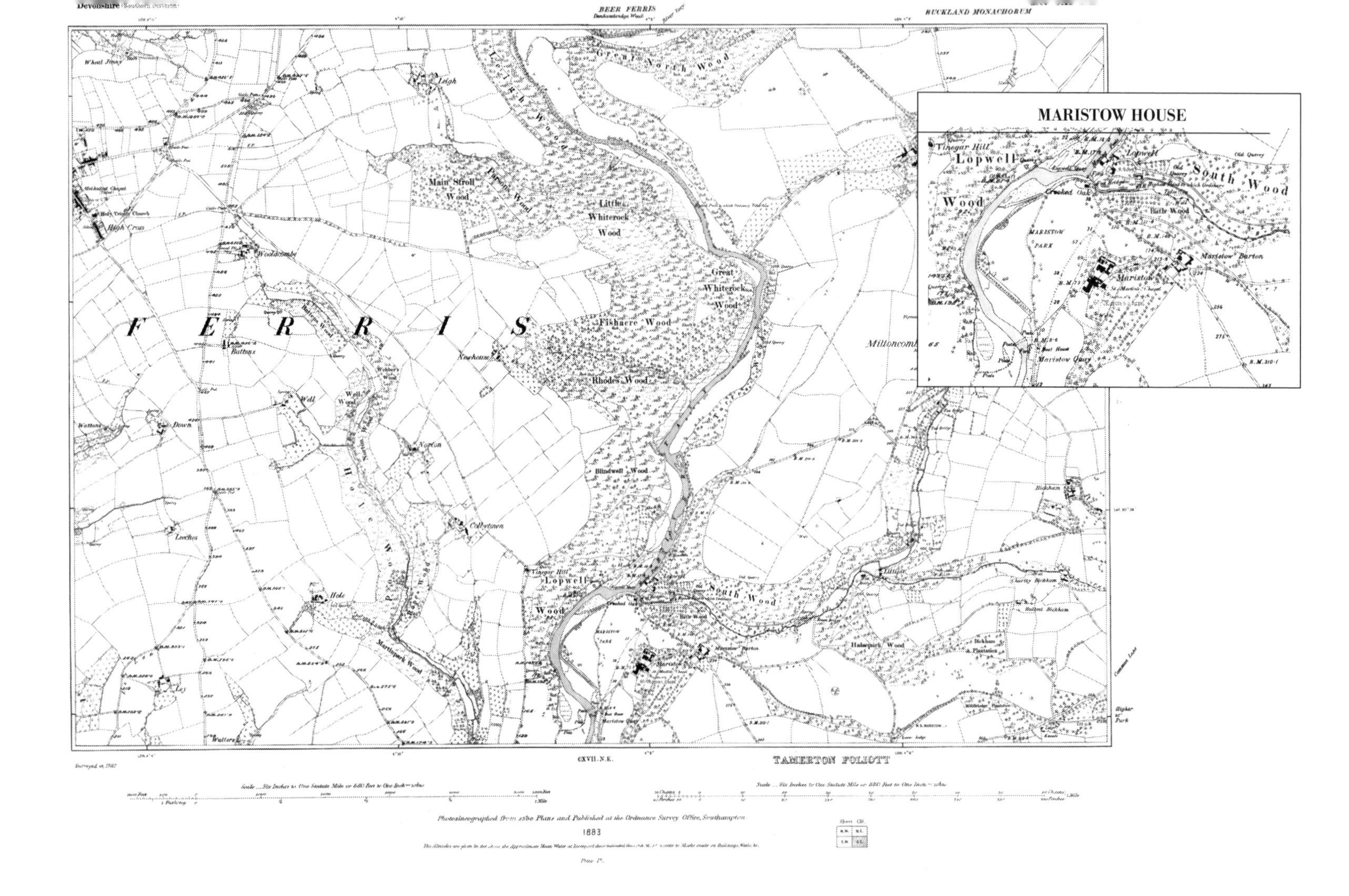
Devonshire
BEER FERRIS
BUCKLAND MONACHORUM
MARISTOW HOUSE
Vinegar Hill
Lopwell
South Wood
Wood
Crooked Oak
Bathe Wood
MARISTOW PARK
Maristow Barton
Maristow
Maristow Quay
Great North Wood
Main Stroll Wood
Little Whiterock Wood
Great Whiterock Wood
Fishacre Wood
Rhodes Wood
Blindwell Wood
F E R R I S
Whiterock
Newhouse
Woolacombe
High Cross
Leigh
Well
Down
Norton
Colytown
Leeches
Hole
Martinpark Wood
Ley
Miltoncombe
Halsepark Wood
Bickham
Charity Bickham
Higher Park
CXVII. N.E.
TAMERTON FOLIOTT
1883

Introduction

The history of a house for any but the most ardent student of architecture appears at first sight to be an eccentric pursuit. But once it is seen as the physical embodiment of those it shelters, the story becomes more engaging. Houses are perhaps one of the most critical components of material culture; they express identities, tastes and predilections but more important, where they embrace the wealthy and are viewed over time they can become a portal through which to appreciate economic and social change on a much larger canvas. Large estates and the houses they contain confirm wealth, reflect prestige and establish credentials for asserting the right to titles and political influence. In the case of Maristow House, located on a tongue of flat land on the eastern banks of the River Tavy in West Devon, just before its confluence with the Tamar, each of those processes, namely wealth creation, the quest for societal esteem and the demand for entry into the halls of political power, is part of a West Indian-British story dating back to the very earliest years of engagement with the Caribbean in the first half of the seventeenth century and ending in the middle of the twentieth (Plate 1).

Studies based on country houses and estates are not unusual but they tend to be either *sui generis*, perhaps concentrating on their unique architectural features, or examined through the prism of one social class, perhaps a lord of the manor from one particular family. Maristow is unusual in being owned over this period by three separate families each of which illustrates one vital strand of this West Indian encounter. To argue that three themes capture a tale over three centuries is doubly disingenuous. It might suggest to some that there is a comfortable fit; one topic per century. That is an obvious fiction. Even more fictitious is the proposition that any one theme is the hallmark of any period, however defined. And yet, when some historians can cheerfully till a field as small as a suburban lawn, simplification and an element of abstraction are essential in order to justify the selection of events from which the narrative of history is constructed. In those that have been selected for this study, some may detect an echo of that great German political economist and historian, Max Weber, who presented in the early years of the twentieth century a survey of European civilisation from Antiquity onwards that revealed an unrivalled grasp of the links between economic opportunities, social prestige and political institutions.[1] Social groups, be they based on kin, community, ethnicity or religion, could lay claim to legitimacy on various grounds including their pre-eminence in controlling wealth, in social esteem or in their mastery of political institutions. Clearly all three operate at the same time and interact, so that accepted social position might influence access to avenues to wealth and political position or the other way round. What made Weber particularly important was the realisation that one or other of these claims to power and authority could emerge as central in one period or in one location, while in others the profile might change. While money might frequently matter above all when it came to making the greatest difference to historical events, at other times political clashes affect all, and in some other circumstances cultural forces, such as religious beliefs, might come to shape how money was made and how politics were practised.

Examining the flow of events on such a wide canvas undoubtedly has its attractions but it also has profound weaknesses. Looked at through the microscope, as it were, two additional variables immediately come into focus. The first is that individuals make a real difference; they make inspired or stupid decisions, they curtail options because of beliefs, they order and reorder priorities on the basis of sentiment and affection, as well as material or other interest

1 Max Weber (1956) *Wirtschaft und Gesellschaft* translated as Roth, G and Wittich, C (eds) (1968) *Economy and Society*, Berkeley, University of California Press. What is remarkable about Weber's threefold categorisation of modes of ascent into the bastions of power is that they are the only pathways available. They may, of course, be mixed at any historical moment, and in the vast majority of cases will be.

and, above all, they disagree with each other, so that outcomes may become a matter of who can win the day. What actually happens at the ground level at any particular time will be constrained by decisions made earlier, but a second factor also enters the picture: that of the unexpected or of chance. An early death can affect inheritance; an act of dishonesty can derail well-laid plans; a chance encounter can open options that were never before considered. People make history but not entirely as they choose; they are in practice constrained by the pressures and opportunities of the age they live in, by beliefs that they have internalised and by options that appear one day to be open and by the next, closed.[2]

The Context

The seventeenth century in England was marked by political, economic and religious turmoil. Men of property in particular were likely to become embroiled in political struggles leading up to and during the Civil War, which in turn had a marked effect on economic fortunes, while religious tensions produced both internal and external crises. Reform meant controlling the over-weaning power of the monarch. Politics, if not exactly pointless, was not very appealing. Were you on the side of the king or the families and interests who opposed his unbridled power? Whatever space there was for social mobility was limited. If you were not part of these struggles why not seek your fortune overseas? If you could use political preferment to make money, so much the better, and if more could be made by using slave labour to cut costs then for many the end justified the means.

One option was to seek one's fortune in the newly established colonies in the Caribbean and one family, closely linked to Maristow, did precisely that and by so doing played a leading role in inventing

2 It was Karl Marx who first made this observation in *The Eighteenth Brumaire of Louis Napoleon* (1869). The usual translation runs as follows: 'Men make their own history, but they do not make it just as they please; they do not make it under circumstances chosen by themselves, but under circumstances directly encountered, given and transmitted from the past.'

plantation slave society. Many fine houses nestling in the English countryside owe their existence to the exploitation of slave labour but this one was built, or rather rebuilt, by pioneers of the art. The mechanism for extracting wealth from unfree labour was the plantation itself and the seventeenth-century owner of Maristow House worked assiduously with his older brother to create it. They were not alone but remarkable nonetheless for their success.

The eighteenth century may have lit the fuse for the industrial revolution but that was not its *leitmotif*, whereas the frippery and foppery of Georgian England certainly was. Sex and sensibility sounds Austenesque, and the author herself has a walk-on role in what follows, but the lead players were much less discreet, redolent in fact of what was to be rerun nearly two centuries later in the 1960s. In the eighteenth century consumption mattered as much as, or in some cases more than, production. If you had land, then it was to be used for display, particularly for that of a fine house. And if the house wasn't fine then it could be made so. If your land made money so much the better, as long as you didn't have to get too involved in its generation. Better still, extract profit from your plantations overseas when no one you knew personally was actually involved. Politics was a pastime best suited to those with the connections that really mattered. It was enough to get as close as possible to members of those elites. Towards the end of the century, disruption, even revolution, was afoot, but in the country the season mattered more than the pursuit of office. Sensuality in all its forms charted a family's rise to influence or its fall from grace.

On the Maristow estate in the opening years of the eighteenth century the scene was set for the return of a significant part of West Indian wealth; a process that was anything but smooth and led to tensions with the survivors of the old ruling class. Conflicts and reversals took up the best part of half a century before the paramount importance of the new Age of Elegance became clear. By the 1750s, trade and production had become transformed among the local elites into preoccupations with fashion and consumption, possibly captured for posterity by the man from nearby Plympton,

Sir Joshua Reynolds (1723–92), or the young man causing a stir around the Abbey Fields of Bath, Thomas Gainsborough (1727–88). What mattered now was how to penetrate the higher echelons of high society, including the royal family, rather than getting one's boots muddy in reversing decades of under-investment in modernising agricultural production. The scene was set for the landed family to be found more often in the salons of London or Bath than in the sparsely populated fields and valleys of the Devon countryside. And yet the country house itself mattered, but needed to look fine and elegant set within its own parkland. Major figures, such as the architect John Soane or the landscape designer Humphry Repton made significant contributions to the estates of the West Country. Towards the end of the century, innovations and inventions that laid the groundwork for the industrial revolution emerged, but it was revolutions elsewhere that figured in the tea rooms and coffee houses of fashionable watering holes. The independence movement in America persuaded many to repatriate their profits from the plantations of the New World while the fate of the *ancien régime* in France shattered the complacency of wealthy elites. To attempt to capture all this in the phrase 'sex and sensibility' is intended as a gloss on Jane Austen's world, but it does serve to focus attention on what were considered the essential pathways to preserving privilege. At Maristow, many hours from London, a family with four attractive daughters and no surviving male heir had to work hard to create the introductions that would lead to the maintenance, or preferably enhancement, of family fortunes.

The complexities of the nineteenth century make it harder to read but in the early years land and money mattered for they gave access to politics, and politics could be an avenue to preferment. Whatever your origins, if you could corner political influence you stood a chance of being blessed with the titles that could be used to consolidate your family's claim to social status. While it was indeed the age of empire, and of the manufacturing and trade that it both inspired and fed, from a more constrained perspective, that of political power, it was an age before the great reform of 1832 when land holdings were still of immense importance in conferring political privilege.

In the first years of the century Maristow House played host to a more authentic West Indian, but a most unusual one: not a serious slave owner but a financier of those who were, and a highly successful supplier of the goods and services they required, who used his enormous wealth to try to prise open the door of parliament itself. Being Jewish, the door slammed in his face, but by then he was not to be denied. Remarkably, he managed to found a dynasty that married low cunning with good works to become quintessentially English, but at some considerable material and personal cost. Rising above antisemitism proved to be exceptionally difficult but Manasseh Lopes can claim to have been a pioneer in outwitting this enduring prejudice, entering parliament in 1802, 35 years before Benjamin Disraeli and 45 before Lionel de Rothschild – indeed, when the slave trade and slavery itself were still very much extant.

Later in the century land became more of a burden, unless you could discover beneath it the resources that new industries needed or could use it to facilitate the movement of people or goods over its surface. Gradual emancipation based on social class added to costs and therefore the burden of land. You could hang on by reforming its use, or seek to maintain your position by educational excellence and good works. But the writing was on the wall and the country house that had accommodated each of these three phases namely the accumulation of money, prestige and political power, began to look ill-suited to any of these tasks.

The Central Focus

While the academic literature on Caribbean slavery and the trade in human beings that sustained it is now commendably substantial, that is not the main focus of this study. It is worth noting, however, that great strides have recently been made in systematising the knowledge base of what is a complex field with the intention of unearthing its effects. For example, the 'Legacies of Slave Ownership' database run by the history department at University College London is a particularly valuable resource now providing detail on more than 11,000 estates in the English-speaking Caribbean.[3] Its work started with the end of slavery in 1833 and worked back, focusing on the compensation paid to slave owners when manumission eventually occurred and its implications for Victorian Britain. This case study is concerned with earlier periods for by the time the slave trade ended, as far as Britain was concerned, in 1807 or slavery itself in 1833, no one on the Maristow estate would have had first-hand experience of the Caribbean nor would have been inclined to recognise its significance in generating their fortunes.

This database has now been complemented by an equally impressive data archive of slave voyages for the whole Atlantic world. Based at Emory University in the US, it builds on the work of many individuals on both sides of the Atlantic and now carries information on more than 36,000 such passages from the late sixteenth to the middle of the nineteenth centuries. Inevitably more information is available on the slave traders and the ships' captains than on the tens of thousands of Africans whose capture and forced transportation were the whole purpose of these voyages.[4] While it can be argued that it has taken centuries for the voices of their descendants to be heard, it would be wrong to conclude that slaves were passively submissive, as Jamaican history so clearly demonstrates.

It has taken time too for the realisation that slave-derived wealth really did affect rural Britain, as well as companies and corporations in major urban centres. It has long been known that port cities, including Bristol, Liverpool and London itself, were shaped by the constant arrival and departure of merchantmen engaged in the triangular trade. What, until recently, was less well recognised was the dependence of grand country houses on plantation wealth. In this regard, the publication in 2013 of a report financed in part by English Heritage (Historic England), *Slavery and the British Country House* (Dresser and Hann, 2013), marked a turning point. Initially, the intention had been to commemorate the bicentenary of

3 https://www.ucl.ac.uk/lbs/
4 https://www.slavevoyages.org/

the abolition of slavery by examining more than 30 country houses in the care of English Heritage to review their connections with the trade. In the vast majority of cases links with slavery were unearthed, nearly all from the West Indies, and a subsequent conference was held to consider what implications arose for improving the communication of these important facts to visitors and the public in general. Inevitably, given this brief, the publication focused on describing links rather than understanding their variability. In other words, the English Heritage report is commendable but amounts to little more than a gazetteer of country houses that benefited from slave-generated wealth. It tells you very little about the modes of extraction of that wealth or why it varied over time.

The link between the wealth generated from the enforced shipment of African labour to the plantations of the New World and the enhancing of life in the colonial metropolis is hardly a surprise, since that was often its main intention. Early scholarly attention concentrated on the contribution of slave-generated wealth to the industrial revolution, but encounters of that importance and duration inevitably had more wide-ranging effects.[5] Modern authors, writing from the vantage point of today's sensibilities, understandably view the exploitation of captured Africans as a moral outrage, but a side effect of this approach is that both sides of the relationship can become over-simplified. In fact, each phase of the encounter had different implications for both sides. Thus the early mercantilist phase of plantation development could not have been dependent upon absentee owners but demanded a physical presence, which in turn affected both life in the colony and that 'back home'. Some years later, when systems of production were sufficiently profitable to be left in the hands of paid staff, the beneficiaries were free to indulge themselves in fashionable pursuits among their social peers, thereby avoiding the oppressive heat, poor facilities and inadequate diversions from tropical agricultural production.

5 A long-standing debate on this issue was triggered by the DPhil thesis written by Eric Williams, subsequently prime minister of Trinidad and Tobago (1961–81), and published in 1944 as *Capitalism and Slavery.*

Similarly, huge tranches of West Indian wealth could not always be easily transmuted into a genteel life in the metropolis unless other conditions were fulfilled. True, this was the standard pattern, particularly after the Slavery Abolition Act of 1833, which showered even greater wealth upon slave owners for the loss of their 'property', but not all West Indians could readily avail themselves of this opportunity. European settlers in the Caribbean included some who lacked family connections in the 'mother country', and in the case considered here faced major discriminatory barriers in many walks of life, however much wealth they had accrued. One avenue to acceptance might be via political representation on both the local and national stages, but only after bending to the cultural and religious dictates of the majority. Even then, victory had to be achieved at the constituency level. Buying entry in 'pocket boroughs' was one way but only for those whose pockets were deep, and only then when the franchise remained comfortably restricted. Timing therefore mattered and in the early nineteenth century, the coming of the Great Reform Act of 1832 mattered more in effecting change than the abolition of slavery the following year.[6]

An Overview

A keen-eyed observer cannot help but notice that the spire of a chapel sits almost dead-centre in the first of the images collected in this book. A chapel, but not the one shown, predates the main focus of this study. The first chapter provides a summary of what is known of these early years. It is no exaggeration to suggest that the first house on the present site, or very close to it, owed its existence to this place of worship rather than the other way round. A reader with a constitution hardy enough to reach the final chapter will note that the chapel features again in a very different but similarly symbolic guise. What becomes clear is that by the end of the seventeenth

6 While the debates at the time rarely recognised a link between the two pieces of legislation, they were both born out of parallel thinking in the sense that broadening the franchise brought new issues on to the national agenda, including ending slavery in the colonies (see Tewari, 2013).

century, the Maristow estate was substantial, having been assiduously enlarged and developed by the Slanning family whose rocky fortunes channelled the inheritance down unexpected paths.

Chapter 2 deals with the rather convoluted fortunes of the two eldest sons of John and Marie Modyford of Exeter in their Caribbean adventures. Thomas, the elder of the two, was a larger than life figure who combined financial acuity and political nous to an unusual degree, with little attempt to hide how the latter was put to the service of the former. He rose, however, to high office in Barbados, one of the richest jewels in the English-speaking West Indies at the time, before being catapulted into the much larger but much less developed resource of Jamaica as governor, only a few short years after its seizure from the Spanish. His younger brother, James, driven by the same ethic of financial success, served as the London end of the family trading arm and later as his older brother's deputy. Together the two brothers became the architects of the Jamaican sugar plantation system and the trading nexus that sustained it. They were not solely responsible for the African slave trade but no history of this vicious mercantile system for the European possessions in the new Atlantic world could be written without them. As Chapter 3 points out, it was James who initiated the connection between Maristow House and the Caribbean in 1655 by marrying Elizabeth Slanning, the younger daughter of the civil war hero Sir Nicholas Slanning; a connection that was to survive for at least a century and a half.

The vicissitudes of inheritance are examined in the following chapter as the male line of the Slannings came to an abrupt and dramatic halt. At the turn of the century it became Elizabeth Modyford's responsibility to turn to estate management, which she appears to have done with a conservative ethos that was more concerned with convention than with profitability or good husbandry. Shortly afterwards, Lady Modyford designed a marriage settlement for her granddaughter that was both generous and, as things turned out, disastrous. On top of that, her wish 20 years before to be rid of anything to do with the slave estates of Jamaica assiduously created by her late husband and brother-in-law, created another nightmare inheritance by bringing the island back into her life through unexpectedly passing to her youngest daughter's West Indian son, the reputedly badly behaved but ambitious James Heywood. The opening of the Heywood years was anything but peaceful. An unhappy marriage with the daughter of one of the most successful West Indian trading dynasties, the Eltons of Bristol, produced a male heir, but the earlier legal settlements continued to haunt the family and new court cases cut the family in half. After a brief respite, the estate itself went into a further period of decline, overshadowed by a serious fire that made the house uninhabitable for a number of years.

The second half of the eighteenth century has been called the 'Age of Enlightenment' and it was certainly a period when both the arts and sciences blossomed as never before. All this seems to have passed the periodic occupants of Maristow House by, for they seem to have been preoccupied with fashion and in using their undoubted wealth to penetrate the highest attainable echelons of 'society'. Not for them membership of the Royal Society but rather the society of royals. Given the entrenched prejudices of the aristocracy, this must have been hard work for the head of the household was born and died without a title. That he appears to have done no other serious work is perhaps testimony to the commitment that this entailed. It also explains the wish to bathe, as much as was seemly, in the glory reflected from his brother-in-law, Earl Howe. It is true, however, that his attractive daughters were successfully elevated by arranged marriages, but even there wealth rather than aristocratic standing was the dominant currency. The eldest, however, was a reluctant party to this scheme and she managed to become one of the most fashionable women of her age largely by ensuring that she played this role on the most eminent of stages.

Chapter 6 explores the life of this extraordinary woman. Her public persona is relatively easy to trace. Married early on the command of her father to a man who was as boring as he was rich, she nonetheless maintained throughout her life a love and commitment to an earlier partner and they together conspired to ensure that plentiful opportunities arose to satisfy this relationship while at the same time seeming only to provide personal support to the royal family. This produced plenty of gossip not least because by dint of personality and persistence Sophia became a fixture in the swirl of hedonism that surrounded the Prince of Wales, later Prince Regent and, after her death, George IV.

For the historian with ambitions to follow only secure sources, the sex lives of key players are a nightmare. Individuals frequently make statements concerning their conquests that may not be true and, more commonly, seek to conceal those that are. There is no question that the evidence for some of the possibilities that this chapter explores is circumstantial and appropriate caveats are included. It is all too easy, however, to dismiss the eldest daughter of the Modyford Heywoods as either promiscuous or a flibbertigibbet, or indeed both. This is often how she was perceived in contemporary publications but it would be a mistake. While it is true that her taste for the very extremes of fashion make her appear monstrously vainglorious, it has to be remembered that she operated in a world of entitlement while herself sporting nothing more than the appellation 'Mrs'. In this day and age, where grandiose titles have a pantomime quality, in eighteenth-century London or Bath they were taken very seriously indeed. Sophia, known always after her marriage as 'Mrs Musters', was the only one of the 'three graces', whose exploits were diligently followed by the nation at large, not to have been a duchess.[7]

Chapter 7 explores some of the key points of the remaining three daughters, Emma, Maria and Fanny. Of these the most illuminating is the first, for Emma had a critically important role in helping to save the life of a distant relative, Peter Heywood, like her great grandfather of the same name, a Navy man. This Peter was arguably

7 While Antonio Canova's famous depiction of the 'Three Graces' was completed towards the very end of Sophia's life, the portrayal of the three Charites (Graces) is found in many earlier works, usually in association with concepts of beauty, creativity and sensuality. It might be argued that she had earned her place in relation to Zeus by her earlier depiction by Reynolds as 'Hebe', the bringer of wine to the gods.

the third most famous officer, albeit only a lowly midshipman, on board that most infamous of vessels, the *Bounty*. Almost always overlooked, the young Peter Heywood, a distant relative of the Heywoods of Maristow and someone who had consulted them before embarking on his ill-fated naval career, was, like Fletcher Christian, a Manxman. What emerges as they mutinied against their Cornish commander, Captain Bligh, is a tale to stir the interest of every schoolboy's imaginings. Emma's role was more prosaic but nonetheless critical for it revealed another offspring capable of being her own person and not adhering to the passivity of expectations for someone of her social class. Unhappily she paid a price that brought about her early demise.

In the final section, that dealing mainly with the nineteenth century, the house became home to a dynasty of unusual West Indians whose descendants are happily still to be found in West Devon. Chapter 8 describes the background and emergence of a true pioneer, Manasseh Lopes, the oldest son of a Jewish family of traders based in St Jago de La Vera (later Spanish Town) and Kingston. Forced by dint of antisemitic rules to be entrepreneurs and by xenophobia to rely on family connections, they became leading lights in trading companies and eventually in sustaining networks of finance and credit that supported investment in plantations and the trade in tropical produce more generally. Inevitably they were drawn in to financing the slave trade that at the time was widely perceived as just another branch of importation. Their struggles against discrimination were particularly significant elsewhere and it is no exaggeration to say that by demonstrating the economic benefits that accrued from freeing trade from restrictive burdens, they played a role, albeit unwittingly, in undermining archaic forms of labour exploitation, including slavery itself.

The following chapter focuses on the remarkable transition of Manasseh Lopes from London-based money lender and private banker to MP, baronet and aspirant member of the landed upper classes. He was helped in this quest by the archaic system of political representation that included seats that were blatantly traded, electorates that were laughably restricted and procedures for entry to the House of Commons that frequently depended on patronage from government ministers. For a variety of reasons, Manasseh Lopes's path to political influence was bumpy and wound its way from Kent to Cornwall with stops in between. In many ways he was remarkably successful, changing seats with apparent ease although at great financial cost. The obstacles he faced were also significant, mainly because he was the outsider's outsider; failing to command the loyalties offered to local squires on the one hand and triggering the prejudices of antisemitism on the other. The overwhelming impression is that of a remarkable man who, despite nearly three decades of engagement, made almost no contribution to national debates. What he did do, however, was to cultivate a dynasty of those who did, despite having no children of his own.

The next century was one of consolidation, rather than startling innovation. Sir Ralph Lopes, ever grateful for his elevation to great wealth and ready-made political access, soon lost his early liberalism and moved to become a quiet and unassuming bastion of Tory causes. He defended landed interests, opposed free trade and took a hard line against Catholic emancipation. Nothing underlined the length of the journey he had travelled more than his equally powerful opposition to freeing Jews, with whom he had once been happy to identify, from the discriminatory rules that prevented them from accessing parliament and many other walks of life. His was not an illustrious political career but gradually as the century progressed, his heir and, in turn, his son moved the occupants of Maristow House towards more significant national and local roles. Sir Massey, 3rd baronet, was a leading spokesperson for improved estate management and, although perhaps overly preoccupied with what he felt were injustices in the burden of taxation between town and country, nonetheless played a leading role in modernising agricultural practice as well as making significant contributions to charitable causes. His son, Sir Henry, failed to find a national voice but made a wide ranging contribution at county level. Hospital wards and educational buildings that still bear his name suggest just two of his and his father's many charitable contributions. These heavy commitments were, however, at the expense of the estate itself, and towards the close of his long life, much of the land was sold off and the eventual abandonment of the house itself became inevitable.

This is not a book about slavery or the trade in human beings that so disfigured many of the years that it covers. By the time the slave trade was abandoned in the English-speaking Caribbean (1807), let alone when, as part of an era of wider reform, slave owners were compensated for their lost human assets (1833), all the occupants of Maristow House had – as it were – cashed in their chips. Indeed, it can be argued that the dependency on slave-generated wealth actually declined over the period with which this study is concerned. And yet it runs through each generation, albeit in rather different ways. As is well known, the trade in slaves from Africa both helped to generate and over time was sustained by mythologies of racial inferiority. Racism was the belief structure that promoted violence as a means of control, just as sexual exploitation was a function, as it so often is, of disparities in power. Slavery is therefore with us still. It lingered and reformed in the Americas and on some estimates there are more slaves in today's world than there were in the heyday of the sugar plantations of the New World. No one should be surprised by its relevance and persistence, nor indeed that the British class structure with all its rigid demarcations fed off the slave system. In this sense, the story of Maristow House and its fine estate has become familiar. What is less well known is that it was not a static system, as archaic as it now appears. It involved buccaneering in all its forms, it helped sustain the burgeoning of the arts and sciences as well as the building or remodelling of many of the finest country houses in the land. Interestingly, it also opened doors of opportunity for those with financial acumen to squeeze under the wire of discrimination and to emerge, chameleon-like, on the other side as champions of conformity to the ways and wiles of their previous detractors.

By taking one house over three centuries, these transitions can be captured on a small scale through the stories of individuals who made a difference, particularly those who in one way or another were 'outsiders'. At the same time the story reflects larger pre-occupations that for the most part they could not have identified. The house meanwhile rose and ultimately fell; only eventually, after appalling indignities, to become a housing estate, albeit one that still to this day has elegance and beauty. As mass society in the twentieth century triumphed over rigid aristocratic elites from the century before, many country houses bit the dust and Maristow very nearly went the same way only – almost accidentally – to be saved as a retreat for the new 'ruralites', a few select members of the urban middle class.

Chapter 1

A Chapel with a House

Prior to the mid-sixteenth century, it is not entirely clear what existed on the site of the current house at Maristow. The one exception is the ancient chapel to St Martin which was located just to the east of the present chapel. This building and its surrounding land were part of the extensive holdings of the Plympton Priory. Before Henry VIII's dissolution of the monasteries, the priory of Saints Peter and Paul in Plympton, an establishment of Augustinian canons, was among the most significant ecclesiastical institution in the county. As Allison Fizzard writes, it was an 'integral part of the social fabric of the counties of Devon and Cornwall, attracting benefactions, holding extensive lands, possessing the rights of presentation to numerous churches, receiving tithes, and exercising considerable control over economic activity in the town of Plymouth' (2007: 1). The priory was re-founded in 1121 by William Warelwast, Bishop of Exeter (nephew and chaplain of William the Conqueror), and became one of the richest Augustinian houses in England (Fizzard, 2007: 9).[1] Originally established in the ninth century, Plympton St Mary in its later incarnation was unusual in receiving more than half its income from the parish churches and chapels it controlled, one of which was at Maristow (or *Martinstowe*). Chapels at Plympton, Brixton, Wembury, Plymstock, Sandford Spiney, Egg Buckland, Lanhorn, Tamerton, Thrushelton and many others were also part of its domain, each paying yearly tithes. Fizzard (2007: 61 Note 21)

1 At the time of the dissolution the priory received an annual income of £912 whereas the average income of most other Augustinian priories was little more than fifth of that sum. It is said that Bishop Warelwast was appalled at the reluctance of the existing canons to live apart from their concubines and sent them off to Bosham in West Sussex while re-founding the priory with brethren from Holy Trinity at Aldgate in London.

records that a pagan donated land at Blakestana (Blaxton) as well as the *Capellam S. Martini de Blakestana* and she goes on to say that this was a reference to the chapel at Martinstow or Martynstowe, which became corrupted into Maristow. Exactly when the grant of the chapel at Martinstowe was given to Plympton Priory is not known but there are references in the *Archaeological Journal* (Vol. 5 1848: 57–8) to two charters which confirm grants of the chapel of St Martin in the manor of Blakestane (Blaxton). The grants were made by Sibilla del Pyn, the mother of Gilbert de Ferrers, and include 'common pasture' and fisheries as well as the chapel itself, suggesting that the holdings may have been extensive (cf. Polwhele, 1797: 448). The grants were made during the period when the dean was Prior Anthony, which places them sometime before 1225, when he was succeeded by Richard de Brugiss. It was common in that period for grant documents to be re-assertions of ownership and rights, and that appears to have been the case here, so it is quite possible that the original transmission was as early as the late twelfth century. What occurred in terms of construction, alteration or land holdings over the following three and a half centuries remains something of a mystery, although the priory itself consolidated its pre-eminent position as a religious order.[2] By 1534, the struggle between the king and the pope looked doomed from the latter's point of view and on 5 August of that year, John Howe, the last prior at Plympton, acceded to the king's supremacy when the total annual revenues amounted to £912 12s and 8d (Oliver, 1846). The surrender took place on 1 March 1539 when Howe, who had been prior for just under 18 years, handed over all the properties owned by the priory to Henry VIII and retired to Exeter College, Oxford, on a substantial annuity of £120. What happened to the 20 other canons, let alone lesser staff who lived with him, is not recorded.

Just before giving up control, John Howe appears to have ensured that all the properties had valid leases and details of

2 It is relevant to note that Augustinian houses were distinctive in their belief in engaging with local communities more than would be the case for other orders (see Brooke, 2006).

these provide some information on what was contained in the Martinstowe/Maristow estate at that time. First, some of the property was assessed for annual tithes, which at the time of the abolition were leased to Edmund Langeford for 21 years at a rate of £8 per annum (Oliver, 1846: 133). Curiously, Maristow is described as a 'rectory' and is bracketed for this purpose with a chapel at Thrusselton near Okehampton (see *Lists of the Lands of Dissolved Religious Houses* PRO, 1964 No III, Vol 1, 87). Second, St Martin's chapel itself, listed as the chapel of Martynstowe under a heading of 'Plymouthe at Tamerton Folyat', was leased separately to Richard Hoper for 13s 4d per annum. Finally, 'the grange and domain' (demesne lands) at Martinstowe were leased to Thomas Whitehede for 18 years at a rent of £5 13s 4d, while the manor of Martinstowe, with all its manorial rights, was leased for a term of 40 years to Richard Eggecumbe and Thomas Whitehede at the yearly rent of £11 (with 20 shillings more at Michaelmas) (Oliver, 1846: 133). While it is important not to attribute modern meanings to some of these terms, it would appear that the priory's control extended over much more than the chapel and would have included land holdings, and associated farm buildings, together with proprietorial manorial rights and the possibility of a residential property associated with the chapel. The lessee identified here was presumably the MP, Sir Richard Edgcumbe (c. 1499–1562), born at Cotehele but busy in his mature years in building a new seat at Mount Edgcumbe.

When the monasteries were abolished an extraordinary quantity of lands, estates and buildings became available at the king's pleasure. Those of noble birth who had demonstrated their solid adherence to the Protestant cause, and who were close enough to the court to catch the king's ear, stood to gain handsomely if they offered unquestioning support for his religious stance. As far as the West Country was concerned, few were more obsequious and fawning than members of the Champernowne (sometimes Champernon or in the sixteenth century Campernulph) family from Modbury in south Devon. The Champernownes were an ancient family with numerous branches, all of which were adept at fortuitous marriages and other means of acquiring estates. Sir Philip Champernowne (1479–1545), together with his second son Arthur Champernowne (1524–78), applied to the king to purchase the manor of Martynstow (or *Marystow*) on 14 August 1544, together with tenanted lands amounting to 55 acres which were woods called Scorne Clyff Copp (16 ac.), Okeridge Copp (6 ac.) Westwod (6 ac.) Hylles Woode (3 ac.), Byckehan Grove (5 ac), Thynwood Copp (2 ac.), Martyns Wood (4 ac.) and Okeridge Wood (11 ac), within the said manor, in the parishes of "Tamerton Buckland Abbots and Martynstow, Devon, all which belonged to Plympton priory".[3]

Specifically excluded from the sale were the advowsons (right to appoint clergy to a particular benefice) and 21 acres hitherto held by the priory at Esthales Park Wood. The contract was signed and sealed at Hampton Court on 19 August 1544 for the sum of £255 11s and 6d. Just over two years later, when he was a steward of the Inner Temple, another staunch royalist, John Slanning from Shaugh, was similarly granted by Henry 'various portions of the property of the dissolved Cistercian Monastery of Buckland' (Jones, 1887: 452). In the meantime the Champernownes had lost little time in divesting themselves of their royal favours, leasing first to Rychard Eggecomb 'the Grange of Martynstow and Mansion House there with pasture in the woods' (PWDRO 70/196) for 60 years in 1546 and subsequently selling 'a wood and underwood at Maristow' in May 1549 to a syndicate of four local citizens (PWDRO 70/197).[4] By May 1550, the Champernownes had succeeded in persuading the new king, Edward VI, to grant them a licence to sell what was left of Maristow to John Slanning, whose heirs subsequently held the

3 Gairdner, J and R H Brodie (eds) (1905) 'Henry VIII: August 1544, 26–31', in *Letters and Papers, Foreign and Domestic, Henry VIII, Volume 19 Part 2, August-December 1544*: 61–87 (*British History Online* http://www.british-history.ac.uk/letters-papers-hen8/vol19/no2/pp61-87 [accessed 10 February 2020]). According to some accounts the great Sir Walter Raleigh's (Ralegh's) father (also Walter) married three times, the third being to Katherine, daughter of Sir Phillip Champernowne of Modbury, who was the great navigator's mother (Brushfield, 1883: 172).

4 This may have been the 21 acres of Esthales Park Wood hitherto reserved.

property for nine generations over one and a half centuries.[5] One of these was Nicholas Slanning, born in 1523, a nephew of John.

Nicholas Slanning was the eldest son of Nicholas Slanning of Ley in Plympton St Mary, who was in service to Plympton Priory.[6] He married Margaret Amadas and had a daughter by her. He was town clerk of Plymouth in 1546 and mayor of the town in 1564–5. In 1558 he was elected MP for Plymouth and was returned again the following year. At that time his uncle, John Slanning, owner by then of the Maristow estate and other properties at Bickleigh and elsewhere, had recently died and Nicholas' father inherited the main part of his brother's holdings, passing on a significant proportion straight away to his eldest son in May 1559 and October 1560 and the rest when he died at Plympton St Maurice in 1565. Some three years later, Nicholas made a provision of the manors of Bickleigh and Shaugh and the advowson of Bickleigh to his wife during her lifetime, but in 1579, four years before his death at Bickleigh in 1583, and not having a male heir, he left nearly all his properties to his younger brother John and his heirs but entailed thereafter to the heirs of his youngest brother, William. However, he specifically left the mansion house at Maristow to William's son Nicholas, who died in August 1589.[7] Some complexity was added to the line of inheritance because John also had a son called Nicholas and he inherited from his father in 1584 the manors of Walkhampton, Shaugh Prior, Maristow and Bickleigh and a few years later the mansion house as well on the death of his cousin.

5 The Champernownes appear to have specialised in entreaties to the king for property favours following the dissolution. John, the son of Philip Champernowne, is said by Carew in his history of Cornwall to have 'followed the court, and through his pleasant conceits, of which much might be spoken, won some good grace with the king', kneeling and begging with others for preferment in the allocation of these ill-gotten properties (Carew, 2004; 127).

6 Nicholas Slanning the elder at the time of the dissolution became entitled from the priory to a pension, livery gown, meat and drink, 4s for the shoeing of his horse yearly and grass for his horse or 5s yearly in lieu.

7 When Nicholas died on 8 April 1583 he also left a daughter, Agnes, who received £200 and an annuity of £10. In addition there were charitable donations to the poor and sick of Plymouth and Plympton and a modest sum for the church at Bickleigh where he was buried. See *History of Parliament 1558–1603*.

This Nicholas Slanning came to an untimely and unfortunate end. He was apparently murdered in 1599 by John Fitz from Fitzford in Tavistock in a drunken brawl on his way back from a tavern in Tavistock to the family seat at Ley(e) near Bickleigh. This encounter has entered the folklore of Devon and it is therefore hard to tell what precisely occurred. According to Sabine Baring Gould, Fitz was dining in Tavistock with friends in June 1599, including Nicholas Slanning, when he boasted that all his lands were held freehold. Slanning, knowing this to be untrue since Fitz held 'copyhold' (leasehold) property of his, contested this assertion and an argument ensued. The quarrel was patched up but Baring Gould writes:

> They had not ridden far when they came to a deep and rough descent, whereupon Slanning bade his man lead the horses, and he dismounting walked through a field where the way was easier. At that moment he saw John Fitz with four attendants galloping along the lane after him. Without ado, Slanning awaited the party and inquired of John Fitz what he desired of him. Fitz replied that he had followed that he might avenge the insult offered him. Thereupon Fitz called to his men, and they drew their blades and fell on Slanning, who had to defend himself against five men. The matter might even then have been composed, but one of Fitz's men, named Cross, twitted his master, saying, "What play is this? It is child's play. Come, fight!" Fitz, who had sheathed his sword, drew it again and attacked Slanning. The latter had long spurs, and stepping back they caught in a tuft of grass, and as he staggered backward, Fitz ran him through the body. At the same time, one of Fitz's men struck him from behind (1908: 188–9).

Slanning died of his wounds and was buried in Bickleigh Church where a monument was erected to his memory. He had been married to Margaret, daughter of Henry Champernowne of Modbury, and he died leaving as his heir a male child (Gamaliel). The administration of his estates was committed to that son's great-uncle. Although he died intestate, he owned at his death the manors of Walkhampton,

Shaugh Prior, Maristow and Bickleigh and under the terms of the earlier will these properties descended to William's heir, the owner of the mansion house. Jones comments on the 'fine Slanning place Ley' adding that by the nineteenth century nothing existed,

> except the balls that stood on the entrance gates, that have been transferred to the vicarage garden at Bickleigh. The situation was incomparably beautiful, and it is to be regretted that the grand old Elizabethan mansion has been levelled with the dust (Jones, 1887: 456).

If these events were as recorded, then Nicholas Slanning was murdered since he was attacked by five men. Astonishingly, however, John Fitz, the probable murderer, obtained a pardon from Queen Elizabeth I on 16 December 1599 and was knighted by James I in July 1603 (Jones, 1887: 456). Worthy, however, contends that Slanning's widow brought an action against Fitz for the loss of her husband, whereby she procured the surrender of a portion of the Fitz estate to herself and her family (Worthy, 1887: 9–10).

John Fitz himself also came to an untimely end. In 1605, on a visit to Surrey, he had made his way from Kingston-on-Thames to Twickenham, arriving in the early hours. Having persuaded an innkeeper to give him a room, he instructed the man to wake him early. On hearing the knock at the door he assumed it was the police come for him and charged out with his sword drawn and killed the unfortunate innkeeper. So mortified was he by this turn of events that he fell upon his own sword. In the opinion of the Slanning family, the owner of Maristow had indeed been murdered since the original memorial to Nicholas Slanning in Bickleigh Church contained a Latin inscription reading in translation the following:

> The author of my death was its avenger too,
> First me he foully killed, and then himself he slew,
> Thrusting into his guilty breast the fatal sword,
> Which pierced my heart; such was heaven's just reward
> (Jones, 1887: 457).

Unfortunately, the plaster memorial fell to pieces when the church at Bickleigh was refurbished in the nineteenth century. Although Jones refers to sketches of it showing the arms of Slanning and a copy of the Latin inscription, nowhere does it refer to Nicholas Slanning and in the opinion of some it was not Nicholas Slanning but his son Gamaliel who was the victim of Fitz and his men (cf. Worthy, 1887: 9–10). This seems rather unlikely since it is usually recognised that Gamaliel was the father of perhaps the most famous Slanning, another Nicholas, who distinguished himself on the Cavalier (royalist) side in the Civil War. This Nicholas Slanning was born in 1606 so his father cannot have died seven years earlier. Moreover, Gamaliel Slanning is claimed by Winslow Jones to have been born on 17 April 1589 and therefore to have been ten years old when his father died, although Jones later accepts that he may have been born in 1586, which would still have only made him 13 in 1599 (Jones, 1887: 456). Either way he is unlikely to have been the Slanning killed by Fitz in that year.

While it is clear that Maristow at this time was owned by the Slanning family, it would appear that only one branch of the family actually resided there. This appears to be Prince's view writing in the seventeenth century:

> Ley, which is in the parish of Plympton St. Mary, continued to be the residence of the family of Slanning after the purchase of the Bickleigh Estate at the dissolution of monasteries ; but after that period was probably the residence of a younger branch, the elder having removed to Bickleigh and Maristow (Worthy 1887: 10 quoting Prince, 1810).

This seems very probable, but it is not entirely clear when the Slannings of Ley moved into Maristow House. Gamaliel Slanning married Margaret, daughter of Edward and Agnes Marler of Kent, probably in 1604, when he could not have been more than 18 years old. Agnes, however, was also a Slanning, being the daughter and heir of the Nicholas Slanning of Maristow who died in 1583 (Wolffe, 2004; Jones, 1887: 459). Gamaliel therefore married his second cousin and by so doing reunited the two wings of the family and of the original inheritance. Winslow Jones records that Gamaliel settled Maristow on himself and his wife and heirs by indenture dated 20 October 1609, although probably continued to live at Ley until his death in 1612 (Jones, 1887: 459).

When Gamaliel Slanning died he left a widow and two children, Elizabeth, born in 1604–5, and Nicholas, born on 1 September 1606. This Nicholas, the most famous of the Slanning dynasty, thereby stood to inherit the West Country estates from both sides of his family. He was married on 23 September 1625 when he just turned 19 at St Andrews Church in Plymouth to Gertrude, daughter of Sir James Bagge of Saltram. He was admitted as a student of the Inner Temple in 1628 and was knighted at Nonsuch Palace on 24 August 1632 after serving in the Low Countries when, in Mary Wolffe's terms, he became 'proficient in the art of war' (Jones, 1887: 46; Wolffe, 2004).

At the age of 26, Sir Nicholas was appointed vice-admiral of both Devon and Cornwall and in April 1635 he became also governor of Pendennis Castle. Sir Nicholas sat in the House of Commons from 1640 to 1642. In April 1640, he was elected MP for Plymouth Erle and later in the same year he was returned for both Plymouth Erle and Penryn (October 1640), choosing to sit for the latter. This was a period of intense activity by many MPs against the reluctance of Charles I to heed parliament, culminating in John Pym's manoeuvrings to curtail the power of the Earl of Strafford, a powerful voice defending the rights of the monarch. Pym accused Strafford of treason through the use of a 'Bill of Attainder' (a device for determining guilt by vote of parliament). Slanning was one of a number of royalist MPs who voted unsuccessfully against this bill which had the effect of making civil war more likely. By April 1642, Slanning and others were debarred from parliament and by August, royalist forces under Sir Ralph Hopton had recruited Slanning and others to their cause, and by November he was leading one of the five loyalist Cornish regiments of foot known as 'the Tinner' from their prior employment as tin miners. Thereafter, in a series of conflicts

Colonel Slanning earned for himself a formidable reputation as a military leader in Devon and Cornwall. As the Civil War approached, Slanning's sympathies were uncritically royalist. Indeed, he played a central role early on by using his naval connection to secure much-needed supplies. It is even claimed that this support went so far as organising a fleet of privateer vessels to apprehend merchant shipping in order to seize materials for the king's service (Wolffe, 2004).

After relatively easy dominance in east Devon, the Cavaliers faced more significant opposition in January 1643 but proved supreme at the first field offensive at Braddock Down (just to the west of the village of East Taphouse off the present-day A390). The following month, when in command of two of the Cornish regiments, Slanning led a retreat at Modbury against superior parliamentary forces, but lost 250 men in the process. He was more successful when he again led the two regiments near Launceston in April 1643 although ultimately, after a battle at Sourton Down, the royalists were forced to retreat. The next test of royalist strength was at Stratton, near Bude in north Cornwall, on 16 May. Here, at a hill just north of the village, the parliamentarians had established a strong deployment under the command of the Earl of Stamford but the Cavaliers under Hopton eventually carried the day with the Roundheads losing 2,000 men (estimated 300 dead) and considerable arms. This victory, which left Cornwall in royalist hands, marked perhaps the beginning of a dominant chapter in Cavalier fortunes in the South-West. Moving east into Devon, royalist successes followed in Taunton, Bridgwater, Wells and eventually Bath. The last, fought at Lansdown Hill just outside the city, was more of a stalemate. Parliamentary forces, under their most successful commander, Sir William Waller, had established themselves on the high ground and an encounter ensued on 5 July. Eventually Waller was forced to retreat at night and Hopkins' men with Nicholas Slanning still in command of his 'Tinner' regiment claimed the ground and the city, although at a high cost in men and equipment. Worthy reports that at the battle 'Col. Slanning is recorded to have performed prodigies of valour, to have led on his followers in the mouth of cannon and musketry' during which his horse was killed under him (Worthy, 1887: 12–3). A week later a more decisive Cavalier victory at Roundway Down near Devizes in Wiltshire opened up the possibility of the king's men moving further eastwards, but in the meantime the cities of Bristol and Gloucester had to be suppressed. On 26 July, after Hopton had left the West Country and Slanning had joined Prince Rupert's forces, the storming of Bristol commenced and although the city eventually fell after 13 hours of fighting, in the process both Slanning and Trevanion, another commander of one of the original Cornish regiments, were mortally wounded.

Nicholas Slanning lived on for some days, during which time he is supposed to have declared his 'great joy and satisfaction in the losing of his life in the King's service to whom he had always dedicated it'. Lord Clarendon in his history of the royalist rebellion described Slanning and his Cornish compatriot John Trevanion as 'the life and soul of the Cornish regiments, whose memories can never be enough celebrated'. In September 1643, the king himself wrote to all churches and other institutions in the West Country saying in part, 'We are so highly sensible of the extraordinary Merits of Our County of *Cornwall*, of their Zeal for the Defence of our Person, and the Just Rights of Our Crown'. As things turned out, it was fortunate that neither Devon nor Cornwall had ever retained strong Catholic sentiments for otherwise they might have suffered the fate of Ireland in the hands of the puritan hegemony that was eventually to follow.

Sir Nicholas Slanning had a son again called Nicholas who died in infancy in 1637 or 1638 and another son born in 1643, on the very day that his father was fatally wounded, who was also called Nicholas, along with two older daughters, Margaret and Elizabeth, the latter figuring prominently in the later story of Maristow.[8] His widow, Gertrude, married Richard Arundell, 1st Baron Arundell of Trerice, a close friend of her former husband. This triggered an attempt under

8 It may have been the day but probably not the year for, as Jones (1887: 462) points out, he must have attained his majority before being knighted by the restored monarchy which would have meant an earlier date of birth.

the Commonwealth regime to sequester the Maristow estate and all properties owned at the time of Sir Nicholas' death but ultimately this did not happen; rather, in 1650 the Parliamentary Commissioners appeared satisfied with a composition payment of £1,197 13s.11d (*Calendar of the Committee on Compounding*: 2210).

In 1660 Nicholas Slanning, having inherited all of his father's estates, bought the manor of Buckland, formerly belonging to Buckland Abbey and owned after the dissolution by Richard Crymes. Winslow Jones claims at this time that he established himself at Maristow but it is more likely that the existing house at that time was already the family home (Jones, 1887: 463). After the Restoration, Nicholas Slanning gained significantly from his father's loyalty by being made one of the Knights of the Order of the Bath at the coronation of Charles II, and having a baronetcy conferred on him in 1662. This preferment, a minor role at court and a string of equally obscure administrative appointments, may have arisen as a result of his first marriage to Anne, daughter of Sir George Carteret of St Owen's Jersey, a powerful member of the prime minister, Lord Clarendon's, inner circle[9] (Plate 2).

Of greater note is that he was elected a Fellow of the Royal Society in 1664, largely because like his father he had a passion for practical chemical processes including 'a cheaper and more excellent way of melting, forging, and refining iron and other metals with turf and peat, to the great preservation of wood and timber' for which in later life he was awarded a patent. Samuel Pepys mentions being present on the occasion of his being elevated to the FRS (*Diary*, 4 August 1665). In the following year on 22 March, Sir Nicholas Slanning, like his father before him, became governor of Pendennis Castle with reversion to his stepfather, Richard Arundell, suggesting his influence in this appointment. On 4 October 1666 he stood at a by-election for Plympton St Maurice but was defeated by Sir Edmund Fortescue, although the mayor was persuaded to send in two returns which the House elections committee recorded as 'absurd and usual'

9 These included Commissioner for Assessment in Cornwall (1661–78) and Devon 1661–2; 1665–80; both counties, 1689–90; Commissioner for Recusants, Cornwall and Devon, 1675; Commissioner for Rebel's Estates, Devon 1686, Vice-Warden of the Stannaries from 1686.

and a 'pretended counterpart'. In the event, Sir Edmund died the following year and Slanning was offered the seat (cf. Jones, 1887: 463). Subsequently he was returned for Penryn on 17 September 1679, on 3 March 1681 and again on 9 May 1685. Throughout this period his parliamentary career was reasonably active, if never spectacular. He was appointed over the years to nearly 70 committees and appears to have been a loyal court supporter, although never with an outstanding record of attendance in the House. Slanning, as Lieutenant Governor of Plymouth from 1687, was present at the landing of the Prince of Orange in 1688 professing 'at first his devotion to James II, although on the suggestion of Secretary Blathwaite, he soon became an adherent of the Prince' (Jones, 1887: 463).

In addition to his first wife who died in 1668, Slanning married a further three times. His second wife, whom he married on 22 June 1670, was Mary, daughter and co-heir of James Jenkyn of Trekenning in St Columb Major, Cornwall. She died on 9 July 1672 and on 23 September 1673 he married another Mary, this time daughter of Sir Andrew Henley of Bramshill, Hampshire, who bore him a son and heir. Finally, on 16 November 1679 he married a double widow: Amy, a daughter of Edmond Parker of Boringdon, Plympton. She was the widow of Walter Hele, from a well-known local family of South Pool in Devon, and also of Sir John Davie of Creedy in Devon.

Some of these marriages brought Sir Nicholas significant dowries and so it is improbable that Maristow House was not at this early stage a house of some substance. For example, Mary Henley brought him a dowry of £5,500 but in return he was required to declare his property to her no doubt sceptical father. Made in 1673 on the occasion of his marriage with Mary daughter of Sir Andrew Henley, the 'Particular of Sir Nicholas Slanning's Estate of Inheritance' provides a rare insight into the scale and profitability of his holdings at this early date (DHC 346M/F534–550).[10]

The figures entitled 'an estimate of my estate' give the following

10 Interestingly a note on the file declares that the information was taken from 'letters of Philip Edgcumbe in the possession of Lord Mt Edgcumbe' which is presumably a reference to the 4th Earl's *Records of the Edgcumbe Family* published in 1888 but dealing primarily with the seventeenth century and before.

annual values:

	£
Barton of Maristow	200
Barton of Blackson (Blaxton)	40
Bickham also adjoining land	25
Pound tenement	25
Lillapitt	20
Ringmore Down (about 700 acres)	40
Coppice Woods adjoining Maristow more than 100 acres sometimes sold at £12 per acre	50
Tythe corne, graine, wool and lambes of Budock and Gluvias (Cornwall)	100
Coppice woods with the manor of Bickleigh, Shaugh and Walkhampton being more than 500 acres (sometimes sold at £7–£8 per acre)	200

	700

Old rents of Assize[11]

Manor of Maristow	£16 – 8 – 2
Manor of Bickleigh	£68 – 8 – 2
Manor of Shaugh Pryor	£16 – 16 – 4
Manor of Walkhampton	£55 – 3 – 10
Manor of Pennance in Cornwall[12]	£26 – 9 – 6
	£199 – 11 – 11

'These rents are some 4d in the pound but now about 12d in the pound except Plymouth and Modbury'.[13]

The Royalty of the Hundred of Roborough	£600
The Royalty of the River Plymm which abounds with all sorts of fish	£700

	£1,300

Although acreages of only 1,300 are identified, it is not unreasonable

11 The sums paid by conventionary tenants.
12 This may be a reference to an area near Gwithian in north-west Cornwall.
13 On this basis the income is rounded up and multiplied by three. The total in income terms in 2020 would be in excess of £4 million.

to suppose, given the rental incomes achieved, that the estate was more than 2,000 acres in extent at this time. The association with Pendennis Castle is reflected in the land holdings at Budock and Gluvias close by (just to the north of Penryn).

Sir Nicholas died in April 1691 and is described as 'of Maristow' in his will, which left nearly all his possessions to his only son, Andrew (Prob 11 28/1079). In a legal indenture dated 1696, the estate is described as 'all that capitall messuage of Maristow House called Maristow or Martinstow with its gardens and orchards thereto belonging' together with Maristow Barton 'containing by estimation 250 acres (more or less)' (PWDRO 70/122). The will is dated 10 February in the second year of the reign of William and Mary (1690). It appears to have been proved on 29 November 1692. His son was not of age when the will was made and therefore Andrew is placed into the care of Sir John Molesworth, his uncle by marriage, Sir Josiah Calmady of Langdon and John Quirke (looks like), the trustees and executors of the will. The will contains so many references to debts that it seems likely that these may have amounted to a considerable sum, notwithstanding the multiple marriages and the dowries they may have brought in. On the other hand, Sir Nicholas clearly owned numerous houses and lands in Cornwall as well as the estate itself that stretches over four parishes (Bickley, Shaugh, Walkampton and Maristow). On his majority, Andrew Slanning, was to inherit the estate and should he not have a son of his own but daughters then it was devised that it would pass to the eldest of these. Failing that the estate was to pass to his beloved wife Amy Slanning during her life, and if all else fails then to his brother-in-law Sir John Molesworth. There is a lack of clarity in the will at this point, compounded by difficulties of legibility, but it would seem that the testator was not enthusiastic about leaving a significant proportion of his estate to Molesworth and here the terms of the will make a turn towards charitable causes, including a house for the poor of the four parishes identified above, two from each. It was no doubt these clauses that caused the will to be contested (Molesworth v Seymour), almost certainly unsuccessfully.

Sir Andrew, was married in April 1692 at the age of 19 to Elizabeth Hele of South Tawton in Devon who died in May 1700, possibly in childbirth. Sir Andrew died in the same year in November in rather peculiar circumstances and both he and his young wife were buried at Bickleigh. According to *Burke's Extinct Baronetage* he is said to have died on 21 November 1700 as a result of a fight in the Rose Tavern in Covent Garden three days before. The story, which drew a great deal of public attention, was that the recently widowed Sir Andrew, after attending a play at Drury Lane, struck up a conversation with an orange-seller (*pace* Nell Gwynn) and asked her to join him. This seemingly aroused the ire of one John Cowland, who placed his arm around the woman's neck as a result of which swords were drawn on both sides, but tempers were calmed by the intervention of other men present. The story from a popular publication of the day (see Borrow, 1825) continues:

> They all now agreed to adjourn to the Rose tavern; and Capt. Wagget having there used his utmost endeavours to reconcile the offended parties, it appeared that his mediation was attended with success; but, as they were going upstairs to drink a glass of wine, Mr. Cowland drew his sword, and stabbed Sir Andrew in the belly, who finding himself wounded, cried out "murder". One of Lord Warwick's servants, and two other persons who were within the house, ran up immediately, and disarmed Cowland of his sword, which was bloody to the depth of five inches, and took him into custody.

On 5 December 1700, Cowland appeared at the Old Bailey charged with murdering Sir Andrew Slanning, who was supposedly described at the trial as having possessed an estate of £20,000 a year and of being 'a gentleman of great good-nature, and by no means disposed to animosity'. Cowland was found guilty of murder and 'though great interest was made to obtain a pardon', he was hung at Tyburn on 20 December 1700.

Slanning died intestate and without issue thereby bringing to a close the Slanning dynasty at Maristow. His legal heir was decreed to be his aunt, Dame Elizabeth Modyford (née Slanning), by then a widow aged 66. She was already living in Maristow House where, after the death of her father in 1643 and her mother's remarriage, she had come to play the dominant role in its management, even before her husband's death in 1673, due to his frequent absences in the Caribbean. A devout Protestant of very firm views, she lived on as chatelaine of the estate into her 91st year eventually passing away in 1724 in favour of her two daughters equally, Mary, the elder and Grace, her younger sister. There was to be no rebuilding or restoration of note during her reign, lest this might detract from the simple, abstemious adherence to the Christian faith that was the hallmark of her tenure.[14] But the estate was extensive and produced a handsome gross revenue when assessed in terms of rents and tithes. In 1690, at about the time of the death of Sir Nicholas Slanning, the total value of the estate to Sir Andrew Slanning was £1,563, substantially above the value 20 years earlier mainly because his father's fourth wife had brought substantial land holdings in the Barton of Hele near Modbury, to which were added incomes from the Forest of Dartmoor and Lydford Mills (£100 per annum) and other tithes making a total value per annum of £1,743 (PWDRO/3434).

It may be queried why this valuable asset passed to the younger of Sir Andrew's two aunts. The answer is that Elizabeth's sister Margaret was indeed older having been baptised at Plympton St Mary on 20 February 1630. However, she died before 12 February 1682 and was buried at Egloshayle on the River Camel near Wadebridge in north Cornwall on that date. She was therefore dead by the time of Andrew Slanning's demise. She had married Sir John Molesworth at the age of 38 on 7 July 1668 and there were no known children of that

14 Throughout her later life, Lady Elizabeth supported charitable institutions, particularly primary level schools to instil Christian virtues and familiarity with the catechism. She started with Lady Modyford Hall School in Buckland Monachorum in 1702 and this was followed by a Church of England Primary in Walkhampton for '20 poor boys'. The latter still exists, celebrating its tercentenary in 2019, although in a later building. Her daughter, Mary, continued this tradition by supporting a primary school herself in Tamerton Foliot that also still survives.

marriage. Similarly, when Gertrude, the mother of both sisters, was remarried to Richard Arundell of Trerice (an Elizabethan country house near Newquay) after the early death of their father, she had a son, John, born on 1 September 1649 in Richmond, Surrey, but he also died before Sir Andrew on 21 June 1698 in Piccadilly, London aged 48. His mother by that time had been dead for some years, so that the widowed aunt, Elizabeth Modyford, was the only potential heir remaining.

Chapter 2

Plantations and Pirates

At first sight the connection between the Modyfords and the fortunes of the Maristow estate appear somewhat tenuous, since it is unlikely that anyone born into this family ever owned it and lived there at the same time. Actually the decision by Elizabeth Slanning to marry the family's second son, James, was destined to change the fortunes of the estate forever and to open up a connection to the Caribbean, and in particular to Jamaica, that lasted for three centuries. Moreover, the way this occurred was not only financial; Caribbean culture intersected with English landed estates in important ways creating particular dynasties that projected somewhat unlikely families into the higher echelons of English society (cf. Amussen, 2007).

The Modyfords were a family of successful Exeter merchants well known in the city for their overseas trade connections. John Modyford eventually rose to be Mayor of Exeter in 1622; he died on 10 May 1628 and was buried in St Mary Arches, Exeter. The family was notably loyal to the king and identified with the royalist side in the emerging feud between parliament and monarchy that was to lead to the Civil War. They had in their family a 'cousin' (George Monck), although the exact relationship is not clear, who was to play a significant role in the fortunes of both sons. George Monck, born on 6 December 1608, was the second son of Sir Thomas Monck and his wife Elizabeth, daughter of Sir George Smith (Smyth) and his first wife Joan (née Walker). Smith, a merchant, particularly in tin, was one of Exeter's most famous sons, elected MP for the city in 1604 and mayor on three separate occasions (1586, 1597, 1607) following in the footsteps of his father, John. Sir George, who died in March 1619, was reputed to be Exeter's richest citizen and used some of his wealth to build a fine Elizabethan mansion on the

Wonford Road, Heavitree. The house was later usually referred to as 'Madford' but earlier as 'Maydford' and after Sir George died, and while his widowed second wife still lived there, it was also used by Bishop Joseph Hall of Exeter, who held the bishopric from 1627 to 1641. He referred to his temporary residence there as 'Maydeworthie' or 'Madforde'. Sir George's second wife, Grace, was the daughter of Jane Arundell of Trerice in Cornwall and their only child, also Grace, was the wife of Sir Nicholas Slanning's great friend and equal Civil War royalist hero and MP for Cornwall, Sir Bevil Grenville of Bideford and Stowe, killed just before Slanning himself at the Battle of Lansdown (1643). Slanning's widow, it will be recalled, married Richard Arundell of Trerice. With all these entangled relations and friendships it is highly probable that George Monck (later after the Restoration the first Duke of Albemarle), even if he was not directly related, thought of himself as a relation of the Modyford brothers and it is tempting to suggest that it was through them that Elizabeth Slanning met her future husband.[1]

Thomas Modyford, the eldest son, was born in 1620 and his younger brother, James, one of five sons, was born around 1623–4.[2] Their mother, Marie, who bore her husband 12 children, was the daughter of Thomas Walker an alderman of Exeter (mayor 1601, 1614 and 1625) and a leading member of another well-known local family at this time.[3] Fittingly, Thomas Modyford, served in the king's army rising to the level of colonel. He trained as a lawyer and served briefly as a barrister in Lincoln's Inn. His younger brother, James, also had some training in law but took an even earlier interest in trade, originally being apprenticed to the Turkey Company in Constantinople where it is claimed he also mastered the language

1 A topic equally worthy of further exploration is whether the name 'Modyford' is itself connected to the famous residence at Heavitree, particularly since the surname itself was spelt in alternate ways (e.g. Maddiford, Modiford, Muddiford).

2 The year James was born is not recorded but he is mentioned in his father's will dated 1625.

3 The Modyford brothers' grandfather, Thomas Walker, was related to George Monck's grandmother and Sir George's Smyth's first wife, Joan Walker, but exactly how is unclear.

(*CSP* 30 June 1666). He returned to London in the early 1650s and at his marriage to Elizabeth Slanning in 1655 he is described as a 'merchant' of Chelsea, although elsewhere his location in London is often given as 'of Chiswicke'. The entry in the *Dictionary of National Biography* reads in part:

> ... under the Commonwealth (he) was employed in Ireland, presumably through the interest of his cousin George Monck, first duke of Albemarle. On 18 Oct. 1660 he was appointed 'clerk of the first-fruits in Ireland', was knighted about the same time, and on 18 Feb. 1660–1 was created a baronet in consideration of his having 'liberally and generously provided and sustained thirty men for three years for the care and defence of Ireland' (*Patent roll*, 13 Car. II, pt. i. No. 2).

Thereafter, James' life and fortune became entwined with those of his older brother, Thomas, whose role in the development of the Caribbean colonies was of major significance and as a consequence rather better documented than that of most settlers at this time.

Arrival in the West Indies

Thomas Modyford, who had married Elizabeth daughter of Lewin Palmer of Devon in 1640, migrated to Barbados in 1647 with his wife, young children and a business partner called Richard Ligon (sometimes Lygon), who was to go on to write the earliest account of the island's history (1657) (Plate 3). Very soon after arriving aboard the 350-ton vessel *Achilles*, he bought from Major William Hilliard a half share in a large sugar plantation of 500 acres containing 96 African slaves, 3 Indians, 28 Christians (white indentured labourers), 45 cattle, 8 cows, 12 horses and 16 *assinigoes* (a breed of donkey originating in the Azores) for a total payment of £7,000 (with £1,000 immediately payable and the balance over three years) (*Caribbeana*, 4: 340). Ligon stayed on this plantation and he reports that Hilliard soon left for England 'and left Colonel Modyford to manage the employment alone; and I to give what assistance I could for the benefit of both' (1657: 67).

Announcing to the world that 'he would not set his face for England till he was worth £100,000', Thomas Modyford began life as a planter in a colony that was at that time experiencing an economic boom (*Caribbeana*, 4: 340).[4] There is little doubt that once in Barbados he applied himself ably to the complex task of cultivating sugar cane and producing sugar with considerable skill and aptitude. Richard Ligon reports, 'to do him right, I hold Colonel Modyford as able, to undertake and perform such a charge, as any I knew' (DNB; cf. Ligon, 1657: 67). Modyford's subsequent career, however, suggests very clearly that his financial ambitions dominated all others. In this he was not alone, but what subsequently marked him out as unusual was the extent to which he used his considerable political talents in pursuit of this goal, even to the point of seemingly acting against the planter interest when more lucrative opportunities for trade presented themselves and, at a later stage, ignoring the express instructions of the King of England, leading eventually to his incarceration in the Tower of London. In these activities his brother James was an active and enthusiastic partner.

Barbados at this time was among the first English colonies to introduce sugar cane and had already become a preferred destination for young adventurers seeking to make their fortune by helping to meet the seemingly insatiable demand for the multi-purpose product derived from it. In 1636 alone, 6,000 English settlers arrived in the island and many were to receive free grants of land as an inducement to grow this valuable crop (see Mintz, 1985). Henry Hawley, who served as governor from 1630 for a decade, is reported to have had no arable land left at the end of his period in office (Dunn, 1972: 49). The island had a reputation for being strongly royalist during the Civil War years and, partly as a consequence, was a favoured destination for officers from the king's regiments in the late 1640s as their fortunes declined back home. Under the

4 In price terms £100,000 would be worth in excess of £10 million in today's money.

staunchly royalist leadership of Governor Francis Lord Willoughby, who took office in 1650, the island refused to submit to Cromwell and the parliamentarians in that year and in 1652 put up a stout but unsuccessful defence against Commonwealth forces under Sir George Ayscue.

Thomas Modyford was a complex figure. On the one hand, he was clearly very ambitious and politically able. Although Barbados was small, it was not at this time economically insignificant. His curriculum vitae suggests that only a few years after his arrival he was playing a leading role in the island's affairs becoming a Member of the Council in 1650, briefly governor in 1660 and Speaker of the Assembly in 1661 and 1662. On the other hand, he was not well liked for what was seen as his financial opportunism and fickle political loyalties. Nothing reveals the former better than the example of the Royal Adventurers.

The Modyfords as Merchants

The Company of Royal Adventurers in Africa, set up in 1662, was a trading company that was among the first to attempt to exploit the raw materials of Africa whether this was elephants' teeth, wax, Malagueta pepper[5] or initially gold. Stockholders in the Royal Company of Adventurers, and in the Royal African Company which superseded it, included the king, members of his family, court dignitaries, the chief politicians of the day and the principal merchants and traders of London and Bristol. The king's brother, James, Duke of York, was the nominal head of both organisations. As one commentator put it, 'company policy was therefore Government policy: both had vital colonial interests, both sought quick colonial profit, both hated the name of a competitor' (Thornton, 1955: 374). Although these and other items sold well in England, they came to be displaced as a primary objective by the trade in human beings for work on the plantations in the New World. Prior to this, planters had to make do

5 *Amomum melegueta* – an aromatic seed of a plant in the ginger family sometimes used to flavour beer or other drinks and then often referred to as 'grains of paradise'.

with white indentured workers who coped poorly with the climate and diseases of the tropics, and in any event had to be paid wages.

From its foundation, the Royal Adventurers Company achieved a Royal Charter and hence obtained the sole right of trade between England, the English colonies and Africa including the monopoly of the slave trade. Moreover, 'not only did the company supply the planters with slaves, their greatest necessity, but in exchange for these it took sugar and other plantation products which it carried to England' (Zook, 1919: 207–8). In this sense, therefore, the company was the founder and main bulwark of the triangular trade. The important point is also that what had become the Royal African Company came to dominate this trade. This was not because of its efficiency or farsightedness but rather because of the powerful figures which stood to gain from it. As Violet Barbour put it,

> As the king, the Duke of York, other members of the royal family and prominent men at court were shareholders in the Africa Company, it is not surprising to find it exerting paramount influence on British policy in the Indies (Barbour, 1911: 543).

Among these 'prominent men at court' was George Monck, the fellow Devonian of strongly royalist beliefs who was to play a critical role in the careers of both Modyford brothers and who, like them, had no qualms at using his favoured position at court to further personal gain[6] (Plate 4).

The original company ran into trouble as a result of the war against the Dutch, who had attacked its forts and infrastructure on the West African coast and by 1668 it was not much more than a holding operation. The Royal African Company, which emerged out of the wreckage after paying £34,000 for the assets of the Adventurers with a flotation of 200 new subscribers, played a critical

6 His son, Christopher Monck (1653–88), succeeded his father in 1670. He was in later life a notorious adventurer becoming hugely wealthy as a result of plundering a Spanish wreck off Hispaniola. He became briefly governor-general of Jamaica on 26 November 1687, dying in post a year later (DNB, 13: 594).

role in forming the plantation societies of the New World. When the Royal African Company was reformed and renamed from the Company of Royal Adventurers in Africa in 1663, it was specifically charged with the supply of 'negro servants' to the plantations on the order of respective governors. It charged £17 per head in Barbados, £18 in Antigua and £19 in Jamaica, with a reduction for taking a whole ship load. The new Royal warrant granted the company sole access to the West African trade to the plantations in the Americas for a thousand years, naming the members of the company at this time. From its foundation in 1672 until 1689 the Royal African Company exported almost 90,000 slaves (25,000 to Barbados and 23,000 to Jamaica). Jamaica's slave population rose from 550 in 1661 to nearly 10,000 in 1673 (Thomas, 1985: 203; cf. Scott, 1912: 17–24).

The Modyford family was deeply involved in both companies. Thomas Modyford, one of the Royal Adventurers' first subscribers, became the company's factor (managing agent) in Barbados and, later, Sir James Modyford successfully lobbied Sir Andrew King, the company's sub-governor (chief executive) in London to make his family agents for the Royal African Company (WAM 11348; WAM 11689). Charles Modyford, Thomas' son, was a trustee and subscriber to the Royal African Company. In addition to the king's family and diverse members of the court, the deed setting up the Royal African Company also names Sir James Modyford as entitled to conduct all trade under the royal warrant (CSP, 'America and West Indies', January 1663, 5: 1661–8: 119–22). The king would himself benefit from a two-thirds share in any gold mined in West Africa, the remainder being retained by the company.

It is probably the case that the motivation to benefit from trade lay behind both Thomas Modyford's emigration to Barbados and his dramatic entry into the island's politics. This strategy was not, however, without cost since the planter interest objected to the monopsony trade with England when it came to supplying sugar, since they felt that better prices might be available elsewhere. They also felt that the monopoly offered to the company in the supply of slaves unduly raised their price. They noted, in particular, that these restrictions on trade did not operate the other way round. Thomas Modyford, for example, felt it was quite appropriate that he, acting on behalf of the company, should be free to sell slaves to the highest bidder, wherever they were from. As Zook puts it, 'Modyford was very enthusiastic about the company's prospects for a profitable trade in Negroes with the Spanish colonies' (1919: 209). This double standard, and its repercussions for their financial health, infuriated the Barbadian planters who petitioned the House of Commons over the unfairness of this policy. Zook summarises their complaints:

> They maintained that previous to the establishment of the Royal Adventurers Negroes had been sold for twelve, fourteen and sixteen pounds per head, or 1,600 to 1,800 pounds of sugar, whereas now the company was selling the best slaves to the Spaniards at eighteen pounds per head, while the planters paid as high as thirty pounds for those of inferior grade (1919: 214).

They became so exasperated that they often refused to ship their sugar to England in the company's vessels, regardless of the freight rates they were offered. Unsurprisingly, Modyford was not universally liked (Zook, 1919: 214).

Political Opportunism

An even greater difficulty was to plague Thomas Modyford's reputation in Barbados. This was the seemingly fickle nature of his political allegiance. Having played an early role on the king's side, it is no surprise that he started out at one with the royalist sentiments of the islanders, even though it could be argued that he left England when defeat loomed. Subsequently he participated in the opposition in 1650–51 to the demands of the Commonwealth for the surrender of the island to the Roundhead commander, Sir George Ayscue. But as Barbour observes,

> After the news of the Royalist defeat at Worcester reached Barbados, Modyford's loyalty became less pronounced. He entered into secret negotiations with Ayscue and finally went over to the enemy, taking with him the regiment of which he was colonel (Barbour, 1911: 544).

Thus in 1651 Thomas Modyford was declaring his allegiance to the Stuarts, co-signing a declaration of support from which 'no hopes of reward, nor fear of future sufferings will ever make them recede', yet under two months later the Governor of Barbados and a staunch royalist, Lord Willoughby, could write to the Commonwealth's chief officer sent to take over the island (Sir Geoffrey Ayscue) that 'neither the treachery of one (Col Thomas Modyford) nor the easiness of many others seduced by him, have so weakened them as to accept either an unsafe or dishonourable peace' (CSP, 'America and West Indies: January 1652', 1: 1574–1660).

This defection contributed significantly to the weakening of the royalist position and to the fall of Governor Willoughby. Rightly suspecting political opportunism rather than a real change of heart, many on the parliamentarian side suspected Modyford's motives, while the traditionalists dismissed him as traitor. Indeed, General Daniel Searle, who was to take over as governor in 1655, had two years earlier removed Modyford from the command of his regiment precisely on the grounds that this 'most restless spirit' was 'much disrelished by the honest party'.

In August 1653, Modyford appealed successfully to Cromwell for his reinstatement.[7] It would appear that James Modyford, writing from St Cullume in Cornwall, was also prepared to change sides to suit the prevailing sentiment, even going so far as to advise the Protector of possible plots against his continued rule, but beseeching the administration not to divulge his role as an informer (CSP, 1656

7 Nuala Zahedieh writing in the *Dictionary of National Biography* claims that Thomas Modyford's opportunism, which marked his entire career, was apparent very early on as some royalists had claimed that his duplicity led to the fall of Exeter in the Civil War. It is also possible, as some commentators always contended, that his true loyalties lay with parliament.

June. *A collection of the State Papers of John Thurloe*, Vol 5: May 1656–January 1657: 96–108).

The governor's actions against Thomas Modyford had the effect of prompting protestations of loyalty by him to the new order. In 1654, when thinking that the royalist cause was lost for good, he wrote a letter to General Venables claiming that he 'utterly abhorred and abjured the interest of the Stuarts' (Macray, *Cal. of Clarendon State Papers*, iii. 26) and two years later he published a document called *Protestation of loyalty to the Protector's government by Thomas Modyford of Barbados, 1656*. After Modyford's reinstatement to his military role, the governor was ordered to admit him to the island's governing council. Further success occurred in early 1660 when in his fortieth year he received a commission to take over from Searle in the role of governor. The Restoration meanwhile intervened and on 9 July Charles II signed a commission returning the governorship to the *status quo ante* in the form of Lord Willoughby. Modyford was arrested in Barbados in 1661 by the Provident Marshall, but bail was permitted as long as he resided on his own plantation (*CSP*, 1661: 1 and 14, 20, 49, 116).

It was unfortunate for both Modyford brothers that the death of Cromwell was to lead to an unravelling of the Commonwealth. In the short run at least, the elder brother, Thomas, whose supposed allegiance to parliament was more open and declared, paid a higher price. In December 1660, he was stripped of the command of his regiment and the minutes of the Council in Barbados for January 1661 show that a motion was passed calling for his impeachment on grounds of high treason (*CSP*, 'America and West Indies: January 1661', 5: 1661–8: 1–4). Modyford's reaction, as in later years, was to turn swiftly to his kinsman, the Duke of Albemarle, to seek support from the king himself on the grounds that prior to the restoration he was only doing Albemarle's bidding; the latter having been one of a small number of senior officials able to bridge the interregnum. It is testament to Albemarle's persuasive powers that this was duly forthcoming; indeed, Charles had decided very soon after his resumption of the throne to confirm Modyford as Governor of Barbados.[8] His reasons were probably financial in that supporters of Modyford's undoubted abilities as a merchant presented a proposal to the king that should he take this course, the island's council would raise a 4 per cent tax on the sale of all commodities payable to the king. Moreover, the king himself wrote to Thomas Modyford as 'Governor of Barbados' as early as December 1660 commanding him to examine all the accounts of those charged with receiving 'prize goods' to ensure that the monarch's share (50 per cent) was received by the crown (*CSP*, 'America and West Indies: 9 January 1662', 5: 1661–8: 66–70). Less fickle royalist stalwarts were quick to spot this plan, informing the king that those who had stood by the former governor, Lord Willoughby, would have continued the defence of the island had it not been for Modyford's role in supporting Cromwell. For some only a harsh judgment was appropriate. Colonel Humphrey Walrond, President of the Council, wrote that 'his treachery in betraying the island to the usurper and his persecution of royalists ever since, has rendered him odious to all honest people' (*CSP*, 'America and West Indies: 29 March 1661', 5: 1661–8: 14–21). Mammon appears to have humbled loyalty on this occasion, although the opposition to Modyford was such as to prevent him remaining governor and he was demoted to serve as Speaker in the Assembly.

Most men would have been defeated by this turn of events, but not Thomas Modyford. Although he was condemned by some, his opponents had not taken account of his cousin, George Monck. As Barbour writes, notwithstanding his protestations of loyalty to the Commonwealth, 'Monck's influence saved him from disgrace' (1911: 544–55). Charles II clearly felt Modyford had leadership qualities, even if his loyalty was suspect, for in February 1664 he was not only appointed Governor of Jamaica with extensive powers and instructions to take as many settlers as possible with him, but he was also honoured with a baronetcy. It is probable that Modyford's

8 It is important to note that although Thomas Modyford was looked upon with intense dislike by many in the political elite, this was not the view of all, particularly merchants and traders who petitioned the king calling him 'full of justice and ability' (*CSP*, 'America and West Indies: January 1661', 5: 1661–8: 14–21).

trading skills also played a part in this decision, particularly his role in the new Royal African Company in which the king and other members of the royal family had such a significant financial interest (DNB, 2004).

The Question of Spanish Trade

It was towards the end of Thomas Modyford's period in Barbados that the issue of trading with the Spanish in the Caribbean first arose. On the one hand the Navigation Act of 1660 and the Staple Act of 1663 made it clear that colonial plantations were not just expected to use the Royal African Company for their labour supplies and for shipping produce back to England, but also that *all* trade should be between England and her colonies. This was not universally popular:

> Even the fact that English West-India sugars dominated the world market until well after the turn of the eighteenth century only made the planter moodily calculate how much greater his profit would have been had his shipping and his produce not been trammelled by the Navigation Act (1660) and the Staple Act (1663), and had he not been debarred from obtaining his own supply of labor for his plantations from Ireland, Scotland, and the Guinea Coast (Thornton, 1955: 375).

What interested the planters was to buy cheap and sell high and this restriction on trade was perceived by them as unwarranted and unjust. Nor was it consistently applied. The Governor of Jamaica before Thomas Modyford, Lord Windsor, was even charged with responsibility for promoting free trade with the Spanish which, if they resisted, he was enjoined to impose by force. Moreover, the king was under pressure on the one hand to avoid purchasing Spanish goods and thereby undermining the suppliers from England but on the other side were contrary pressures. Most notably the Modyford brothers were lobbying Charles for free trade claiming that the duties imposed would bring in £100,000 to the crown. Thomas

Modyford himself was actively involved in this trade both by his role as the local agent for the Royal African Company and in his own right. The Spaniards, Modyford claims, had 'filled our island with money', paying 125–140 pieces of eight a head (£25-£28) and being prepared to take 800 Africans. In this project they were remarkably successful and by March 1663 the king had signed orders allowing for free trade with the Spanish colonies both on the islands and the Main, subject only to customs dues (*CSP*, 'America and West Indies: February 1663', 5: 1661–8: 122–4).

While Barbados was economically very successful, it was clearly overcrowded, which is one reason for Thomas Modyford's plan to colonise the Carolinas south of the Charles River. Thomas Modyford was remarkably entrepreneurial and this was possibly one additional reason why he was liked by some and hated by others. One proposal to Charles II, for example, was for the 'Corporation of Barbadoes Adventurers' led by Modyford and Peter Colleton (another cousin of the Duke of Albemarle) involving '200 hundred gentlemen of good quality' settling the coast of North Carolina and being granted an area 'not exceeding 1,000 square miles' (*CSP*, 'America and West Indies: 12 August 1663', 5: 1661–8: 151–8). Others, too, were looking for new opportunities. A planter travelling to Surinam (then simply regarded as a part of the Guianas) wrote to the king in words that would have been echoed by anyone trying to create a plantation economy based on sugar: 'Were the planters supplied with negroes, the strength and sinews of this western world, they would advance their fortunes and his Majesty's customs' (*CSP*, 'America and West Indies: November, 1663', 5: 1661–8: 166–71).

Jamaica was also under-resourced in terms of both planters and slaves having only been pried from the Spanish eight years earlier. The State Papers record that on 10 May 1655 the English took possession of Jamaica from the Spanish and offered the colonists from that 'desert and barren wilderness' of New England the opportunity to 'remove to a land of plenty' where they would be granted land (20 acres for every male over 12 years old and ten for all others) next to some good harbour, free of rent for seven years and then subject only to a charge of one penny per acre (*CSP*, 'America and West Indies: September 1655', 1: 1574–1660: 428–31). In March 1662, the king set out the his instructions to the new governor, Thomas Lord Windsor, which included the command that 100,000 acres in each quarter of the island should be set aside for the king's plantations 'to be preserved and improved to the best advantage for the use of the King and his successors' (*CSP*, 'America and West Indies: 21 March 1662', 5: 1661–8: 80–84). He also commanded a survey of the island, to be carried out by Sir James Modyford. His report to the king, dated December 1663, was generally very positive pointing out that sugar production in some factories was as high as 20–30,000 lbs. per week of a quality that allowed for prices 50 per cent higher than Barbados. But a new injection of human resources and capital was required because of losses through disease 'and also by reason of the intemperance of the inhabitants' (*CSP*, 'America and West Indies: December 1663', 5: 1661–8: 171–9).

It was this report, combined with his obvious entrepreneurship and a set of specific proposals, that persuaded Charles to overlook Thomas Modyford's chequered history of loyalty and propose him as Governor of Jamaica with instructions to take as many planters as he could from Barbados to help develop the island (*CSP*, 'America and West Indies: 11 January 1664', 5, 1661–8: 179–84). His proposed terms of reference were astonishingly broad and far reaching:

> to give liberty of conscience in Jamaica; to grant land at his discretion; to make declaration in all the Caribbee Islands that there shall be no custom paid at Jamaica for 21 years; to call in all private men-of-war; to proceed against those who refuse and continue pirates or take commissions from other princes; to settle an Admiralty there; to give assurances to Spanish subjects of free trade at Jamaica; and that, for the security of the island, his Majesty keep a ketch there for obtaining intelligence; and that the ship now going be victualled for 12 months, that she may return to the Caribbee Isles for planters.

The Governor of Barbados, Lord Willoughby, was instructed to lend 'every assistance' he could in this project, which he no doubt acceded to with alacrity since it removed an obvious thorn in his side. By mid-February 1664, the king's commission was sent to Thomas Modyford, elevating him to a baronetcy and granting him a salary of £2,000 per annum (over £2 million in real wage comparison for 2020) (*CSP*, 'America and West Indies: 15 February 1664', 5, 1661–8: 184–91).

In this original specification of the role to be played by Thomas Modyford in his new position as governor of the crown colony of Jamaica it is possible to discern the beginnings of the British colonial model of indirect rule which was to hold sway in the Caribbean, Africa and South-East Asia for three centuries. This devolved considerable day-to-day autonomy to the governor and council. It is doubtful whether the planters and settlers wanted more autonomy in practice than this model offered. This was not because some would not have preferred to be rid of the constant reporting to Whitehall, but because the implicit deal in which the crown received financial benefit in return for defence when required had much to commend it, particularly when, as was true in the Jamaican case, there was no guarantee that the previous Spanish colonists would not avail themselves of any chance of repossession. It was proposed that Modyford could make law, subject only to the advice of five or more members of the 12-person council chosen by him; he could establish courts, administer oaths and appoint judges; he commanded the military forces locally with power to impose martial law, he could divide the island into administrative units as he thought fit and establish, towns, ports and defences as required. There was oversight from Whitehall certainly, but these were great powers particularly since he was in charge of granting land not already privately owned, subject only to establishing 'moderate quit-rents to the King'.

Interestingly, a second letter from the king proposed a more limited set of rights and duties which suggested that his officials in Whitehall had done more work on the particular challenges presented by the new colony. Among other things, it halved the governor's proposed salary but paid £600 to a deputy (first incumbent Colonel Edward Morgan). The king abandoned his original wish for royal plantations of 400,000 acres in favour of the existing planters and proposed an allocation of 30 acres of land to each new settler bringing with him (or occasionally her) a servant, the latter to receive the same after four years of service.[9] Both these classes were to receive arms together with training in their use. In addition, there were three instructions that recognised the special circumstances of Jamaica. First, tales of the swashbuckling lifestyle, particularly of the pirates and privateers in and around Port Royal, had obviously reached Whitehall for the new governor was enjoined to 'take care that drunkenness and debauchery, swearing and blasphemy be discountenanced and punished, and none admitted to public trust and employment whose ill-fame may bring scandal thereon'. Moreover, the second requirement also targeted this segment of the population by prohibiting the issuance of 'letters of marque' and keeping in 'good correspondence with the Spanish Dominions'.[10] Finally, however, the potential of Jamaica was recognised by the instruction to encourage trade, particularly that controlled by the Royal African Company (i.e. the slave trade and the shipping of produce to England).[11] Modyford's successful role in this regard while in Barbados was very clearly an important reason for his appointment. In all of this, the role of Sir James Modyford, now resident in England and able therefore to lobby effectively through his relative, the Duke of Albemarle, was critical.[12]

---

9 These were English or Irish men and women, often recruited from the prison population.

10 'Letters of marque' were a form of license used to allow private citizens to apprehend and seize enemy vessels in times of war. 'Prizes' thus obtained could then be brought before an admiralty court to enable the 'privateer' to gain control of the assets.

11 Modyford's role in the local trade is evident in his reporting while still in Barbados to the company's governors and court of assistants. In March 1664, for example, he records very high levels of mortality with 200 Africans in port whom no one there will buy because they are dying. He negotiated a sale of these and a hundred others to Nevis and St Kitts.

12 See *CSP*, 'America and West Indies: March 1664', 5: 1661–8).

From Pure Plantation to Pirates' Nest

The king's instinct appears to have been that Modyford was an energetic and talented leader, whose principles might stop short of anything other than self-interest, but who was ideally suited to take charge of the Caribbean's Wild West. Jamaica, since being happened upon by Columbus in 1494, had been a rather sleepy Spanish possession; the Spanish settlers appearing to spend more time extinguishing the native peoples than in developing the rich agricultural potential of the island. In 1538, they had established their capital at St Jago de la Vega and it was more than a century later after various raids for plunder and slaves that the island succumbed to the English. This was the period of Cromwell's 'Grand Design' for nothing less than the humbling of Spanish colonial ambitions and the freeing of trade to English advantage. While the Protector's attack upon Hispaniola in 1654 was unsuccessful, the unfortified and sparsely populated island of Jamaica was a much easier conquest.

A concerted attempt was then made to populate this large island with English-speaking settlers. In 1656, Governor Edward D'Oyley arranged for 1,000 young men and an equal number of young women to be sent from Ireland. In the same year, 1,600 men were sent from Nevis as settlers and others arrived a few years later from the Eastern Caribbean Windward Islands and elsewhere. In the meantime, the governor had encouraged English buccaneers to move from their base in Tortuga to a newly established harbour at Port Royal and a few years later 1,500 men had taken up this offer (Penson, 1924: 24). In August 1662, the Spanish attempted to retake the island but were defeated by D'Oyley and his royalist colleagues.

It was into this febrile environment that the new governor, Thomas Modyford, stepped, arriving from Barbados on 1 June 1664 with four ships carrying 987 persons; Lord Willoughby, it appears, was only too pleased to see the back of him by helping to organise his trip (*Caribbeana*, 4: 341). It is no exaggeration to say that over the next seven years Modyford was instrumental in helping to create and meld together three vital strands of Caribbean history; namely a plantation society exporting primary products to the Old World, a system of production based upon chattel slavery and a vigorous assertion of England's right to dominate the high seas for the purposes of trade and political advantage. All three were principles embodied in the approach of the new governor but, unlike the rather isolated eastern island of Barbados, Jamaica was far more centrally placed in the Caribbean sea lanes hitherto dominated by the Spanish and the Dutch. It was the presence of these competing nations that had already led to the buccaneering tradition and the question now was how to use these privateers to help protect and promote the interests of the new English colony.

The Spanish fleets were far better entrenched than any other, although it was relatively easy to galvanise anti-Spanish, anti-Catholic sentiment in support of raiding parties and piratical attacks. It was thus easier for privateers to obtain letters of marque, or other papers issued by a sovereign state to those of their kinsmen seeking redress for supposed infringements to rights of property or to violent attack. As Violet Barbour remarks,

> Privateering became a profession having no necessary connection with the politics, commerce, or religion of those that practised it, though all of these motives continued to be used to disguise individual cupidity (Barbour, 1911: 531)

It was not so much that the Spanish made any distinction between those with letters of marque and those without, treating all as *pirates*; rather, the letters enabled those who had gained booty to bring it home and sell it. A particularly troublesome settlement as far as the Spanish were concerned was the island of Providence (*Providencia*), midway between modern Costa Rica and Jamaica. The English puritan colony, set up in 1629, was run by the London-based Company of Providence Island. It did not do well as an agriculture settlement but 'as a base of warlike operations against Spanish ships it proved highly satisfactory' (Barbour, 1911: 537). What was important was that when the Spanish made an attempt to recapture the island in 1635, Charles I wrote of English adventurers in the area that 'whatever they should take in the West Indies by way of reprisal, should be adjudged lawful' (*CSP*, Colonial, 29 January 1636; Barbour, 1911: 537). The Spanish forces briefly took over the islands in 1641.

The conquest of Jamaica, and the base that it offered for privateers to operate, opened up what has been termed 'the great era of buccaneering' initially sanctioned by the early governors as a way of helping to protect the island from Spanish attempts to re-establish their presence (Barbour, 1911: 540). Moreover,

> It is not surprising that the Jamaicans fell into the way of interpreting all signs from the Spanish Indies as war's alarms, and began early to patronize the buccaneers who were willing to fight and rob the Spanish for any one that would give them papers (1911: 541).

The new town of Port Royal, set up on what is now Kingston harbour, burst into life as a base for privateers and pirates themselves and for all the service providers and suppliers that tend to congregate around centres of sudden wealth, particularly when accompanied by significant chances of equally dramatic injury or death (Plate 5).

As a trader from his earliest years, the new governor might have been expected to support this buccaneering tradition for it promised the opportunity of opening up routes and destinations for the Royal African Company to trade in slaves, to supply all colonies and settler societies with goods and to ship produce back to Europe. But, true to his form in Barbados, Thomas Modyford attempted to enhance his fortune in both ways; firstly by becoming a major planter himself and, second, by exploiting the opportunities that arose for trading in produce and supplies. The difference in Jamaica was that he already held the highest political office, although that was ultimately to prove his undoing because it came with the clear suggestion from the restored monarch himself that Modyford's task was to establish a colony of planters, and thereby to entrench English interests, but not to antagonise the Spanish still smarting after the Protector's aggressive policies over the previous decade. For this reason, one of the new governor's first moves was to move the capital back to the old inland site of St Jago de la Vega (Spanish Town) and to condemn 14 privateers from Port Royal to death for piracy. This policy was not to last long and within weeks most of the condemned men were pardoned and the new governor wrote to Whitehall that he now 'thought it more prudent to do that by degrees and moderation which I once resolved to have executed suddenly and severely' (Modyford to Bennet, 30 June 1664, TNA: PRO, CO 1/18, fol. 177; DNB). His reasoning was probably that with only a tiny population of planters, many of them inexperienced, it would have been folly to force out the privateers who brought a very profitable trade into Port Royal from which much needed capital could be extracted. Moreover, while the king never explicitly condoned piracy, other members of the royal family and the court were less circumspect. A few years later, for example, the Duke of York, the admiral in command of 'English maritime forces in the (West) Indies' and the king's brother, sent the powerful man-of-war the *Oxford* to take charge of the privateers to ensure for himself a large slice of the booty.

Although the Minutes of the Legislative Council of Jamaica show that the governor reiterated the king's instructions not to seize as prizes any ships belonging to Spain, it is also quite clear that the pirates and privateers from Port Royal demonstrated no such reserve. A furious communication from Charles II in June 1664, only just after Modyford had arrived, expresses his 'dissatisfaction at the daily complaints of violence and depredations done by ships, said to belong to Jamaica, upon the King of Spain's subjects'. Clearly action against the pirates had to be a priority for the new governor and he issued an appropriate proclamation to this effect at the end of the same month. Meanwhile, Sir James Modyford was very active in support of the new colony. In October 1664, he requested the Duke of Albemarle to ask the king for a special licence from the Portuguese monarch to enable him to procure 600 head of cattle from the Cape Verde islands for Jamaica, and in November he successfully petitioned the king for the privilege of transporting all pardoned felons from the jails of all circuits to his brother in Jamaica. It must be recalled that this was an age when the penalties for relatively minor misdemeanors could include hanging, and courts were often faced with a choice between extreme sanctions and acquittal. Transportation offered a middle way between the two (Smith, 1934: 244).[13]

In the meantime, Thomas Modyford sought to establish a 'model cacao estate that soon took an honored place among the few cacao and sugar plantations already constructed' (Bennet, 1964: 58). Notwithstanding his experience with sugar cane, Modyford was initially persuaded by the virtues of cacao as an easier way to make money than sugar cane, with its seasonal replanting and expensive costs of processing, and felt that the Spanish cacao tree was 'the most profitable tree in the world' and one capable of producing a revenue of £200 per acre so great was the demand for cocoa and chocolate in England (Bennet, 1964: 60). Modyford's cacao plantation was at Sixteen Mile Walk in St Catherine parish and in a letter to the newly-arrived English planter and his neighbour Cary Helyer, he described the life of the planter as 'a happy and innocent way of thriving' (Bennet, 1964: 59, 60). But this was not to be through cacao, which soon began to succumb to the blight that was later to be the fate of almost all other attempts to cultivate this crop elsewhere in the Americas. Helyer describes in a letter to his brother in England how Modyford swiftly reverted to sugar cane cultivation and that he was now 'going upon a huge sugar work having three hundred Negroes, and conveniency of a waterwork'. It was, he says, 'the custome here that hee that has a mil will grinde his neighbours sugar canes and make his sugar at halves'; in other words, Helyer could process sugar cane at Modyford's watermill and pay for this service by giving the governor half the sugar produced (Bennet, 1964: 65).

A survey in 1670 showed that there were 209,000 acres planted and that there were 717 families numbering a total of 15,000 persons. There were at that time 57 sugar works, producing yearly 1,710,000 lbs. of sugar per annum, 47 cocoa walks yielding 180,000 lbs. of nuts, and 49 indigo works, producing 49,000 lbs. of indigo

13 The two brothers refer to Albemarle in their correspondence as 'our Duke' (October 1664).

per annum, besides pepper, salt and other products. The revenue of Jamaica in the same year, arising mostly from duties on wines and spirits, was £1,870, while the necessary disbursements for support of the government, which included a salary of £1,000 to the governor, £400 to the deputy governor, £200 to the major-general and £80 to the chief judge, and other salaries, amounted in all to £1,960, and with incidental expenses for the fort, to nearly £3,500.

In the meantime, a second principal focus of the governor's attention was the preservation and promotion of trade, purportedly for the benefit of the crown but undoubtedly also for his own enrichment. The difficulty he faced, however, was that Charles II, in trying to reach peace settlements with the Spanish, specifically excluded from the outset attacks on Spanish possessions by privateers or pirates based in Jamaica, thereby allowing Spanish vessels to compete with those of the Royal African Company in the provision of slaves and to exclude all others from the profitable business of supplying the Spanish settlements in the Main, Hispaniola and the rest of the Caribbean. While it was true that privateers were difficult to control, settlers in Jamaica felt continually under threat from Spain and fearful of being caught up in the nightmare of the Inquisition. The Modyford brothers used every opportunity to circumvent the official proscription on attacking both the ships flying the Spanish flag and even the settlements in the vicinity of Jamaica. They did this in three ways and, although their motives may have been mixed, they always involved a significant element of personal pecuniary advantage. Violet Barbour summed up the governor well when she wrote that he was 'energetic and capable, but impetuous, short-sighted, and none too honest in the use of his office' (1911: 545). There is no reason to think that James Modyford was that different in temperament or morality.

In the first place, they took full advantage of the periods when the official instructions were suspended. In the early years of his governorship, for example, Thomas Modyford had made some efforts to control privateering by refusing to issue letters of marque and even by arresting and imprisoning a number of sea captains from Port Royal for piracy. These measures were never wholly successful and probably only prosecuted by the governor in a rather half-hearted manner. In any event, the declaration of war between England and the Dutch in May 1665 (until August 1667) saved the day for, even though antagonisms between the two were never as intense as those between either and the Spanish, it provided a justification for official commissions to attack all foreign vessels to be resumed. Thus, the instructions to the new Governor of Jamaica concerning the Spanish were in marked contrast to the attitude adopted towards the Dutch and French in the West Indies. By 1666, the king was advising Modyford in the latter case to 'damnify them to the utmost of his power in their adjacent Plantations' (February 1666). The islanders did not seem prepared, however, to heed the royal instruction regarding the Spanish for by the following month the council minutes report the passage of a motion to issue letters of marque against Spanish ships:

> It seems to be the only means to force the Spaniards in time to a free trade, all ways of kindness producing nothing of good neighbourhood, for though all old commissions have been called in, and no new ones granted, and many of their ships restored, yet they continue all acts of hostility, taking our ships and murdering our people, making them work at their fortifications and then sending them into Spain, and very lately they denied an English fleet bound for the Dutch colonies wood, water, or provisions. For which reasons it was unanimously concluded, that the granting of said commissions did extraordinarily conduce to the strengthening, preservation, enriching, and advancing the settlement of this island.

Moreover, in May 1665 ten vessels and 500 men set out from Port Royal under the command of the deputy governor, Edward Morgan, against the Dutch, and Modyford continued to argue the case for a resumption of attacks against the Spanish as well, since in his view they were an even greater impediment to English traders like himself.[14] As Barbour put it, 'Modyford was delighted to be able to obey orders, conciliate the populace of Port Royal, and obtain his fee from commissions' (1911: 547). The going rate for issuing letters of marque to privateers, thereby providing official sanction for attacking other vessels, was £20 per commission (Barbour, 1911: 545). But monetary gain did not stop there. When the treasure seized by privateers was officially sanctioned by valid commissions from the governor in council, he was entitled to claim in the king's name a fifteenth of the booty, and always did so. Where a valid commission had not been issued or even on occasion when it had, the rewards could be far greater. This was arranged through the placement of family members in positions where they could act in concert for mutual advantage.

Sir James Modyford, having been denied an official position in Turkey had spent some years in Jamaica and had sought through his cousin, the Duke of Albemarle, some more official role, possibly believing that this would open up even greater trading opportunities. On 10 November 1666 he was offered the governorship of Providence after it had again been seized by the English. Travelling via Barbados he was delayed for 11 weeks 'through the ignorance rather than the malice' of the then governor Lord Willoughby and by the time he reached Jamaica on 15 July 1667 he discovered that *Providencia* and *Santa Catalina* were once again in Spanish hands. By this time, his brother was Governor of Jamaica and he lost no time in appointing James as lieutenant general (deputy governor) and, importantly, chief judge of the Admiralty Court. By this time also, the governor's son, Charles Modyford, was back in England representing the interests of Jamaica, a role that James had also played some years before. These posts were strategic, as Violet Barbour points out, since they enabled the family to exploit the colony as if it were a family fief:

> The governor issued commissions and bought in prizes which Sir James had condemned, and then the goods were

14 Edward Morgan did not survive this trip, dying of a probable heart attack while engaged in the attack on the Dutch-held islands of Curaçao and St Eustatius.

> shipped to England to the governor's son, Charles Modyford, who could dispose of them more advantageously than was possible in Jamaica (1911: 554).

In other words, James Modyford used the Admiralty Court to confiscate goods whose origins were said to be unlawful. These were then bought by the governor, possibly through the Royal African Company, and shipped to Britain where they were disposed of by his son at the best price he could obtain. Alternatively, when goods were not confiscated, Sir James would use his privileged position to buy them cheaply. According to the planter John Style, the island trade consisted almost entirely of 'plate, money, jewels and other things brought in [by the privateers] and sold cheap to the merchant' (Style to William Morrice, 14 January 1669, TNA: PRO, CO 1/24, fol. 19; DNB). This family business was clearly very profitable. The governor received £20 for each commission for a privateer, the goods were then condemned by Sir James at his valuation and disposed of by Charles with a proportion going to the privateer, the crown and the balance to the Modyfords. Occasionally the goods were bought in Jamaica by a wealthy planter or merchant (including both Modyford brothers) and shipped to the care of Charles Modyford in England.[15]

These practices are very clearly laid out in Sir James Modyford's correspondence with Sir Andrew King. The latter, presumably in his role as the chief administrator of the Royal African Company or possibly for himself, was keen to ship goods to Jamaica. Sir James, however, felt this was not a sufficiently rewarding trade and preferred to buy from the privateers. He makes this clear soon after his return to Jamaica in late 1667:

> This place continues still its privatiering against ye Spaniard, without which it cannot well flourish, or by a trade with

15 An example was the seizure of the vessel named 'Our Lady of Conception and St Joseph' (*Nuestra Señora de la Concepción y San José*) seized in 1668 by Captain Demster and bought with all goods she contained by the planter Hender Molesworth in Jamaica and sent on to England to the care of Charles Modyford who lobbied the king against the pleas of the Spanish Ambassador that she was a rightful prize.

> them which theyle never (I believe) allow off. Three or four prizes have been brought in since my being here but ye most considerable was one of 200 tuns laden with loggwood chiefly bound from Cartegena to Havanna – and there are now sundrie of our small men of warre abroad a cruising and 5 or 6 more have lately gone out; they return as fast as they get any purchace, and to have a stock of money readie against there (sic) return to buy their purchace (which they commonly sell dogge cheape) is ye most hopeful trade here. I could have bought loggwood at ye prizes first coming in for 10 or 11 (pounds) a tun which now is not to be had for 20 (Pounds); and so much may suffice for a demonstration (Modyford to King, 27 December 1667, WAM 11912).

Whereas goods from England often remained unsold for months, 'ye opportunities wee often meet with by means of our Privatiers do sometimes double nay treble our money without any hazard' (WAM/11922, January 1668). As far as legitimate trade with the Spanish was concerned, there were opportunities and Sir James commends to his friend and mentor the port of Saint Martha (*Santa Marta*) on the coast of what is today Colombia as 'ye properst place for our trade with ye Spaniard'. Here, he says, 'wee can buy wools, cottons, wines, Tobacco, Gold, Pearles, Emeralds and silver'. The way to do it, he suggests, is to buy English goods for, say, £10,000 and 'put them on a good ship of 26 guns at least and send her away with speed'. Make sure the vessel calls at Jamaica for then the ship can obtain 'authentic copies of ye capitulations' from him and the governor. In this arrangement 'my brother and myself will goe halfs of both ship and cargo' (WAM/11918, 11 May 1668).

It is important also to stress that both Thomas and James Modyford took to plantation ownership in Jamaica in the most serious way possible, ranking among the largest landowners in the island by 1670. In that year a survey showed that in St Catherine parish alone, Sir Thomas Modyford owned or controlled plantations covering 6,199 acres, making him the largest landowner in the parish, while his brother's 3,500 acres ranked number three. But some of Thomas' holdings were in the name of the Royal African Company or his first son (also Thomas) while James appears to have owned his outright. Moreover, James had very significant holdings in other parishes; for example, 1,000 acres in St John and 530 acres in St Andrew, making his land holdings at least 5,000 acres. Most plantations were by comparison much smaller. For example in St Catherine in 1670 there were 158 families. Excluding the Modyford brothers and Captain John Noyes who came second with 5,868 acres, the remaining 155 owners shared holdings of 53,982 acres or a mean average of 348 acres per family, with even this figure skewed upwards by a small number of owners with 2,000 acres or more. There is no doubt, therefore, that the Modyford brothers were among the largest landowners on the island.

A second strategy used by the governor to maintain pressure on the Spanish was to seek 'clarification' of his responsibilities not from the king but from elsewhere in the government where there was likely to be a more sympathetic response. One such communication was sent in early 1665 by Governor Modyford to the Duke of Albemarle, who was to be one of the two leading figures in the sea battles with the Dutch in the English Channel some months later. After some unsurprising delay, given what was occurring in England at this time, his cousin responded in June 1665 and advised that privateering could continue at the governor's discretion. Once again, Sir James Modyford played a key role in eliciting this response. He was in London at this time, officially representing the interests of the colony and it is probable that he saw Albemarle in person. In any event, the reply was sent by James with a letter of his own and, as Barbour notes, this decision was probably influenced by the interest that all had in the Royal African Company, which stood to gain much by an enhanced position in the growing trade with the colonies, not least in the continued supply of African slaves. There was clearly a balance here to be struck between the king and council feeling it unwise to continue depredations against the Spanish, and thereby incur the wrath of the Spanish monarchy, which had agreed peace treaties, and the Admiralty, which was led by relations of Modyford and co-investors in the Royal African Company who would gain by seizing trade from the Spanish. The Peace of Breda in 1667 brought an end to the French and Dutch wars and in May of that same year a commercial treaty was signed with the Spanish supposedly to regulate trade relations in both the East and West Indies. Once again letters of marque could only be granted in extreme situations but again the Duke of Albemarle informed Modyford that he could continue supporting privateers as long as it was for the 'benefit of the king's affairs'.

This last justification was tantamount to a complete freedom to do as he pleased, or at least that appears to be how it was interpreted. Nothing reveals this more clearly than the commission offered by the governor to Henry Morgan not just to attack Spanish vessels on the high seas but to capture, loot and destroy Spanish settlements in Cuba and elsewhere, basically therefore to start a war against the Spanish nation. The commission, dated 22 July 1670, is from the 'Governor of His Majesty's Island of Jamaica Commander-in-Chief of all His Majesties Forces within the said Island and in the Islands adjacent Vice-Admiral to His Royal Highness the Duke of York in the American Seas' specifically empowering 'Admiral' Henry Morgan to 'make war' against the Spanish (Malthus, 1683).[16] The commission is justified by reference to an incursion by Don Pedro Bayona de Villa Nueva, Captain General of the Province of Paraguay and Governour (*sic*) of the City of St Jago de Cuba and its Provinces on to the northern coast of Jamaica and charges that he and other Spanish commanders were plotting a more systematic invasion of Jamaica with the intention of retaking it for the Spanish crown:

> to use your best endeavours to surprise take sink disperse and destroy all the enemies ships or vessels which shall come within your view and also for preventing the intended Invasion against this place you are hereby further authorised and required in the case that you and your Officers in your

16 Younger brother of Charles II and later James II.

> Judgement find it possible or feasable to land and attain the said Town of St. Jago de Cuba or any other place belonging to the Enemies where you shall be informed that Magazines and Stores for this War are laid up or where any Rendezvous for their Forces to Imbody are appointed and there to use your best endeavours for seizing the said Stores and to take kill and disperse the said Forces And all Officers Souldiers and Seamen who are or shall be belonging to or embarqued upon the said vessels are hereby strictly enjoyned both by Sea and Land to obey you as their Admiral and Commander in chief of in all things as be cometh them; and you yourself are to observe and follow all such Orders as you shall from time to time receive from His most excellent Majesty his Royal Highness or myself.

The prizes gained by plunder were to be specifically distributed according to rank and were regarded as in lieu of pay as an incentive, if one were needed, to behave piratically. Commenting on one part of the invasion Zahedieh claims, 'the prize from Portobello alone amounted to £100,000, substantially more than the total value of Jamaica's annual agricultural output at the time' (DNB). Slaves were to be granted liberty provided they gave 'assurance of their Loyalty to His Majesty' and a right to possess the estates of their masters after a quarter deduction for the crown to provide defence against external aggressors. Anyone, Spaniard or slave, not swearing loyalty to the English crown would be killed except female slaves who would be brought back for sale. Therefore the third strategy for attempting to avoid the king's wrath was to justify commissions against Spanish vessels and settlements that might have been engaged in planning attacks against the island.

This was certainly not the end of the matter. One Spaniard, Don Juan Ximenes de Bohorques, complained to the English crown of losing his ship, the *Santo Cristo*, to a Jamaican vessel, the *Hopeful Adventurer*, in what the king's secretary (Lord Arlington) described as 'circumstances of inhumanity scarcely credible from Englishmen, and to the great scandal of the nation'. Thomas Modyford was ordered to investigate and provide restitution if the Spaniard's claims were found to be true (16 March 1666). On the other hand, it is clear that the governor was not entirely convinced by a policy of appeasement, partly because he had difficulty in enforcing it, partly because it led to the loss of a major stream of income for Port Royal (and his family) and partly because disregarding it put at his disposal a much larger fleet of adventurers drawn to the island by the promise of commissions against the 'weak and wealthy' Spanish. His response was to try to divert the privateers against the Dutch, particularly by attempting to take the island of Curaçao, and to encourage them to retake possessions seized by the Spanish from the English. The most important of these was the island of Providence off the coast of the mainland in the western Caribbean which was retaken after a period of 25 years under Spanish rule (June 1666). Modyford felt it was his duty to reinforce the garrison left behind by the English and 'to send down some able person to command it'. This he did in the form of Major Samuel Smith but it is quite obvious that the governor was intent on a more general strategy of hostility towards the Spanish in the Indies:

> the Spaniards look on us as intruders and trespassers wheresoever they find us in the Indies and use us accordingly; and were it in their power, as it is fixed in their wills, would soon turn us out of all our Plantations; and is it reasonable that we should quietly let them grow upon us, until they are able to do it. It must be force alone that can cut in sunder that unneighbourly maxim of their Government to deny all access of strangers (January 1667).

The Spaniards, he argues, 'have so inveterate a hatred against the English in those parts that they will not hear of trade or reconciliation, but any of the islanders that they can cowardly surprise they butcher inhumanely'. While events may have occurred to bolster this perception, it must always be remembered that the men-of-war that the governor wished to keep in Port Royal, in the absence of official forces of the crown, would not have come there were it not for continued access to rich prizes. The result was a period of dissembling in which Ximenes de Bohorques was accused of not owning the goods contained on his ship, reference again being made to the Duke of Albemarle's permission to grant discretion to the governor in issuing commissions against the Spanish while Sir James Modyford, now in Chiswick, lobbied the king's secretary to say that 'the governor of Jamaica has done all in his own name concerning the privateers' commissions, in order that nothing may impede any treaty at home' (CSP Domestic, Charles II-volume 170, 1–8 September 1666). In return, Sir Thomas must have proposed his brother as the reliable person to look after the English interest in Providence, for James received a commission in November 1666 to become lieutenant governor of the island, reporting to his brother in Jamaica while both brothers, again through their cousin, successfully argued for militia hardware (powder, ball, gun carriages, firelocks etc.) for both Jamaica and Providence.

Unfortunately, for Modyford this seizure of regal powers occurred at precisely the time that the king himself was engaged in more serious attempts to bring peace to longstanding feuds with the Spanish, culminating in the Treaty of Madrid on 8 July 1670, and perhaps of even greater significance, coinciding with the death of George Monck in January 1670. The upshot was that Modyford's commission as governor was rescinded and the new appointee, Sir Thomas Lynch, was ordered to return him to England under arrest charged with 'making war and committing depredations and acts of hostility upon the subjects and territories of the King of Spain in America, contrary to his Majesty's express order and command'.

For Charles II, struggling to establish peace with the Spanish crown, these events were, to say the least, embarrassing. To begin with the privateers appeared to be convinced that their commissions could be extended to the taking of Spanish-owned towns in Hispaniola, Cuba or the mainland. The governor meanwhile, despite some token gestures against acts of piracy, seemed bent on perpetuating a state of war with Spain, claiming that Spanish vessels were plotting to retake

Jamaica as they had Providence, where they had inflicted appalling acts of inhumanity against the governor's representative (5 October 1668). Thereafter, in a barrage of communications, the governor offered his defence for a policy that clearly ran counter to the king's pleasure, going so far as to say that the official policy of peaceable trade would be to commit 'that saddest error of all Governments', namely 'to weaken ourselves and strengthen our enemies' (23 August 1669). The claims that he benefited financially from the commissions he granted were in his eyes false, he having made only £300 by this means. All this was to almost no avail as in June 1670 the king declared that 'this way of warring is neither honourable nor profitable to his Majesty' and that he wished it to cease forthwith. In the same month, however, Sir Thomas was in receipt of a commission from the Governor of Curaçao purporting to come from the Queen Regent of Spain declaring open war against the English, and by the following month this appeared to be borne out by reports that a Spanish invasion had occurred on the north side of the island with settlers murdered and houses destroyed. The governor felt he had no choice but to grant the open-ended commission to Admiral Henry Morgan 'to attack, seize, and destroy the enemy's vessels' with the support of the Council.

In running specifically counter to the king's instructions, it is not surprising that the governor's future became somewhat fragile. What is of interest is that a series of petitions reached Whitehall, calling for his retention. Perhaps the most interesting of these is one from 'officers, freeholders and inhabitants of Jamaica to the King' that was read in Council on 9 November 1670. It commended Modyford as a planter himself and one who 'daily endeavours to oblige them by many wholesome laws, with a free and unbiased administration of justice; and the loud fame hereof draws great numbers of his Majesty's subjects from all parts to settle amongst them, to the great benefit of this island, his Majesty's revenue, and the English nation'. Although the petition was signed by some leading figures (including Henry Morgan, Theodore Cary, Robert Byndlos, a number of military personnel and 251 freeholders) it fell upon deaf ears and by January 1671 the die was cast, the governor's commission suspended and an instruction sent to Sir Thomas Lynch to become the new governor. The king's pleasure was that Sir Thomas was to be 'made prisoner and sent home under a strong guard to answer for what shall be objected against him' which was that he had made 'many depredations and hostilities against the subjects of his Majesty's good brother the Catholic King' (4 January 1671). By the summer of the same year, an English force had captured Panama and even stronger representations were sent from Madrid because both Sir Thomas and his son Charles were suspected of aiding and abetting this 'outrage'. Charles Modyford, easily accessible in London, was packed off to the Tower of London on 16 May where his father was soon to join him ('Preface', *Calendar of State Papers Relating to English Affairs in the Archives of Venice*, Volume 37: 1671–2).[17]

It is interesting to speculate whether the apparent contradiction of the king's instructions was the only reason for Sir Thomas' removal. There is some reason for thinking that the Modyfords were perceived as having grown (too) rich in the king's service, or even that the governor was corrupt. For example, the king's secretary, Lord Arlington, demanded that Charles Modyford furnish him with an account of his father's wealth in Jamaica. Charles' very suspect reply glossed over his sugar plantations and trading activities, and concentrated on funds owed to his father by the king.[18] It is unlikely that this proved helpful to his father's cause. The same could be said of the new governor's first report which complained bitterly of the old way of surveying and granting land, even though these were in accordance with the king's earlier instructions. More particularly he was fearful of how he was to remove the popular former governor

17 It is testimony to the character and popularity of Sir Thomas that the king felt it prudent to issue instructions to the Duke of York (the future James II) that he was to assist should there be opposition to the arrest of Sir Thomas and if necessary he should destroy all the privateers who were likely to support him (7 March 1671).

18 The claim was that these amounted to £6,250 out of a total European-based estate of £10,732.

without causing mayhem on the island. By enticing Modyford aboard a vessel in the harbour at Port Royal, he appeared to have used subterfuge and casuistry (20 August 1671). He reports that Sir James Modyford in particular was 'frantic' on hearing the news of his brother's imprisonment and subsequent passage to England. Subsequently, Sir Thomas Lynch appears not to have fared very well and was always aware that the previous governor was popular and the king's move the opposite. Sir Thomas Modyford spent two years in the Tower but was never charged; after a further flurry of petitions, he was released in the summer of 1674.[19]

A year or so later, Sir Thomas Modyford was back in Jamaica where, under an order from the then governor (Lord John Vaughan), who replaced the hapless Sir Thomas Lynch in June 1674, he became chief justice in 1675. In the same year his son, Charles, was appointed Survey-General of Jamaica.[20] Thomas Modyford died in Jamaica on 2 September 1679. He is described on his tombstone in the cathedral church at Spanish Town as the 'best and longest governour' and the 'soule and life of all Jamaica who first made it what it now is'. His oldest son and heir, who lived only a little more than a month longer, lies close by.

Loyalty Question

There is some evidence to suggest that both the Modyford brothers were more persuaded by the case of the parliamentarians than by the continuance of a powerful monarchy. The evidence in support of this would include the claim by the royalists on the fall of their home city, Exeter, and the apparent alacrity with which Thomas Modyford went out of his way to publicise his contempt for the Stuarts when in Barbados. James Modyford's unsolicited attempt to betray royalist sympathisers during the Commonwealth years is another example and, of course, there is the seeming indifference of his brother

19 Sir Thomas' son, Charles, was released soon after his confinement.
20 It was reported that although the governorship of Jamaica was a post attracting a salary of £1,000 per annum, four and a half years after assuming this position, Sir Thomas Lynch had yet to receive anything (24 May 1676).

to the king's instructions. The conventional view is that all such behaviour was merely opportunism and, although the evidence is not conclusive, the cumulative case is more persuasive. A curious example was reported in October 1676 when a Captain William Bragg declared to Sir Henry Morgan that Sir Thomas Modyford was guilty of treason because he had told him that while in England he had persuaded two counties (Essex and Suffolk) to rebel against the king because he had opposed acts of parliament. Morgan's deposition, signed 27 September 1676, went on to claim that Sir Thomas had left Andrew Arguile to solicit more counties, in particular Norfolk, although both were certain that they could also count on the support of Cornwall. In this deposition Bragg claimed that Modyford had said that 'he had rather have the love of his subjects than of the King' (Secretary Coventry delivered to Lords of Trade and Plantations [the above] three papers [I., II., III.] concerning Sir Thomas Modyford and William Bragg. *Together, 5 pp. [Col. Papers, Vol. XXXVII., Nos. 73, 73, I., II., III.; also Col. Entry Bk., Vol. XXIX., p. 106.*]).

Modyford's response was to be expected. He declared himself a loyal supporter of the king and entered a suit for £10,000 in damages. Another example, however, is cited by Nuala Zahedieh, who quotes one Mr Nevil in a letter to the Earl of Carlisle commenting on the drunkenness and debauchery that was widespread in Jamaica during the period he was there. Writing in 1677, after Thomas Modyford had returned to Jamaica (and after the death of both his wife and brother) he claims that apart from Modyford's 'avowed antimonarchical principles he is the openest atheist and most profest immoral liver in the world as your Lordship will soon discover if ever you have to do with him' ('The present state of Jamaica in a letter from Mr Nevil to the Earl of Carlisle', 1677, BL, Add. MS 12429, fol. 152 quoted in DNB).

It would not be true to claim that the younger of the Modyford brothers was in the elder's shadow but he was clearly less significant in political terms. He certainly matched his brother as a merchant and possibly as a planter. Both were equally engaged in the slave trade and both profited hugely from it. James had less of the buccaneer about him and by comparison with Thomas might be thought more staid. The male members of the family are not normally viewed together but in Caribbean terms they comprised a formidable team. They were merchant adventurers who played a pivotal role in creating what today is usually termed 'plantation society' with all that meant in terms of generating a system of white privilege and black subjugation for meeting the demand for tropical produce. They were not alone but few had the combination of administrative competence, legal precision and spirit of ruthless exploitation that the brothers possessed.

Chapter 3

The First Plantation Inheritance

In addition to Sir Nicholas Slanning and his sequence of wives, Maristow appears to have been home initially at least to both his sisters. Margaret, who was 14 years old when her father died, and Elizabeth, who was ten years old at the time of his death, spent their childhood years there. By the time of the Restoration in 1660 Margaret was petitioning Charles II for confirmation of a grant made previously to her late father for the profits of Dartmoor Forest in compensation for the number of years the family had lost during the Civil War and its aftermath (*CSP* Domestic 1660–1: 144, 194). Through her mother's new family, Elizabeth became acquainted with James Modyford whom she married when she was 22 in 1655. Although her husband was away making his fortune in Jamaica almost continuously after 1663 until his death ten years later, they managed to have four children who survived birth from twice that number of confinements. Thomas, named after his uncle, was born in 1658, Mary was born in 1660, Elizabeth was born in 1662 and Grace was born one year later in 1663, when her mother was still only 30 years old.[1] None of these children could have seen much of their father and nor could he have played any part in the management of the estate. With his elevation to a baronetcy in 1661, the children's mother became Dame Elizabeth, but male roles in their lives must have been played by their uncle Nicholas or possibly to some extent by their nephew Andrew Slanning, both of whom were living in the mansion house at Maristow.

1 James and Elizabeth had another child, James, who died at birth on 21 May 1664. As a later reference will make clear, Elizabeth is likely to have had eight confinements in as many years.

The only surviving son, Thomas, lived long enough to inherit his father's title but died at the age of 15 in November 1678 while away at Westminster School in London and never returned to Devon or played any role in the estate.[2] Of the three remaining girls the older two both acquired husbands from the village of Mattingley in Hampshire. Elizabeth married a man called Herne, but by 1684 when all heirs of their father's property were described in the deed of transfer to Grace and Peter Heywood, she is listed as a widow, even though then only being in her early twenties. Mary also married a 'Gentleman of Mattingley in the County of Southampton', John Deane, in 1683 at the age of 23. According to a manuscript by P Bebbington,

> Mary lived at Mattingley for a while after her marriage, and a daughter whom they called Elizabeth was born in 1685 and baptised at Heckfield and Mattingley Parish Church (see H & M Parish Registers). Sometime later Mary and John moved their home to the West Country, almost certainly to Maristow to be nearer her mother, a widow living on her own in a large house. John Deane died there in 1702 and was buried in Bickleigh Church (Bebbington, n.d.).

The parish register does indeed confirm that Elizabeth Deane was baptised in the church on 12 April 1685, but depending on when they moved, it might not have been the case that Elizabeth Modyford was on her own. The house was home to Sir Nicholas Slanning and his wife until his death in 1691 and to Sir Andrew Slanning and his wife until 1700. The youngest, Grace, had by then been widowed in Jamaica and had married again to Peter Heywood.

After his marriage to Elizabeth Slanning in 1655, Sir James Modyford spent some time in Jamaica, even prior to his brother's appointment as governor in 1664 as, for example, when he was commissioned by Charles II to prepare a survey of the island in 1663. Indeed, it is very probable that Thomas Modyford owed his appointment partly to his younger brother's lobbying with George

2 Thomas Modyford is buried in the crypt of Westminster Abbey.

Monck, Duke of Albemarle, and there is no doubt that he played a significant role also in helping to populate the island both through the agreement he negotiated for former convicts to serve as indentured servants and through his role in the Royal African Company. Much of this, however, was accomplished while he was in England either at Maristow or at his London address. He was again in England between 1664 and 1666, when he served as agent for the new colony, now governed by his brother.

Following the arrest of Sir Thomas in 1671, Sir James Modyford travelled back to England to lobby the king for his release, returning to Jamaica when this seemed unlikely to be successful. In January 1673, while the former governor was still incarcerated in the Tower, James died and was buried on the 13th of the month at St Andrew in Jamaica (*BM Add. MS.* 27968, f. 30). His estate consisted mostly of his Jamaican plantations and although he died intestate, these appear to have been granted to his widow, Elizabeth (*Caribbeana*, 4: 340). There is no strong evidence that Elizabeth Modyford ever travelled to Jamaica and much to suggest that she was unenthusiastic about the island and what she knew or thought she knew of its way of life.[3] Almost certainly, she continued to live at Maristow because a commitment was made at the time of her marriage that James Modyford would provide £3,000 for 'lands of inheritance' for the benefit of his wife to be held in trust by Richard Lord Arundell of Trerice in Cornwall, Sir George Smith and Sir Andrew King (WAM 11683, 14 January 1666).[4] Dame Elizabeth Modyford would not have been independently wealthy at this time and later evidence suggests she put a great deal of energy into building up properties in Devon. She would not then have known that all of the Maristow estate would eventually become hers.

3 This is not the view of the first author of the DNB entry for Sir James Modyford and it is true that he writes to Sir Andrew King in 1670 that 'my wife intended hither' (WAM 11936, 2 May 1670) but there is no evidence that she did make the journey.

4 Questions of debt and financial loss may have affected the once close relationship between the Modyford family and Sir Andrew King. After James Modyford's death Elizabeth Modyford obtained an order of the Court of Chancery removing Sir Andrew as one of the trustees of this indenture (WAM 11704, 27 October 1675).

Their first child, Thomas, born in 1658, survived until after the death of his father and therefore inherited the title but not the Jamaican properties as he too died prior to the age of majority being buried in the cloisters of Westminster Abbey on 5 November 1678.[5] This left three daughters. The first of these, Mary, born in 1660, was to play a very significant role in her mother's later life and with the Maristow estate. She married John Deane of Mattingley near Southampton. The second daughter, Elizabeth, born in 1662, married a man called Herne also from Mattingley but by the early 1680s she had been widowed. The youngest daughter, Grace, born in 1663, was the only one to show any enthusiasm for her father's career, travelling out to Jamaica in the late 1670s after his death in 1673, perhaps to consider what to do with his huge plantations and their associated houses and sugar factories. As a young women of seemingly very considerable means, and staying with her highly esteemed uncle Sir Thomas Modyford, she must have made an impact on the eligible bachelors living in that part of Jamaica. Indeed, immediately after her uncle's death, she married into the Drake family (Edward Drake) on 5 August 1679. In this choice she turned out to be unlucky since barely a year after their marriage, Edward Drake also died (5 October 1680).

A month after this event on 2 November 1680, a young naval officer, Captain Peter Heywood, of the frigate HMS *Norwich* arrived in Jamaica to assist in the defence of the island, particularly against the incursions of the French fleet in the West Indies. His early exploits in seizing foreign ships breaking the Acts of Navigation by attempting to land African slaves to help meet a steady and growing demand, were no doubt a factor in providing the young officer with a swashbuckling reputation for courage and skilful seamanship. In any event, it was not long before he and Grace Drake were engaged to be married, an event which duly took place on 2 February 1682.

5 They may have had a second son, also called James, who died as an infant and was buried at the parish of St Andrews Undershaft, City of London on 21 May 1664.

In the two years that followed, Captain Heywood's star that had shone so brightly at the outset began to dim, particularly in relation to his naval career. Given the merchant tradition of the family into which he had now married, it is interesting that it was the search for payments due for carrying or seizing goods that produced this crisis. Although the exact date is not known, sometime in the summer of 1682, the *Norwich* was lost off the south coast of Jamaica and it was widely reported that the ship foundered while overladen with merchandise. A report in the *Journal of the Lords of Trade and Plantations* in November 1682 from Lord Finch recorded the loss which he said was caused by carrying merchandise contrary to orders. He went on, in what must have been a reference to Heywood, 'captains sometimes excuse themselves by saying that they take such goods on board by the Governor's order' (*CSP 'America and West Indies'*, 11 November 1682, 11, 1661–5: 317–32). Four days later an Order from the King in Council was issued to all colonial governors 'requiring them to allow no merchandise to be laden on the King's ships in future; also that upon the occurrence of any accident or misbehaviour of any officer or men on any King's ship they do not hold a court-martial on the case, but take the necessary depositions and transmit them home'.

The Governor of Jamaica, Sir Thomas Lynch, received a separate instruction to send Heywood back to London in custody 'to answer for the loss of the ship and other charges'. Given the general edict that the loss of the *Norwich* caused, it was to be expected that the governor would respond with indignation, which he duly did by the following May, denying both that the vessel was carrying goods under his orders or that he should be sidestepped when it came to punishing those who broke naval orders. It would appear likely that the *Norwich* was laden with booty from a captured vessel when she went down. Subsequently, Peter Heywood did appear before a court martial in Jamaica and was also sent back in late 1683 to answer in Whitehall for the loss of his vessel. Fortunately for him, no further action was taken, but by the spring of the following year it was apparent that his naval career was over (*CSP Domestic*, Charles II, 15–30 April 1683–84: 387–400).

It seems probable that Grace Heywood may have accompanied her husband in early 1684 on his return to England to face the king's pleasure in relation to the loss of his ship, for what happened thereafter was highly significant in changing the fortunes of the family. Peter Heywood had to find a new career and his young wife was heir to one-third of the Modyford estate, which must by then have been somewhat run down, particularly after the death of Sir Thomas Modyford in 1679. Whose idea it was is unclear but Grace and Peter proposed to Dame Elizabeth Modyford that they should buy out the other coheirs to the Jamaican plantations in order to establish themselves as planters of some size and note. This they duly did in a transfer dated 1684 between on the one part Dame Elizabeth Modyford, John Deane Esq of Mattingley near Southampton and Mary his wife and Elizabeth Herne of the same place now a widow and, on the other, Peter Heywood of Jamaica Esq. and Grace his wife. The deed of transfer continues:

> Whereas Sir James Modyford was seized of a considerable estate both real and personal in Jamaica it is agreed that Peter Heywood shall have all such and in consideration of 5s. payable to Dame Eliz. Modyford, and of £650 with interest at 6 per cent, payable to John Deane and Mary his wife, and of £650 &c. to Eliz. Herne, they sell and release to him all the lands, houses and goods (in Jamaica).

By any standards this was an astonishingly generous settlement, particularly since no money actually changed hands. Peter and Grace were simply required to sign bonds for £1000 due to both Mary and John Deane and Elizabeth Herne should they default on the payment of the interest due. There is also no question that the Modyford estates in Jamaica were by this date worth many times the sums involved in this transfer.

Peter Heywood and the Pursuit of Power

Peter Heywood came from a family of some considerable note, mainly because of their importance in the history of Lancashire.

Peter Heywood himself, however, was descended from a branch of the family that was more London-based, particularly in relation to the borough of Westminster. His father Thomas was a page to James Duke of York and his grandfather, also Peter, was famous for being credited with the discovery of Guy Fawkes as he hid in the cellars of the Palace of Westminster in 1605 thereby frustrating the 'Gunpowder Plot' to blow up parliament. His anti-Papist reputation, however, also led to his early demise, following his stabbing by the Jesuit John James in Westminster Hall in 1640.

The career of Peter Heywood in Jamaica was one of fortuitous promotion rather than the result of charisma or the product of real leadership qualities. By the early 1690s, approximately a decade after his marriage to Grace Modyford, he was a member of the island's Council and by 1698 a member of the Assembly by virtue of being a judge of the high court. It has to be remembered that most of the population were black slaves. In fact, there were fewer than 2,500 white men from which to choose holders of public office, and many of these owed their presence in the colony to having been imprisoned in England and subsequently banished. As far as Heywood was concerned, an opportunity arose in November 1706 for real preferment with the death of the chief justice. The then governor, Thomas Handasyde, who served in this role from 1702 to 1711, reported to the Council of Trade and Plantations:

> The Chief Justice of this Island, Col. Walters, departing this life, I have been obliged to appoint in his stead Col Peter Heywood, who has been the eldest Assistant Judge these 12 or 13 years; I must confess I have no extraordinary opinion of him, but he was the best I could get, having proffered it to severall other Gentlemen, who I thought were fitter for it, and they all declined it (*CSP*, 23, 1706–8).

From this vantage point, it would not be many years before he could attempt an assault on the highest position, that of governor of the colony, although the path that lay ahead was far from smooth and straightforward.

It is important to note that the closing years of the seventeenth century and the following two decades were profoundly affected by a combination of natural and manmade disasters. On 7 June 1692, for example, Jamaica experienced a severe earthquake. The island Council reported to the Council on Trades and Plantations describing the events in graphic terms:

> On the 7th inst., there was a dreadful earthquake which in ten minutes threw down all the churches, dwelling houses and sugar works in the Island. Two thirds of Port Royal were swallowed up by the sea, all the forts and fortifications demolished and great part of its inhabitants miserably knocked on the head or drowned (*CSP*, 13, 1689–92).

This was followed by a serious fire in what remained of Port Royal and by periodic invasions of the north coast by French forces. On top of that, disease took a particularly heavy toll; so much so, in fact, that that the white population experienced an absolute decline in numbers even though the continued arrival of African slaves boosted the population overall. One report suggests that the island's militia fell in just one year from 2,440 in 1695 to 1,390. The same author goes on to say that 'recovery from these blows was slow. When the next census was taken in 1730, (the) white population had barely increased from 1692' (Burnard, 1996: 771–2).

One manifestation of this unease and the rending of the social fabric was a deep division between the Assembly, which represented the interests of the planters, and the governor and his Advisory Council whose role was to ensure good governance and the interests of the crown. The system in all Crown Colonies was that the Assembly had a legislative function but all representations and communications were sent to Whitehall via the king's representative, namely the governor as advised by his Council. Only in the rarest of circumstances, when the Assembly wished to make an address containing complaints about the governor himself, was it permissible for them to send anything directly to London. The Jamaican Assembly, however,

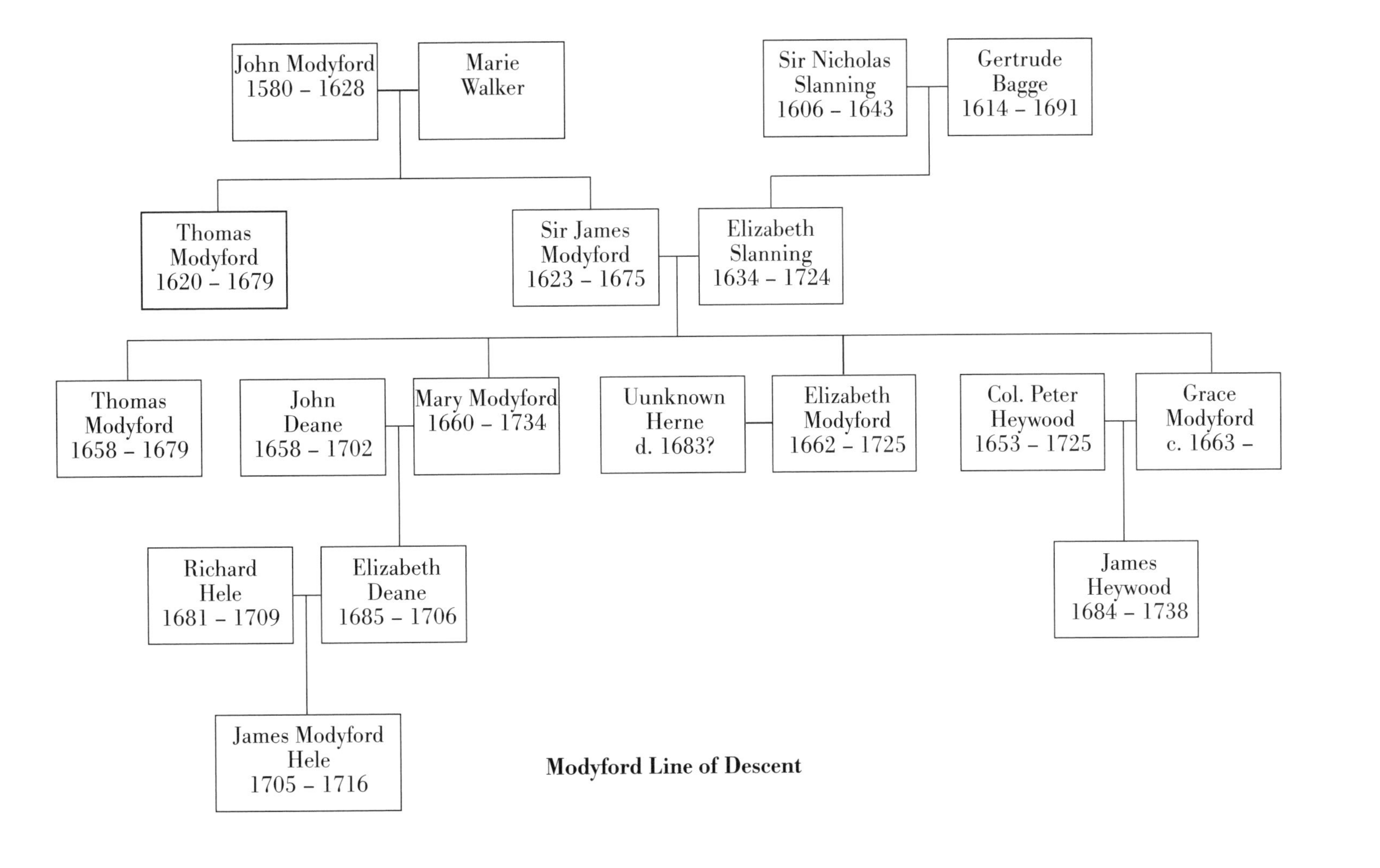

Modyford Line of Descent

was wont to ignore this instruction for which they were criticised for 'pretending to assume new privileges and powers, which if not prevented, may lead to the weakening of H.M. prerogative in those parts'. Unsurprisingly this brought the Assembly into conflict with the governor as it sought to bypass him and make representations directly to the crown. In this regard, the incumbent from 1711, Lord Archibald Hamilton, fared no better than his predecessor. The immediate issue, however, was the role of the Assembly in voting adequate funds for paying the militia and other staff. In the governor's view, they had failed to do this on numerous occasions with the result that in 1715 he had personally been obliged to meet these salaries from his own resources. Again, the majority in the Assembly refused to pass votes allowing for the repayment of this loan. The governor's only other option was to meet these expenses with the revenues from the island's treasury, as had been the case in earlier periods. A vote to this effect was then brought before the Council which was divided equally on the issue. Critically, however, Peter Heywood, although chief justice and a crown appointee, voted against this strategy and therefore with the majority in the Assembly, on the grounds that there was no existing law that allowed public revenues to be used in this manner. The governor construed this as an act of disloyalty to the government of which he was a part and Heywood was suspended both from his role as chief justice and from the Council itself.

In the meantime, perhaps sensing that they had the governor and those loyal to him on the run, two members of the Assembly made direct representations to London to the effect that a ship part-owned by the governor had engaged in acts of piracy by removing booty from Spanish vessels wrecked off the coast of Florida. How they knew this is entirely unclear but the hand of Heywood is not difficult to discern. Having been summarily removed from office he certainly had a motive; he was an ex-naval captain who was closely in touch with the privateers of Port Royal and he was married to Grace Modyford, whose uncle had been arrested and returned to London on similar charges 45 years before.

As things turned out this devious strategy was remarkably successful. Peter Heywood wrote to the Council on Trade and Plantations complaining of his suspension from the government and pleading that 'I always thought that the King in his Instructions to the Governor permitted the Council to have freedom of debate, and that they have the liberty of giving their votes as their judgment directs, without lying under the displeasure of the Governor and being suspended by him and the majority of the Council' (CO 137/11, 19 May 1716). Two days later the commission and instructions were prepared by secretary Stanhope for Peter Heywood to succeed Lord Archibald Hamilton as lieutenant governor,[6] and, even more importantly, he was instructed

> to make inquiry into any robberies or piracies committed by persons commissioned by the Lord Archibald Hamilton upon the Spaniards in the Gulph of Florida or elsewhere, to seize the effects of those concerned therein and send over to this Kingdom the principal persons with their effects and proper evidences against them, and also to send the Lord Archibald Hamilton home under arrest, in case it shall appear he was any ways concerned in those illegal practices.

Although this instruction is both impetuous and poorly drafted, it appears to require Heywood, who was after all the island's principal law officer, to conduct an investigation under due process and where there was a case to be answered send on the suspects to London for further trial. In any event, the Council for Trade and Plantations immediately requested this draft be withdrawn, only to be informed that the commission and instructions to Heywood had already gone. All they were able to do was send a further communication enclosing extracts of letters sent to Lord Hamilton 'for your information and guidance in what may be expected from you'. The Board went on to argue strongly that Heywood's duty was to maintain the militia and promote greater harmony in the affairs of the island:

6 The role of lieutenant governor could be construed as a deputy to an existing governor but as a temporary governor when no other existed.

> The preservation of the peace and safety of Jamaica, is of such consequence, that we hope the Assembly will maturely consider of it with the present circumstance of that Island, in regard to the growing power of the French and Spaniards and the weak condition of your own militia; so that it may be needless for us any more to recommend the taking care of providing the additional subsistance necessary for H.M. Forces there, till the Island shall be better strengthen'd by white people, and that H.M. shall be pleas'd otherwise to dispose of the said troops.

As for the militia, the board insisted on the absolute necessity of retaining them as a protection against 'rebellious negroes or foreign enemies', at least until there were sufficient white settlers to render the island safe.

According to Heywood's own account, he sat with the Council to inquire into the former governor's conduct but appeared not to miss an opportunity to indict him for his alleged connivance in piracy, reporting to London on 11 August 1716 that 'his Lordship being concern'd as an owner and receiving of 468 pound 5 ounces troy weight of plate' had suffered 'vessells that had landed upon and plundered the Spaniards to come in and goe out of port again without any manner of discountenance' (*CSP*, 29, 1716–7: 159–77). What he did not do was dispassionately examine the case against Lord Hamilton in a judicial manner as arguably he was instructed to do, and return him along with his accusers if there was a case for him to answer so that he could be properly examined. Rather, the former governor was packed off home under arrest without knowing what he was supposed to have done, and without an opportunity to defend himself, while his accusers were never asked to justify their case against him.

Because Heywood was only regarded in London as an interim appointment whose preferment rested entirely on his being the longest serving member of the Council, he was forbidden from passing any laws other than those immediately necessary for the peace and welfare of the island. In his speech to the Assembly, however, Heywood announced, contrary to this instruction, that he would pass all laws they chose to send him. This meant that all the bills that had been rejected before, including one that had been annulled by the crown, were re-presented. This incurred the wrath of the new chief justice, Thomas Bernard, with the effect that Heywood lobbied London for his removal, and when this did not work chose to remove all the existing members of the Council and replace them with his friends who could be relied upon to support the charges against Lord Hamilton. The existing seven members were all persons who had been unanimous in stripping him of his Council position and role as chief justice. The first name he proposed to London as replacement was his son James whom he describes as 'my only son, *etc.*, a gentleman of as great honour, integrity and good sence as any man in the Island, and his own estate little inferiour to most of the best'.

None of these proceedings went unchallenged despite the attempt to silence opposition in the Council. In the first place, not all the planters and merchants of Jamaica supported the majority view in the Assembly, despite the fact that it was overwhelmingly drawn from their ranks. Petitions were sent to London very early on when charges were initially laid against the governor in which it was said that 'the complaints against the Governor were not well founded, but were carried on by persons of small credit in Jamaica'. Moreover, if anyone was to replace him it must be a person 'of honour, ability, and integrity' (*CSP* 182, 182 i., ii., 203 i., ii., v.). These views were not without some justice since the Assembly contained a number of members whose wealth rather than selfless commitment to public service was more relevant in their elevation to the Assembly and Council.

Perhaps the best-known of these were the Beckford family whose wealth had been built by the ambition and acumen of Colonel Peter Beckford, a contemporary of Peter Heywood, who became president of the Council in the 1690s and whose son, also Peter, was promoted in his early twenties to become receiver-general only to lose this position after murdering a colleague (the deputy judge advocate, one Lewis). His younger brother Thomas was also accused of murder but neither of Colonel Beckford's sons faced any serious penalty and these misfortunes, which might have been expected to retard the family's political aspirations, merely prevented Colonel Beckford becoming lieutenant governor for a brief period in the early 1700s, and nor did they stop both the sons resuming political careers some time later when they were staunch supporters of the Heywood faction in the Assembly.[7] This, together with Peter Heywood's own behaviour, lay behind the judgment of the Rev William May who wrote around 1720 to the Bishop of London reporting on 'the Principal persons' of the island. His views on a number of key figures were less than flattering. On Peter Heywood and his son James (Jemmy) he was particularly scathing: 'Colonel Heywood, lately Governor, Mammon is his God, and vehement for the present corrupt principles; and, his son, Jemmy, another colonel, and most wicked debauchee, his Heir' (Oliver, (ed) 1914, III: 8).

Once he returned to London, Lord Hamilton was vocal in his protest against his arrest and subsequent expulsion. Noting in September 1717 in a plea to the king that 'Your Majesty was pleased to recall him, and appoint Mr Heywood to succeed him, whom he had some months before by the unanimous advice of the Council removed from the Council and from being Chief Justice', he warmed to his understandable complaint that

> Far from complying with your Majesty's Instructions, the new Governor and Councillors, in the enquiry made by them, acted in the most arbitrary, partiall and injustifyable manner, denying Lord Archibald the common right of the meanest British subject vizt. a copy of their charge or by any means to give him any knowledge of what they had to alledge against him, thereby greatly abusing the trust reposed in them, the measures they took having been with the only view of aspersing him by screening the guilty against your

7 These events are well covered in Parker (2012: 219–33).

> Majesty's just and royall intention of making restitution to the Spaniards. Thus unheard, ignorant of his charge, did Mr. Heywood and new Councillors seize his person, and at a day's warning sent him a prisoner to Great Britain, having granted a very extraordinary if not illegall warrant for his commitment, and all this by a majority of one only, and those new Councillors, the rest protesting.

Since the new governor and new councillors had not pressed any charges after his removal, Hamilton concluded, '... it appears that the complaint was raised thro' their malice without any just foundation, merely to procure his recall' (*CSP*, 30, 1717–8: 30–50).

The Council of Trade and Plantations was similarly appalled by what had occurred. In its report to the king, its address is carefully couched so as not to imply any mishandling of the whole affair by the monarch, but its meaning is unambiguous:

> You will likewise be pleas'd to take notice, how ill an use Mr. Heywood and the Council have made of H.M. Instructions for securing the Lord Archd's. person, wherein in our opinion they were no wise justifiable by those Instrns., because they were not directed by H.M. Orders to send the Ld. Archd. prisoner to England, unless upon examination it shou'd appear to them, that he was concern'd in the piracy complain'd of by the Spaniards, the contrary whereof seems to us to be true. It cannot but be a great misfortune to any Gentleman to be dismiss'd the service of so excellent a Prince as H.M.; but to be remov'd in a manner so reflecting upon his character must add to the mortification; and we are sorry to find the publick has been so little advantag'd by the change. We shall not take upon us to determine how far it might be proper for H.M. to comply with the prayer of my Lord Archibald's Memorial, thô if it shou'd appear to H.M. that Mr. Heywood and the other persons complain'd of by his Lordship have been guilty of the facts by him laid to their charge, we cannot but think it wou'd be for H.M.

> service in that Island and contribute very much to the better supporting H.M. Government there for the future, that H.M. shou'd shew such marks of his displeasure against them as to His Royal wisdom may seem most proper (CO 138/15; *CSP*, 30, 1717–8: 77–96).

In fact, while Peter Heywood was clearly at best a Machiavellian figure, the handling of Jamaican affairs in London cannot be said to have marked a high point in colonial administration. The mishandling of appointments did not end with the treatment of Lord Hamilton. In June 1716, Thomas Pitt was appointed to succeed Hamilton but he never took up the appointment and in the following year a local planter, Colonel Nicholas Lawes, was knighted and arrived back in the island in 1718, thus allowing Heywood two years at the helm.[8] Heywood died in Jamaica in 1725 a very rich man and left his numerous estates to his eldest surviving son, James, who was to play a highly significant role in the fortunes of Maristow House.

The Momentous Events of the Early Eighteenth Century

These were troubled years in many respects. The late seventeenth century was marked by infant deaths of around one in five and in some parts of England up to one in three.[9] The miseries surrounding these losses must have been immense and although possibly ameliorated by devout adherence to the scriptures, as was undoubtedly the case at Maristow, it is equally likely that guilt over the Devil's work would have made things worse. It is also worth emphasising that there is little in common in the late seventeenth and early eighteenth centuries with the explosive growth of the later

---

8 Thomas Pitt, formerly President of Madras, resigned this appointment after the sale of a large diamond (the Regent gem) brought back from India improved his finances. He entered parliament instead becoming known as 'Diamond Pitt'. He was the grandfather of William Pitt, the elder (1708–78) twice Prime Minister of Great Britain. Nicholas Lawes had been a high court judge and member of the Council alongside Peter Heywood since 1668.

9 Measurement errors and differences by social class make generalisations hazardous but a welcome decline after the period 1680–1710 is well documented (see Jones, 1980).

eighteenth century. On the contrary, in rural areas of south-west England, this was a period of faltering incomes based on traditional agricultural practices with static or declining populations and low levels of productivity. Whichever theory of economic growth one prefers to account for the industrial revolution, the technical prowess and population growth that were to come were absent in Devon's landed estates at this time, particularly when they were directed by families more concerned with surviving through opportune marriages than by generating wealth through advances in production techniques. This was not an era of trade, transport innovation or scientific thinking, at least not on rural estates. Even the approaches to specialist agricultural production adopted by the plantations of the New World, with which family members at Maristow must have had some familiarity, were regarded as anathema not because they were founded upon the horrors of unfree labour but because sun-drenched tropical lifestyles ran the risk of undermining Protestant discipline and abstinence.

It is a profound irony therefore that economic survival came to depend on wealth extracted from Jamaican plantations, but this was no linear transition. On the contrary, the exigencies of inheritance and the profound family discord they generated first produced a period of intense upheaval rivalling the best Victorian sagas of Anthony Trollope. A family legal adviser edges his way, possibly through illegal means, to an undeserved inheritance of one of the most prestigious estates in the West Country. An unhappy widow struggles through the courts to extract the ill-gotten proceeds diverted by a politician of dubious morality that should have been expended on the well-being of her ill-fated grandson. An elderly matriarch clashes with her foreign-born relative over the right way to run a large but crumbling estate. A bizarre will reflects years of disappointment in a late marriage that ends in another unhappy widow taking her own pre-teen son to court to try and extract from her late husband's estate enough for her and her daughters to thrive. A major conflagration leads to the near-destruction of a loved country mansion and its subsequent abandonment. All are contained herein.

Chapter 4

Inheritance and its Aftermath

Although having been a widow for more than a quarter of a century, Elizabeth Modyford cannot have ever imagined that aged 66 she would be left in charge of a large and complex estate. Her older brother, albeit not a gifted administrator of the family holdings, had added to them and she must have anticipated that her nephew, Andrew, would have succeeded and in all probability produced a male heir himself. Whatever wealth her side of the family had generated through her husband's Caribbean adventures had long since been passed to her youngest daughter and her second husband, but now, unexpectedly, she was responsible both for running the family estates and for deciding where within her family they would best be preserved. Her daughter, Elizabeth, was out of the picture through widowhood and her favourite daughter, Mary, was nursing her sick husband John, only for him to die in 1702. During her married life Mary Deane had given birth to four children, but three of them did not survive infancy and therefore the choice focused on Mary Deane's daughter, another Elizabeth.

In 1704, two years after her father's death, Elizabeth Deane at the age of 19 married Richard Hele from Holbeton in Devon. The Heles of south Devon were one of the largest and most affluent families in the county. The family had numerous branches locally including at Gnaton and Holwell, Newton Ferrers, Brixton near Plymouth and Wembury. Richard, however, was a descendant of the Heles of Flete or Fleet Damerel(l) near the village of Holbeton on the River Erme. He was the oldest son of the Rector of Helland in Cornwall, also Richard. His father had inherited Flete House, one of the most beautiful and substantial estates in south Devon, from his uncle Sir Samuel Hele, who had been MP for Plympton

Erle in the seventeenth century and for Okehampton later (Plate 6). Richard, after inheriting the family estate in 1682 at the age of three, went on to New College, Oxford, and entered parliament for Plympton Erle himself in 1701–2. He became member for the pocket borough of West Looe in 1702 and again sat as MP for Plympton with Richard Edgcumbe in the first parliament of Queen Anne in 1702–5.

The 1704 Marriage Settlement

The lack of capital that appears to have been a hallmark of these years of the Maristow estate is nowhere better exemplified than in the marriage settlement that was agreed between Elizabeth Deane and Richard Hele. As the undisputed head of the family and the owner of the Maristow estate, this settlement was designed by Elizabeth Modyford. It consisted of two parts. First, there was a sum of £8,000 to be settled on the younger Elizabeth as a marriage portion but which was promised rather than paid by selling part of the estate or from other resources.[1] Second, the whole of the estate was placed in the hands of trustees with a clear sequence of inheritance in which Richard Hele was located. He was thus entitled to become a member of the family and one who might under certain circumstances benefit financially, in addition to the promised cash component. The quadrapartite deed is dated 13 June 1704 between Elizabeth Modyford, Richard Hele, the trustees and Elizabeth Deane (PWDRO 70/293). The trustees were a mixture of male relatives and family advisors (James Kendall, Henry Manaton of Harwood, John Woolcombe, James Bulteel of Tavistock, John Snell of Exeter and William Langford of Bratton Clovelly). Kendall was related to the Modyford family and Woolcombe was to become Richard Hele's brother-in-law after marriage to his sister, Ann. The others were estate, financial or legal advisors or administrators.

1 It is likely that this would have been matched by a jointure or payment from the husband to pay for his wife's maintenance should she be subsequently widowed. The marriage portion is high, probably because Hele was a wealthy landowner (see Habakkuk, 1950).

The deed grants to the trustees the mansion of Maristow including Maristow Barton and 250 acres; also Bickham and associated lands and properties in Tamerton Folliot, Shaugh Prior, Bickleigh and Walkampton totalling 400 acres together with lands in Roborough and Buckland Monachorum and in Cornwall (Penryn). Essentially, this included everything that Elizabeth Modyford had inherited two years before. The sequence of inheritance, however, specified that Dame Elizabeth would have sole rights to the property for her remaining life which then passed to Mary Deane and then to her heirs including her daughter, Elizabeth. Richard Hele then became named as the successor in title for 99 years after his marriage or for however long he should live, providing he remained a widower. After that the Maristow estate would pass to the surviving sons and then daughters of Elizabeth Deane. At this point for the first time the children of Grace Heywood are identified in the sequence of succession, although clearly not in any expectation that they would benefit. James Heywood and his successors then became entitled to inherit the estate, which if he did not survive then passed to the trustees. Only subsequently does the line of inheritance move to Grace Heywood's daughter, Elizabeth Morgan Byntloss.[2]

The Will of Richard Hele

Very soon after this marriage took place there began a sequence of family tragedies that led to quite unexpected outcomes. Richard and Elizabeth Hele produced a son in 1705, James Modyford Hele, presumably while living at Flete House. A daughter, who died immediately after birth, was also born to the couple but Elizabeth herself passed away while still only in her early twenties on 6 February 1706 as a consequence of this confinement. Her husband, no doubt highly distressed by his wife's death, did not have long to live himself. In October 1709 he was reported to be in a 'raving' state at Bath and he died on 12 November of that year. He was just 30 years old.

2 See also PWDRO 70/294, dated 12 August 1704, which covers the contents of the principal mansion house in a similar sequence of inheritance.

Richard Hele's will, dated 17 June 1709, is vitally important in understanding what subsequently transpired (TNA: PRO 11/525). He appointed his 'dearest friend', James Bulteel, who since November 1703 had been one of two MPs for Tavistock, to arrange for the education and upbringing of his four-year-old son, and four other trustees including 'my most honoured Grandmother the Lady Elizabeth Modyford (and) my honoured mother in law Mary Dean' to use the sale of all his goods and chattels to meet his debts, funeral expenses and small legacies.[3] Elizabeth Modyford is specifically entreated to oversee the upbringing of his son, and all the properties, which were very considerable, were left to his son and any heirs he may eventually generate. Should his son not survive then all his estates were to pass to his sister Anne, who in 1707 had married John Woolcombe of Pitton near Yealmpton in Devon (a lawyer and MP for Plymouth 1702–05) and then onwards through her male line. In the event of her having only daughters then they would receive substantial legacies on attaining the age of majority and some of the properties would pass to his cousin Walter Hele with the residue, which included Flete House, then descending to James Bulteel and his heirs.

James Bulteel was a Tory lawyer of Huguenot descent and a legal advisor to several landed families in Devon including the Modyfords and the Heles. He stood unsuccessfully for parliament in the two elections of 1701, but was returned unopposed for Tavistock at a by-election in November 1703. Although born in Tavistock, he was not universally respected there, losing the 1708 election but going on to gain a seat on petition in 1710. Precisely why Bulteel was disliked is unclear but events that unfolded in relation to the occupants of Maristow House certainly add some credence to this reputation.[4]

3 Other trustees were his cousin Walter Hele of Widdecombe and John Snell, clerk, of Exeter.

4 James Bulteel married Mary Crocker, heiress of Courtenay Crocker, the owner of Lyneham in Yealmpton, Devon. Later descendants founded the banking dynasty of Bulteel which became the Naval Bank of Plymouth that collapsed amid allegations of fraud and conspiracy in the years immediately preceding the First World War.

He was re-elected in 1713 but retired at the dissolution of that parliament.[5] That he was extremely ambitious is uncontroversial; his methods of achieving his goals were much more questionable.

What then occurred was remarkable. James Bulteel interpreted his responsibility under the will of his client, Richard Hele, to arrange for the 'care, tuition and education of my son and only child', James Modyford Hele, as a licence to occupy the grand mansion of Flete House and to receive the rents and other payments from tenants on the extensive estates. The will gave the trustees the right to sell the estate, to repay any debts and to ensure that the money raised passed to James Modyford Hele and a specific clause was added requesting that 'I do most earnestly request the said Lady Modyford not only to be assisting but contributing towards the discharge of the same (repayment of debts) for and on the behalf of my said son and her great grandson for the preservation of the more of my lands for him so long as it shall please Almighty God to continue him or any issue of his body in this transitory world.' In other words, the interests of his son were paramount, but Elizabeth Modyford was expressly requested to ensure this came to pass.

In fact what transpired fell far short of this aspiration. First, Richard Hele's sister Anne and her husband died mysteriously without issue a few days apart in April 1713. She was 31 and her husband, John Woollcombe of Pitton and Ashbury near Yealmpton and MP for Plymouth and High Sheriff for Devon in 1712, was 33. In the meantime, James Modyford Hele was sent off to boarding school at Tiverton (Blundell's) and died there soon after his arrival in 1716. The way was now clear for James Bulteel to occupy the mansion house at Flete as the legitimate owner. Clearly, it was not at all unusual in this period for young people to succumb at an early age, but some commentators have regarded this event as suspicious. For example, the official history of Flete House, noting that Bulteel seemed 'an unlikely recipient of such a responsibility', points out that 'there were those who wondered if, perhaps, the boy might

5 James Bulteel was an early ancestor of Lady Diana Spencer on her mother's side.

have been assisted on his way' (Watt-Carter, 1987/2013: 6). The very frequency of early and unexplained deaths might serve as an excellent cover for those that might not have happened without third party intervention. These suspicions might have been enhanced if the sudden deaths of Richard Hele's sister and her husband had also been considered, since they too were obvious impediments to Bulteel's continued occupation of Flete House.

There was also the issue of whether James Bulteel while occupying Flete House and benefiting from its income, really busied himself with ensuring that James Modyford Hele was duly cared for and educated. Dame Elizabeth Modyford did not believe she had been consulted over this or other issues and some years later in 1727, after she herself had died (1724) and the Maristow estate was run by her daughter and heir Mary Deane, the latter felt compelled to sue James Bulteel and others named in the will in the Court of Chancery for failing to uphold these responsibilities (TNA: C11/610/15).[6] As the plaintiff in this case, she is described as 'Mary Deane, widow of Maristow, Devon (grandmother and adminstratrix of James Modyford Hele, esq. deceased, who was only child and heir of Richard Hele, esq. deceased, late of Fleet Damerell and Elizabeth Hele his wife, deceased, who (was the) daughter of said Mary Deane)'. Mary Deane's deposition in this case is clear and compelling. She claimed that after Richard died, she took over a small part of his estate which she sold for £2,174 using these funds to pay Richard's debts amounting to more than £2,628, thereby leaving her out of pocket by more than £450. But

> James Bulteel possessed himself of all or the greater parte of the rest of the goods, chattels and personal estate of the said Richard Hele amounting to a very great value and the said James Bulteel after the said testator's death entered upon

6 The Court of Chancery met for nearly all of its existence in the famed Westminster Hall. It was a court of equity, whose origins go back to the medieval period, which provided greater flexibility for issues of civil complaint that were not covered by common law proceedings. Dogged by high charges and slow proceedings, the court was eventually abolished in 1873.

> all the testator's real estate which was of the yearly value of two thousand pounds and received the rents and profits thereof to the death of the said James Modyford Hele (20th August 1716) amounting in the whole to the sum of twelve thousand pounds and upwards.

She goes on to claim that she educated the son and received nothing from Bulteel. He argued that he owed nothing because of mortgages and debts on the estate but no proof was ever forthcoming of these obligations and even if they had existed there were provisions in the will for the trustees to sell all or part of the estate and to use the proceeds for that purpose. Mary Deane was in no doubt that these claims were fictitious and that the other trustees, whom she refers to as 'co-conspirators', knew this to be so. This bill is dated 1727, long after all the curious deaths that led to Bulteel's improbable inheritance, and it is significant that the language used by Mary Deane or her legal advisors hints at foul play. She identifies Walter Hele as a 'co-conspirator' because he stood to inherit valuable properties alongside Bulteel but after naming the other trustees as being in cahoots she uses the phrase 'the rest of the confederates when discovered' (TNA C 11/610/15).

Although Mary Deane won this case, Bulteel refused to pay either these debts or make any reparations for the rents and profits he had illegitimately obtained from Richard Hele's estate, which properly should have come to his son. It is interesting also to note that Bulteel announced his retirement from Parliament in 1715 at the comparatively early age of 39 following the death of Queen Ann the preceding August, possibly knowing that he had other pressing matters to attend to in order to maintain his prestigious country seat.[7]

The Role of James Heywood

At this point, it is important to reflect on the position of James Heywood, the only surviving son of Grace and Peter Heywood. He was in fact the second son but his older brother Thomas (born 1682)

---

7 James Bulteel died in 1757.

died young.[8] James, sometimes referred to as 'Jemmy', was born in 1685 and became a member of the Jamaican Assembly in his early twenties (1709 for St Thomas; 1714 for St Catherine; 1716 Port Royal; 1718–19 for St Mary and 1721–23 and 1726 for St Dorothy). During that time, however, and possibly earlier during military training, he appears to have lived at Maristow where he played a role in managing the estate in partnership with his aunt Mary Deane but no doubt under the watchful eye of his grandmother, Dame Elizabeth Modyford. It is sometimes assumed that James Heywood returned to Maristow House from Jamaica a short time before the death of his aunt Mary, which occurred in October 1734. The implication here is that he returned to assist her in her final illness or, more negatively, that he returned in order to be available to claim his inheritance since the 1704 settlement and the subsequent fatalities made this the inevitable outcome. Thirty years later, however, in lawsuits discussed below there are sworn affidavits by estate staff declaring their awareness of his presence at that time. Given his political role in Jamaica, it is probable that he returned to the colony on a number of occasions before settling full-time after his father's death in 1725.

James Heywood was then a mature bachelor just turned 40 and it would appear that he felt the time was right to find a wife. In common with many other eligible West Country men, he may have participated in the fashionable circles based in Bath or Bristol and while there visited the Elton family at their country seat, Clevedon Court, some ten miles from the latter city. Sir Abraham Elton, the head of the family, was a prominent Bristol merchant who became sheriff of the city in 1702, master of the Society of Merchant Adventurers in 1708, mayor in 1710 and High Sheriff of Gloucestershire in 1716. Created a baronet in 1717, he went on to be a member of parliament for Bristol for the five years before his death in 1728. He was a self-made entrepreneur famous for his brass and iron foundries, glass and pottery works and weaving factories. As such he was deeply enmeshed in the port of Bristol,

8 In some accounts, Grace Heywood experienced 12 confinements but only two other children are known to have reached maturity.

including the slave trade. Abraham Elton's three sons followed in their father's footsteps and the eldest, also Abraham, specialised in shipping brassware and other goods to Africa to pay for slaves, while he and his brothers, Isaac and Jacob, also invested in the slave ships themselves and had estates in Jamaica where the family would have been known to James Heywood.[9] The eldest brother, who became the second baronet, had a daughter, Mary, born in 1705 and it was she who caught James Heywood's eye (Elton, 1974). James Heywood (misspelt as Haywood in the parish register) married Mary Elton on 17 August 1727 at St Nicholas' Church, Bristol; he was 43 and she 22 (Plate 7).

One possibility is that the couple then returned to live at Maristow House where James' aunt, Mary Deane, had succeeded her mother in running the estate. It is highly likely, however, that Mary's father made available one of the many properties that comprised the Clevedon Court estate. Her grandfather had bought the estate in 1709 and added to it considerably by the time of his death in 1728 when Mary's father, also Abraham, inherited responsibility and also added further properties. Indeed, her grandfather's will, dated 29 October 1727, is an astonishing testament to the quantity of properties he had amassed during his lifetime. It distributes many houses, farms and lands; nearly all to his two surviving sons (Abraham and Jacob) and numerous grandsons and, although Mary and James are mentioned only in relation to £100 as a mourning allowance, it is quite clear that she could easily have had a choice of properties on the estate either through the bequests to her father or her grandmother. The properties were mostly in Somerset but also in Gloucester and in the city of Bristol. It does appear, however, that the house they occupied was in or closer to Bath since from this time onwards there was a family connection with the village of Claverton, near Bathampton, 30 miles away from the Elton family home at Clevedon Court, but only two miles from Bath city centre.

9 For example, the *Jason Gally*, a ship of 120 tons and 16 guns co-owned by Abraham Elton, paid duty of £178 on a voyage commencing in December 1711 with the intention of delivering slaves to Jamaica (Richardson, D.)

The Clash of the Old and the New Styles of Estate Management

The will of Dame Elizabeth Modyford, dated 1718–19, makes it clear that after modest bequests (including £100 to James Heywood and his sister in Jamaica, Elizabeth Morgan Byntloss, and £200 for charitable activity amongst the poor of Buckland Monochorum, Walkhampton, Bickleigh and Shaugh) all her goods and chattels should pass to her 'dear and most entirely beloved dutiful daughter' Mary Deane (PWDRO 722/8). The transfer of the estate itself also passed to her in accordance with the sequence of inheritance set out in 1704.[10] Dame Elizabeth died on 30 March 1724, aged 91, and Mary Deane appears to have managed the estate in a very similar manner to her mother; that is to say, very conservatively with no sales or investments, very modest rentals and little encouragement for improving the land. To James Heywood, used to the concept of active land management and investment in new technologies, this must have seemed a feudal way of proceeding, as indeed in many ways it was. He was not in a position, however, to improve things all the while his aunt remained firmly in charge. He appears to have concentrated instead on starting a family.

A daughter, Mary Slanning Heywood, was born, possibly a little early, in January 1728 and baptised on 13 January at St Nicholas', Bristol.[11] Little is known of her life but she appears to have lived at one time in Hitcham in Buckinghamshire (now subsumed by the larger village of Burnham, near Maidenhead) and to have married one John Andrews on 14 September 1756 at St James, Piccadilly. This was after her mother's death but the place of baptism where her parents had married a few months before goes some way to confirm that the couple were living in or near Bristol or Bath at this

10 A codicil dated 17 June 1722 adds that monies owing to her 'shall be bestowed and applied for and towards the purchasing of some rents messuages land or tenements in fee simple to be insured and set forever as a Foundation upon and for the use of the charity school lately created in the Borough of Tamerton Foliott by my daughter and Executrix, Mary Dean Widow". She is referring to a debt for rent of property at Maristow owed by the heirs of Richard Hele (i.e. James Bulteel).

11 If this date is correct then Mary Elton would have been at least four months pregnant at the time of her marriage.

time. This conclusion is confirmed by the birth of their son, James Modyford Heywood, who was born in March 1730 and baptised on 13 April at St Mary's, Claverton.[12] Another daughter, Lucy Heywood, who was born later and on some accounts after her father's death in 1738, married Sir Robert Throckmorton on 20 February 1764 at St George's, Hanover Square, close to where she was living.[13] She was his third wife but possibly some compensation was derived from his immense wealth. She was, however, between 26 and 28 years old while he was 62, although he did survive until 8 December 1791, aged 89.[14] Her brother James was one of the witnesses to the marriage, which no doubt gave him some satisfaction, particular because the marital home was Buckland House, a magnificent newly constructed mansion designed in the Palladian style by John Wood of Bath and his son, also John. The house, later described by Pevsner as 'the most splendid Georgian house in the Country', had 15 bedrooms, one of which was reputed to have been modelled on that of Marie Antoinette in Versailles.

Mary Deane died at Maristow at the age of 72 in October 1734 and probate on her will was granted on the 28th of that month. This will, drafted only two months before in August, contained no great surprises; the line of succession from 1704 and subsequent early deaths made it clear that James Heywood would inherit the estate (PWDRO 512/2). After declaring her wish to be buried in Bickleigh Church alongside her mother ('my honoured mother the late pious and charitable Lady Elizabeth Modyford in a vault there already made') she left the contents of the mansion house to her nephew, apart from one or two individual bequests. Four-year-old James Modyford Heywood was to receive 'my grandfather Slanning('s) pictures and dymond crown, dymond lockett and dymond ring, the dymonds in the crown and locket to be set

12 If the birth date was before 25 March then it would have fallen legally into the year 1729 under the Julian calendar that operated until 1752.

13 Later legal documents suggest Lucy was alive in 1738 and may have been born no later than 1736.

14 Lucy Heywood did not survive very long after her husband despite the disparity in their ages. Her will was probated in December 1795.

around the said pictures' together with a purse containing two pieces of gold, while his sister, who was six at the time, received other lockets including those owned by Mary's daughter Elizabeth. The charitable works instigated by her mother were to be focused on endowing the primary school that still bears her name with £480 raised from the sale of her silver plate.

James Heywood was to live for only three more years, dying on 1 February 1738.[15] It is quite clear that prior to his demise he had set about improving the estate with funds derived from his plantations in Jamaica. There was little to suggest that there was sufficient income from the Maristow estate itself to make these provisions. A survey was carried out very soon after James died and it showed that the rental income from the various manors amounted to exactly what it had been 50 years before.[16] Although, the rents from the many bartons (manor lands and farmhouses), farms and woodlands would have increased this figure, the total would not have been enough to make the investments that were so desperately needed. Moreover, although wages were very low, Maristow house and estate itself employed 15–20 people. We know the names of many of them, together with their respective roles and wages as the following table shows. In addition, James Heywood was said to have had several other servants hired by the day and three apprentices (TNA: C 11/413/2).[17]

	Wage per annum
Cook	£6.50
Dairymaid	£3.00
Waiting maid	£8.00
Nursemaid	£4.00
Housemaid[18]	£3.00

15 This was the 1737–38 year and is sometimes recorded as 1737.
16 Approximately £200 per annum (PWDRO: 407/715 'Lands of James Heywood 1740').
17 Including one William Coffee, 'a Black'.
18 Wage estimated.

Horseman	£6.30
Coachman	£6.50
Gardener	£8.00
Under gardener	£5.00
Carpenter	£11.00
Carpenter (jr)	£8.00
Hind (skilled farm hand)	£10.00
Ploughmen (2 at £5.25)	£10.50
Labourer	£5.25
Ploughboy	£3.00

From the death of Mary Deane onwards, the records show that new leases and rental arrangements were signed by James Heywood.

There is evidence that the role of Heywood in assisting in the running of the estate was a major cause of ill feeling prior to Mary Deane's demise and long before when Elizabeth Modyford was still alive. A remarkable passage in James Heywood's will makes this point abundantly clear.[19] In it he points out that he has granted 99-year leases for three lives since he came into 'the possession of the severall and respective manors lands tenements hereditaments and premises on the death of my aforesaid aunt Deane lying in the several counties of Devon and Cornwall', which under the terms of the 1704 settlement made by his grandmother he may not have been entitled to do, presumably because she had laid down the correct way in her view for these leases to be determined or more probably because they were already covered by agreements signed by Lady Modyford.

Heywood's will goes on to state that either his grandmother or his aunt had believed that 'the reason which induced me to grant

19 The will was proved on 10 March 1738 (1737–8).

such leases was for that I was an entire stranger to and did not well understand the management of estates'. But he believed that the reason the Maristow estate was in such a parlous state was because the two women had failed to utilise the economic potential that all the lands possessed. Fearful therefore that his heirs would be burdened with the poor returns generated by his forebears and possibly concerned that antiquated practices were commonplace in rural Devon, he instructs his son on reaching his majority to 'confirm all and every such lease and leases which I have so granted or executed' with the dire penalty that should he fail to do so he would be disinherited ('He shall not have or obtain any benefit or advantage from, by or under this my will') (TNA: Prob 11/693).[20] So passionately did he believe that the settlements made by Dame Elizabeth were the wrong way to go that he instructed his trustees to seek to renew other leases issued by Elizabeth, presumably at far more advantageous terms for his heirs and descendants. If this proved difficult because of the legal settlements entered into by his grandmother then he suggests his trustees should seek an act of parliament to allow this to happen, with the costs thereby incurred to be charged to his Jamaican estates.

Evidence on the state of the lands at Maristow in the 1730s comes from sworn statements of staff employed by James Heywood submitted after his death at the time of numerous court cases concerning financial problems commented on below. For example, Robert Duins, a 38-year-old gardener employed by Heywood, relates that 'the mansion house called Maristow and the Barton and demesne lands called Maristow' together with 'three tenements called Lillipitt, Bickham and Dunwood' belonging to the estate were 'very much out of repair' when James Heywood took possession (TNA: C11/413/2). He continues that his employer 'did in his lifetime at severall times and almost every month lay out and expend severall sums of money in repairing and improving the said Barton

20 The will contains a provision that should his son not inherit through early death then his daughters too will be excluded from the benefits of his will if they do not honour these leases for the full term.

and lands'. Another witness, George Austin, who worked for James Heywood as a hind or labourer, echoed these comments saying that when Heywood took possession of the mansion house, barton and six tenements (Lower Bickham, Dinwood, Lillipitt, Milltown, Mt Jessop and Sellmans) they were all 'very ruinous and out of repair'. He also said that the land 'was very much impoverished for want of dressing and good husbandry'. There is no reason to disbelieve these affidavits that suggest a long period of decline, possibly going back more than 30 years.

The parlous state of the Maristow holdings were not in any way assisted by a disastrous fire that occurred in the house on 5 March 1736, 'which consumed two parlours, the best stair case, a dining room, a hall, five bed chambers, a store room, a green house, pantry and one closett'.[21] It was claimed that the damage was far worse than at first realised and that although James Heywood had spent £550 on rebuilding when he died in February 1738, almost the same sum again was required to complete the repair works.[22]

The other issue that James Heywood battled with during the short period of his tenure in charge of the Maristow estate was to do with debts unpaid or credits not received, and both entailed dealing with someone who must have been his nemesis: James Bulteel. It has earlier been noted that Bulteel had lost a case brought in Chancery by Mary Deane for monies he illegitimately received from the estate of James Modyford Hele, prior to the young man's mysterious death in 1716. Despite the success of her case, this debt had never been repaid and James Heywood struggled to negotiate an appropriate sum and extract the funds from Bulteel. In a deposition in a later court case after Heywood's death, his agent, one Thomas Mangles, describes going with James Heywood and Joseph Blissett on 24

21 Testimony of Robert Duins (TNA: C 11/413/2).

22 The historic opportunity cost of £1,000 in 1737 (the value foregone by spending this amount at the time) is equivalent to £150,400 in 2020 while the more appropriate labour cost, or what would have to be expended on labour charges in 2020, amounts to over £1.7 million. Since materials would have comprised an important part of the total expenditure, an accurate estimate lies between these two figures depending on the ratio of labour to materials.

March 1735 to confront Bulteel over this debt and after he and Heywood were in discussion it was agreed in order to avoid another lawsuit that he, Bulteel, should offer Heywood the sum of £1,500 in full compensation for the rents he had received from the Hele estate. Mangles declares that James Heywood agreed to accept this amount in full payment of what was owing but this agreement was only done by word of mouth and 'not reduced into writing' (TNA: C 11/413/2). In October 1737, when he was suffering from the illness that killed him, James Heywood and his agents went to see Bulteel again since he had not paid up. Once again he promised to pay but nothing was forthcoming.

Matters were further complicated by the fact that Bulteel, as the seemingly undisputed heir of Richard Hele, was entitled to claim the payment for the marriage portion owed to the latter under the ill-fated agreement of 1704. This amounted to the significant sum of £8,000, presumably plus interest, unless this had already been paid. James Heywood was clearly very well aware of this debt and had gone some way to meeting it, according to his agent. In the same case cited above, Thomas Mangles records that he was present when Joseph Blissett delivered to Bulteel two bills of exchange one for an amount of £1,450 drawn in James Heywood's favour on Messrs Benjamin Hoare and Company bankers in London and the other for the sum of £550 drawn on Captain James Pearce also from London and both of them made payable to James Bulteel 15 days after their signing and for which the recipient provided a receipt.[23]

After the fire at Maristow House in 1736, it must have taken some time before it was again habitable and since work was outstanding when James Heywood died in 1738, it must be assumed that it never became his residence again. James Heywood died on 1 February and in his will of 5 November 1737, only a short time before he died, he describes himself as 'sick and weak in body'. This was precisely during the period when the house at Maristow was being rebuilt and

23 There is a divergence of opinion as to whom drew the second bill of exchange. Joseph Blissett claimed it was drawn on Abraham Elton and not James Heywood (TNA: C 11/413/2).

it seems likely that he had moved with Mary to Bath before his death. Their son and heir was almost certainly born in the city, since he was baptised at Claverton, but where they were living at this earlier date is not entirely clear. Certainly by the late 1730s, Elton House may have been available. The house is situated opposite Abbey Green in the heart of Bath. It was built by Edward Marchant in the 1720s and in the latter's will dated 1735, just before his death in the same year, the lease was left to his widowed daughter Elizabeth Brydges. Elizabeth married Jacob Elton (marriage contract dated 2 April 1739) who was Mary's uncle, five years younger than her father, and it is very probable that this was where James and Mary Heywood stayed when in the city. Certainly it was never home to Jacob and Elizabeth Elton who always remained in Bristol, even when they bought the lease of the property from the Duke of Kingston in 1749. It remained in the family until after Jacob's death in 1765, and in Mary Heywood's will of 1754 she is described as 'of the city of Bath'.[24] James Heywood was interred in the Church of St Mary's in Claverton, an elegant Bath stone village just to the south and east of Bath. On the north wall of the tower of the church there is a marble tablet that records his burial nearby aged 52, and on the chancel floor within the altar rails is another memorial stone above a vault which was later to contain two further members of his family.

The Rift between James and Mary Heywood

James Heywood's will was cited earlier when he used this final chance of applying pressure to modernise what he saw as the archaic system of running the substantial lands comprising the Maristow estate. It is remarkable in another sense too, for Heywood constructs an elaborate method for extracting money owed to the estate and for freeing it from the enormous burden imposed many years before when Elizabeth Modyford rashly committed so much money to her granddaughter's marriage portion. At the same time, he carefully ensures that his Caribbean wealth is not swallowed up

24 Following a later bequest, the property is now owned by the Landmark Trust.

in meeting these obligations, but more importantly it sets a very high bar for his family, other than his son, to inherit enough on which to survive.

At first sight the will reads in a very traditional manner. His wife, Mary, should receive an annuity of £700 payable not from the meagre profits of the West Country estates but 'out of my several and respective estates and plantations in the island of Jamaica' (TNA/PRO 11/693). His trustees and executors (his wife and her brother Abraham Elton) were instructed to keep up the 'full stock of negroes and cattle on my respective estates and plantations'. If for some reason there was a shortfall, his wife – who had never been to Jamaica or possibly ever outside the West Country – was entitled to intercede with the plantations to secure her annuity. The three children were instructed to ensure that this annuity was paid. His son, James Modyford Heywood, received in his father's will, subject only to the payment of his mother's annuity while she lived, 'all my several and respective estates and plantations situated lying and being in the island of Jamaica aforesaid with their and every of their appurtances together with all the plantation utensils and stock of negroes and cattle thereon'. These were certainly substantial, amounting to 5,611 acres spread over seven counties.[25] All his other properties in Britain were also left to his son, subject only to his living until his majority, with his trustees responsible for ensuring his appropriate education and upbringing.

Meanwhile, his two daughters were to receive £3,000 each if and when they reached their majority. What is particularly interesting is that these substantial legacies were not to be paid from the sale of property in the Caribbean or by dissolving a part of the Maristow estate but from the money owed to his aunt, the then late Mary Deane, by James Bulteel of Fleet Damerell, the guardian and trustee of the late James Modyford Hele, her grandson. In so doing he reiterates that Bulteel had taken over Richard Hele's estate and received the income from it and had not

25 St Catherine 200, St Andrew 80, St Thomas in the East 168, St Mary 3,711, Vere 80, St Dorothy 12, St Thomas in the Vale 1,360.

paid the 'said moneys to my aforesaid Aunt Mary Deane in her life time or to me who are now become entitled thereunto since her death'. He instructs his executors to go after this money using 'all lawful and equitable ways and means for the recovery thereof' and to put it towards the payment of his daughters' legacies. However, these handsome payments were not actually to be paid to his daughters. Rather, as soon as these funds were to be extracted from Bulteel then his executors should 'pay and apply the same for and towards and as part discharging the sum of £8000 unto the executors administrators or assigns of the said Richard Hele and for which the capital messuage Barton farme and lands of Maristow and all other the lands, manors, soigniories and royalties lying in the Counties of Devon and Cornwall which were my grandmother's the late Dame Elizabeth Modyford deceased stand charged' (TNA: Prob 11/693). In other words, the marriage portion arranged for Elizabeth Modyford's granddaughter had never been paid and was therefore still owing, regardless of whether the couple and their only child were deceased. These loans to the heirs of Richard Hele (i.e. James Bulteel) should be interest bearing at the rate of 4 per cent payable to his wife 'for the maintenance and education of my said daughters during their respective minoritys', or should she die before they reached 21, then to her brother Abraham Elton for the same purpose. Any shortfall, which in theory would be £2,000, should be payable from his personal estate in Jamaica.[26]

What is clearly ingenious about this scheme is that it does not depend on any actual repayment of debt by Bulteel, something that no one had achieved for the preceding 20 years, but rather it applies this debt to the payment of monies owed to the same person and charges the recipient substantial interest for the privilege. The problem with the scheme, and indeed with the will in general, is that nothing in cash is then available for his daughters other than interest on a loan that may not be repaid in their lifetimes.

26 The payment of £2,000 to James Bulteel by James Heywood via two bills of exchange would suggest that this part of the debt had been settled after the will was written but before his demise.

Moreover, his wife has to depend on the profits of the distant Jamaican plantations for her income and nothing is available to meet the needs of his family in the meantime, except the meagre returns from the run-down Maristow estate.[27] These problems were to cause Heywood's widow great anguish for the rest of her life and were not finally resolved until James Modyford Heywood took over the estate in 1751.

Interregnum and Family Rifts

The period of 13 years from the death of James Heywood in early 1738 until his son, James Modyford Heywood, came of age is one of stasis and family conflict as inadequate resources and a lack of clarity over who was in charge led to what was at best marking time and at worst a further deterioration in the estate's fortunes. The sworn statements of staff in court cases commented on below paint a very gloomy scene. For example, Robert Duins, the carpenter, in a deposition in late February 1739, just over one year after James Heywood died, records how staff were relieved of their duties by the trustees sometimes ostensibly because of failing to carry out their duties but mostly for no other reason than to save money. For example, six staff members were dismissed in 1738 'to lessen the family and the expenses thereof' (TNA: C 11/413/2).

These statements were deposited in a case brought by Abraham Elton and James Modyford Heywood, then aged ten, against his mother and James Bulteel. The latter clearly had a case to answer for not honouring commitments to return the profits of an estate that was previously not his, but what is also suggested is that Mary Heywood was thought to be in possession of funds which could have been made available to help sustain the precarious fortunes of the

27 The will was signed on 5 November 1737 but seemingly proved on 10 March of the same year. This apparent discrepancy is explained by the old ecclesiastical calendar which commenced the New Year on 25 March (Lady Day). Thus, a death in February 1737 would actually have occurred in 1738 on the Gregorian calendar. A note in the margin for 28 February 1750 says that the will was further proved on that date and gives the reason that by then the major beneficiary, James Modyford Heywood, had attained the age of 21.

Maristow estate. As far as the former was concerned, evidence was produced of the £2,000 paid by James Heywood to Bulteel suggesting that Abraham Elton was not aware of the marriage settlement of 1704 and the obligations it placed on the Maristow estate. As far as Mary Heywood is concerned, the claim was that she must have received monies from James Heywood because when they were married there had been a provision for her to receive a payment of £700 a year, and what had happened to that?

Mary Heywood strenuously denied these accusations and it is a measure of the degree to which financial hardships had eroded family trust that she took out another case against her brother, her son and her two daughters in connection with what she considered onerous conditions applied to payments to her under the will of her late husband (TNA: C 11/356/22). The affidavit entered in support of her claims, dated 27 June 1738, suggests that family loyalties were not simply frayed by money worries but that they had by this time broken down entirely. She notes that her late husband as the beneficial owner of estates in Devon and Cornwall was in receipt of £1,200 per annum 'and estates and plantations in the island of Jamaica'. She goes on to say that her father, knowing that her intended husband would receive properties owned by his aunt Mary Dean(e), had agreed a marriage portion of £4,000. In return it had been arranged that within six months after the marriage James Heywood would commence payment to her of £700 yearly as a jointure from the profits of the estates in Devon and Cornwall or elsewhere. She claims, moreover, that the settlement showed that this payment would continue should her husband die and in the event of his executors failing to meet this payment within six months of his passing, then they would be liable to pay her £10,000. However,

> your oratrix showeth that the annuity or rent charge was not settled upon or secured to your oratrix within six months after the said marriage in pursuance of the said articles or at any time after during the marriage and your oratrix further

> showeth that on or about the month of March in the year 1737 the said James Heywood dyed without having made any settlement (TNA: C 11/356/22).[28]

The fact that she gets the date of her husband's death wrong suggests that they were not cohabiting at the time. She then notes that his will states that she must receive her annuity of £700 yearly from his Jamaican estates in full settlement of his obligations towards her, which meant that any claim for payments under the terms of the original marriage settlement become null and void.

The problem from Mary Heywood's point of view is that this implied a choice that had to be made within six months when the first annuity payment would have been due under the terms of her husband's will. Either she accepted the terms offered by the will or she fought to uphold the conditions contained in the marriage settlement. She writes, however, that she is 'entirely ignorant of the nature, value and condition of the aforesaid Jamaica estate' and that therefore six months is far too short a time to undertake the necessary enquiries to ascertain whether she can agree to these conditions. She therefore 'cannot with safety make her election to surrender and release the provisions made by the aforesaid marriage articles and accept of a rent charge of seven hundred pounds'. What she had hoped for was that 'Abraham Elton, and the rest of the defendants would have consented to have allowed your oratrix such further time as was reasonable and requisite within which to make her election'. This was particularly problematic because she believed there were debts on the Jamaican estates, the details of which had not been given to her. But she observes in a very telling phrase that 'Abraham Elton combining and confederating with James Modyford Heywood, Mary Slanning Heywood, Lucy Heywood and severall other persons unknown to your oratrix' turned down this request. She goes on to contend that the defendants 'endevouring (sic) to distress and injure your oratrix and to deprive your oratrix of her just right sometimes

28 The year '1737' is a reference to the 1737–8 year but it is curious that the month of her husband's death is wrongly given.

pretend no such articles were intended' and that James Heywood had no estates in Devon and Cornwall and therefore had no power to grant her anything from them. She continues that 'sometimes the said James Modyford Heywood pretends that his father the said James Heywood made no such will'. She complains that all the defendants 'absolutely refuse to allow your oratrix any longer time although they know in their conscionces (sic) that it is absolutely impossible for your oratrix to obtain a tolerable knowledge and discovery of the value state and condition of the estate in Jamaica as well as the incumbrances which are thereon within so short a time as six months'. Their position is, she says, 'contrary to equity and good conscience'. She concludes by demanding that the defendants should be brought to the court to say whether the marriage existed and the marriage portion paid, whether the annuity was paid or not and whether she should be entitled to the said £10,000. When one considers that those she is indicting for this behaviour were her fellow executor and hitherto beloved brother, her eight-year-old son and his two sisters, it is hard to imagine a more distressing situation, whatever the rights or wrongs of the claims being made.

The reply (dated 28 January 1738–9) consists of a statement by Thomas Hurrell on behalf of James Modyford Heywood acting as his guardian dismissing the claims by his mother to any money from James Heywood's will on the grounds that it is her son and not her who was entitled to inherit. The counter claim then reiterates the contents of the infamous 1704 settlement setting out that the Maristow estate passed to the trustees, of whom Bulteel was the sole survivor, after the prior claims of the Modyford family, Richard Hele and James Heywood, now all deceased.[29] This meant that prior to James Modyford Heywood coming of age the estate would be controlled by Bulteel and that she was not entitled to anything

29 Listed as 'the capital messuage or mansion house called Maristow and the Barton and demesme lands called Maristow Barton and the manors of Maristow and Buckland otherwise Buckland Monachorum and diverse other Manors Bartons messuages lands woods advowsons tythes hereditaments and premises therein mentioned lyeing and being in the severall counties of Devon and Cornwall'.

except the annuity of £700 per annum paid for out of the Caribbean estates. The deposition also mentions the marriage settlement between Mary Elton and James Heywood confirming the belief that it had been paid, 'but whether any settlement was made on the said complainant in pursuance of the said articles other than what appears by the will of the said James Heywood this defendant cannot sett forth'. It concludes, 'this defendant by his said guardian doth deny all unlawful combination and confederacy in the said bill charged against him' and he 'humbly hopes that this honourable court will preserve to and for him this defendant all such right and title as shall appear to be belonging unto him this defendant out of in or to the severall estates of the said James Heywood his said deceased father...' and further prays that the bill will be dismissed.

The evidence suggests that the appeal by Mary Heywood was indeed lost. It seems likely, however, that she subsequently extracted some financial support from her late husband's estate, although not on the terms detailed in his will. Bulteel was untroubled by the legal turmoil in which he became embroiled, neither repaying more of his ill-gotten gains from the Flete estate, nor receiving anything that he could claim was his due from his mentor's marriage portion. There is also no evidence, such as his name on lease agreements, to suggest that he pursued the possible claim he may have had to control of the estate until James Modyford Heywood attained his majority in 1751. The waters closed over these torrid events and Bulteel went on to found a dynasty based upon the Flete estate and the wealth brought to him by his marriage at Lyneham House, Yelverton.

Mary Heywood in the meantime, although she continued to sign leases with her brother as and when they arose from the estate at Maristow, did not choose to live there permanently or play any part in day-to-day management. There is no evidence that she ever travelled to Jamaica in pursuit of her annuity. Rather, she became permanently settled in Bath, almost certainly in Elton House, either paying a modest rental to her uncle and aunt or possibly as a family concession. Her children, ten, eight and an infant when their father died, would have been with her, although James spent most of the year away at school or university. He was later to develop a profound attachment to the city and it is unlikely that the unpleasant experience of being a mother and son arraigned on each side of a legal dispute would have impacted much upon their relationship. Mary's target in litigation was not her son but those who acted in his name. It is perhaps significant to note that Gainsborough's rather fine portrait of Mary's only son has long been displayed in Clevedon Court, where it is to this day. The likelihood of reconciliation could not have been said for the relationship between Mary and her late husband. She was clearly appalled by how she had been treated after his death, but her sworn affidavits suggest an unhappy marriage long before that time.

Maristow House, half repaired after the fire of 1736, fell empty but the estate would have continued as before. There was, after all, an estate manager and all the farmsteads were let and generating modest rental income. Mary and her brother, destined to become the 3rd baronet after their father died in 1742 and therefore in charge of the vast family estate, visited from time to time, staying either in part of the house that had been restored on in one of the associated properties.

Mary Elton died on 27 February 1755 aged 49 and was buried in the Elton family vault in the St Thomas chapel of St Andrew's Church, Clevedon, on 2 March.[30] Significantly, she chose not to be interred with her husband at Claverton. A memorial tablet on the wall of the chapel lists her along with her father (Sir Abraham Elton 2nd Bart who was buried on 24 October 1742) her brother (also Sir Abraham Elton 3rd Bart, 4 December 1761) and six other later members of the family.[31] In her will, Mary Heywood is described as 'of the City of Bath'. It was signed on 30 September 1754. She left £1,000 to her daughter Mary Slanning Heywood and the same sum in trust to James Modyford Heywood, her son, to be invested

30 Her burial entry is dated 1754 because Clevedon retained the old ecclesiastical calendar until the 1770s which started the New Year on 25 March. Thus, she died at the end of the 1754–5 year or 1755 in the Gregorian calendar.

31 I am grateful to Helen Pegg of St Andrew's Church for her help in locating this memorial tablet.

at interest for her other daughter, Lucy Ann Heywood, who at the time of the will had not reached the age of her majority. Apart from small bequests to her family (£100 to her sister Elizabeth Elton and £50 each to her two remaining brothers Sir Abraham Elton and Abraham Isaac Elton) godchildren and servants, the remains of her estate went to James Modyford Heywood who was also executor of the will which was proved in his presence on 7 March 1755 (Prob. 11/184).[32]

There is so much in the events just described that raises more questions than it is possible to answer. How much turns on the duplicity of James Bulteel and his exploitation of the trust placed in him as the legal adviser to both the Modyford family and that of Richard Hele? What role, if any, did he play in the early deaths of those who blocked his path to such a magnificent inheritance? That Elizabeth Modyford was stultifyingly pious and conservative is evident, but how much of her dislike for her grandson, James, was in fact a reflection of what she no doubt perceived as the lax morals of plantation life that may have contributed to her husband's early death? The tragedies of premature deaths no doubt generated a sea of misery that washed over all subsequent events but did any of that justify the failure of James Heywood to offer the financial support he had committed to provide for his wife? Above all the separation, isolation and grief that came to Mary Heywood seems hard to justify, even though it was in part another reflection of a clash between Caribbean exuberance and English reserve.

32 Mary Elton's other brother Jacob Elton died on 29 March 1745 in action as a result of a sea battle with the French. It was her uncle, also Jacob Elton, and his wife who owned Elton House in Bath. He died on 15 June 1765, a decade after her.

Chapter 5

High Society and the Absentee Owner

In accordance with tradition, James Heywood's treatment of his son in his will was straightforward. His son, James Modyford Heywood, would inherit all his properties in Britain, subject only to surviving until his majority, with his trustees responsible for ensuring an appropriate education and upbringing. Much more importantly in financial terms, and subject only to the payment of his mother's annuity while she lived, he would also enjoy all his father's Jamaican possessions amounting to more than 5,000 acres of land. James Heywood thereby reunited the wealth of the Slannings and their Devon and Cornwall estates, with the two accumulations of capital derived from plantation slavery in Jamaica, those of James Modyford and those of his father Peter Heywood. James Modyford Heywood was subsequently to dispose of these assets over the subsequent years to fund the rebuilding of Maristow House and to sustain a luxurious lifestyle, sometimes at the country seat, but more often not.

In the immediate aftermath of his father's death James Modyford Heywood spent some time with his mother and afterwards from 1742 until 1747 he was sent off to Eton College. From there he entered Trinity College, Cambridge, on 8 June 1747 aged 17 as a Fellow Commoner, successfully matriculating but failing to graduate. Where he spent his vacations is not known but his later enthusiasm for Bath suggests that his mother's residence was his most likely destination, although it is very probable that some of the time was spent at Clevedon Court, where his portrait still hangs among other family members on the main staircase. It seems certain, however, that soon after he attained his majority, and therefore became the owner of the Maristow estate, he returned to his property in Devon, still in a state of ruinous decline.

It is probable that he came alone as soon as possible since he began signing leases for properties on the Maristow estate as early as July 1751 (PWDRO 70/227). On the other hand, the manor house itself may not have been habitable following the fire of 1736. We know that some years later rebuilding was not complete and funds to cover these works would only have become available with the unlocking of James' inheritance. This may be the reason why in January 1751 he took out a lease on Walkhampton Rectory at a peppercorn rental only to let it again when he assumed ownership of the property in the summer of the same year (PWDRO 874/83/10; 874/83/17). It is clear that by the time James reached his majority the relationship with his mother had been repaired following the court cases of the late 1730s, since Mary Heywood is thought to have provided financial support to her indigent brother during the 1740s, suggesting that she had succeeded in extracting her annuity by this time.[1]

Three years later James married Catherine Hartopp from Melton Mowbray in Leicestershire at the house of her father, Chiverton Hartopp, by special licence from the Archbishop of Canterbury. Chiverton Hartopp was an army major born in 1690 to Thomas Hartopp of Quarndon, a village north of Derby, and Anne Bennett, who was also from a local family. He married Catherine Mansfield of West Leake, a small village in the Rushcliffe parish of Nottinghamshire, on 14 February 1726. The marriage produced two daughters who survived their early years, Catherine, born 20 June 1728, and Mary, born 20 July 1732. Between 1747 and 1754 Hartopp held the post of Lieutenant-Governor of the Citadel, a fortress overlooking Plymouth Sound. The actual governor at this time (Sir John Ligonier) was mostly absent and Major Hartopp was required to be in residence with his family and was responsible for day-to-day management.

1 Abraham Elton (3rd Bart) had been negatively affected by the losses sustained by his and Mary's father in the South Sea Bubble crisis of the 1720s.

The Citadel, built between 1665 and 1671, incorporated an older fortification (Plymouth Fort) dating from the time of Drake but was being strengthened and refurbished in the 1750s, eventually bristling with 113 guns. Hartopp's tenure was not without controversy since he was determined to reinstate the sloping land between the Citadel and the sea (*glacis*), thereby alienating some local citizens who did not want to lose their access to this land. After a petition was raised for his removal, he was sent back to Nottingham in 1754. The family occupied a fine early Georgian mansion in the centre of Nottingham that had descended to the family through his wife (19 Castle Gate). James Modyford Heywood, then in his early twenties, had met the Hartopp family after his return to Devon in 1751 and no doubt invited them to Maristow to explain his plans for its total refurbishment. He would have welcomed the opportunity to impress and consult the two attractive daughters of the family.

James and Catherine were married on 21 December 1754 in the Castle Gate house, rather than in a church.[2] The ceremony was performed by a relative, Thomas Myddleton, a vicar from Melton Mowbray. The house in Castle Gate was also to figure in another important relationship. It was where Richard Howe courted Mary Hartopp, Catherine's younger sister. Howe was born in Albermarle Street, London, on 8 March 1726, the second son of Emanuel Scrope, the 2nd Viscount Howe of Langar Hall, which lies just to the east of Nottingham and north of Melton Mowbray. The Hartopps were known to the Howes, particularly through Richard Howe's elder brother, George Augustus, and it is probable that the latter used the Hartopp house in Castle Gate as a base for his campaign to be re-elected Whig MP for Nottingham Central, which he succeeded in doing at the election on 18 April 1754.

2 An application to the Faculty Office of the Archbishop of Canterbury for a special licence to marry was only possible from January 1755 so this must have been an exceptionable case. It would have avoided a calling of Banns but was probably done in this case to stress the status of the bridegroom rather than for any other purpose. The fee was higher and it was granted as 'a special act of grace and favour' that became so popular later that it became much restricted after 1759.

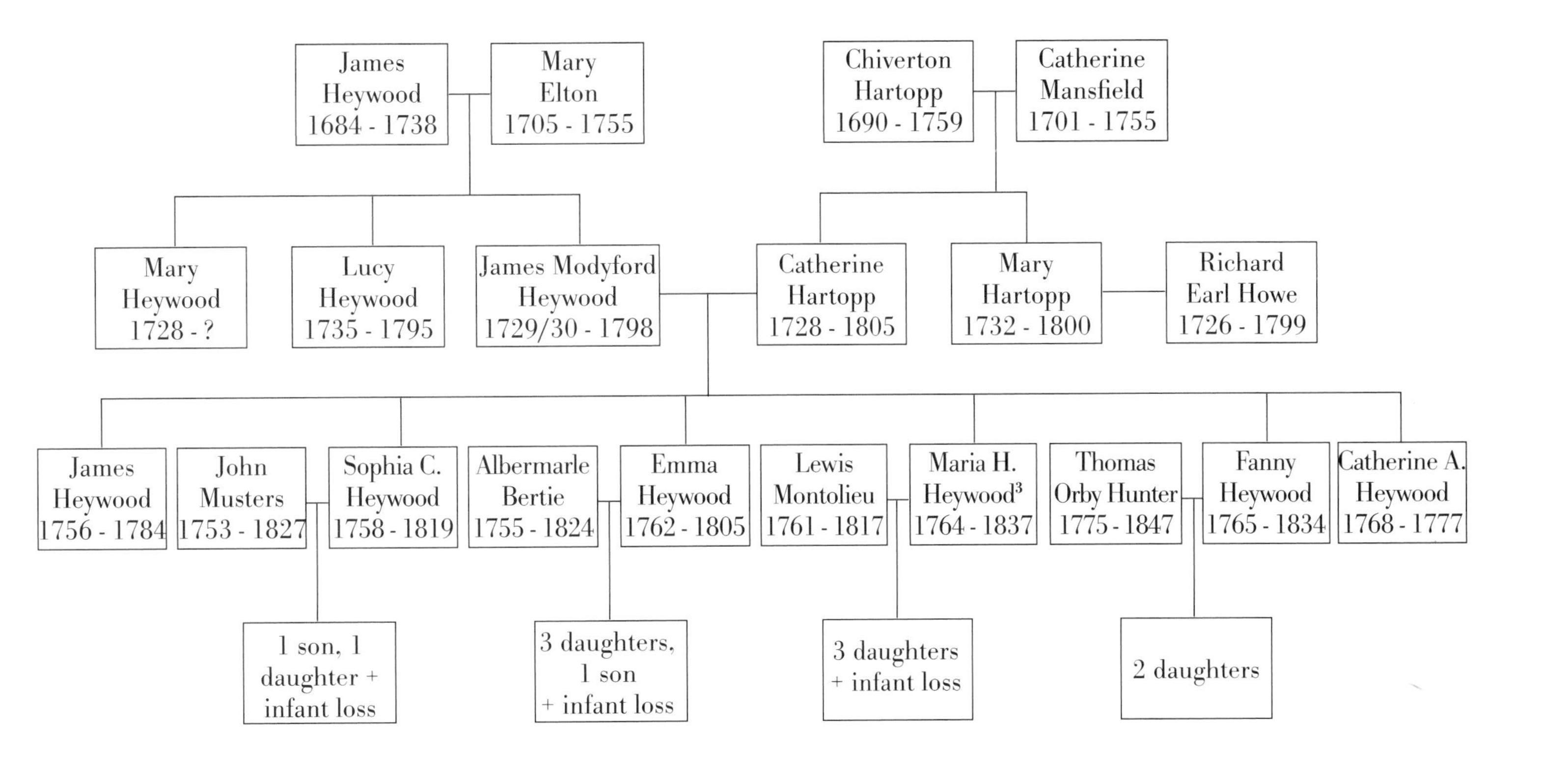

Heywood Line of Descent

3 Secondly Henry C. Clifton

The Hartopp sisters were very close and Mary became a frequent visitor to Maristow after her sister's marriage to James. When she and Richard Howe were married on 16 February 1758, they chose St Mary's parish church in Tamerton Foliot, partly because of its proximity to Plymouth, where Captain Howe was based in the early stages of what was to become an exceptionally illustrious naval career, and partly because of its closeness to Maristow. In the same year (6 July), George Augustus Howe, the 3rd Viscount, was killed at the Battle of Ticonderoga, an unsuccessful and poorly-led confrontation between the British at Fort Carillon and the French defending their holdings in Canada. Lord George Augustus Howe was a brigadier-general in the British Army, and second in command of the British troops. After his death Richard Howe succeeded to the title as the 4th Viscount Howe.

The following year on 2 April, Major Hartopp died and was buried six days later at Melton Mowbray, leaving the house in Castle Gate to his daughters. The two young husbands collaborated in its sale and the friendship between James Modyford Heywood and Lord Howe was to be sustained throughout both their lives, although it has to be said that the former must have gained far more from it than the latter. Howe was a somewhat reserved figure who played an important role in political administration after becoming MP for Dartmouth in May 1757, a position he was to hold until April 1782. Clearly a leader of immense capability, his naval career gave him more satisfaction than the compromises and manoeuvrings of politics. His bravery in battle and combat skills made him hugely respected in the country and he swiftly progressed to the highest levels; by 1765, while still in his late thirties, he was treasurer of the Navy. He was appointed a vice-admiral in 1776 on his appointment as commander-in-chief of the crucial American war; he was promoted to admiral in 1782 and the following year he became first lord of the admiralty. His undisputed qualities and his close relationship with the king produced a flood of honours. He was rewarded with an earldom in 1788 and later the Order of the Garter, among many other signs of preferment (Plate 8).

Earl Howe's greatest claim to fame was yet to come. Returning to command the Channel Fleet in the early 1790s, after two unsuccessful attempts to engage with the French fleet in 1793, he succeeded in May the following year in bringing them to battle, eventually claiming the famous victory of the 'Glorious First of June' which decimated the French fleet under Rear-Admiral Louis-Thomas Villaret de Joyeuse. Howe was a favourite of George III, despite being a man who, when faced with those he considered incompetent or idle, had no hesitation in resigning or in shifting his loyalties from one side of the political spectrum to the other. The remarkable fact is that he maintained amicable relations with James Modyford Heywood, perhaps because beneath his stern and unforgiving exterior he was in fact rather shy and even warm. It would have to be admitted that his brother-in-law was non-threatening to a fault, and for Earl Howe family loyalty, even for a perfectionist, counted for a lot. One example, of which there are a number, is worth repeating. Between 1760 and 1772, the noted – if subsequently controversial – architect Sir Robert Taylor was building a number of elegant mansions in Mayfair as a speculation for the Duke of Grafton. Four exceptionally large ones had been completed and one of these was reserved for Lord Howe, but numbers 1–14, which were still grand but slightly smaller, were awaiting completion and Howe resolved to take two of them, one for his widowed mother and sister and the second for James and Catherine, thereby ensuring that the families saw more of each other than might normally have been the case.[4]

Following his marriage, James seems to have been swayed by the delights of fashion in London as much as by the need to return to Devon and the demands of resurrecting the dilapidated and damaged estate at Maristow. For example, he commissioned the

4 There is no suggestion that Modyford Heywood did not pay for the lease, only that Earl Howe used his good offices to secure it. The suggestion that Earl Howe's property was one of the larger ones derives from the comparison of rates paid. In 1790, he paid £52 10s in rates for his property in Grafton Street whereas James Modyford Heywood paid £18 and the Hon Caroline Howe, his sister, paid £16.00 (Westminster Rate Book, 1790).

fashionable portraitist, Joshua Reynolds, to paint both himself and his wife in the 1750s after the artist had returned to London. In fact, he was present for his fifth sitting on 27 February 1755 at the painter's studio on the day his mother died in Bath (Waterhouse, 1966–8: 153).[5] He managed to be present on 7 March for the proving of her will, of which he was the sole executor and prime beneficiary, before resuming sittings on six occasions from 15 until 31 March. The result of these endeavours is unknown since the portrait now appears to have been lost, but not necessarily destroyed since new identifications of sitters for Reynolds still appear from time to time.[6]

Unlike some portrait painters, Reynolds preferred to invite his clients to sit for him for a maximum of two hours but to repeat this arrangement on a number of occasions until a portrait was finished. Since even in the 1750s, not long after he had returned from his sojourn on the Continent, his diary was crowded with appointments, this necessitated an arrangement some time in advance for all the expected sittings. As things turned out, those arranged for Catherine could not be used due to her first pregnancy, and James made use of these slots to fit in Thomas Mangles of Plymouth (whom we encountered in the previous chapter). This was an unusual thing to do because Mangles had been his father's steward and in fact had managed the Maristow estate on a day-to-day basis after his death. As such he had become unusually close to Mary Heywood during her long period as a widow but before James reached his majority. In fact, Mary Heywood's will signed on 30 September of the preceding year (1754), recognised Mary Mangles, the daughter of Thomas, as her goddaughter and left her a modest bequest. The fact that the estate's steward was acknowledged in this way suggests that mother and son had well and truly healed their earlier divisions.

5 He did cancel an appointment on 13 February which may have been associated with his mother's final illness.

6 One of the most celebrated scholars on Reynolds, E. Ellis Waterhouse, reportedly discovered 25 'lost' Reynolds painting between his first major work on the artist published in 1941 and a subsequent volume published in 1973.

Very fortunately, the portrait by Reynolds of Mr Mangles has survived and it shows a rather gruff, unpolished figure in his fifties, very different from the usual aristocrats and military men who comprise the greater part of the artist's extensive *oeuvre*.[7]

Catherine must have postponed her appointments with Reynolds as soon as she realised her impending confinement and did not sit for the portrait until after the birth of their first son, another James, on 2 January 1756. The painting by Reynolds shows a determined young woman with aquiline features in spotted silk, her hands firmly clasped within a fur muffler. The plucked eyebrows and the hooded eyes appear to have suggested to Reynolds someone of almost Oriental origins (Plate 9).

Eight more pregnancies were to follow, marred as was so commonly the case in those years, by frequent early deaths. Their second child, however, stayed very much alive, as we shall see. Sophia Caroline was born almost two years to the day after her elder brother but another daughter, Lucy, born one year later in January 1759 was less lucky, surviving for only two months. A pause then ensued before Emma was delivered on 8 May 1762, to be followed by two more girls, Maria Henrietta and Frances ('Fanny') born respectively in 1764 and 1765.[8] These four surviving girls all married and lived into the following century but fate intervened with the three final pregnancies. Catherine Ann Heywood, born on 21 January 1768, died as a child of nine, while two more boys, Richard born December 1769 and Francis born May 1771, did not survive past infancy.

A continuing issue after James' return to Devon must have been the completion of works to Maristow House initiated immediately after the fire of 1736. It seems very probable that a 20 year interregnum ensued after his father's death and that when he returned in the early 1750s, and particularly after he was married, the plan was not restoration but substantial rebuilding.

7 In fact so unusual is this portrait that none of the catalogues raisonnés for Reynolds identify this sitter or even suggests his first name.

8 Many years later a death notice records Emma's birth date as 1757 which would have made her the eldest surviving daughter.

Certainly by the end of the 1760s, the house had acquired a mid-eighteenth-century appearance and had been substantially enlarged. A fine new staircase was constructed and principal rooms on the ground floor now had ornate plasterwork and expensive marble fire pieces. The mansard roof was added at this time and the southern elevation in particular, facing down river towards the estuary, now had an unmistakably Georgian look, albeit lacking the precise symmetry that often characterised this genre elsewhere (Plate 10).

The question arises as to how this major transformation was financed. No doubt the estate continued to return a steady profit but, as his father had found, this would prove insufficient for major expenditure and the evidence suggests that income from the Jamaican plantations would have been critical in meeting rebuilding costs. In fact in September 1761, he was granted a further 820 acres in St Mary, again on the eastern side of the island. A little later, no doubt when building costs became due, some of the estates were sold. For example, the Rio Magno Pen in St Thomas in the Vale was sold in 1766 and in 1769 he disposed of Langley's Plantation (including Boyne Park Pen) at Port Maria Bay in St Mary in the county of Middlesex to one George Ogilvie (PWDRO 90/396). Langley's Plantation along with Heywood Hall were inventorised and appraised in 1740 two years after his father's death and Heywood made much from the sale of the latter (Heywood Hall 1,589 acres) to Donald Campbell for £18,000 in 1765.[9] In neither case, however, did they find it easy to extract the funds owed to them. In an agreement dated Christmas Eve 1783, James had secured the services of Daniel Singer to establish that the unpaid £18,000 had now risen with interest to £23,355. By May 1789, the capital sum had still not been paid by Campbell and James employed Robert Mckay and Co. of Glasgow to eject Campbell if he failed to makes payments for the crop of 1788 and

9 £18,000 in 1765 equates to between £18 million (RPI-based) to £38 million (GDP per capita-based) in 2020.

1789.[10] Eventually, it was bought by Mckay in 1792 for the original price.[11]

The Modyford Heywoods presided over the Maristow estate for nearly half a century during a period at the national level of important transformations in political and social life. On the one hand this was an age for the elite of fashionable consumption, but it was also a time when the seeds of the industrial revolution were sown, when new constitutional constraints were imposed on monarchy and when the privileges and pretensions of the wealthy were shaken as never before by events across the Channel. To all intents and purposes, James appears to have been oblivious to these tumultuous changes and to have settled comfortably into a rather undemanding life either in the Devon countryside or, as was more likely, at one or other of the more fashionable centres for meeting the landed gentry from amongst whose number it might be possible to position one's daughters in the quest for a good marriage.

James did manage to occupy a number of public roles, although on inspection each turns out to have been a sinecure, or to have entailed a modest commitment of time or to have been held for a very brief period. For example, he was made Sheriff of Devon in 1759 when only in his thirtieth year (*London Gazette* No. 9866, 30 January – 3 February 1759). This role, whose history goes back to William the Conqueror, is largely ceremonial, is filled by nomination and held for one year only. Previous occupants had included male representatives of almost all the leading local families, including the Edgcumbes of Cotehele and Maker, the Carews of Anthony, the Drakes of Buckland Abbey, the Parkers of Saltram and the Radcliffes of Warleigh, but Heywood was the first from Maristow perhaps

10 See also Scottish Record Office TD1/88 Articles of Agreement between JM Heywood and R McKay & Co). Much of the Scottish wealth from Caribbean plantations was funnelled through Glasgow but was often destined to end up in baronial mansions and estates in the Highlands (see Devine, 1978). By 1811, under its new ownership, the estate had a mill powered by wind and cattle and 196 slaves. It was then valued at £23,513.

11 There are no records of other sales extant but it must be assumed that all the plantations had been disposed of by the time of James Modyford Heywood's will (1796) since no mention is made of any further Caribbean possessions.

because he was the first for a century and a half to have been of the right gender and sufficiently locally born to have been considered acceptable as the monarch's representative in the county.

James Modyford Heywood also had a brief and very low profile political career. At the parliamentary election held on 18 March 1768, he was returned for the seat controlled by George Edgcumbe for the port constituency of Fowey. This was a pocket borough with approximately 100 voters and Heywood appeared to receive the support of 61 of these in this election. The result did not, however, go unchallenged and the losing candidates unsuccessfully petitioned parliament for the 'unfair, unwarrantable and illegal practices and proceedings' when it was alleged that qualified electors were refused the suffrage, while unqualified ones were permitted to vote (*Journal of the House of Commons* 32, 10 November 1768). Fowey in these years was experiencing considerable economic distress and as a port town was wont to ally itself with candidates who could help develop trade and shipping. It would appear that James was seen as someone with important overseas connections in the Caribbean. In Lewis Namier's *The History of Parliament: the House of Commons 1754–1790*, he writes,

> In the end Edgcumbe's candidate was J. M. Heywood, a *West Indian* – and according to Thomas Pitt, discussing Fowey in 1747, there was a club of West Indian merchants who made it a rule 'to promote the trade of any borough where a friend may be chosen' (emphasis added).

It seems highly improbable that James delivered on these expectations. There is no record of his having voted before February 1774 and he did not stand again at the next election on 10 October the same year. He did not speak in the House of Commons and, other than being defined as a 'friend' of King George III, he does not appear to have played any serious role in political affairs. The only other public role that he held was during a very brief period when he was made a lord commissioner of the Admiralty on 30 December 1783 (*London Gazette* 30 December 1783). This appointment was entirely due to the influence of his brother-in-law, Admiral Lord Howe, who had been a member for 20 years and by this date was first lord. The prime minister, William Pitt the Younger, writing to the king just after assuming office, damns this appointment with the faintest of praise and makes it entirely clear that it was a temporary expedient: 'Mr. Pitt flatters himself that the Admiralty commission is expedited, the name of Mr. Heywood, a relation of Lord Howe, out of Parliament, had been added to fill the vacancy for the present.'[12] By 2 April, only three months later, James Modyford Heywood's name had disappeared from the list of lord commissioners. This may have been simply because he was a stopgap appointment, but it could also have been due to the ill-health of his only son, James, who died from unknown causes at the age of 28 at Kempsey, near Worcester, on 11 May 1784.

It is unlikely that James needed a career for financial reasons. Capital expenditure for the rebuilding of Maristow House had been paid for by the sale of West Indian possessions, and throughout the whole of his period of ownership the Maristow estate consisted of 8,300 acres of agricultural lands and more than 10,000 acres of common lands and woodland. By the time it was sold after James' death in 1798, it was producing £5,200 annually and almost certainly not much less for the preceding 30 to 40 years.[13] In addition, for some of the period there may have been other holdings of sugar plantations in Jamaica, although how much he derived from these is not entirely clear. Certainly, there is no evidence that he ever made the journey to Jamaica and, even if he had done so, his 'West Indian' heritage would not have prepared him for the harshness of either slavery or the average planter's life. This would have meant that he may have had major difficulties in extracting the annual surpluses from the sugar crop as well as from the proceeds of sale.

12 Quoted in Namier, L and Brooke, J (eds) (1964), *The History of Parliament: the House of Commons 1754–1790*.

13 In standard of living terms this income equated to £463,500 in 2020 while in 'economic power' terms, which measures an amount relative to that of others in the economy, it is in excess of £26 million.

Also in the 1790s, the income from tenanted farms was boosted by the newly rediscovered copper, silver and lead mines of the Tamar and Tavy valleys which, together with large parts of Dartmoor, were to play such a significant role in sustaining local incomes for at least a century to come. For example, as early as 1793, James Modyford Heywood was issuing 21-year mining leases at Wheal Fanny and Wheal Emma on Roborough Down to London-based entrepreneurs (PWDRO 874/48/1/2). Royalties were usually set at between one-twelfth and one-sixteenth of sales although in the early years these mines had yet to discover the copper lodes that brought such high returns 50 years later when the two named above became part of Devon Great Consols, the richest copper working in Western Europe (cf. Hamilton Jenkin, 1974).

See and Be Seen

Importantly, the Modyford Heywoods appear to have laid a great deal of store by being seen in the most fashionable places and this itself may have prevented any alternative career. From the 1760s onwards, they appear to have spent the autumn and winter months (the 'Season') in either Bath or London. In the earlier years this would have helped secure arrangements for their daughters to marry 'appropriate' partners, but later it appears to have simply become a preferred alternative to life in Devon.

Up until 1765, when Elton House in Bath was sold after the death of James' uncle Jacob Elton, it seems very probable that they continued to lease this accommodation. Brother–in-law Richard Howe also visited Bath when his busy life allowed and it was there in 1764 that he and his young wife commissioned the young Thomas Gainsborough to produce portraits of them both. His portrait of Lady Howe in particular is a stunning demonstration of his craft and it is known through x-ray radiography that capturing the fine layers of material from which the sitter's gown is fashioned caused him to make many revisions (Plate 11). Gainsborough moved to Bath in October 1759 (although he appears to have been there also for the previous season). Bath's advantages as the place to be were clear to

Gainsborough as they must have been to the Modyford Heywoods. Its season ran from October through the winter months when the diversions of the city must have seemed so much more appealing than the damp of West Devon. Sloman quotes Horace Walpole, who apparently did not like it, but had to admit 'the place is healthy, everything is cheap, and the provisions better than I ever tasted' (Sloman, 2002: 7).

Gainsborough rented a large house in Abbey Street owned by the Duke of Kingston from 1760 until just before he left the city, although at the end of 1766 he moved his 'painting room' and eventually his family to a newly built house at 17 The Circus, just around the corner from Gay Street, where the Modyford Heywoods' daughter Emma died 35 years later (Sloman, 1997: 326).[14] Abbey Street, right opposite the abbey itself, continues into Abbey Green, and Elton House was thus only yards away. The Modyford Heywoods must have been aware of the young up and coming artist a few doors up the road from them when they were in Bath. After 1765 when they would have been forced to move their lodgings in the city, Gainsborough still worked in Abbey Street even though for reasons of health and quiet he had by then moved with his family to Lansdown Road just out of the city centre (Sloman, 2002: 51–3).

As before, the Modyford Heywoods soon emulated their esteemed kin and also sat for Gainsborough during his Bath sojourn. The portrait of James Modyford Heywood dating from the late 1760s, when he would have still been in his late thirties, is the one by which his appearance is usually known. The painting (possibly a copy) found its way eventually by way of the Elton family to Clevedon Court. The picture shows Heywood against a rustic backdrop wearing a naval officer's jacket to which he could scarcely have been

14 Originally he was thought to have lived in No 24 but later opinion shifted to No 17. While a plaque was erected first on the former and then on the latter, certainty was not aided by the fact that the houses in Bath and elsewhere at this time were not numbered. Gainsborough's financial fortunes rose with his reputation but he was able to afford a large house in the city centre because his wife, Margaret, was the illegitimate daughter of the 3rd Duke of Beaufort who paid an annuity of £200 per annum to the couple.

entitled (Plate 12). It is wrongly identified on the picture itself as James Heywood, the sitter's father, who died when Gainsborough was ten. The companion portrait of Catherine Heywood found its way by inheritance to Newburgh Priory, the long held residence of the Wombwell family.

On 25 April 1777 Modyford Heywood wrote 'from Bath' to his neighbour the Rev Walter Radcliffe of Warleigh House thanking him, inter alia, for 'the concern you are so good as to express on account of the late distresses in my family. The children, I thank God, are recovering fast, and, I trust, will soon regain their strength by the air of Clifton, where I propose to remove them in a few days' (PWDRO 407/1316–1357 [407/file 2/M]). This was a reference to the loss of his daughter, Catherine, who had died a few days earlier and been buried in Claverton, near Bath, where James' father also lay. It seems highly probable that the Heywoods never owned a property in Bath or Claverton since it was customary at this time to lease one for the Season, but it was certainly a frequent destination. Even much later towards the end of his life, James and his wife made frequent visits to the city. Anne Robinson, writing from Saltram House in December 1789, reports that when he called at the house to visit her, Modyford Heywood told her that he and his wife were going to Bath and 'meaning to come again (to Maristow) next summer' (PWDRO 1259/1/41; 1259/1/46).[15]

Other trips were made on a regular basis to London for extended periods. In 1762 and 1767 James Modyford Heywood is listed in the Rent Book for a house in Hertford Street in the parish of St George's, Hanover Square, at a rent of £60 per annum and later in the same parish and at the same rent for properties in Tilney Street and Grosvenor Street.[16] The Modyford Heywoods also stayed

15 Anne 'Nanny' Robinson was the elder sister of Theresa Parker, both daughters of Lord Grantham. Theresa was the second wife of John Parker, first Baron Boringdon, who inherited Saltram House from his father in 1768. He married Theresa the following year but she died in 1775, very soon after giving birth to their second child. Her sister Anne then moved to Saltram to look after the children.

16 Emma Heywood's birth was registered in the parish of St James' Piccadilly.

regularly with their daughter, Maria, in Albemarle Street, just off Piccadilly, after she married in 1786 and a little later they took a lease on the house just around the corner in Grafton Street, Mayfair, where Earl Howe also resided. James Modyford Heywood died there in April 1798 and his widow, Catherine, continued to live in Grafton Street until just before her own death seven years later. Indeed, the Modyford Heywoods' commitment to life in Devon, insofar as it was ever strong, seems to have been on the wane for some years. Anne Robinson writing from Saltram on 21 November 1789 reported that Modyford Heywood wanted to sell the Maristow estate, where she was a regular visitor, but was thinking of asking £80,000, which in her view was very much more than it was worth. While she thought it was 'a very pretty place and good house' even £60,000 was much more than its then value as the estate is 'all let out on leases for lives and is full lived so that it must be a great while before it all drops in, in which case it would be a very good estate' (PWDRO 1259/2/81). A short while later, Modyford Heywood had apparently dropped the price he would accept to £70,000 (PDWRO 1259/1/41).

Consequences of Absence

One consequence of all these absences was that relatively straightforward administrative problems in Devon took an inordinate time to be resolved. A good example concerned the fishing rights from Blaxton Quay, which lies on the Tavy south of the main Maristow estate at the boundary with Warleigh House. The Rev Walter Radcliffe had asserted in the 1760s that at least part of the quay was owned by him, together with the rights to extract fish. These rights were especially valuable because of the seasonal arrival of Atlantic salmon making their way up the Tavy to spawn in the shallow waters upstream from Maristow. Heywood replied that Blackston (Blaxton) had come 'to them upon the whole upon the purchase of it' and that therefore the estate owned all the quay and the fishing rights ever since the transfer to the Slannings from the Champernons (sic) after the dissolution of the monasteries in the sixteenth century (PWDRO 2320/1):

> My family has been in quiet and uninterrupted possession of that estate upwards of a hundred years and it has not paid a pepper corn acknowledgement or done suit or service (as appears by my deeds) to any other manor court than that which was formerly held at Maristow (PWDRO 407/1645, 8 September 1768).

The point is that although appropriate deeds were produced at the time, the dispute was still rumbling on 23 years later when acrimonious correspondence was exchanged between Radcliffe and Modyford Heywood, addressed to him at Albemarle Street, blaming each other's tenants for infringing the rights of the other, but still based upon the unresolved question of the boundary between the two properties (PWDRO 407/1648; 407/1651; 407/1653).

In addition to his frequent absences, unresolved problems of this sort, together with what appears to have been a rather passive and 'hands off' administration of the estate as a whole, may also have reflected aspects of Modyford Heywood's character. His first and middle names were often the target of waggish humour. 'Janus' Modyford Heywood, as he was sometimes known, suggests a perception on the part of some that he may not have been given to decisiveness, while James 'Mudd' Heywood could also be taken to suggest an incapacity for clear decision making. He died on 22 April 1798 and his obituary published in the *Gentleman's Magazine* does nothing to dispel these impressions. It makes no mention of his role as a landowner, nor of any of his public roles, focusing entirely on his character, about which all that the anonymous obituarist could think of saying was that it was that of an 'English gentleman'. It continues,

> Such were the pleasing preludes to more solid virtues, to the piety of the religious, the integrity of the moral, the bounty of the charitable, man; to the tenderness of the husband, the affection of the father, the kindness of the master, the munificence of the patron, the generosity of the landlord, the warmth of the friend, the urbanity and hilarity of the companion. Beside the merits already recorded,

> be remembered the last, but not the least amiable in the catalogue, a gentleness of manners, and an harmlessness of disposition, not to be described by a single term, unless, possibly, by that of innocence; but which all who were intimately acquainted with him will perfectly understand, and own the propriety of the application (*The Gentleman's Magazine* April 1798: 356).

Translated from its flowery inflexion, it is clear that this journal saw itself recording the life of a man of childlike simplicity with no discernible accomplishments.

In one important respect, however, this would be an unfair assessment. As a man of property but without the recognition thought to be bestowed in the eyes of his peers by a title, James together with Catherine placed enormous importance on determining to whom the surviving daughters should marry. In this, with one or two hiccups along the way, they were remarkably successful, or at least seemingly so, since all four daughters married men who had substantial resources in their own right, rather than simply depending solely upon the vagaries of inheritance. Whether they were suitable in all other respects is more doubtful although by the standards of the day they may have fared no worse than their peers.

In any event, James and Catherine went to great pains to ensure that each daughter was sustained by a significant marriage portion and, as was always his practice, these resources were spread equally among their daughters. James' will, dated 2 April 1796, contained no pretence that any of his family should continue to hold the Maristow estate, or for that matter his substantial remaining slave plantations in Jamaica. Rather, he instructs his executors (his wife Catherine, the Rev Abraham Elton, Lord Howe and Thomas Dunn, his London-based lawyer, to sell his estates both in England and Jamaica and with the proceeds make up the marriage portion of £8,000 to each daughter, some having already been paid at the time of marriage.[17]

17 This sum is equivalent when measured by standard of living to £666,000 in 2020 and to many millions in terms of 'economic power'.

After a bequest of £5,000 to his wife, to which £200 per annum was added in a codicil to the will, any remaining resources, after small annuities and costs were met, were also left to the four daughters in equal shares (TNA Prob 11/1305).

The close of the century or thereabouts brought further deaths within the family. Catherine's brother-in-law and fellow trustee of her husband's estate, Earl Howe, died on 5 August 1799, aged 73. His second daughter, Mary Juliana Howe, died a few months later aged 35 on 9 April 1800, followed in another few months by Catherine's sister, Mary Howe, who died on 9 August of the same year, aged 67. All were buried in the family vault at Langar in Nottinghamshire. There was then a short interlude before the passing of her daughter Emma, the estranged wife of Admiral Bertie, who died in Bath on 15 March 1805 and was buried at Claverton near Bath where she joined her sister and grandfather.

Catherine's daughter's premature death and the circumstances that appear to have led to it that are referred to later, must have been hard to bear especially after the loss of her sister and so many other intimates. In any event, she had her own will prepared very soon afterwards, dated 14 May 1805, and died late in the same year, probate being granted on 13 January 1806. The will is straightforward; it divides the greater part of her wealth (£10,000), mostly in government securities, into four parts, one each to the three surviving daughters, who were also the executors, with the remaining quarter held in trust by Admiral Bertie for the four children of his marriage to Emma Heywood (PWDRO 407/1316–1357;407/file 2/M).

By this time, the Maristow estate had been sold and the proceeds divided in a similar way, thus bringing to a close a period in its history where large sums were expended on the fabric of the building itself, arguably creating its most architecturally appealing presence. Yet the attention to the house and its immediate surroundings did not reflect an equal concern for the estate that sustained it. Had he lived, Modyford Heywood's father would have behaved differently for although he was not born to it, he appears to have understood that active management was required and that it was simply not possible to leave everything to professional staff. One indicator of this apparent indifference was the lack of investment in productive lands and another was the falling into abeyance of the manorial court system that, although fundamentally medieval in origin, nonetheless served to provide a framework of rules and procedures for tenants (Scott, 1997: 131). With all surviving offspring married off to men who all owned their own estates, it is perhaps no surprise that the Maristow estate changed owners. What is perhaps more startling is that in at least two cases the daughters of less than adventurous parents preoccupied with conventional pursuits were unafraid to pursue paths that became the *subject* of gossip rather than its mere purveyors.

Chapter 6

Mistresses and Marriage

Very little is known about the Modyford Heywoods' oldest surviving daughter's childhood years. Sophia Caroline, born in January 1758, was almost certainly educated at home in Maristow House. At some time during her teenage years she met George Pitt, seven years her senior and the only son of the diplomat and politician of the same name, when he was quartered in Plymouth. George junior was both good looking and worldly, having been born in the French city of Angers and having called Turin his home between 1761 and 1768, where his father had been envoy-extraordinary and minister plenipotentiary to the Kingdom of Sardinia, based in that city. As subsequent events would show, Sophia seems to have fallen seriously for George Pitt and these feelings were reciprocated. She was uncommonly good looking, prepossessed, with a lively wit and generous personality, but this match did not suit her father. This may have been because James Modyford Heywood believed that George Pitt, although a first-born son with an exceptionally wealthy father, was a long way from an appropriate inheritance, or that there was some other impediment to a match.[1] In any event, he arranged an introduction to John Musters of Colwick Hall in Nottinghamshire and declared to his beautiful daughter that 'with Mr Musters she would be happy, but with Mr Pitt she would be miserable' (NRO, HMN5/235/5).

---

1 Other possibilities are that George Pitt had an older brother who died young or that Pitt's father had gained notoriety through his friendship when young but married with the eighteenth-century beauty and traveller Lady Mary Wortley Montagu. Walpole, the great essayist, often praised George Pitt's mother Penelope (née Atkins) for her beauty but called George Pitt senior 'her brutal, half-mad husband' (DNB, 345).

John Musters, who was the son of Mundy Musters, a former Sheriff of Nottinghamshire, and his wife Mary (née Grey), came from a well-established family of Tory country squires from Colwick, just north of the Trent and two miles to the east of Nottingham city centre.[2] At the age of 17, John inherited Colwick Hall and its surrounding estates, which had been bought from the Byron family by his ancestor Sir John Musters in the mid-seventeenth century. As far as one can judge, John responded enthusiastically to the possibility of marrying this vivacious girl whose eyes were said to have been 'as blue as a blue ribbon' (NRO, HMN5/235/5). By 1775, the arrangement had been made and in July of the following year John and Sophia were married. He was 23 and she was half way through her eighteenth year. Feeling that the ancient Colwick Hall, with its motte and bailey, was too dated for his new bride, John had it pulled down and completely rebuilt to a design by John Carr of York, probably the most famous architect of domestic buildings in the north of England at that time. The lake in front of the house was fed by waters diverted from the Trent to the annoyance of other residents of Colwick, who claimed this left them short of supply (Plate 13). As they settled into their magnificent new home, with its massive Palladian portico, fashionable Georgian symmetry and Robert Adam-inspired interior, the bride's father could have been forgiven for congratulating himself on his perspicacity. Indeed, Sophia appeared to settle for the country life of horses and gardening surrounded by her beloved spaniels, while her good looking young husband began his subsequently lifelong passion for hunting with hounds and offering help to the Tory cause when required.

Before she was 20 years old, her new husband had delightedly paid for two portraits of his young wife and one of himself by Joshua Reynolds (Plate 14). He also commissioned George Stubbs to produce no fewer than seven pictures, two of which are discussed later. The first half length portrait captures an elfin-faced young lady with

2 It may not have been the case that Mary Grey came from such elevated origins. It has been said of her that she had been 'employed to weed the garden' (NRO, HMN5/235/5).

tousled hair in a creamy-yellow silk dress. Although not a classical beauty there is a suggestion in the direct gaze beneath the hooded lids of her mother, of someone with an impish wit and enquiring mind. It is said that the artist certainly found her beguiling and even offered to guide her in acquiring basic art skills herself (Plate 15).

In the second portrait, the image is more bucolic as she plucks *Syringa* (lilac) in a spring garden at Colwick, watched adoringly by her brown and white spaniel[3] (Plate 16). This first phase of married life was, however, busy. Three children were born in as many years: John ('Jack') in 1777, Sophia Ann in 1778 and Frances Catherine the following year, she dying tragically in the year of her birth. Whether it was the understandable distress over this loss, or a growing realisation that her husband, despite his wealth and steadfast support for her artistic temperament, was rather dull no one can be sure, but at the close of this dutiful, domestic period Sophia's life became more exotic and diverting.

Sophia in London

For many years the Musters family had retained a townhouse at 22 Grosvenor Place in London's Belgravia and very soon after the loss of her third child, Sophia took to spending an increasing amount of time in the capital while her sporting husband was preoccupied with his estate and in building his reputation as a huntsman of note. Despite the fact that Sophia was brought up in the countryside, and appeared to have had a love of rural pursuits, she is often reported as being unhappy during this period, possibly as a result of post-natal depression, bereavement or simply boredom with her country squire.[4] She appears, however, to have made a positive impact on

3 An early variant of the breed that went on to be called the 'Springer' after its use in raising game from the undergrowth.

4 In the volume identified below, the editor (her niece, Charlotte Barrett) refers under 'Mrs Musters' in the biographical notes to an occasion in Brighton when a gentleman attending a ball reported to Miss Burney that when he had handed Sophia a class of water that was rather turbid and chalky, she had commented, 'Chalk is thought to be a cure for the heartburn: I wonder whether it will cure the heart-ache?'

Plate 1. Maristow House 2020

Plate 2. Sir Nicholas Slanning aged 17-18 by a follower of David Scougall, 1660

Plate 3. Barbados (Ligon, R. 1673)

Plate 4. George Monck, 1st Duke of Albemarle from studio of Sir Peter Lely (1665-66) (© NPG No 423)

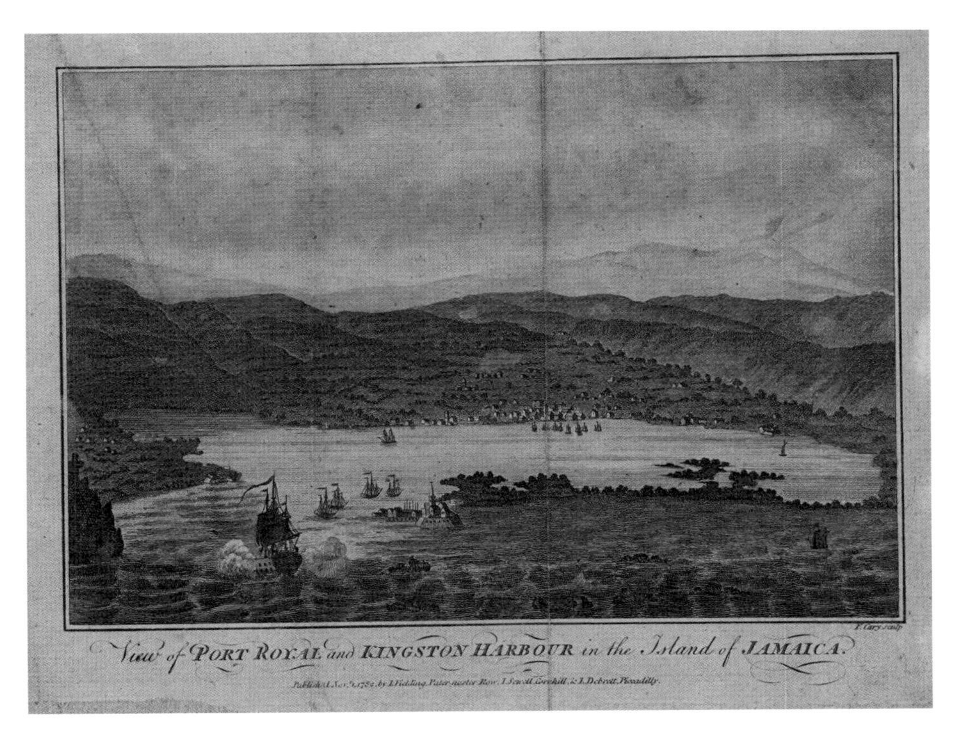

Plate 5. View of Port Royal 1782

Plate 6. A View of Flete House, Modbury, Devon

Plate 7. Mary Elton (Heywood) c. 1735 by Michael Dahl (© NT 624155)

Plate 8. Admiral Lord Howe by John Singleton Copley, 1794

Plate 9. Mrs Catherine Heywood (1756) by Sir Joshua Reynolds (© Liverpool, Walker Gallery, Sudely House, Holt Bequest)

Plate 10. Maristow House (1831) drawn by W.J. Lea; engraved by J. Bingley

Plate 11. Mary Lady Howe by Thomas Gainsborough c.1764 (© Kenwood, Iveagh bequest)

Plate 12. James Modyford Heywood by Thomas Gainsborough c.1768 (© NT Clevedon Court) (1270mm/ 50inx1016mm/ 40in)

Plate 13. Colwick Hall in 1790s

Plate 14. John Musters by Joshua Reynolds, (© NG 1777- c.1780)

Plate 15. Sophia Musters by Sir Joshua Reynolds, 1777

Plate 16. Sophia Musters in the gardens at Colwick by Sir Joshua Reynolds 1777 (© NT Petworth) (Mezzotint engraved by John Raphael Smith from Reynolds' original April 1779 © NPG)

Plate 17. Marine Pavilion, Brighton (Henry Holland, 1801)

Plate 18. George, Prince of Wales by Sir Joshua Reynolds, 1785 (© Tate Gallery)

Plate 19. William Thomas Beckford, c. 1781 by Sir Joshua Reynolds (© NPG 5340)

Plate 20. Tomb stone of George Dean Pitt in Symonds Street Cemetery, Auckland, NZ

Plate 21. Major-General George Dean Pitt KH (1836) (unknown artist)

Plate 22. Louisa Beckford by Sir Joshua Reynolds 1782 (© Lady Lever Gallery, Liverpool)

Plate 23. John Musters and Sophia Musters in front of Colwick House by George Stubbs, 1777 (restored 1935) (© Bridgeman Gallery, London)

Plate 24. John Musters and the Reverend Philip Story riding out from the stable block at Colwick Hall 1777 by George Stubbs and later significantly modified by the same artist (private collection).

Plate 25. Mrs Musters as 'Hebe' by Sir Joshua Reynolds, 1778 (© Iveagh bequest, Kenwood)

London society and is referred to approvingly by the diarist and novelist, Fanny Burney, on a visit with her family to 'Brightthelmston' (Brighton) in 1779. In a slightly waspish comment on the others invited with her to afternoon tea, she writes,

> The folks of most consequence with respect to rank, were Lady Pembroke and Lady Di Beauclerk, both of whom have still very pleasing remains of the beauty for which they have been so much admired. But the present beauty, whose remains our children (i.e. nieces) may talk of, is a Mrs. Musters, an exceedingly pretty woman, who is the reigning toast of the season.[5]

This was the period before the Prince of Wales had transformed the sleepy small town of Brighton into an extremely fashionable watering hole focused on the royal court. He did not visit the town until 1783 at the age of 21 but three years afterwards acquired a lodging house near the sea and in 1787 commissioned the architect Henry Holland, who had worked for him on the reconstruction of Carlton House in London, to transform this building into a neo-classical residence that was to become the Marine Pavilion. It was this building to which Sophia went on many occasions as a member of the prince's retinue[6] (Plate 17).

Both the family of her birth and the one into which she was now married were wealthy but not obviously linked to the aristocratic circles whose members normally could expect to become courtiers. Yet she did achieve this status and the reason was again her sexual allure. There is no evidence that she became one of the long line of sequential mistresses of the Prince of Wales, but she does appear to have been an early conquest that permitted her to become a valued member of his social circle for the rest of her life. Unlike

5 The ladies referred to were both daughters of the Duke of Marlborough. See *The Diary and Letters of Madame D'Arblay* (Fanny Burney), 1778–87, Vol. 1: 154) (http://www.gutenberg.org/files/5826/5826-h/5826-h.htm).

6 This is not the building identified today as the 'Brighton Pavilion'. This is an architectural confection created by John Nash between 1815 and 1822 in a lavish, theatrical Oriental style complete with minarets and domes. Sophia may have known this building but only before it was completed.

her husband, Sophia was very much at home in London society, and in 1781 she was invited to join the royal household as one of a number of ladies of the bedchamber to Queen Charlotte. How this came about is not known although if propinquity played a part then it may be relevant that the front elevation of the house in Grosvenor Place was opposite the boundary wall to Buckingham House (later Palace). In any event, she was granted an apartment in the house in order to be available when required by the queen.

At this time George Augustus, Prince of Wales, four years her junior, had been permitted to occupy a small separate set of rooms in Buckingham House.[7] On the subject of the seduction of young female palace staff, the prince already had form. In Robert Huish's life of the future king, published just after his death in 1831, he describes the undoing of 'the beautiful but ill-fated Harriot Vernon', a 17-year-old maid of honour who on one day 'ceased to be an honourable maid (and) the day subsequent to it was no longer a Maid of Honour' (1831: 50).

While it cannot be said that Huish, a prolific social commentator and author, should be relied on for unvarnished historical truth, in the light of subsequent events his report is not implausible, even though unsupported by others. Huish relates what nearly went horribly wrong when the prince's eyes settled on 'one of the most celebrated beauties of the British court at this time', one Mrs M(usters). According to this account, Mr 'M', who had also been staying at the palace, was expecting to be away for the night on business, thereby presenting an opportunity that could not be missed.[8] As Huish delicately puts it, 'the sleeping apartment of the Prince was on that night to be tenantless'. Mr M, however, returned unexpectedly at midnight and knocked at the door in the courtyard for entry to the rooms he shared with his wife. Since 'a detection would be the inevitable ruin of one of the parties, and the indelible disgrace of the other', 'Prinny' dressed and hid in a small

7 George's contacts with the staff of Buckingham House would have been lessened by his move to his own residence at Carlton House on attaining his majority in August 1783.

8 Huish explains his use of the abbreviated name because John Musters was still alive when the book was written but not when published. He died in 1827.

adjoining room.[9] A rescue was at hand, however, because George James Cholmondeley, later to be chamberlain to the prince, on hearing the knocking and being aware of the circumstance, is reported to have said, 'My dear Musters, I am truly rejoiced at your return; something rather of an unpleasant nature has happened to the Prince, and he commanded me to desire your attendance in my apartments immediately on your return. Accompany me, therefore, thither without delay, and I will hasten to apprize the Prince that you are in attendance.' This achieved, 'the Royal lover' was liberated while Mr M was informed that his services were not in fact required that night (Huish, 1831: 54–5) (Plate 18).

At about the same time Sophia appears to have renewed her relationship with George Pitt, whose prospects in the meantime had changed significantly. His father, also George Pitt, was MP for Dorset but was elevated, after much petitioning of the king, to the peerage in May 1776 as Baron Rivers of Strathfieldsaye in Hampshire, and his son took over his father's parliamentary seat, retaining it until 1790. Although a relationship with a married woman was fraught with danger, there is little reason for supposing that his affections for Sophia were anything but genuine. He is known to have kept a miniature portrait of her all his life, and many years later when their affair was but a distant memory and Sophia a matronly grandmother, it was reported that one of the grandchildren as a young girl 'remembered driving in London with her grandmother, the beautiful Mrs Musters, when Lord Rivers, the latter's old admirer came up to the carriage. Mrs Musters told him these were her little grand-daughters, to which he replied, "I didn't come to see them but to see you"' (NRO, HMN5/235/5). By this time, George Pitt's career had become even more elevated as Lord of the Royal Bedchamber, but he died unmarried in July 1828.[10]

The latter fact is clearly not the same as being deprived of

9 'Prinny' was a popular diminutive for Prince of Wales.

10 In March 1802 his father had obtained a second patent as Baron Rivers of Sudely Castle in Gloucestershire with remainder in default of male issue from his son to his brother Sir William-Augustus Pitt and after him to the male issue of his daughter Louisa, Mrs Beckford. George Pitt inherited both titles on the death of his father in 1803 when the first title became extinct while the second devolved according to the limitation upon his nephew. Part of the condition for the inheritance was the change of name of the title to Pitt-Rivers.

the pleasures of paternity. It has to be admitted that George Pitt's immediate family was not a model of conjugal bliss. The *Royal Register* in 1781 said of his father,

> He possesses an immense landed property, and has ever been esteemed a model of a modern fine gentleman. He is well-bred, accomplished, and debauched. He ill-treated his wife, the most charming in the world, who loved him till he deserved to be hated.

In addition to his father's indiscretions, at least two of George's three sisters were unfaithful to their respective husbands in a manner that provided much grist for the gossip mill of high society. His sister Penelope, who had married Edward Ligonier, Earl Ligonier of Clonmell, in December 1766, was discovered *in flagrante* with her Italian lover, the dramatist Vittorio Amedeo, Count Alfieri, leading to a duel in Green Park in May 1771, while another sister, Louisa, married to the Hon Peter Beckford, had a much remarked upon affair with his cousin, William Thomas Beckford.[11] Possibly in order to provide chaperone cover for her brother's visits to Grosvenor Place, Louisa Beckford and Sophia became close friends and it was through this association that Mrs Musters was drawn into the web of the prodigiously talented William Thomas Beckford, the young heir to one of the largest West Indian fortunes ever amassed and certainly one of the most interesting eccentrics that England, a bastion of the breed, has ever produced.

The Encounter with William Beckford

William Thomas Beckford, born on 29 September 1760, was the eldest son of William Beckford of Fonthill Splendens in Hampshire, former Lord Mayor of London on two occasions and owner of the largest acreage of plantations ever amassed in Jamaica. William *père* died in 1770 leaving all of his massive wealth to his eldest son

11 The duel was not fatal to either party although Alfieri was injured. Ligonier succeeded in obtaining a much publicised divorce by Act of Parliament in November 1771 when such an act was highly unusual.

when he reached his majority. Young William's grandfather was the infamous Peter Beckford, speaker of the House of Assembly in Jamaica while his great-grandfather, also Peter Beckford, was briefly lieutenant governor and commander-in-chief of Jamaica. It was he who accumulated the family's enormous wealth from Jamaican slave plantations.

So much has been written about William Thomas Beckford's controversial life, each author seeking a new slant or reinterpretation, that simple conclusions are elusive. Nearly all commentators, however, appear to concur on three basic propositions. First, that he was a young man of huge energy and very uncommon talents. Educated at home, he was a noted linguist (particularly in French and Iberian languages), a devoted student of the arts and architecture becoming one of the greatest connoisseurs and collectors of his day, a travel writer of distinction and an able musical performer with a talent for charming female companions.[12] Second, despite, or perhaps because of, the fact that he was descended from a line of hyper-masculine men, he revealed a complex sexuality. In today's world, he would almost certainly have been proud of his homosexuality; in Georgian England, where such leanings were regarded as an aberration wholly worthy of the law's repressive provisions, this could not be declared, but there was much that made him highly suspect to purportedly 'straight' males, particularly those of an older generation. As Guy Chapman (1937), in one of the best books on Beckford, writes, 'he neither drank, whored nor gambled, and he did not follow the life of the clubs. He was inordinately rich; he sang like a professional; he mimed like an actor; he played the piano and enchanted the women' (1937: 121).

Finally, even his most generous and warmest of friends would never have concluded that William Beckford was careful with money. While there is no evidence that he gave a second thought to the human exploitation that generated his inheritance, he certainly disposed of it with unrivalled determination and vigour. He died in debt having

12 In addition to his extraordinary ability, he received instruction from unrivalled tutors, including – at the age of five – from a nine-year-old Mozart.

consumed more than the million pounds that came to him when he turned 21 at the end of September 1781.[13] Even his birthday party celebrating this event was reputed to have cost £40,000 (Plate 19).

Some years before, Beckford had formed a romantic attachment to William Courtenay, a beautiful boy eight years younger than him and destined later to become the 9th Earl of Devon (from 1788–1831 he was known as the 3rd Viscount Courtenay of Powderham). The only boy from a family of 14 children, 'Kitty' as he was known was eventually forced into exile abroad in order to survive England's repressive laws against 'unnatural' sexuality, but at this time Beckford planned to celebrate their relationship, and his newly acquired freedoms, with an extraordinary 'Christmas party'.

The phrase does not do justice to the occasion that Beckford planned. This was an age not merely of reason but one of experiences beyond reason. As a precocious lover of the arts, Beckford would have been very conscious of Edmund Burke's then recently published essay that drew a distinction between beauty, characterised by order, proportion and harmony, and the sublime or the experience of the extreme, the unreal and the inexplicable; that which lay beyond the everyday senses and brought us to a new level of experience. Burke's claim that this was a distinction 'never to be forgotten by any whose business it is to affect the passions' appeared to Beckford as a rallying cry that could not be ignored.[14] Similarly, the *Castle of Otranto*, published in 1764 and normally regarded as the first 'Gothic' novel, marked a return to a more imaginative, medieval conception of romance in which a web of improbable events take place in hauntingly dark settings where the natural vies with the supernatural and realism is tempered by magical forces.[15] Moreover, one enduring fascination with the Gothic theme was that

13 This would be more than £100 million in today's purchasing power.

14 Edmund Burke *A Philosophical Enquiry into the Origin of our Ideas of the Sublime and Beautiful*, Dublin, 1779: 171.

15 Originally published as a translation by William Marshall of a sixteenth-century Italian manuscript by 'Onuphrio Muralto' Canon of the Church of St Nicholas at Otranto, the novel was eventually revealed as the work of Horace Walpole, the Whig politician, essayist and man of letters whose life and character were in some respects not dissimilar to Beckford's.

it allowed followers to move beyond the restrictions of convention and repressive sexuality. As John Bowen has commented in the introduction to an exhibition in London in 2014 on 'Terror and Wonder: the Gothic Imagination', this genre undermined the taboos of sexual 'normality':

> Sexual difference is thus at the heart of the Gothic, and its plots are often driven by the exploration of questions of sexual desire, pleasure, power and pain. It has a freedom that much realistic fiction does not, to speak about the erotic, particularly illegitimate or transgressive sexuality, and is full of same-sex desire, perversion, obsession, voyeurism and sexual violence.[16]

To this heady mix, Beckford added the exoticism of the Orient and elements of the *Arabian Nights* with their references to the literature and folklore of the Arab, Persian and Egyptian worlds, again set within an explicitly sexual framework. Clearly, this was not going to be a Christmas party in the conventional sense.

Beckford's staggering wealth and contacts in the fashionable circles of London enabled him to recruit those who, perhaps uniquely, could have brought off an event which he described as 'the realization of romance in all its fervours, in all its extravagance' (quoted by Chapman, 1937: 105–6). Chief among them were Alexander Cozens, the artist who taught him to paint, and Philippe de Loutherbourg, another artist but also the chief set designer at Drury Lane. De Loutherbourg was a master of illusion using hidden lights shining through stained glass and scrims or gauzes that could be made to seem solid or transparent according to how light fell upon them. In this way, he could conjure up vistas with what seemed like running water, changing cloud formations and the passage of time as leaves turned from green to russet. All this had been made possible by a dramatic change in the way theatres operated. David

16 John Bowen 'Gothic motifs' *Discovering Literature: Romantics and Victorian*', British Library, 2014 (http://www.bl.uk/romantics-and-victorians/themes/the-gothic).

Garrick at Drury Lane, even before hiring Loutherbourg, had done away with seats on stage and separated the lighting of the sets from that in the auditorium itself. For the first time, the 'scenographer' had a chance to create a sense of the sublime, an altered state of reality. As Beckford wrote to his increasingly besotted cousin, Louisa Beckford, de Loutherbourg would transform the massive rooms of the Palladian mansion, Fonthill Splendens, with 'all the wildness [that] his fervid imagination can suggest or contrive to give our favourite apartments the strangeness and novelty of a fairy world'. He continued,

> This very morning he sets forth with his attendant genii, and swears... that in less than three weeks... [to] present a mysterious something that the eye has not seen or heart of man conceived (his own hallowed words) purposely for our own special delight and recreation (quoted in Chapman, 1937: 99).[17]

In creating this 'mysterious something' de Loutherbourg was joined by musicians and singers of international fame and by the smells and tastes of the Orient. Chief amongst the former was the great mezzo-soprano castrato, Gaspare Pacchierotti, whose capacity to move an audience through the subtlety and sensitivity of his voice was legendary.[18] The action centred on the 'Egyptian Room' filled with appropriate treasures by his late father but spread throughout the mansion whose rooms were to be sealed against the intrusion of natural daylight for the whole of the three-day extravaganza.

William Beckford went to a great deal of trouble to compose a guest list for his great event of those who combined physical beauty with emotional sensitivity and, in the case of a few, as a cover to provide the pretence of social respectability. Apart from the prime

17 See McCalman, I. (2007) 'The Virtual Inferno: Philippe de Loutherbourg, William Beckford and the Spectacle of the Sublime', *Romanticism on the Net* 46 (www. erudit.org/revue/ron/2007/v/n46/016133ar.html)

18 Lord Mount Edgcumbe spoke of him as 'decidedly the most perfect singer it ever fell to his lot to hear'. Beckford had met Pacchierotti in Lucca in 1780 during the former's 'grand tour'.

object of his attentions, his beloved 'Kitty', Louisa Beckford, was to complete his personal *ménage à trois* but Sophia Musters was also seen by him as a central figure.[19] He wrote many years later when recalling the occasion,

> Immured we were *au pied de la lettre* for three days following – doors and windows so strictly closed that neither common–day light nor common place visitors could get in or even peep in – care worn visages were ordered to keep aloof – no fallen mouths or furroughed foreheads were permitted to meet our eye. Our society was extremely youthful and lovely to look upon – for not only Louisa in all her gracefulness, but her intimate friend – the Sophia mentioned in these letters – and perhaps the most beautiful women in England – threw over it a fascinating charm... (quoted by Chapman, 1937: 104).

Sophia appears to have offered Louisa some comfort in her ill-fated relationship with Beckford, although she herself was very preoccupied with George Pitt, who accompanied her to Fonthill. In Louisa's eyes, she appeared determined to become pregnant by him, even though her recent experiences and the scandal that would have ensued would seemingly have made this a dangerous project. Being unsuccessful in this endeavour at the great occasion, Louisa comments amusingly that she was '... resolved to do her best to-morrow night at Salthill in her way to town... and hopes with the help of George and the grace of God to succeed in the pious undertaking' (Louisa to Beckford 25 January 1782 quoted in Chapman, 1937: 111).[20]

A little later in an undated letter to Sophia, passed on by her

19 Louisa Beckford was suffering from the early stages of tuberculosis but was clearly unhappy with her husband about whom Guy Chapman writes that he '...filled his house with large parties of his hunting neighbours to the infinite disrelish of his pretty delicate wife, who held with the famous Lady Suffolk "smoking drinking and hunting to be the life of a country brute"' (1937: 61).

20 Salthill was a village with a famous coaching inn on the Bath Road to London now absorbed by Slough.

to William Beckford, Louisa alludes to this assignation and the problems of concealment to which it gave rise:

> I am rejoiced at the pleasure you seem to experience and sincerely hope it will last this long while undisturbed and undiscovered. I long to know how you got to Salt-Hill and how long you stayed there. I suppose you could not afford to spend much time there the next morning – as your delay might have given cause of suspicion to the *caro sposo*. How did you manage about your maid? Will she not think you suspect something on seeing G? [Pitt] there without any apparent business? However that may be I do not dread her much – she seems to be so good humoured and to have a real regard for you (Bodleian, MS Beckford c. 17, folios 5–10).

It is also true that whatever discretion may have been attempted early on, the affair could not remain unnoticed, at least in the circles in which all relevant parties mixed. In a letter to William, Louisa Beckford noted that John Musters had already reacted to his wife's infidelity: 'finding himself repulsed by her, [he] has abused her with all the virulence of malice and disappointment'. She went on, 'If she escapes with her liberty and George with his life, it is more than I expect' (quoted in Chapman, 1937: 117).

Louisa, however, was to be an unreliable friend. Finding herself inevitably sidelined in William's eyes, she was not going to stand by and watch Sophia enjoy her brother's affections in perpetuity, declaring that 'Sophia's reign is almost over', for what he 'mistook for the stings of conscience were in fact the loathings of satiety':

> Yet some small remains of honour and pity still attach him to her – and he rattles his chains without daring to break them. That he would is my most earnest wish. Her husband is on the watch. My father terrified and incensed – her character going to the dogs – and my own following with hast strides.

Writing here to William Beckford only four months after the

'Christmas party', and with a singular absence of self-awareness, she concludes that the scandal is now such that 'forsake her I must – however cruel it may be' even though 'I hate myself for being capable of withdrawing my support and assistance from one, whom I myself have encouraged in wickedness, and urged on to ruin and contempt' (quoted in Chapman, 1937: 126). It is clear that something rather dramatic must have occurred for this *volte-face* to be declared when memories of Christmas past must have been fading.

Given the earlier ambitions, the most likely candidate is that the affair with George Pitt produced a tangible human outcome. As Brockman drily observes, 'Sophia Musters was in love with George Pitt, and wished, in the fashion of the time, to have a child by him' (1956: 42). If so, then considerable ingenuity would have gone into its concealment so that all that there may be to go on would be a birth, the most likely date for which would be the autumn of 1782. In fact, a grave in the improbable location of the Symonds Street Cemetery in Auckland, North Island, New Zealand may provide an answer. The place of interment lies adjacent to the grander tomb of William Hobson, the distinguished British naval officer who was appointed the first Governor of New Zealand on its promotion from a protectorate of New South Wales in 1840, but lasting only two years in the post before dying from a stroke at the age of 49 in 1842 (Plate 20).

The grave in question is surmounted by a simple cross bearing the inscription:

> In memory of his Excellency George Dean Pitt K.H. Lieutenant-Governor of the Northern Province of New Zealand and Commander of Her Majesty's forces in the colony.
> He died January 8th 1851
> Aged 70

The date, or even the year, of his birth is not entirely clear but genealogists, of whom many show an interest in this question, consider 24 October, in the early 1780s, the most probable time of George Dean Pitt's birth, which might reasonably be assumed to place his conception in January of one of those years.[21] This makes it highly probable that if George Pitt was this gentleman's father, then Sophia Musters was very likely to have been his mother.

In exploring this question, it must be stressed that certainty is elusive, not least because the parties involved would have gone to great lengths to conceal a scandalous pregnancy and subsequent birth. The undisputed facts are that George Dean Pitt was illegitimate and that George Pitt was his father.[22] The latter became clear sometime after George Pitt had been elevated to become Baron Rivers on the death of his father in 1803. On 29 January 1819, the year of his probable mother's death, Major George Dean, as he then had become, was granted a Royal License to take the surname 'Dean-Pitt', which was recorded by the College of Arms after receipt of a letter dated four days earlier from Baron Rivers acknowledging him as 'my natural son'.[23]

In recognition of this fact, searches have been mounted on

21 The professional genealogist, Gervase Belfield (2014: 177) cites family correspondence giving his birth year as 1780. The difficulty of discovering where and when George Dean's birth was registered is considerable. The date itself is unclear as is the location, the names given as parents and even the surname itself. It is quite plausible that the name 'Dean' may have been that of a wet nurse or surrogate in whose home the child was raised. Simply to order possibilities by date we find a George Dean son of John and 'Nanny' baptised at Batcombe, Somerset on 22nd (month not given) 1781 or George Dean, son of John and Anne born on 13 May 1781 at Winterslow, Wiltshire. If we take the middle period there is George Dean son of George and Jane Dean baptised on 27 September 1785 at Winscombe Somerset or George R Dean, son of Thomas and Sarah Dean, baptised 10 July 1786 at St George's Hanover Square. If the later period is preferred then the options are George Dean, son of George Dean and Jane his wife, at Brixton in Devon on 25 December 1787, George Dean, son of George and Mary Dean, baptised in London on 18 December 1788, George William Dean, son of George Dean and 'Christian', baptised 29 May 1789 at St Marylebone, George Dean, son of George and Sarah Dean, baptised at Wooburn, Buckinghamshire, on 5 July 1789, and George Dean, son of John and Jane Dean, baptised on 27 May 1790 at St George's Hanover Square, London.

22 In the custom of the day, the surname 'Dean' varies slightly, sometimes with a final 'e', sometimes without.

23 See Belfield (2014: 178) for the most valuable summary of George Dean's life and career.

parish records near to the Pitt family home at Stratfield Saye on the Hampshire-Berkshire borders.[24] Some genealogists have discovered a 'Mrs Deane' in the Land Tax return for the parish of Stratfield Saye in the early nineteenth century, while others have targeted a Patience (sometimes 'Patianse') Dean born on 24 September 1749, who it is claimed was the mother of both George Dean and his older sister Susannah Rivers, both fathered by George Pitt. As far as the children of Patience Dean are concerned, there is no compelling evidence to suggest the accuracy of the proposition that she was George Dean's mother. It is true that a Patience Dean, the daughter of John and Susannah Dean, was baptised in Swallowfield on 24 September 1749, but she only appears to have produced two generations of girls with the same name. A girl called Patience Dean was born in Swallowfield on 14 November 1779 whose father was given as James Dean, and another Patience Dean was baptised on 12 August 1802 in Swallowfield, the daughter of John Dean and mother Martha. This last named Patience Dean married David Reed in Swallowfield on 12 May 1822 and appeared in the 1841 Census with her husband, a farm labourer, and seven children. In other words, none of this effort comes to very plausible conclusions, not least because birth and baptism records have not been found to provide any corroboration. The name 'Rivers' was not reconnected to George Pitt until more than 20 years after George Dean was born. Moreover, on the other side of the issue, the surname 'Dean' was well known in the Modyford Heywood family as the married name of Sophia's great-great aunt on her father's side.[25] Her grandfather on her father's side was James Heywood, the son of Grace, the sister of Mary Deane (née Slanning). Even if the household of Patience Dean did provide accommodation and care for George Dean in his early years, this does not mean that he was born into that household, particularly since it can be shown that his father was intensely engaged in an affair with Sophia Musters at the most likely period

24 The name of the house and the district used to be given as one word but became divided in the late eighteenth century.

25 It is true, however, that in an earlier incarnation of the earldom, the surname 'Rivers' had existed.

of his birth.

As far as his birth year is concerned, the most valuable and compelling evidence comes from military records. Discharge papers reveal a George Deane who served as a private in the 15th or Kings Regiment of Hussars until 12 June 1804 (TNA WO 97/39/64). This document shows that he was born in Oakingham (Wokingham), East Hampstead, Berkshire, in 1782. East Hampstead lies eight miles to the north-east of Swallowfield and 13 miles from Stratfield Saye. Unfortunately, the record provides no information on his parentage nor does it tally with the reconstruction of his early career by Belfield (2014: 179). On the other hand, as will be shown later, Census reports reveal that he may have been born even later than this date, rather than earlier as Belfield contends.

There are two other considerations that point to the conclusion that this Deane was indeed the natural offspring of Sophia Musters. The first is her later entry into the inner sanctum of the royal court. There were plenty of fine looking women in the circle of the Prince of Wales so that beauty itself would not be enough to generate royal preferment. It is known, however, that George Pitt was one of the prince's favourites when it came to drinking partners. Horace Walpole, the diarist and social commentator, describes a 'debauch at Lord Chesterfield's' in May 1781 when the two were joined by other young aristocrats in a drunken revelry that led to Chesterfield falling and fracturing his skull, while the king, on hearing of these events, supposedly endured ten sleepless nights (Walpole, 1910: 361). The probability that George Pitt was the connection whereby Sophia Musters came to the attention of the royal household does not prove anything itself about the parentage of George Dean-Pitt, but it does provide reason to suppose that the couple had both the opportunity as well as the incentive to maintain a relationship for longer than is commonly supposed.

A second clue comes from a comment made by George Dean-Pitt's commanding officer during a period when he was serving as aide-de-camp to Lieutenant-General Robert Ballard Long (1771–1825). The two of them travelled together to Portsmouth in January 1811 to set sail to join the Peninsular War where Long was to play a distinguished role. The general wrote to his father, Edward Long, the author of a well-known history of Jamaica, remarking,

> The officer who accompanied me as my Aide de Camp is Capt. Dean, a natural son of Lord Rivers. The Howe family take such an interest in his welfare that I could not resist so favourable an opportunity of making them a small return for all their kindness and attention to me (McGuffie, 1951: 51; quoted in Belfield, 2014: 182).

General Long had earlier in his career served as ADC to General Sir William Augustus Pitt, George Pitt's uncle, and it is entirely possible that Belfield is right in concluding that this was the reason for the family's interest in the welfare of George Dean. It is possible but improbable, for why should Sir William, a distinguished military figure, be kindly disposed towards his nephew's illegitimate son? Much more probable is that the consideration and concern came from Sophia's aunt, Mary Howe (née Hartopp), wife of Admiral Lord Howe, the highly distinguished and applauded hero of the American War of Independence and much else. Mary Howe spent a considerable time with her sister, Sophia's mother, both in Devon and London during her husband's service overseas.

Be all this as it may, there is no denying that George Dean-Pitt had a remarkable career. Belfield (2014) establishes that George Dean as he then was enlisted as a private in the Portsmouth Division of the Corp of Marines on 14 November 1797, claiming to be a 19-year-old plumber and glazier born at Swallowfield, Berkshire.[26] This may have been a reference to Swallowfield Park or one of the cottages associated with it, or to Stratfield Saye itself just over the county border.[27] He was described as six feet tall with light brown hair, grey eyes and a fair complexion. As an image as a middle-aged man shows (Plate 21), he

26 Swallowfield is just into Berkshire and very close to Stratfield Saye, which is just into Hampshire.

27 Swallowfield Park was once home to Thomas Pitt (1653–1726) the line of the family that led to his grandson William Pitt, first Earl Chatham (1708–78) and his great-grandson William Pitt the Younger (1759–1806). Thomas Pitt sold Swallowfield Park in 1737.

had fine features and a confident aristocratic bearing with looks that bore a striking likeness to those of Sophia Musters; a likeness that is considered a little later.

After a series of minor postings, his name appears as a sergeant in the Marines where he is described as 'a young man and very active' while General Long had earlier described him as 'willing and intelligent'. He was recommended for promotion to lieutenant 'without purchase', an unusual advancement for penurious but talented young men (Belfield, 2014: 179). From there he was sent to the Windward Island of St Lucia in the Royal African Corps, part of which subsequently became the Royal West India Rangers where he remained and during which time he participated in a number of expeditions against French Antillean possessions. In August 1809, he was promoted to captain and as Belfield rightly comments, 'within a dozen years, he had come a very long way from being a lowly private in the marines' (2014: 181). In January 1811, he took up the post of ADC to General RB Long. In later military actions he distinguished himself for bravery and presence of mind for which he was mentioned in despatches and awarded an army gold medal. His support for General Long was reciprocated when the general wrote to his twin brother CB Long that he liked him very much (McGuffie, 1951: 92). He was promoted to major in January 1814 but by the end of the year was retired from active service as a consequence of the reduction in personnel following the defeat of the French. On 20 May 1818, Major George Dean married Susan Baillie in Bristol (St James') and it would appear that he was living at Rushmore Lodge on the estate of Rushmore House owned by his father, by then Lord Rivers.[28] He was employed by his father as steward of the Stratfield Saye estate, which had been sold to the crown and then awarded to the Duke of Wellington in recognition for his success at Waterloo.

Major George Dean-Pitt, as he was then styled, returned to

28 Later in the century the estate was inherited by great grandson of the first Lord Rivers, Lieutenant-General Augustus Henry Lane-Fox who added Pitt-Rivers to his name and is often regarded as the founder of modern English archaeology for his work at nearby Cranborne Chase.

active service in August 1819 and for the following decade, he and his young wife were posted to Gibraltar, Malta and Corfu. Clearly, this service was regarded as distinguished for in April 1822 he was promoted to lieutenant-colonel and in 1836 he was granted the title of Knight of the Hanoverian Guelphic Order (KH), an honour of preferment in the monarch's personal gift. The following year he was made a full colonel. During this period he and his wife produced eight children, the youngest of whom, Clara Eliza, was born in Clevedon near Bristol in 1838.[29] He was then awarded a senior staff post in 1840 and eventually promoted to major-general on 9 November 1846. During this period Dean-Pitt and his family lived in Sloane Street, Chelsea, from where the 1841 Census, recorded on 6 June that year, lists him with his six daughters and three servants.[30]

In January 1847 the final stage of Dean-Pitt's remarkable career took shape when he was appointed commander of British troops in the colony of New Zealand. He arrived with his family on the barque *Minerva* on 8 October that year. This was a period when the new governor, Sir George Grey, was seeking to quell Maori uprisings with considerable subtlety and skill. He needed a military force that combined both a reserve of fighting skills with a capacity to use this potential with intelligence and care.[31] Dean-Pitt in this regard was a sound appointment but he also played an important role in the administration of the colony. In February 1848, he was appointed

29 Clevedon was the birthplace of Mary Elton, Sophia Musters' grandmother on her father's side.

30 The Census return of that year clearly shows his age as 55 and that of his wife Susan as 40, making his birth date 1785. Given his background, it is conceivable that he was unaware of his true birth date but if not, another puzzle emerges as the narrative of his career would have to be rethought since he could not have presented himself in 1797 as a 19-year-old recruit (Belfield, 2014: 177).

31 There is likely to have been a bond between Dean-Pitt and Grey since the latter's father, Lieutenant-Colonel George Grey, whom he never knew, was a friend of the former and both served together at the Siege of Badajoz (1812) when Anglo-Portuguese troops under Arthur Wellesley (Duke of Wellington) laid siege to this French-occupied citadel. Colonel Grey was killed there along with more than 4,500 allied troops. The victory was marred by the savagery of the victors who killed 2–300 civilians after the battle was won.

Lieutenant-Governor of New Ulster (the North Island) and in 1849 he became one of the appointed members of the Legislative Council for the colony as a whole. Seemingly, the last two years of his life were plagued by ill-health to the point where a local obituarist wrote that 'for about two years past his health had been so broken down that the continuance of his life for any lengthened period could not reasonably have been anticipated' (*New Zealander* 11 January 1851). He died on 8 January 1851 and the chief mourners at his funeral the following day were his namesake and eldest son, Captain George Dean-Pitt, and his two sons-in-law, Captain JH Laye and Lieutenant George Hyde Page.[32] Although there is no doubt that his paternity provided considerable assistance to his career, Belfield (2014: 187) is surely right to note that the major-general's career is 'a remarkable and very unusual story of how a young man of real ability and determination could rise from working as a tradesman to very senior positions in the British army and colonial administration'. What is much less clear is what role, if any, his mother may have played in fomenting his ambitions.

The Aftermath of Fonthill

Ironically, it was not Sophia who appears to have greatly suffered at the time from her liaison with George Pitt or from her participation in the events at Fonthill, other than by infuriating her husband, from whom for some years she became periodically estranged. As for both Louisa and William Beckford, lady luck was less evidently present. William appears not to have been a match for his ferocious mother who, together with all other relatives who could be mobilised in the cause, demanded a return to the straight and narrow. Despite the rumours of the horrors that had taken place at Fonthill, it is probable that none had the imagination to appreciate his true nature and simply had in mind that he should forego affairs with married

32 While in England, George Dean-Pitt junior had married Louisa Jones in Richmond, Surrey in 1842. He went on to a distinguished military career, later serving in the Tower of London as keeper of the Crown Jewels. He died on 4 April 1883.

women. Their demand was that he was now expected to marry a young aristocrat, Lady Margaret Gordon, to which he duly acceded on 5 May 1783. He was already an MP and the family's expectation was that this would soon be followed by elevation to the Lords. However, his entanglements with the prejudices of the age dictated otherwise. On a visit to Powderham Castle in Devon in 1784, he was apprehended in 'Kitty's' bedroom in what may have been a pre-planned 'sting' and the resultant orchestrated scandal drove him and his new wife into exile on the Continent. Although he fathered two children with her, Margaret died of a puerperal infection after giving birth to their second daughter.

William eventually returned to Fonthill where he lived the life of a reclusive eccentric for many years, rebuilding the house into a pseudo-medieval edifice complete with a 90-metre tower which mirrored that in his most famous work, *Vathek*, where the eponymous caliph erects a tower so high that he can survey the known world. Tellingly, given his understandable views on the persecution of homosexuals, this astonishing Gothic fantasy tells the tale of a mighty leader confronting Mohammed, thereby leading to his banishment into the subterranean world ruled over by Eblis, prince of darkness. Outlined in just three frenzied days of creativity immediately following the great event of December 1781, there are clear parallels between the novel's mysterious cast and the more interesting of the invitees (Landry, 2008: 180).[33]

Louisa, meanwhile, returned to rural life and the husband she found so distasteful. Her fortunes were dogged by periods of severe

---

33 A sympathetic and insightful description of Beckford's later life in which he documents for posterity the repression of homosexuals in England during the early years of the nineteenth century can be found in Rictor Norton, 'William Beckford's Gay Scrapbooks', *Gay History and Literature*, updated 16 November 1999 <http://www.rictornorton.co.uk/beckfor2.htm>. See also the same author's overview of his life and the dramatic fortunes of Fonthill Abbey in 'William Beckford: The Fool of Fonthill', *Gay History and Literature* <http://www.rictornorton.co.uk/beckfor1.htm> and 'A Visit to Fonthill', *The Great Queens of History*, updated 30 June 2000 <http://www.rictornorton.co.uk/beckfor3.htm>.

illness with tuberculosis first contracted in the late 1770s.[34] Seeking to gain some improvement in a gentler climate she and her husband spent considerable time in northern Italy but she died there in Florence in 1791 aged 35, and was buried at the Old English Cemetery in Livorno[35] (Plate 22).

Louisa's prediction that Sophia would pay a heavy price for her well-advertised indiscretions certainly appears to have been borne out in her public, if not private, profile. Intriguingly, this can be seen in her portrayals by some of the nation's leading painters. The first of these, and in many ways the most straightforward, concerned the studies done by George Stubbs very soon after Sophia's marriage to John Musters. In 1777, Stubbs was commissioned to produce seven paintings amongst which were two studies that have become exceptionally well known. The first of these shows Sophia in a spectacular red outfit riding ahead of her husband in front of the newly rebuilt Colwick Hall (Plate 23), while the second now appears to show two gentlemen riding to hounds in front of the stable block at Colwick (Plate 24). Such was John Musters' fury when news of Sophia's infidelities reach him that he reacted by having her expunged from both paintings. In the former case, he hired a lesser artist to remove both Sophia and himself from the painting and to have both horses led by grooms. It was only in 1935 that the original was discovered beneath centuries of dirt and varnish and the painting restored. As far as the second was concerned, Stubbs himself was commissioned to remove Sophia and replace her with John's hunting friend, the Rev Philip Story. Originally, Sophia was highlighted by being on the grey mare in the centre of the composition but clearly Stubbs was disconcerted by his new instructions for the Rev Story's right leg appears stiff and wooden and he omitted to add an appropriate saddle flap on the right hand side, which would not have originally been necessary with a side-saddle rider, although he did remember to remove the pommel used to give support to ladies in skirts (Egerton, 2007: 392).

34 In 1781, William Beckford had commissioned Joshua Reynolds to produce a portrait of her when he was himself sitting for the great artist. Reynolds chose to portray her making libations to Hygeia, the goddess of health.

35 Where her mother, who died in 1795, is also buried.

Artists themselves were not immune to reflecting the change in Sophia's public reputation. She sat for Joshua Reynolds on many occasions for at least four portraits and there seems little doubt that her elfin looks, vivacious personality and good humour made her one of his favourite sitters. Moreover, her artistic temperament gave her a particular interest in Reynolds' technical skills and there is some reason for supposing that she may have used some of their time together for acquiring a basic understanding of how he worked. In the late 1770s, Reynolds produced the two portraits that reflected Sophia's youthful innocence. The one showing her in a yellow silk dress was exhibited at the Royal Academy in 1885 while the other has a particularly amusing history.

Sophia and John's daughter, also Sophia, married a Colonel Vaughan and their daughter recalled the history of the painting in a note written in the 1860s (WSA PHA/9551 *nd*):

> When we came from abroad my mother (Mrs Vaughan) on seeing the Print at Colwick asked where the picture was, when her father (Mr Musters) said 'Sir Joshua came to Grosvenor Place, saying there was some fault in the painting and begged to have it to correct'. Your Mother very reluctantly let him have it , and keeping it for some time, sent for it, but Sir Joshua came himself saying 'I am come to return the money, the Picture I never can, for it has been stolen from my studio'. All was tried but they never could trace it (and), after their death, my mother met a Mr Chapman who said 'was your name Miss Musters', Yes, 'then I have seen a beautiful Picture of your Mother, now to be sold. It was found in George the 4ths Gallery of beauties, and bought by a Mr Bullock, because it was like one of his family, who spoilt the likeness of your mother by having the nose altered'.

She goes on to explain that she and her mother accompanied by her uncle, Jack Musters, went to see the portrait and they urged him to buy it, but he refused on the grounds that it might not be her and that in any case he had no money.[36] Her mother, however, was convinced, despite the alterations to the face, saying that she remembered her little spaniel 'Busy'. After confirming that the painting was bought eventually by Lord Egremont, she concludes that the 'King admired my Grandmother, and they say bribed Sir Joshua'.[37]

This story in a rather garbled form is often wrongly relayed in the context of Sir Joshua's most famous portrait of Sophia Musters where he depicted her as 'Hebe', bringer of ambrosia to the gods along with eternal youth. Completed in 1778, during her well-publicised affair with George Pitt, this painting has been referred to as 'the ultimate male fantasy'[38] (Plate 25). The goddess of eternal youth and of pardons or forgiveness, the offspring of Zeus and Hera brings nectar and ambrosia to the mighty eagle representing Zeus himself. Although Reynolds had tried this device before in 1772, in this huge canvas (239cm x 146cm) she is depicted as a free spirit as she seeks to escape the lowering rain clouds of public opprobrium.[39] At least three identical versions of this extraordinary painting were produced by Reynolds' studio. The first was bought in 1778 by Sophia's husband John Musters and may indeed have been commissioned by him. This one was inherited by Jack Musters and stayed at Colby until it was auctioned after his death in 1849. The details of the sale of the contents of Colwick Hall included this painting and a full-length portrait of the elder John Musters also by Reynolds and both were sold to a 'Mr Weeks' for 600 guineas and 580 guineas respectively (*Gentleman's Magazine* January-June 1851). The whereabouts of this painting is not now known. Another version was bought by Philip, 3rd Earl of Hardwicke (1757–1834), and passed on inheritance to Charles 5th Earl of Hardwicke (1836–97), who sold it privately on 19 June 1888 to the Wertheimer brothers and Thomas Agnew and Sons. The latter firm were the principal agents for Sir Edward Cecil Guinness,

36 She says delightfully as an aside, 'people with £15,000 a year never have'.
37 This is why the portrait, presumably still with the emendations to the nose, is in the current Lord Egremont's private collection at Petworth House.
38 A mezzotint was produced by Charles H Hodges three years later.
39 In 1772 he showed 'A Portrait of a young lady in the character of Hebe' (Miss Meyer).

Earl of Iveagh, who acquired the painting four days later. In 1925 he bought Kenwood House on the northern part of Hampstead Heath to save it from demolition and to provide a home for his outstanding collection of paintings. In 1927 on his death he left to the nation both the collection and the house, which is where this version now is located. A third version was retained by Reynolds himself and sold on 16 April 1796 for £36.15.0 (lot 46) at the sale of the contents of his studio after his death four years previously. Passing through a dealer, it was bought by the artist John Hoppner and eventually sold at auction after his death in January 1810. It is not clear what happened to it immediately after that but it was eventually bought by the Dowager Countess of Chesterfield, the widow of the 6th Earl of Chesterfield, and brought to Bretby Park in Derbyshire. This property passed by marriage to the Earls of Carnavon and the painting was transferred to their seat at Highclere Castle near Newbury in Berkshire, where it appeared in a new catalogue of paintings prepared in 1939. This is the setting for the TV serial *Downton Abbey* so the painting will have been viewed many times by adherents of this classic soap opera, and by the many thousands of visitors who now help to pay for the upkeep of the enormous house itself.[40]

The symbolism of this painting suggests that Reynolds himself did not share the public censure that was coming to haunt Sophia Musters. Indeed, there is evidence that she identified herself at this time with the free spirit of 'Hebe' since she signed herself as the goddess in correspondence with intimates.

What happened, however, to another portrait by Reynolds suggests that darker forces were at work, either within the studio or within the world of collectors. Baldry (1900) in his book on the great artist lists five portraits of Sophia, the last of which is described as 'Mrs Musters and Child' and its location is given as the National Gallery. The note is rather cursory and reads, 'Child looking over her shoulder' (Plate 26).

40 I am most grateful to Laura Houliston, Senior Curator of Collections at English Heritage, and to David Rymill from Hampshire Record Office and archivist to the Highclere Estate for assistance with establishing the provenance of these two versions of the 'Hebe' portrait (cf. Bryant, 2003: 352–8 and Mannings and Postle, 2000: 349).

The picture is not now recorded as one of the five works by Reynolds held currently by the National Gallery but the 1901 catalogue (No. 891) lists a Reynolds under the heading 'Portrait of a Lady' and goes on to describe it: 'In a low russet dress, showing the left profile; the head and arm of a child seen resting on her right shoulder (bust, life size 2ft 5½ inches high by 2ft ½ inches wide)'. The really interesting part of the entry is, however, the following:

> A duplicate of this, known as the Hon. Mrs Musters and Son, formerly at Colwick Hall, Nottinghamshire, the residence of the Musters family was sold at Christie's in 1888. The same portrait, without the child, was engraved by S.W. Reynolds in 1825, from a picture at Holland House, as Mrs C.J. Fox.

There are three features of this portrait that deserve comment. The first is that the image of Sophia is of someone with an older and fuller figure suggesting that it was painted well after those mentioned above when she was still in her early twenties. This is a portrait of a woman at least a decade older. The second feature is the child himself. Reynolds was a highly intelligent, even scholarly, man and he would not have made this figure so shaded and hidden unless he was reflecting a parallel feature of that life itself. The child is not a young baby with such a head of hair and could easily be five years of age. The third feature is the way it was subsequently amended and retitled.

The duplicate version, which also includes the child, was acquired by the National Gallery with the purchase in 1871 of 77 paintings from the collection of the late prime minister, Sir Robert Peel. It is now at the Tate Gallery and is listed as 'Mrs Fox' in the manner of Reynolds. The Holland House version from which the mezzotint was taken, without the child, was bought by Dr GWA Clowes in January 1933 from a bookseller in Indianapolis called Arthur Zinkin, owner of the Meridian Bookshop. It is now in the Indianapolis Museum of Art where it is listed as a Reynolds of 'Mrs Charles James Fox'[41] (Plate 27).

41 I am most grateful to Dr Annette Schlagenhauff, Associate Curator of Research at the Indianapolis Museum of Art, for this information.

At first sight it is remarkable that a portrait by the country's leading artist should appear simultaneously in two versions as two different people. How this occurred has not been fully documented but what is particularly significant is not just that this should have happened but rather *with whom* the confusion existed. 'Mrs C.J. Fox' was born Elizabeth Bridget Blane (sometimes reported as 'Cane') in Greenwich on 11 July 1750. She may have worked in London as a model for a fashionable hairdresser before becoming a dresser for the actress Frances Abington and possible also for Mary Robinson ('Perdita') at Drury Lane. In this way she herself took to the stage under the name 'Mrs Elizabeth Armstead' (sometimes given as 'Armistead') but not before receiving financial and other support from a number of aristocratic lovers. Her role as a courtesan did not go unnoticed by the popular press and in 1776 the gossipy magazine *Town and Country* suggested that she could lay claim to the conquest of 'two ducal coronets, a marquis, four earls and a viscount' possibly all at the same time. These friendships produced rich rewards, including houses and annuities, and by 1785 she was able to buy a relatively small country house at St Anne's Hill, Chertsey, that sat within a 90-acre estate.[42] It was here that she entertained Charles James Fox, the outstanding Whig politician sometimes referred to as the 'best Prime Minister England never had', eventually marrying him and settling down to a life of gardening and other domestic endeavours.[43] The important issue is that whoever changed and mislabelled the portrait of 'Mrs Musters and Child' was making a far from innocent point about Sophia's perceived morality.

From the foregoing the possibility must exist that the child in the first two versions of this picture is not Jack Musters but George Dean. Some light may be thrown on this far from certain conclusion by trying to establish when Reynolds completed this painting and whether or not he, or a member of his studio, was responsible for its subsequent emendation. Reynolds produced an extraordinary

42 Reputedly with a loan of £2.000 from the Duke of Marlborough.
43 She outlived her husband by many years, eventually dying in 1842 at Chertsey in her 92nd year.

number of portraits and his fame and pre-eminent position in the late eighteenth century motivated many specialists to produce descriptive studies of his work. By no means the best, but perhaps the most detailed, are those by William Cotton. In 1856, Cotton published a work derived from his diaries including information on sittings and much else besides (Cotton, 1856). Unfortunately, Cotton was not exhaustive and was overly impressed by the social standing of those attracted to Reynolds' painting room. As a result, there is no mention of either Sophia Musters or her husband, who also sat for him. In a subsequent volume that reveals, *inter alia*, the artist's account book there is more promising information (Cotton, 1859). What this publication shows is that work for the Musters was billed on two occasions. The first was in the middle period of Sir Joshua's output when his work commanded rather moderate prices. In December 1777, an account was presented to Mr and Mrs Musters for £157.10s, which almost certainly included more than one work and would account for at least two of the portraits completed when Sophia was still in her early twenties (Cotton, 1859: 97).[44] However, more than ten years later in May 1788, there is another account issued in Sophia's name only for £78 15s which, given the artist's fame and accompanying inflated prices, would then have sufficed for a rather modest work. The date and the single name are significant and it is not unreasonable to suppose that 'Portrait of a Lady' was the work in question. If so, Jack Musters was at least ten years old and the child must have been the only other son, George Dean(e).

The scandal that Sophia may have had to endure as a result of her long-lasting affair with George Pitt probably influenced what happened in relation to another famous likeness of Sophia, that produced by George Romney, usually considered England's third greatest contemporary artist after Reynolds and Gainsborough. This painting like the early ones by Reynolds was paid for by John Musters and it stayed at Colwick, passing eventually to Jack Musters and after to his sister Sophia Vaughan. Like one version of 'Hebe'

44 The peculiar circumstances surrounding the 'Hebe' portrait may have meant this painting was not included in this invoice.

it was acquired by Earl Iveagh and now hangs in Kenwood House. Again, she is portrayed demurely, the only hint of her larger than life personality being the extravagant headgear, but even this passes as more fashion than passion (Plate 28). Immediately after it was finished a mezzotint engraving was prepared by James Walker. The run of 300 priced at three shillings sold out almost immediately and the plate was destroyed. In the meantime, however, another version of the original portrait was produced by an unknown artist.

As the illustration shows, this version is totally different in tone and composition (Plate 29). The demure look has vanished and what we now behold is an ostrich-feathered hussy with rouged cheeks, a low cut dress and ringulets. Anyone seeing this painting at the time, which is now in the Tullie House Museum and Art Gallery Trust in Carlisle, would be in no doubt that this painted beauty was a lady of the town. Thus, by being painted out of existence, redefined as someone with an even more scandalous reputation or simply by being 'tarted up', Sophia Musters became the target of salacious innuendo. As a recent exhibition of paintings by Reynolds brilliantly observed, the age of 'celebrity' has a history of at least two centuries.[45]

With a Prince by the Sea

If a celebrity is someone who is well known for being well known, he – or particularly she – may also be known for being known well. Sophia is not normally listed among the many conquests of the Prince of Wales (later Prince Regent and, after his father's death in 1820, George IV).[46] The bane of government accountants and his staid parents, 'Prinny' was a wit, *bon viveur* and lover of the arts who, despite his philandering, captured the spirit of the 'Georgian' age with its zest for style, refinement and taste, regardless of the cost.

45 'Joshua Reynolds: The Creation of Celebrity', Tate Britain, 26 May–18 September 2005.

46 Sophia did not fall into his normal categories of conquests. She was neither one of his actress friends (*inter alia* Mary Robinson, Elizabeth Billington, Elizabeth Armistead and the redoubtable Maria Anne Fitzherbert) or an aristocratic wife (e.g. Lady Melbourne, the Marchioness of Hertford, Frances Lady Jersey, the Marchioness of Conynham etc.).

There is no doubt that Sophia knew him well and frequented his circle both in Carlton House in London and at the Marine Pavilion in Brighton. She became a close friend of Georgiana Duchess of Devonshire and there was even a report that as a consequence of the high spirited conversation between the two of them while present in the public gallery of the House of Commons, ladies were forbidden from attending (NRO, HMN 5/235/1–33, 738X5). In the summer of 1793, when Georgiana was regarded as the leading light of fashionable society, Sophia was often to be found at social events featuring the prince, particularly when they took place at Brighton. For example in August of that year, during his affair with his older muse, Lady Jersey, a reporter detailed an 'amazing influx of company' featuring the prince, his mistress and Mrs Musters, who 'take the lead here in point of beauty as well as fashion' (*The World* 14 August 1793).[47] After her death in September 1819 press notices recalled in these years, 'the late Duchess of Devonshire, the present Duchess Dowager of Rutland and Mrs Musters, who were contemporaries and associates, were distinguished in high life by the appellation of the Graces' (*Leeds Intelligencer* 4 October 1819).

The prince gave her a silver filigree jockey cup, which passed down through the family for a number of generations.[48] There were so many press reports of Sophia's participation in the fashionable world of high society that it is clear that she had graduated beyond the demi-monde. One example was a masquerade held in Mayfair at Mrs Walker's home attended by 700 people identified as 'the whole of the fashionable world'. Chief among them as one of those that excited the 'greatest interest' was Mrs Musters dressed as an Indian queen:

47 *The World* was a periodical with Irish roots published by Robert Dodsley in Pall Mall between 1753 and 1756 and again between 1789 and 1793. It was edited by Edward Moore (Adam Fitz-Adam) but frequently included essays by Horace Walpole, the Earl of Chesterfield and others with personal knowledge of royal events (cf. Clarke, 2016).

48 Other mistresses received more substantial presents but Sophia was not without financial resources and it would not have been lost on her that this gift could be construed as possessing an obvious sexual innuendo.

> The dress uncommonly beautiful and appropriate: the robe of Indian grass; the vest of silk; a profusion of jewels, particularly pearls, as ear-rings, necklaces etc. the hat made of grass, the crown running up to a spire, from which issued forth a plume of Indian feathers; around the rim gilt bells (*London Courier and Evening Gazette* 3 June 1801).

Of course, the Prince of Wales was also present and Sophia is often mentioned near or in his box at the theatre, opera or other occasions. The social whirl in Brighton during this period was described in great detail in the press including who was seen promenading on the Steyne; inevitably Mrs Musters is identified.

What is remarkable is that she appears to have continued her association with the royal court well into her middle age, or even to the end of her life. There is a report, for example, that she was present in August 1806 with other ladies of his circle when a grandmother of 48 with the Prince of Wales at Brighton Pavilion.[49] Later on, press reports would sometimes identify her with one or other of her sisters as, for example, with Fanny, Mrs Orby Hunter, at Cheltenham in September 1807 (*British Press* 18 September 1807). Even as late as 1816, when 58, she still appears to have been able to turn heads:

> Seldom have we witnessed so many fair and elegantly dressed women as in Hyde Park, from the hour of 4 till 5, on Sunday last. Among the most admired were the beautiful Mrs Musters of Cadogan Place and her lovely sister, Mrs Montague (Montelieu), lately returned from the Continent (*Morning Chronicle* 13 November 1816).

The reference to Cadogan Place in Knightsbridge is interesting for about the same time a press report, almost immediately denied, appeared claiming that she – without her husband – was moving to Cleveland Square, north of Hyde Park. This was perhaps

---

49 *The Jerningham Letters: Correspondence and Diaries of the Honourable Lady Jerningham*, Vol 1: 290 (cf. Boyes 1987).

further evidence that it was only towards the very end of her life that a rapprochement had been negotiated with her husband, although occasionally it was reported that she was attending a social event with him, as in Margate in 1808 (*Morning Post* 31 August 1808).

In addition to this evidence of her closeness to the royal circle, it is also relevant to note that artists and craftsmen of the day, whose livelihood depended upon royal patronage, were often at pains to ensure they included a dedication to Mrs Musters or included her in their selection of public offerings. For example, Edward Jones, 'Bard to his Royal Highness the Prince of Wales', dedicated his *Lyric Airs* (1804) to Sophia Musters and a year later a piece for harp or piano forte music featuring national songs from southern Europe was dedicated to her (*Sun* 19 December 1805). William Bate, the Irish miniature artist and 'Painter in Enamel to the Princess Elizabeth and the Duke of York', included one of her at his exhibition at the Royal Academy in 1817, along with royals and other public figures.

Intriguingly, satirical observations of the day when looking back on her life would compare her favourably to other women, even though at the same time including salacious innuendo. The best of these appeared in 1824 where she is compared with 'Lady Bertram', the venomous anti-heroine of Mansfield Park:

> (Mrs Musters) the wife of three husbands, one of the most brilliant beauties of the day, witty, wise and wicked, who has since figured in a new banking firm of *Drummond, Hore and Child*, was the self-elected leader. The only one who could dispute the palm with this formidable rival was our heroine – perhaps two finer women were never seen. Mrs Musters was taller, higher bred, and wore a more dignified carriage. She had the tone of the best society, and all the accomplishments of the day, to set off a beauty glowing and matured. (Lady Bertram) was more piquant and professional in her appearance. She had a dash to vulgar audacity in her

> manner that set her admirers quite at ease in their addresses (*Bell's Life in London and Sporting Chronicle* 24 October 1824).

The fictitious bank is a reference to the fact that Mrs Musters, late in her life for reasons that are not clear, sometimes referred to herself as 'Mrs Drummond'. The italics are in the original but they are probably a reference to the fact that Sophia, as she aged, appears to have been in need of the flattery provided by younger consorts. The most publicly scrutinised of these affairs was that with Peniston Lamb, the eldest and spoilt son of Elizabeth Milbanke and Sir Peniston Lamb, later Viscount and Viscountess Melbourne. This attention was partly because the activities of the Melbourne family usually provided good copy. Peniston himself was said to be the only one of eight children born to Elizabeth Milbanke who was actually fathered by her husband, who in turn was dubbed a 'Paragon of Debauchery' in a satire of 1812. Twelve years her junior, a portrait of Peniston by Sir Thomas Lawrence shows him to have been a rather petulant as well as privileged young man, but no doubt Sophia saw what the sculptress Anne Seymour Damer did when she sculpted a bust of him as Mercury, messenger of the gods, but also a Roman deity associated with financial gain. The latter came to pass as he left a generous bequest to Sophia when he died of tuberculosis, reputedly in her arms, at the early age of 34 in January 1805. There is no evidence that this liaison was anything but platonic.

Remarkably, despite all these activities, Sophia found time later in life to return to Colwick Hall and to her long-suffering but besotted husband. There she appears to have given fuller rein to her artistic temperament. Remembering the guidance she had been given by Reynolds many years before, she took to painting on stained glass in a similar fashion to his designs showing the Nativity and the Seven Virtues that were used by Thomas Jarvis for the great west window of New College, Oxford. Some of the panels Sophia created were used in Colwick Hall itself and others in Colwick Church. The latter were moved to Annesley's All Saints Church at Southwall when the old church next to the hall fell into disrepair (Plate 30). Perhaps surprisingly, while at Colwick she appears also to have taken a lively interest in the running of the house itself. A later descendant, Lina Musters (1842–1912), writing in the 1890s, includes the following anecdote:

> I remember an old hairdresser at Nottingham, Driver by name, who used to say he had cut the hair of five generations of the Muster's family. He used to go to Colwick every morning to powder and dress old Mr Muster's head, and on one occasion he noticed the stablemen carrying water in pails from the backwater to the house and spilling some. Mrs Musters saw this and objurgated them, and old Driver used to say he 'never thought to hear such foul words come out of such a beautiful mouth' (NRO, HMN 5/235/1–33, 738X5).[50]

Another issue that appears to have pre-occupied her, and on which perhaps she was well qualified to comment, were the fragile fortunes of her son's marriage. Jack Musters clearly had a lively sporting temperament, commented upon from quite an early age.[51] While at Eton in the early 1790s he is reported as having had a fight with T Assheton Smith, another athletic young man, which lasted nearly an hour with no decisive victor. The battle was duly relayed to his parents and even made the national press many years later. Assheton Smith, who went on to become a life-long friend, was apparently a rather plain young man who was reported as saying, 'that fellow,

50 Lina Musters was the wife of John Chaworth Musters (1838–87). She was the author of an historical novel set at the time of the Civil War (*A Cavalier Stronghold: A Romance of the Vale of Belvoir*) that has itself become a noted text in feminist commentaries on the role of women in the writing of British history. See Devoney Looser [2000] *British Women Writers and the Writing of History 1670–1820* Baltimore and London, Johns Hopkins Press: 58–9.

51 It was said of him: 'Mr Musters' active and athletic powers were extraordinary. It was in his younger days his standing challenge to run 50 yards, he carrying a man of any weight, against another's running 100 yards; and another general challenge of his was to run 50 yards against any horse's 100' (obituary appearing in *Bell's Life in Sydney and Sporting Reviewer* 15 June 1850).

Jack Musters, spoilt my beauty' (*Glasgow Herald* 7 March 1860). Like his father, Jack became master of the local hunt and was known as the 'king of gentlemen huntsmen'. He was master of South Nottinghamshire hunt for 16 years and of other local hunts for a total of more than twice that period, during which time he built an enviable reputation not only as a huntsman but also as a breeder of fine hounds.

Mary Ann Chaworth is possibly best known for her relationship, if that is what it could be called, with Lord Byron. In fact, her family had a darker link with the Byron dynasty. She was the grand-niece of William Chaworth of Annesley who had been killed in 1766 by the 5th Lord Byron after an argument and subsequent duel in the Star and Garter inn in Pall Mall.[52] In any event, the poet developed an adolescent passion for Mary Ann during a six-week period over his summer vacation from Harrow School in 1803 when he was 16 and she two years older. He saw her only once more in the following year but it was enough to stimulate him to write 'The Dream' extolling her virtues just before her marriage to Jack Musters. His first published collection of brief verse (*Hours of Idleness*, 1807) contains the following fragment;

> Hills of Annesley, bleak and barren,
> Where my thoughtless childhood stray'd,
> How the northern tempests, warring,
> Howl above thy tufted shade!
>
> Now no more, the hours beguiling,
> Former favourite haunts I see;
> Now no more my Mary smiling
> Makes ye seem a heaven to me.

Although Mary Ann rejected Byron in no uncertain terms before her marriage, she changed her mind after his rise to celebrity and her

52 He was acquitted of murder but indicted for manslaughter. See Outram, T (1905) 'An Old Mystery in a New Light: The Byron-Chaworth Affair', *The English Illustrated Magazine* 34: 122–37.

later despair at the philandering of her husband. The couple had an unhappy marriage and separated for nearly three years between 1813 and 1816, during which time she sought to arrange a meeting with Byron, who initially resisted but eventually agreed. Claiming that had he been successful in marrying her 'the whole tenor of [his] life might have been different', he is reported as saying,

> I remember meeting her after my return from Greece, but pride had consumed my love, and yet it was not with perfect indifference I saw her. For a man to become a poet he must be in love, or miserable. I was both when I wrote the *Hours of Idleness*.[53]

Given his later life, it seems probable that this was merely an adolescent passion, but Mary Ann did appear to harbour regrets. There is a story that on a visit into Nottingham in July 1824 her carriage was stopped by a crowd of mourners in Pelham Street, opposite the Byrons' town house. On learning of the poet's early death, it is said that she burst into tears and kept the blinds of the carriage down as the funeral passed.[54]

Mary Ann Chaworth married Jack Musters in August 1805 when she was a pretty 19-year-old.[55] They produced over the coming years seven children, six of whom survived their childhood, although the eldest son died in his late thirties. The oldest three (two girls and the eldest son) all married members of the Hamond family of Westacre in Norfolk, cementing a family connection that lasted for two centuries. The youngest son, Charles, died aged 14 of malaria

53 T Medwin *Journal of the Conversations of Lord Byron, detailing the principal Occurrences of his Private Life, his Opinions on Society, Manners, Literature, &c., noted during a Six Months' Residence with him at Pisa, in 1821 and 1822.*

54 There is a peculiar connection between Sophia and Lord Byron. Lady Caroline Lamb, with whom the poet had a wild affair in 1812 and after, was married to William Lamb, Peniston's older brother and the country's future prime minister. It may have been loyalty to him that caused her to dismiss Mary Ann's claim that the poet still had feelings for her after she left her husband in 1813.

55 There is a portrait of her by John Hoppner now in Dublin (National Gallery of Ireland) labelled 'Mrs Musters or Mary Chaworth'. Catalogue 1981 inv.no 256.

in 1832 as a midshipman aboard HMS *Beagle* on the ship's second survey voyage with Charles Darwin. It is indicative perhaps of a rift with his family that Jack changed his name (and that of all his children) by royal licence to that of his wife on 3 October 1806, just over a year after he was married, only to change it back again in August 1823, four years after his mother died.[56] Since his father lived for some more years, this might suggest that it was Sophia who objected more strongly, although there is no evidence for this theory. Another possibility, perhaps borne out by the disinclination to assist in the purchase of his mother's portrait noted earlier, is that Jack Musters had another reason to reject his family name to become Jack Chaworth.

Jack Musters was reputedly born in Grosvenor Square on 6 July 1777, one year after his mother's unhappy marriage to John Musters at a time when, as later, she was besotted by George Pitt.[57] In 1987, an article appeared in a newsletter produced by Nottinghamshire's Rural Community Council entitled 'Sophia Musters – friend of the Prince Regent' (Boyes, 1987), where the author advances this speculative proposition:

> It was the Prince Regent himself who was said to be one of her most devoted admirers and there were rumours that her only son, the attractive, athletic, woman-loving Jack Musters was the Prince's son and, although this is difficult to prove at such a distance of time, the fact remains that the older Jack grew, the more he resembled the Prince, as did many of his descendants after him (Boyes, 1987: 96).

Warming to the theory, Ms Boyes continues, 'he was also as much unlike the old squire of Colwick and Jack's rather plain sister, later Sophia Vaughan, as it is possible to get'. Unfortunately, when Jack

56 The announcement in the *London Gazette* declared that his Majesty granted John Chaworth the right to resume the surname Musters 'from affectionate regard to his own family' (14 August 1823).

57 In fact this must be mistaken as official records show that he was baptised on 29 June 1777 at St George's, Hanover Square and, on the same day, at St John the Baptist Church in Colwick, Nottinghamshire.

Musters was conceived, presumably in October or thereabouts of 1776, the Prince of Wales had just turned 15 years of age and this was some years before Sophia had entered his social circle. George Pitt, however, was an equally athletic, tall, handsome 25-year-old at that time. Unlike the man who may have been his younger brother, George Deane Pitt, it would have been quite impossible to acknowledge any other paternity than that of a new husband.

It is tempting to ask whether the two gentlemen looked as if they might have shared the same parentage. Unfortunately, Jack Chaworth-Musters was not given to the indulgence of sitting in artists' studios but in the mid-1840s his love of hunting did get the better of him and he commissioned the well-known animal painter, Richard Barrett Davis, to depict him and his two whips together with his beloved hounds at Annesley Park, Notts (Plate 31). A detail from that painting shows the face of a gentleman with the same aquiline features as George Deane Pitt but, of course, that could have derived from having one rather than two parents in common. On the other hand, the straight back and disciplined demeanour does not immediately suggest a royal lineage, or at least not the one proposed above. Given Sophia's personality and temperament, the balance of probabilities might suggest that her long standing allegiance to George Pitt did indeed produce two sons separated in age by four to five years. In fact, the evidence, albeit circumstantial, is that Sophia and her early paramour maintained an intimacy not shared with her husband until the end of her life. Sophia Musters died while in Brighton on 19 September 1819. Her body was brought back to Nottinghamshire and interred ten days later in the family vault in the St John the Baptist church next to Colwick Hall where it came to light in the 1970s when workmen were making the ruined building safe for visitors (Boyes, 1987: 97). Both she and Lord Rivers were still enmeshed in the social circle of the Prince Regent when she died. At that point he resigned from his longstanding role as Lord of the Bedchamber to the prince but lived on unmarried for another nine years.

A Troubled Outcome

The 1820s saw the growth of gradual but determined pressure to reform the antiquated electoral system which was not only demonstrably undemocratic but also corrupt and quixotic. In Nottingham, 9,000 people signed a petition in favour of reform. Eventually in September 1831 the House of Commons with a Whig majority passed the Reform Bill only to see it defeated by the Tory-dominated House of Lords. Immediately, disturbances broke out in a number of cities, including Nottingham. A public meeting took place in the market place on the 10 October to condemn the decision and, although most participants dispersed quietly afterwards, some did not and resolved to attack the houses of known Tory opponents of reform. Colwick Hall was their first destination since Jack Musters, who had moved his family there following the death of his father in 1827, was a vocal critic of reform and a Tory stalwart. The rioters destroyed much of the house's contents including a second portrait of Sophia Musters by Romney. They also broke into pieces two of the stained glass windows she had painted, which were above the main stairs, although they did not reach the version of the Reynolds portrait of Sophia as Hebe nor one by the same artist of John Musters senior because Mrs Musters and her daughters locked themselves in the ballroom to which the rioters were unable to gain entry (*Morning Post* 17 October 1831).

Jack Musters was absent at the time but Mary Ann and the children spent part of the night hiding in the shrubbery outside as the rioters tried unsuccessfully to burn the house down. She had been ill for some considerable time and suffered from what appears to have been severe depression, a condition that was certainly not helped by this experience. She and her husband moved to Wiverton Hall, but Mary Ann died there under four months after these traumatic events, on 6 February 1832. After the mob left, they moved on to burn down Nottingham Castle, owned by the Duke of Newcastle, who had voted in the House of Lords against the Reform Bill. It remained a burnt out shell looking down on the city for the next 50 years.[58] Jack moved back to Colwick after his wife's death and lived many more years, dying at the age of 72 in 1849.

As for Sophia, a memorial to her in white marble was sculpted by Richard Westmacott and originally erected at Colwick but moved to All Saints Annesley at Southwall when the church was abandoned in 1937. It contains three medallions on the base, one for each of her accomplishments – music, dance and painting.[59] The commemorative text, not without irony, reads, 'To the memory of Sophia Catherine Musters this monument was erected by her affectionate husband if truth, if goodness, charity and grace can in Heaven's holy record find a place thy name, Sophia, with an angel's pen is traced on leaves of bliss by saintly men' (Plate 32).

While observers of the day might not have missed the reference to 'saintly *men*', this interpretation of her life would be as unfair to her as it was erroneous about the men involved. Her achievements were actually remarkable. She came from a wealthy but untitled background with an intelligent and characterful mother but dull and dictatorial father. Clearly a women of great character and wit, she used her sensuality to advance in society, but did so with spectacular success. Many examples have been cited but she may have been a more discreet influence behind the scenes. The visit of King George III, Queen Charlotte and three of their daughters to south-east Cornwall in August 1789, for instance, is sometimes regarded as the 'most memorable visit of the last century' (Worth, 1873: 91). The king was entranced by his navy and regularly reviewed its progress but on this occasion the royal party visited Saltash, Mt Edgcumbe and Cotehele but came to Maristow on two consecutive days and identified it as the highlight of their West Country sojourn. It is

58 The Reform Act, when it was eventually passed in 1832, enfranchised the middle classes for the first time. It was not until the Chartist Movement over the next 15 years that progress was made towards mass participation in parliamentary elections.

59 Westmacott (1775–1856), a former pupil of Antonio Canova, was a prolific sculptor, particularly of commemorative works, including a number in Westminster Abbey (Charles James Fox, William Pitt the Younger etc.). He also produced the reliefs on the north side of Marble Arch and on the pediment of the British Museum (*The Rise of Civilisation*).

true that Earl Howe was part of the welcoming party and may have suggested to officials a visit to his brother and sister-in-law's estate, but in the circumstances it is hard to imagine that Sophia's hand did not also play a part for she must have had many conversations with the queen and almost certainly with her daughters.

Above all, she captured the spirit of the eighteenth century and the regency years. It was an age of wit, fashion and privilege in all of which she was at home. She was a 'woman who was the toast of her generation and who amused her friends and contemporaries by the brilliance of her wit and her many talents' (Boyes, 1987: 97). Despite all the fripperies and frivolities of those about her and in which she indulged to the full, it may also be said that she arranged her life with great skill, mixing in the highest social circles, marrying into great wealth and, at the same time, honouring a teenage romance to the end of her days. It is probable that she entertained the young Prince of Wales but that was an entry ticket to his circle that she used all her life without having to worry about its renewal. Her popular portrayal as a hussy was more to do with explaining how she could otherwise inhabit rarefied social circles without a title. She was, in an age of romance, one of its greatest exponents.

Chapter 7

Defending the Family Name

The only thread that runs through the lives of the four daughters of the Modyford Heywood family is that each married a man more of her parents' choosing than her own. Otherwise their characters appear to be very different. Sophia was determined to overcome the boredom inflicted by her selected spouse by liberally spending his money and living apart from him for much of the time after providing an heir. The others were more dutiful but not necessarily happier. The next in line, Emma, suffered at least as much if not more than her elder sister but in her own way made an equal contribution to the social standing of the family.

As with her elder brother and sister, any details of Emma Heywood's early life are unknown. She was born on 8 May 1762 when her brother, James, was six and Sophia four years old. In her early years, she would no doubt have been conscious of being joined by two more sisters and at the impressionable ages of seven and nine witnessing the births and early deaths of two more brothers. Despite not having had a naval career, James Modyford Heywood had always imagined himself to be a man of the sea, partly perhaps through the reflected glory of his brother-in-law's illustrious career. It was no doubt with great pleasure, therefore, that he arranged for the introduction of Emma to the ambitious young officer Albemarle Bertie. Bertie was one of two illegitimate sons of the 3rd Duke of Ancaster, half-brother to Lady Jane Mathew. He was born on 20 January 1755 and after officer training was appointed a lieutenant a little before his 23rd birthday on 20 December 1777. His career got off to an unsteady start as soon after his first posting as first lieutenant on board HMS *Fox*, the vessel was captured by the French warship the *Junon* at the Battle of Ushant in September 1778. As a result he and other officers became prisoners of war, only returning to England the following January when he gave evidence in the highly politicised courts martial of Admiral Augustus Keppel, in whose fleet he had served, and Sir Hugh Palliser. Although both were acquitted, Bertie's evidence helped to destroy the future career of the latter. With the fall of the Tory administration in March 1782 and the rise to greater prominence of Admiral Keppel as first lord of the Admiralty in the new Whig administration, Bertie was appointed captain of his first command, the frigate HMS *Crocodile*.

Exactly when Bertie became acquainted with Emma Heywood is not known but it must have been after he was released by the French in late 1778 and before he took up his appointment as captain in 1782. The marriage settlement between the two, dated 4 June of that year, consisted of £12,000 bequeathed by the late Duke of Ancaster to his son (LA 2ANC3/C/71).[1] Their marriage followed on 1 July 1783 and his residence at that time was given as Nether Hall, Dedham in Essex. The couple had three daughters in quick succession, Emma, Louisa and Catherine, and eventually on 29 October 1795 a son, Lyndsey-James Bertie, who became an infantry officer in the 12th regiment of Dragoons, only to lose his life on 18 June 1815 at the Battle of Waterloo.

There seems little doubt that Bertie's ambition was matched by a ruthless streak. It was apparent in his undermining of Sir Hugh Palliser in support of his superior, Admiral Keppel, and again some years later after serving on a number of vessels on defensive duties in the Channel. Having been made a rear-admiral in April 1804 and a vice-admiral four years later, he was posted as commander-in-chief to the Cape of Good Hope. Two years into this posting he was aware of the preparations being made for an assault against the French-held island of Mauritius and took it upon himself to sail the 2,500 miles to join the fray in the frigate *Africaine*.[2] Although well beyond the boundaries of his station, Bertie assumed command when all the

1 One of the trustees of the settlement was John Musters, Sophia's husband.
2 Mauritius had been in French hands for a century and during the Napoleonic wars had become a base for French corsairs harrying English trade routes around the Cape into the Indian Ocean.

planning and much of the successful action had been accomplished by the commander-in-chief in India, Vice-Admiral Drury, and the actual commander Josias Rowley. Although careful to praise Rowley, Bertie took much of the credit for the operation to the accompanying fury of Drury who wrote home to the Admiralty that he had been 'insulted and injured' by these claims. The Admiralty was sympathetic but, following the crisis in the Tory administration in May-June 1812 involving financial problems, the commencement of war with the United States and the assassination of Prime Minister Spencer Perceval, sentiment shifted in Bertie's favour and he was awarded with a baronetcy in December that year.[3]

Whatever the justice of Drury's claims, there seems little doubt that Emma's husband was a man wedded to a successful career which, together with his extended periods away from home, must have made their marriage less than easy. As with her three sisters, Emma was herself not without aspirations beyond the humdrum confines of domesticity. She found her cause in the role she played in the most famous maritime drama of her age and, arguably, that of the Navy itself – the mutiny aboard the small merchant vessel originally called the *Bethia*, built in 1784, but rather better known by the name she was given when bought and refitted by the Royal Navy three years later – the *Bounty*. Arguably, Emma's intervention helped to save the life of the third most famous crew member of the *Bounty* and the one who bore the family name, Peter Heywood. The story of how she managed to achieve this and what effects it had upon her later life are often glossed over or ignored by the scores of authors who have written about this extraordinary tale, combining as it does perilous journeys, violent conflict and illicit sexual relations in the South Pacific.[4]

3 Although he never saw active service again he continued to find favour being promoted to a KCB in January 1815 and an Admiral of the White (second only to the Admiral of the Fleet) in 1821 (obituary, *Gentleman's Magazine* May 1825).

4 Even a cursory search of the secondary literature on the mutiny will reveal more than 2,000 items. It is not the purpose here to add anything of substance to that corpus but only to reflect on the Heywood connection.

Perhaps the first question to ask is whether Emma and Peter Heywood were in fact related. The answer is in the affirmative, but very distantly. Both were descended from a Lancastrian family. While the Heywood dynasty goes back for many prior generations, in the sixteenth century Peter Heywood of Heywood in Lancashire and his wife Margaret produced ten children including two sons, Peter and Robert whose subsequent marriages and offspring brought one line of the family by way of depleted financial circumstances to the Isle of Man where they prospered and became highly influential in that island's government, administration and legal service (*Iter Lancastrense*, 1845: Notes: 19–21). The other son, Peter, came to London and it was he who is credited with apprehending Guy Fawkes in the Palace of Westminster in 1605. His grandson was the Peter Heywood discussed in Chapter 4, great-grandfather of Emma Bertie. In other words Emma and Peter were cousins five times removed. There is no evidence that until the saga of the *Bounty* brought them together, they had maintained any contact, or indeed were aware that they shared common ancestors. It is worth stressing, however, that Peter Heywood came from a family whose origins in terms of social class were not that dissimilar to Emma Bertie's. His father, Peter John Heywood, had been one of the Deemsters (judges) of the Isle of Man (1765–8) and Seneschal (head steward) to the Duke of Atholl, who until 1765 was the proprietor of the island. Peter John's father in turn had been Speaker of the House of Keys (the lower branch of the parliament), his grandfather attorney general and his great-grandfather governor of the island.

Peter Heywood, the second son of Peter John Heywood and his wife Elizabeth, was born on 6 June 1772 at the family home, the Nunnery, near Douglas, the capital of the Isle of Man. Possibly influenced by his aunt's husband, Captain Thomas Pasley, and despite being rather intellectual by nature, he developed a passion for a naval career and after a period of training in Plymouth was offered the position of midshipman aboard a vessel newly acquired by the Royal Navy on a journey to the South Pacific to acquire saplings of the breadfruit tree (*Artocarpus altilis*), a staple food crop of the South Pacific islands, in the hope that the fruits could provide a nutritious and low-cost solution to the problem of feeding slaves on New World plantations.[5] This idea had come from the renowned botanist, Joseph Banks, who had accompanied James Cook on his first voyage to the South Pacific in search of the mythical land mass *Terra Australis*. On his third and last voyage, his sailing master aboard HMS *Resolution* was the young William Bligh who went on to witness Cook being killed on a beach of the Sandwich Islands (Hawaii) by local people in February 1779.

William Bligh was born on 9 September 1754 at St Tudy, near Bodmin in Cornwall, and went to sea from a very early age, on some accounts as a seven-year-old servant to a captain. In his late teens he trained as a midshipman specialising in navigation and cartography, a skill in which he excelled and which led to his appointment at the age of 22 on Cook's final voyage. After serving on a number of other vessels as a lieutenant and a spell in the merchant service, William Bligh was appointed lieutenant in command of HM Armed Vessel *Bounty* on 16 August 1787 for a return voyage to Otaheite (Tahiti) to acquire the breadfruit saplings and transport them to the Caribbean where it was believed they would grow well and fulfil the needs of the planters for a nutritious addition to slave diets. During the four years he was in the merchant service, Bligh had been given command of the ex-convict ship *Britannia* now owned by the uncle of his wife, Elizabeth (née Betham). During this time, he had recruited a volunteer midshipman by the name of Fletcher Christian and sailed with him twice to the West Indies supplying goods to the planters of Jamaica. Christian, although born (25 September 1764) in Cockermouth, Cumbria, was like Peter Heywood a Manxman and the parallel does not rest there. Both came from families of high social status that had fallen on very hard times. In Christian's case, his widowed mother faced the prospect of debtors' prison through profligate spending and had to flee back to Man to escape her creditors, while Heywood's father had been forced to flee the

5 This problem had become more acute with the cessation of supplies of salted fish following the American War of Independence.

other way to Whitehaven for embezzling funds belonging to his employer, the Duke of Atholl. In happier times, the families had been on friendly terms and there is good reason to believe that Peter Heywood and Fletcher Christian retained personal warmth towards each other throughout subsequent events.

The *Bounty* was a very modest vessel, just under 91 feet (27.7 metres) in length and 24 feet (7 metres) at her widest point with minimal armament and a complement of 45 men, of whom just over half were able seamen, most of the remainder being warrant officers. She had been modified to carry the breadfruit plants and this added to her feeling of being overcrowded. Her size also dictated a major departure for a vessel destined for a voyage of some years' duration; she carried no means of imposing internal security other than the will and determination of the commander. On a larger ship on an extended voyage, it would have been more usual to include a body of marines amongst the ship's company together with additional commissioned officers.

Expecting to set off no later than mid-November 1787, the *Bounty* was held back by a delay in delivering Admiralty instructions until later, finally leaving from Spithead on 23 December with Captain Bligh (33) in command, Fletcher Christian (23) as one of two Master's Mates and Peter Heywood (14) as one of two midshipmen (the most junior crew granted officer status).[6] Bligh's orders were to round Cape Horn and then to cross the Southern Ocean to the South Sea Islands, particularly Tahiti, where ample supplies of breadfruit saplings could be found. From there, it was intended that they would continue around the Cape of Good Hope and then cross the Southern Atlantic in order to offload their cargo in the Caribbean.

Rounding Cape Horn is always difficult but the delayed departure made it especially so and faced with powerful headwinds and sickness among the crew, Bligh eventually abandoned this plan and turned back towards the Cape of Good Hope, making landfall on

6 There were at least two other young men on board with this title which was often seen as an apprenticeship for an officer's commission.

22 May 1788, approximately six months after leaving Portsmouth. After a month's restocking and repairs, the *Bounty* set sail eastward, passing south of Australia and calling briefly at Adventure Bay on the southern tip of Van Diemen's Land (Tasmania) in August. Later there were reports that some challenges to Bligh's authority had been made during these months at sea, but none seems to have been made by Fletcher Christian. On the contrary, Bligh had promoted him to acting lieutenant and master on the basis of his seamanship and commitment to the wellbeing of the ship's company, demoting the previous incumbent (John Fryer), one of those who had challenged his authority. After taking on water and some supplies, the ship headed eastward and then north towards the Pacific islands, arriving at Matavai Bay in Tahiti on 26 October 1788 (Plate 33).

One can only speculate on how these young men felt on arriving in Tahiti after the trials and tribulations of so many months at sea. The issue arose, however, of how to pass the time while the young breadfruit plants were established, a period that the botanist on board suggested would be from four to six months. With the wisdom of hindsight, Bligh at this point made a profound error. He simply permitted the ship's crew to mingle and enjoy the company of the friendly South Sea islanders with few other duties other than maintaining the ship and tending to the saplings. The result was that the men swiftly 'went native', eagerly availing themselves of opportunities for sexual liaisons, some very short-term but others accompanied by much more serious levels of commitment. Fletcher Christian may have been among the latter, for some time during this period he established a relationship with the women who was eventually to become his wife, Mauatua (called by Christian 'Isabella' after his cousin but often referred to as 'Mainmast' because of her height and statuesque figure, sometimes abbreviated to 'Miamiti'). In addition, tensions had arisen with both warrant officers and petty officers, particularly in relation to an attempted desertion by three crew members. Although these men were swiftly found and punished, Bligh revealed a personality trait that was perhaps his greatest fault. It was not, as is so often portrayed, that he was a sadistic exponent of extreme punishments; indeed, as far as the able seamen were concerned, he was relatively lenient. It was his incapacity to accept joint responsibility when things went wrong, and to blame his junior officers in the most virulent of terms, which both undermined his authority and the morale of others. Many months later when preparing his account of events, he was to write, 'such a neglectful and worthless petty officer I believe never was in a ship as in this'. As JC Beaglehole says of Bligh, 'he saw fools about him too easily, and the thin-skinned vanity that was his curse through life was already with him. He never learnt that you do not make friends of men by insulting them' (1992: 498) (Plate 34).

Eventually, amidst grumblings from the rest of the crew on having to leave their paradisiacal lifestyle, the *Bounty* set sail westward on 4 April 1789 intending to complete the journey to the Caribbean to deliver her valuable cargo. Some two weeks or so out and approximately 30 nautical miles from Tofua/Tofoa in the Tongan archipelago, Bligh's relationship with Christian took a severe turn for the worse. According to John Fryer's later report, they argued frequently with Christian complaining at one point, 'Sir, your abuse is so bad that I cannot do my duty with any pleasure. I have been in hell for weeks with you'. A trivial event on 27 April led to Bligh accusing his acting lieutenant of theft which appears to have been the final straw. Although the original plan was simply to abandon the vessel on a makeshift raft, a full-scale mutiny took place at dawn on 29 April while Fletcher Christian was on watch. In Bligh's own words,

> Just before sun-rising, Mr Christian, with the master at arms, gunner's mate, and Thomas Burket, seaman, came into my cabin while I was asleep, and seizing me, tied a cord behind my back, and threatened me with instant death, if I spoke or made the least noise: I, however, called so loud as to alarm everyone; but they had already secured the officers who were not of their party, by placing centinels (sic) at their doors. There were three men at my cabin door, beside the

> four within; Christian had only a cutlass in his hand, the others had muskets and bayonets. I was hauled out of bed, and forced on deck in my shirt, suffering great pain from the tightness with which they had tied my hands.[7]

He goes on to describe how he and 18 other warrant officers and petty officers were set adrift in the ship's launch while 25 men, including nearly all of the able seamen, stayed on board the *Bounty* now under the command of Christian. At no time did Peter Heywood take an active part in the mutiny, but in Bligh's later narrative of events he is specifically mentioned as one of the 'pirates', as were all those who remained behind on the *Bounty* with the exception of four men, who in the captain's estimation would have come with him had they been allowed to do so.

Subsequent events are rather well known. Fletcher Christian first tried to establish a settlement on the island of Tubuai, the largest of the Austral Islands 640 kilometres south of Tahiti, which he had identified from Bligh's charts drawn during the journey the latter had made with Captain Cook. After an initial conflict with islanders while the ship was at anchor, the *Bounty*'s crew returned briefly to Tahiti to obtain what they considered the essentials that they had been unable to beg, buy or steal on their first visit. The second time they landed and established a fort ('Fort George') but again internal conflict and the hostility and resentment of the local people sapped morale to the point where a new plan had to be concocted. Eventually it was decided to return to Tahiti where whoever wished could stay, with the risk that they would be apprehended, while Christian and the ship would move on to another island with those who elected to join him (Dening, 1992: 94–5). In the event, 16 of the 25 men stayed in Tahiti, including Peter Heywood and his fellow midshipman, George Stewart, and four of those who had vociferously opposed the mutiny but had not been allowed to enter the overcrowded launch with Bligh. Christian was joined by the remaining eight men, 'Miamiti' with whom he

7 http://law2.umkc.edu/faculty/projects/ftrials/Bounty/blighnarrative.html

had now been through a local marriage ceremony, and a further 11 Tahitian women and six local men (five Tahitian and one Tubuaian). It was this motley crew that after months of searching eventually settled on the uninhabited island of Pitcairn.

Bligh, meanwhile, in one of the most remarkable voyages ever made, drew upon his undeniable skills as a navigator and with no chart managed to navigate the open 23-foot launch 3,618 nautical miles through the Endeavour Strait with its masses of shoals and islets, making landfall eventually in Coupang (Kupang) in south-west Timor (Java), arriving on 14 June 1789 and losing only one man in the process. After a period of recuperation, Bligh purchased a local schooner and sailed back to England, arriving to a hero's welcome in March 1790. In Otaheite during these months, Peter Heywood and the other men had settled back into a simple but comfortable life. Heywood, in particular, appears to have been genuinely interested in the culture of the Tahitian people and prepared to absorb as much of it as he could. He learnt the language, adopted the clothing, respected and observed their rituals and – along with others – had himself extensively tattooed. He also took a local woman as his partner and fathered at least one child. For all these reasons, he was remembered with affection by local people for many years after his departure from the island.

This leaving was inauspicious. The Royal Navy could not allow mutineers to go unpunished and in the summer of 1790 Captain Edward Edwards was commissioned to set sail in HMS *Pandora*, a 24-gun frigate, in search of the *Bounty* and as many as possible of the alleged mutineers as he could manage to find. He arrived in Tahiti on 23 March 1791. Immediately on sighting the vessel, Peter Heywood and his fellow midshipman, George Stewart, took a canoe and made themselves known to Edwards and the crew. For their pains they were immediately clapped in irons. Edwards was a man unprepared to make distinctions; as far as he was concerned anyone who did not accompany Bligh was a suspected mutineer and helped him meet the tally that he felt duty bound to reach. Eventually his crew tracked down all of those still alive who had opted to stay in Tahiti, an additional 12 souls.[8] They were confined in irons in a specially made box only 18 by 11 feet on the aft deck where they were to remain for five months in appalling conditions while the *Pandora* sailed westward in an attempt to find Christian and the remainder of those 'piratical villains' who had dared flout the legitimate orders of a senior officer. On 28 August, disaster struck as Edwards was trying to find a way through the northern part of the Great Barrier Reef, just to the east of the northern tip of what is now Queensland. The ship bilged on the reef and after some hours of frantic pumping, the *Pandora* sank with the loss of 31 crew members. At the very last moment, an armourer on board tried to free the prisoners from their shackles and Peter Heywood and nine other prisoners made it out of '*Pandora*'s Box' through one of two small access ports, but four including Heywood's great friend, George Stewart, were not so lucky and went down with the ship.

After the wrecking of the *Pandora*, Peter Heywood found himself adrift clinging to a plank before being picked up by one of the ship's smaller boats and ending up with 99 other survivors on a spit of sand. The regular crew fashioned makeshift coverings from the vessel's sails but Heywood and the other prisoners were shackled in the open where they suffered considerably from sunstroke after months in the semi-darkness of their former prison. They then had to endure a 1,000-mile journey in open small boats to Coupang and then onwards for a further 33 days to Batavia (Jakarta) where they were imprisoned in the local castle by the Dutch colonists. After that the prisoners we sent, via the Cape of Good Hope, on Dutch merchantmen to England, arriving at Spithead on 19 June 1792 whereupon they were transferred to await their fate to the *Hector*, a 74-gun third rate ship of the line, moored in Portsmouth Harbour.

Having survived the ill-fated return of the *Pandora*, it was inevitable that Peter Heywood would appear alongside all the other prisoners at the subsequent court martial. This was especially so because William Bligh had clearly gone out of his way to indict

8 Two of the original *Bounty* crew had been murdered in Tahiti.

Heywood as one who played an active role in the staging of the mutiny itself. As early as March 1790, Bligh had replied to a letter from James Holwell, Peter's uncle, in the following terms:

> ... I inform you that you nephew Peter Heywood is among the mutineers: his ingratitude to me is of the blackest Dye for I was a father to him in every respect and he never once had an angry Word from me thro' the whole Course of the voyage as his conduct always gave me much pleasure and satisfaction. I very much regret that so much Baseness form'd the Character of a young Man I had a real regard for (William Bligh to Colonel James Holwell, 26 March 1790).

Even to Peter Heywood's mother, Elizabeth, he had written in a similar vein, to the point of anticipating his eventual fate: '... his Baseness is beyond all description, but I hope you will endeavour to prevent the Loss of him, heavy as the Misfortune is, from afflicting you too severely' (William Bligh to Elizabeth Heywood, 2 April 1790).[9] It was fortunate indeed that by the time the court martial of the *Pandora*'s surviving prisoners commenced on 12 September 1792, Bligh, whose public standing had been greatly enhanced by the story of his remarkable survival and voyage home, had been sent off yet again to the Southern Ocean to repeat the quest for breadfruit saplings.

In the meantime, faced with these charges from Bligh, the Heywood family in the Isle of Man was quick to try and mobilise support for Peter, as well as to learn whether the indictments were to be believed. It becomes clear that James Modyford Heywood was approached not simply because he was seen as a man of influence in naval affairs, but rather because he had played a role in Peter's original decision to pursue officer training. Precisely how this came about has been lost but Peter's indefatigable sister, Hester (Nessy), makes reference to it in a later letter to him when she writes of James Modyford Heywood as one 'by whose Interest you first went

9 This letter was kept from Elizabeth by other members of her family.

into the Navy' (Nessy Heywood to Peter Heywood, 3 June 1792).[10] Because of his incarceration on the *Pandora*, Peter Heywood was well aware prior to his return to England that he was being blamed for not having gone with Bligh in the launch following the mutiny. In his first explanation of the reasons why this occurred, written in a letter to his mother from Batavia (Jakarta) dated 20 November 1791, he concludes by beseeching her to pass on this explanation to 'my ever honoured and much respected Friend Mr Betham (William Bligh's father in law)' and also to 'my Uncle (Thomas) Pasley and Mr Heywood of Plymouth' since 'their timely Aid and friendly Advice might be the means of rescuing me from an ignominious Lot...'

It was precisely during these months that the Modyford Heywoods of Maristow came into their own in offering rather more than advice. Emma Bertie, in particular, played a major role in three ways. First, she clearly influenced her father who changed from being convinced of Peter Heywood's guilt to being prepared to offer both material and other forms of support. For example, in a letter to Nessy Heywood in the Isle of Man, who had written to him seeking his aid, he replied that according to his inquiries, 'you have every reason to believe that he has been in this Instance drawn aside to join in the Mutiny...' He went on gloomily, 'Feeling as every true Friend of his Country does for the discipline upon which must depend the prosperity of the Navy, who of distinguished Character will be ready to intercede for Men who shall be found guilty of such an Offence?' (James Modyford Heywood to Nessy Heywood, 22 June 1792). Under a week later, however, Emma, at that time living aboard her husband's ship the *Edgar* then being refitted in Portsmouth Dockyard and – by chance – moored alongside the *Hector*, intercedes with a letter to Peter's mother in which she says that 'a 'Friend of mine' went to see Peter and he was in good health but requiring a few things which 'at My father's request he has been and will be supplied with'. Crucially, these included a naval uniform appropriate to his rank so that he

10 All this correspondence, plus other original documents and much else besides, can be read on the remarkable website www.fatefulvoyage.com compiled by James Galloway.

could appear distinct from the other prisoners at the impending court martial.

The second contribution Emma made was to serve as a means of communication between Peter Heywood, who had just turned 19 in the summer of 1792, and his family and to befriend him in what must have been a period of great alarm and distress. The letter cited above makes this clear:

> I think it will be a great satisfaction to you to know, that he has a Friend and relation on the Spot, who will do everything she can, to make his present Confinement as comfortable as possible (Emma Bertie to Elizabeth Heywood, 28 June 1792).

Emma's role did not go unrecognised by those it most directly affected. On 22 July, Peter wrote to his sister, 'How kind my dear Nessy is Mrs Bertie – I need but express a Wish for any thing and I have it immediately – she sends me Vegetables &c every Day – & Yesterday she sent me some Books to soften my Confinement and amuse the tedious Hours'; and just before the conclusion of the trial Nessy wrote to him a letter that included the following paragraph:

> My Mama wrote on Saturday to your charming Friend Mrs Bertie, in answer to the most delightful letter you can possibly have an Idea of from her. I call her *your* Friend in particular, my Love, but she has been the Friend of us all, the sweet soother of our fears, and, by paying you the tender Attentions of a Sister, has loaded us with Obligations, which can never be sufficiently admired and gratefully remembered, and which a whole Life of thanks cannot possibly repay (Nessy Heywood to Peter Heywood, 17 September 1792).

The emissary who carried out Emma's wish was an officer of her husband's ship, the *Edgar*, with whom she was clearly close. He was Robert Larkan, the *Edgar*'s first lieutenant, and there is some reason for supposing that he was a friend of some years' standing. In a letter to his mother, dated 29 June 1792, Peter Heywood describes him as 'being an intimate Friend of Mr Heywood of Marristow' (*sic*) which might suggest that Emma knew him from before she was married.[11]

It appears that thereafter, Emma spent more time at Maristow, where her youngest sister Fanny was still unmarried and living at home. It is probable that her friendship with Larkan also continued through these years when he was not at sea. A fascinating suggestion of this arose as a result of a love affair that Fanny was conducting whenever possible with a young army officer named William Dyott. Dyott kept a daily diary for more than 50 years and an edited version was published in 1907 (Jeffrey, 1907). He describes his infatuation with Fanny Heywood in July 1794 on a posting to Plymouth. He declares that he 'never passed so pleasant a time; being in love, and having the object of your adoration present, makes any place cheerful; I certainly never knew what it was to love till I saw the best creature existing (Lovely Fanny)' (1907: 76). A little later in June 1795 on a return visit when he was staying at the Citadel with General George Lennox, Governor of Plymouth, it becomes quite clear that his affections were directed at Fanny Heywood as he writes, 'I renewed my visits to Maristow with a pleasure that I cannot express'. In October the same year he records with great melancholy having to leave Plymouth for the West Indies and therefore 'parting from the woman of all others I ever did or ever shall love'. He was accompanied on visits to Maristow by another officer whose name was transliterated from the original diary as 'Markham', with a note from the editor that it was barely legible. The context suggests it was actually Robert Larkan, whom Dyott describes as 'the finest fellow in the world'. His diary records how they

> got into a chaise and proceeded to Maristow, where we dined and supped, and afterwards I passed the most dreadful trial I ever experienced. I cannot – words cannot – express what I felt on taking leave of Sweet Fanny (Jeffery, 1907: 81).

11 Larkan served with great distinction in sea battles under Earl Howe including on the 'Glorious 1st of June'. He retired as a post-captain in 1819 and died in 1841.

As things turned out the appalling gale of 18 November 1795 in which a number of Royal Naval vessels were lost along with more than 200 men (including 14 officers) meant that Dyott's departure was delayed.[12] He immediately disembarked and headed for Maristow 'where I remained till 23rd (November), and four happier days no man ever passed'.

The final role that Emma played was the influence she undoubtedly had over her husband, Albemarle Bertie. Bertie's previous career suggests that he would have been a wholehearted supporter of the naval maxim that passivity in the face of a mutiny was akin to aiding and abetting the actual overthrow of a ship's command. Peter Heywood's defence, first set out in the letter to his mother of 20 November, turned on three arguments. First, he claimed that when inquiring from others who were active in the mutiny what was to become of those who wished to have no part in it, he was told that the captain would 'be sent ashore to Tofoa in the launch and those who wou'd not join Mr Christian, might either accompany him, or be taken in irons as prisoners to Taheite and be left there'. Since he knew the Tofuans to be aggressive towards foreigners, while he had felt very much at home on his previous time in Tahiti, he felt the latter was a better option.[13] Second, when he spoke to his fellow midshipman George Stewart, with whom he was very friendly, he was told that this choice might be construed as not being supportive of Bligh so both young men went below to collect some belongings with the intention of joining the captain's party in the launch. They then discovered that armed sentinels had been posted to keep them from going back on deck and that when they were eventually allowed to do so, the launch was well astern of the *Bounty*. As testimony to his original intentions, when the ship eventually returned to Tahiti to collect supplies and female partners for the mutineers, he and Stewart both opted to stay on the island knowing that a ship would eventually be sent there in search of the

12 The storm is sometimes referred to as 'the Christian Storm' after Admiral Christian who was unlucky enough to be in charge of the fleet on that occasion.

13 Subsequent events proved this point as Bligh lost the only man on his epic voyage to the Tofuans.

mutineers. Finally, when that vessel, the *Pandora*, arrived some 18 months later, both young officers immediately made themselves known to the ship's commander, only to find themselves thrown into irons. In other words, his defence was that he had played no active part in the mutiny and that when he, somewhat belatedly, decided to join his captain, he was prevented from so doing but made himself known to the authorities at the earliest opportunity.

The court martial lasted for only five working days and was held aboard HMS *Duke*, a 98-gun ship of the line, under the presidency of Vice-Admiral Lord Hood, the commander at Spithead. The panel consisted of 11 other naval officers, including Albemarle Bertie, Emma Heywood's husband and captain of the *Edgar* moored alongside the *Hector*. Heywood had attempted, unsuccessfully, to be tried alone but there was some recognition of his status as a junior officer in that he was heard last, which allowed him to contest anything that had been said against him in prior questioning. During the previous testimonies a number of questions were related to his conduct and designed to ascertain whether he could truly be said to have been a 'mutineer' as Bligh had contended. For example, the first witness was John Fryer, the ship's master and one of those who had accompanied the captain in the open launch. Interestingly, he testified that 'I had frequently told Captain Bligh in Our Conversations that I had not seen the Youngsters on Deck' at the time of the ship's seizure. The second witness also, William Cole, the ship's boatswain and another who accompanied Bligh, when asked who, in addition to three men he had named, were 'detained against their inclinations', replied, 'I believe Mr Heywood was, I thought all along, he was intending to come away.' In reply to the question, 'Have you any other reason which induces you to think that Mr Heywood was detained contrary to his Will?', he did not at first mention Heywood but said, 'I heard Churchill call out "Keep them below" – who he meant I do not know.' Pressed again with the question 'Do you think he meant Heywood?' he replied, 'I have no reason to think any other.' He then confirmed a view that the reason Heywood and three others helped with getting the launch prepared was because they wished to go in it with Bligh. The remark 'keep them below' was also heard by William Purcell, the ship's carpenter and another warrant officer who went with Bligh. He confirmed too that it was only ten to 15 minutes after Heywood went below that the launch was cast off. Purcell then said, 'I by no means considered him as a Person concerned in the Mutiny or Conspiracy.' Importantly, these benign interpretations of Heywood's role were all made by witnesses for the prosecution.

But this would not have been good enough to save Peter Heywood since passivity was no defence and moreover a prosecution witnesses, Thomas Hayward (3rd lieutenant on *Pandora* and midshipman on *Bounty*), testified that he was unaware of any reason why Heywood could not have joined Bligh if he so wished. He also argued that James Morrison, the ship's boatswain's mate, was assisting the mutineers. Hayward was not, however, entirely convincing since he went on to say that Heywood looked sorrowful but still thought he was on the side of the mutineers just after he had testified that one McIntosh, also a prisoner, looked depressed and this was the reason he thought him not of the mutineers' party. Another witness, John Hallet (midshipman), tried to undermine Heywood's passivity defence, testifying that he laughed and turned away after Bligh had spoken to him. Again he also testified against James Morrison saying that he was armed with a gun.

Heywood did not give evidence in person because he argued that his confinement had made him unable to deliver it with 'that force of expression which it required'. Therefore Mr Const, a lawyer hired by Thomas Pasley, Peter's uncle, read to the court martial a document prepared by himself, Heywood and another lawyer, Aaron Graham a friend of Thomas Pashley and well versed in court martial proceedings. The statement is very similar to the letter to his mother from nearly a year before but emphasised his youth (16 at the time of the mutiny). His final statement to the court was as follows:

> It has been proved that I was asleep at the time of the Mutiny and waked only to confusion and dismay. It has been

> proved, 'tis true, that I continued on board the Ship, but it has also been proved I was detained by force – and to this I must Add, I left the Society of those with whom I was for a time obliged to associate, as soon as possible, and with unbounded satisfaction resigned myself to the Captain of the 'Pandora', to whom I gave myself up, to whom I also delivered my Journal (faithfully brought up to the preceding day) and to whom I also gave every information in my Power.

The result of the trial was that half of the ten men before the court were found guilty of mutiny and condemned to die by hanging, one was freed on a legal technicality and four were acquitted. Peter Heywood and James Morrison were among the five condemned men but were recommended for the king's mercy. This outcome was undoubtedly influenced by the limitations of naval statute that allowed only for a guilty verdict or acquittal, unless a technical plea was successful. Clearly, the court martial could have acquitted Heywood, which they chose not to do presumably because, even though they may have believed that both Heywood and Morrison were detained against their wishes, neither provided evidence that they had sought to regain the ship or come to the aid of William Bligh.

Heywood's escape from the noose depended therefore upon the wording of the plea to the king for mercy, as well as the monarch's ultimate decision. The verdict, delivered on 18 September 1792, was unequivocal: 'the Court, in Consideration of various Circumstances, did humbly and most earnestly recommend the said Peter Heywood and James Morrison to His Majesty's Royal Mercy' – which was about as strong a recommendation as it was possible to achieve. On the same day, Emma Bertie wrote to Peter's mother in these words:

> I have the Happiness of telling you that the Court Martial is this Moment over, & that I think your son's Life is more safe now, than it was before his Trial: – as there was not sufficient proof of his Innocence, the Court cou'd not avoid condemning him: but he is so strongly recommended to

> Mercy, that I am desired to assure you (by those who are judges) that his life is *safe*.

We may never know for certain what role Albemarle Bertie played in this outcome but, at the very least a potentially negative influence was neutralised by Emma Bertie's role and it may well have been that the part he played was far more positive. Certainly, she had every intention of following up her role in Peter's eventual acquittal by drawing him in to the family circle at Maristow, which she could not have done against the will of her husband. The day after the verdict she left Portsmouth and wrote to Peter on her way back to Devon:

> I am on my way to Maristow (my Father's Place near Plymouth) & as you will most probably on your Enlargement go round to the Isle of Man by Water, I beg therefore you will take the very *first Opportunity* of getting round to Plymouth, & coming to Maristow, as it is the Wish of us all that you shou'd come there for a Variety of reasons, I will give you when we meet.

We do not know what those reasons were since no record survives, even of whether Peter did visit Maristow although it seems very probable that he did.

While it is certain that the Heywoods, on their own admission, mobilised all friends and contacts to aid their relation where humanly possible, there is no evidence, as some believe, that they sought to corrupt the trial itself.[14] This rumour was put about largely by relations of William Bligh, the most curious of whom was Francis Godolphin Bond, the son of Bligh's half-sister Catherine who served as first lieutenant on Bligh's second breadfruit expedition. When writing in December 1792 to his brother, Thomas, Francis Bond opens by attacking his captain's insolence and arrogance claiming in words that could have been those of

14 It is also important to record that if the sentence had been carried out, there would have been a real risk of alienating Earl Howe, Emma's uncle.

Fletcher Christian, that 'every dogma of power and consequence has been taken from the Lieutenants, to establish, as he thinks, his own reputation', which he terms an 'imbecility' in someone of his uncle's rank but then goes on to say, in an account of the court martial's outcome, that 'Heywood's friends have bribed through thick and thin to save him, and from publick report have not been backward in defaming our uncle's character'. Even among those who did not sense actual corruption there were many who felt that the outcome was a reflection of class privilege well expressed by an anonymous correspondent in the local Manx newspaper who reported that 'great murmurs are carefully breathed, and assiduously promulgated on the pardon of the midshipman and boatswain's mate according to the vulgar notion [that] money bought their lives; and that others fell sacrifice to their poverty.'[15] But to this correspondent, and to middle-class opinion more generally, the reprieve was just and what was remarkable was that Heywood and Morrison had not been acquitted. Heywood himself, when the death sentence had just been passed and therefore before his reprieve, eloquently captured this sentiment in a letter to Patrick Scott, a physician and family friend from the Isle of Man:

> I have not been found guilty of the slightest act connected with that detestable crime of mutiny, but am doomed to die for not being active in my endeavours to suppress it. Could the witnesses who appeared on the Court-martial be themselves tried, they would also suffer for the very same and only crime of which I have been found guilty (Peter Heywood to Dr Scott, 20 September 1792).

Peter Heywood had a complex personality. Clearly highly intelligent and singularly diligent, he was also given to flights of emotional language and the attachment of the romantic to indecision. The charge against him largely concerned what he did *not* do, rather than what he did. Few, other than Bligh, labelled him a mutineer

15 Letter published in the *Manks Mercury and Briscoe's Douglas Advertiser* on 19 and 20 February 1793.

and a number were quite willing to swear under oath to the opposite. Yet he seems to have made no serious effort to join Bligh in the launch and certainly none to rally the men against Christian and the other mutineers. Perhaps that is expecting much of such a young man, as indeed he claimed, and it should never be forgotten that he much admired Christian and felt a bond of loyalty to him that was at least as strong as that to the captain.

There are two pieces of evidence that support this proposition. The first was his determination to counter the negative interpretation of Christian's conduct which he did by writing, while still staying at Aaron Graham's house in Great Russell Street, to Christian's elder brother, Edward (a distinguished lawyer), only a few days after his own pardon:

> I am sorry to say, I have been informed you were inclined to judge too harshly of your truly unfortunate brother, and to think of him in such a manner, as I am conscious, from the knowledge I had of his most worthy disposition and character (both public and private) he merits not, in the slightest degree: therefore I think it my duty to undeceive you, and to rekindle the flame of brotherly love (or pity now) towards him, which I fear the false reports of slander and vile suspicion, may have nearly extinguished (Peter Heywood to Edward Christian, 5 November 1792).

As a result the two men met and Edward took upon himself the task of interviewing many of the survivors who had returned, guaranteeing them anonymity but ensuring their words would be believed by including high status and well-known witnesses. He then persuaded William Muspratt's attorney to allow him to publish his verbatim minutes of the court martial, in the absence of an official version. The results of his interviews were published as an appendix. Since this was the first publication after Bligh's own account of the mutiny, it began a line of thinking that cast Bligh as less a victim of other men's villainy and more the instrument of his own undoing.

The second point is not as clear cut and may have been the result of wishful thinking. In the early 1800s, rumours had been rife in Cumberland, that Fletcher Christian had been seen visiting an aunt. These stories built upon other rumours that Coleridge's epic poem 'The Rime of the Ancient Mariner' (first published in 1798) was in fact inspired by conversations with William Wordsworth, who had attended the same school in Cumberland as Christian and had connections with his family. On one interpretation the poem tells of the mariner's return which further fuelled speculation. Nothing did as much, however, to give the story impetus as Peter Heywood's report that while in Fore Street, Plymouth, in 1808, he had been walking behind a man who appeared to have Fletcher Christian's characteristic gait.[16] When he called his name, the stranger turned, confirming Heywood's suspicion, but then ran off to be lost in the maze of alleyways and tiny streets that then characterised the dock area. Edward Barrow, the first to publish a history of the mutiny that appeared just after Heywood's death, and which depended in large part on interviews with him, reported the supposed sighting and commented,

> ... the resemblance, the agitation, and the efforts of the stranger to elude him, were circumstances too strong not to make a deep impression on his mind. At the moment, his first thought was to set about making some further inquiries, but on recollection of the pain and trouble such a discovery must occasion him, he considered it more prudent to let the matter drop; but the circumstance was frequently called to his memory for the remainder of his life (Barrow, 1831, reprinted in World Classics edition, 1935: 327–8, note 1)

Later reports from John Adams in Pitcairn, who changed his story concerning Christian's death on several occasions, plus the fact that

16 Bligh himself had described Christian as having bandy legs. Cf. Gilmour, R. (1983) 'Fletcher Christian's Last Days', *Isle of Man Family History Society Journal* 8 (2): 55–6.

no one to this day has discovered his grave, all served to bolster the rumours but none more so than Peter Heywood's supposed encounter in Plymouth.[17] There seems little doubt that Heywood hoped that he had truly seen Fletcher Christian on English soil.

Unfortunately, even after more than two centuries and millions of words of commentary, we still do not have a balanced view of Peter Heywood. At the time of the trial and immediately afterwards he was portrayed in a very positive light. As Aaron Graham, the lawyer retained by Thomas Pasley, Peter's uncle, to prepare his defence put it, '...everybody who attended the trial is perfectly satisfied in his own mind that he was hardly guilty in appearance, in intention he was perfectly innocent' (Aaron Graham to Dr Patrick Scott, 18 September 1792). More recently, however, as the caricature of William Bligh as a sadistic tyrant has been questioned, the pendulum has swung the other way. For example, Caroline Alexander's (2003) account paints a much more positive portrait of Bligh and assiduously attempts to indict all of those who were tried for mutiny, particularly Heywood. In this she errs in the opposite direction and her 'true story' is no more authentic than those that it attempts to supersede. First, in describing William Cole's evidence she fails to mention that he had supported the interpretation that Heywood and Stewart had been kept forcibly below days before he was interrogated on this point by Heywood himself. She plays

17 Remarkably, the jury is still out on whether Fletcher Christian did return to England. The reports from Pitcairn are unanimous in believing that he was murdered in 1794 while working on his vegetable plot on the day his daughter was born. The most compelling evidence for this proposition comes from 'Jenny', one of the local women alive at the time ('Pitcairn's Island – the Bounty's Crew' [1829] *United Services Journal and Naval and Military Magazine*: 589–93). On the other hand, she herself left the island by a whaling ship, a means of escape that would have been available in theory to Christian. Supporters of this argument point not only to Heywood's testimony but even argue that William Butterfield (1814–1900), the meticulous architect of the restoration of St Bridget's Church in Brigham, Cumbria, where Fletcher was christened in 1764, believed the story on the basis of local reports of a mysterious funeral in September 1824 when two dozen mourners had supposedly attended a funeral at night believed to be that of Fletcher Christian. The body of a man of about 60 was purportedly interred in an unmarked grave next to that of Fletcher Christian's father.

up the information that Peter had his hand on a cutlass which he immediately dropped when challenged, which is hardly the behaviour of someone 'under arms' as she asserts (2003: 246). She then boosts the status of Heywood and Hallett, declaring them 'young professionals' who chose to go to sea, whereas Heywood and Christian had to do so to avoid debtors' prison without a shred of evidence that this fate might have befallen them if they had not gone to sea (2003: 239).[18] Hallett's improbable assertion that Heywood had scornfully laughed at Bligh's predicament to his face is given greater weight than the trial judges or any commentator since felt it deserved. Finally, she muddles the timing of Heywood's decision to follow his captain into the launch in order to claim, in the face of much contrary testimony, that Heywood perjured himself when claiming that he was prevented from so doing (2003: 257).[19] It is hardly surprising that these assertions have given rise in turn to a powerful critique from Rolf Du Rietz, a Swedish author who has spent more than 30 years researching the story of the *Bounty* (Du Rietz, 2010).[20] Moreover, if Heywood's evidence was as inconsistent and illogical as she contends then it is rather surprising that after his pardon, Lord Hood, the president of the court martial, offered Heywood employment on his own vessel, as did at least two of the other captains on the panel of senior officers who had heard the evidence for and against his supposed involvement in the mutiny.

What is more remarkable is why Bligh took so violently against young Heywood. The most plausible answer is that he bracketed him with his fellow Manxman Fletcher Christian as if all such

18 It is hard to prove a counterfactual but this fate did not befall any of either man's siblings.

19 William Bligh himself in an early draft of his evidence when he was court martialled over the loss of his ship had said that officers had 'endeavoured to come to my assistance but they were not allowed to put their heads above the hatchway' (quoted in Tagart, 1832: 151). In relation to Heywood, Alexander prefers the contrary assertion of John Adams, the self-confessed murderer and longest survivor of the mutineers on Pitcairn (2003: 398).

20 See also Maxton, DA and Du Rietz, RE (eds) (2013) *Innocent on the Bounty: The Court Martial and Pardon of Midshipman Peter Heywood, in Letters* North Carolina and London, McFarland and Co.

islanders had the same predilections.[21] Heywood himself pursued a successful naval career, eventually retiring after nearly 30 years of service in 1816, when he also married the widow Francis Joliffe, a relative of Aaron Graham.[22] The couple settled in Highgate, North London, where they stayed until June 1829, moving eventually to 23 Cumberland Terrace, Regent's Park, where Peter died aged 58 in February 1831[23] (Plate 35).

One interesting vignette reported by Alexander concerns the supposed encounter between Albemarle Bertie, then a rear-admiral, and Jane Austen:

> In a delightful crossing of paths, Bertie would later make the acquaintance of that most discerning judge of character, Jane Austen, who declared there was "nothing to like or dislike" about him. And it would have to be allowed that, with his somewhat pampered expression and vague unfocused gaze, he was not a man naturally to command attention (2003: 215).

The connection almost certainly came through one of Jane's six brothers, all but one of whom saw military service. Her brother Francis (Frank), for example, was commissioned a lieutenant in 1792 and eventually was to be knighted and become an Admiral of the Fleet. The encounter to which Alexander refers appears in a

21 Hence his oft-quoted comment: 'I have now reason to curse the day I ever knew a Christian, a Heywood or any Manxman'. Other commentators have identified more intimate reasons for Bligh's comments on both men (see e.g. Hough, 1972) *Captain Bligh and Mr Christian: The Men and the Mutiny* London, Hutchinson.

22 In 1794 when still a midshipman, he was captain's aide-de-camp in Earl Howe's flagship *Queen Charlotte* at the Battle of the Glorious First of June. He was promoted to lieutenant the following year. He later worked as a surveyor and was offered but declined the position of Admiralty Hydrographer. He was appointed captain in 1803.

23 Peter Heywood's literary gifts were evident in his writings long after his retirement. Two pertinent themes stand out. One was his steadfast support of Tahitian peoples against growing nationalist and racist sentiment ('the liberal-minded man will not allow his judgment to be obscured by national partiality') and the other, reflecting the burden of his critique of William Bligh: 'nothing is so inimical to improvement, as that pride which presumes on supposed superiority and merit, or that haughtiness which indicates unqualified contempt of others' (Tagart, 1832: 295).

letter from Jane to her sister, Cassandra, dated 7–8 January 1807. Referring to Frank's return home soon after she had moved with her family to Southampton, she writes,

> Our acquaintances increase too fast. He (Frank) was recognised lately by Admiral Bertie, and a few days since arrived the Admiral and his daughter Catherine to wait upon us. There was nothing to like or dislike in either (Austen, 2011: 163).

While it is true that Albemarle Bertie had a daughter called Catherine, there is no evidence whatever that he lacked decisiveness or an 'unfocused gaze'. It is far more probable that this is a reference to Thomas Bertie whose family home was in Southampton and who also had a daughter of the same name. Thomas Bertie was not a Bertie by birth; he was born Thomas Hoar (1758–1825) but changed his name on his marriage in 1788 to Catherine Bertie in order to comply with her father's will. Thomas Bertie's daughter, named after his wife, would have been in her teens at the time of their encounter with Jane Austen. Although Thomas Bertie, who had an illustrious naval career and was a close friend of Nelson, was not made a rear-admiral until shortly after the meeting described above, Jane reports in a later letter to her sister – in a typically insightful and amusing way – on another visit, this time by Catherine Bertie herself:

> Soon after I had closed my last letter to you, we were visited by Mrs Dickens and her sister in law Mrs Bertie, the wife of a lately made Admiral; – Mrs F(rancis).A(usten) I believe was their first object – but they put up with us very kindly, and Mrs D – finding in Miss Lloyd a friend of Mrs Dundas had another motive for the acquaintance. She seems a really agreeable Women (*sic*) – that is, her manners are gentle and she knows a great many of our Connections in West Kent. – Mrs Bertie lives in the Polygon, and was out when we returned her visit – which are *her* two virtues (Friday 9 December 1808; Austen, 2011: 163).

The Polygon was a Georgian area of 22 acres in Southampton planned as an equivalent to Bath's Royal Crescent, although only a very few houses and an hotel were actually built in the eighteenth century. Emma Bertie had no sister-in-law and, tragically, had been dead for three years when this meeting took place.

Ironically, anyone wishing to make a connection between Albemarle and Emma Bertie on the one hand and Jane Austen on the other could point out that they were in fact related, albeit somewhat distantly. Jane Austen's oldest brother, James, born in 1765 and therefore ten years her senior, followed their father into the Church becoming vicar of Sherborne St John in Hampshire in 1791. In March of the following year he married his parishioner the slightly older Anne Mathew, daughter of the irascible Lieutenant-General Edward Mathew and his wife, Albemarle Bertie's half–sister, Lady Jane Mathew.[24] Soon after the birth of their first and only child, Jane Anna Elizabeth Austen, Anne Austen died (1795) and James subsequently remarried. Their daughter, known as Anna, became close to Aunt Jane, particularly during the period she lived at Chawton, just south of Alton in Hampshire (1809–17) and eventually received an inheritance from her great uncle and godfather Brownlow Bertie, 5th and last Duke of Ancaster, Marquis Kesteven and Earl of Lindsey.

Emma Bertie's fate was as tragic as it was improbable. Sometime after the *Bounty* saga, a naval officer with whom she had a close friendship, possibly as his lover, was serving in a vessel lost at sea when amongst the flotsam was discovered a desk containing incriminating correspondence. It is possible, even probable, that the man concerned was the former Lieutenant Larkan on whom she had lent so heavily in her support of Peter Heywood and with whom she was in any event close. The supposedly indecisive Admiral Bertie acted swiftly and without apparent tergiversation. The only reference we have to these events is from her older sister's branch of the family. Lina Musters wrote nearly a century later:

24 Edward Mathew is often thought to have inspired General Tilney in *Northanger Abbey*.

> Mrs Bertie was discarded by her husband Admiral Bertie, in consequence of a letter she had written to one of his post-captains, which was found in a desk floating on the sea after a shipwreck, and the poor women took her disgrace so much to heart, that she died soon after (HMN 5/235/1–33, 738X5).

We do not know the degree to which her death was related to her exclusion from her husband's household, but it is certainly the case that she was living alone when it occurred on 15 March 1805. The *Gentleman's Magazine* for that month (1805: 293) noted the death thus: 'In Gay Street, Bath, after a long and painful illness which she bore with exemplary patience and resignation, Mrs Bertie, wife of Rear-Admiral Bertie and daughter of the late James Modyford Heywood'. In a curious twist of fate this was the very month, soon after her father's death, that Jane Austen with her mother and sister moved into 25 Gay Street.[25]

Maria Henrietta, the Author

The remaining two Heywood daughters had lower public profiles than their older siblings, although both in their own way showed some signs of their mother's creative instincts. Maria Henrietta, the third daughter, made an adroit but somewhat exotic marriage to Louis Montolieu de St Hippolite. The Montolieus were a Protestant family who could trace their roots from the twelfth century through numerous military figures in defence of the Huguenot cause. After many battles against Catholic adversaries in the Languedoc region of south-west France, the military prowess of David, Sieur de St Hippolite, and his sons was brought to the attention of Emperor Joseph of the Holy Roman Empire, who conferred upon him the patent as Baron of St Hippolite on 14 February 1706. Following

25 The Rev George Austen died on 21 January 1805 when they had been living at 3 Green Park Buildings East in Bath. See Le Faye, D (2006) *A Chronology of Jane Austen and Her Family: 1700–2000* Cambridge, Cambridge University Press.

the Revocation of the Treaty of Nantes in 1685, life for Protestants in an expanding France under Louis XIV became increasingly insecure and David eventually fled the country to Holland, thereafter accompanying William of Orange to England in 1688 and subsequently becoming a general in his army at the Battle of the Boyne in 1690 (Agnew, 1871). His son, the 2nd Baron, Lewis Charles Montolieu, was also an army man serving as a lieutenant in the 2nd troop of Horse Guards and it was his son, also Lewis, born in 1761, who married into the Heywood family on 3 March 1786 at St George's, Hanover Square, London, when he was 24 and Maria Henrietta, 22.[26]

Lewis, the 3rd Baron, was for a time an officer in the Yorkshire Light Dragoons after matriculating to Christ Church, Oxford, aged 17 on 23 April 1779. Subsequently, he worked for Hammersley's Bank in Pall Mall, eventually becoming a partner.[27] Four years later he stood unsuccessfully as MP for Leicester, although his brother-in-law, second husband of his sister Anne, Sir James Bland Burges, was a far more successful politician and statesman becoming under-secretary of state at the Foreign Office (1789–95). Lewis and Maria had a son, Charles, who died at their then residence, 26 Albemarle Street, while a student at Oxford on 15 April 1809, and two daughters, Maria Georgina who trod a similar path to her mother when she married Hugh Hammersley in January 1822, and Julia Fanny, who in 1817 married William Wilbraham, a captain in the Royal Navy and, after his death in 1824, Sir Henry Bouverie,

26 After resettlement in England the family dropped the 'de' from their name and 'Louis' was anglicised to 'Lewis' for both generations with this first name. Hanover Square in Mayfair figured prominently in the Heywood family's history. Lewis took over the mortgage of 20 Hanover Square from Lord Henry Stawell on 29 September 1787. This was where his father Lewis Charles Montolieu and grandfather David Montolieu had both lived prior to their deaths. Subsequently the same house was taken over by Lewis' brother-in-law, John Musters, in 1796.

27 This private bank, originally based at 57 Pall Mall, became banker to the Prince of Wales in 1787. The bank was founded as Ransom, Morland, Hammersley and Co when Louis Montolieu joined it in 1786. He became a partner in a new banking venture with Hammersley in 1796, resigning from the bank in 1806. On the death in 1840 of Hugh Hammersley, the eldest son of the founder Thomas Hammersley, this firm was taken over by Coutts & Co.

one time Governor of Malta (Lart, 1924–5: 64). Both daughters had a number of offspring; the former three daughters and the latter three children by her first husband and a son and a daughter by her second.[28]

As with her older sisters, Maria Henrietta was not entirely content with domesticity. She wrote poetry, specialising in romantic verse linked to botanical themes. Her volume *The Enchanted Plants, Fables in Verse*, inscribed to her daughters, was first published in 1800 and is still in print. The book explores themes of human emotion through the characteristics of flower forms, scents and habits of growth. For a work of poetry, it became a bestseller, perhaps partly because of the implicit social commentary that the verses reveal.[29] In any event, more volumes followed, notably in the year following *The Festival of the Rose*, while she also undertook translations including *The Gardens* (1805), a long poem by the Abbé de Lille (Plate 36).

The wider family contained another author, with whom Maria Henrietta is sometimes confused, Isabelle de Montolieu (1751–1832) who was her husband's first cousin once removed. She wrote the novel *Caroline de Lichtfield, ou Mémoires d'une Famille Prussienne* (1786), which was published in English in the same year and reprinted on numerous occasions. She is credited with over one hundred translations into French including a rather free translation in 1816 of Jane Austen's *Sense and Sensibility.* John Hoppner produced a portrait of Maria Henrietta Montolieu simply called 'Mrs Montolieu'. The painting's whereabouts is now unknown but it was described at the beginning of the twentieth century in the following way: 'Seated in White Dress with lilac ribbons, her head resting on her hand'.[30]

---

28 For a genealogy see Bannerman, WB (ed) (1908) *Miscellanea Genealogicaet Heraldica* Vol. II, 4th Series, London, Mitchell, Hughes and Clarke: 160.

29 It is, for example, hard not to think of her elder sister, Sophia, when reading of the Painted-lady sweet pea under the heading 'Scandal'.

30 The portrait was purchased from the late Lord Oxenbridge, of Burton Hall, Lincoln, and sold at Robinson and Fisher's auction on 27 June 1901 (see McKay and Roberts, 1909: 174).

It seems improbable that Maria Henrietta and her husband spent much time in France. Their main residence was at 26 Albemarle Street, Mayfair, and subsequently at 10 Stratton Street, a short distance to the west, but the French Huguenot community in London was substantial. Although many were highly successful in finance, industry and the arts, some escaped from persecution in France with little more than the clothes they were wearing at the time. For many years it was expected that the wealthier citizens would contribute to the needs of the less privileged and the Montolieus played a full role in this endeavour, particularly in relation to the French Hospital in Bath Street, Finsbury, which the 1st Baron Montolieu had helped to establish in 1718. Lewis died on 20 May 1817 at his house in Stratton Street in his 55th year, and his will concentrates on passing his fortune and properties to his two daughters and their families.[31]

Although Maria inherited more than £16,000 as her share of the sale of Maristow House and over £2,000 from her mother's will in addition to a portion of her late husband's wealth, there is a small hint that she found life after 1817 particularly trying. For example, her name appears under Chester Street (parish of St George's, Hanover Square) in the Rate Book for 1822 in the category of 'Persons in Arrears'. This is unlikely to have been for reasons of financial embarrassment. On the other hand, it does seem very probable that she became emotionally entangled with someone more interested in her wealth. Sometime in the late 1820s, she married a man 23 years younger than herself, Henry Crockett Clifton, and moved with him from Mayfair to Montpelier Row, Twickenham. These houses comprised a row of terraces built in brown and red brick in about 1720 as part of a speculative venture to open up the villages around London to those seeking a leafier lifestyle. While they are highly desirable in today's world, at that time they must have seemed a long way from the capital's *beau monde*. In any event, when Maria died in 1837 the sole executor of her will was Henry C. Clifton, who at the age of 50 married Elizabeth Scott, a minor, on 1 January 1838 at St George's, Hanover Square, only weeks after

31 Although it also recognises his nephew by marriage, John Chaworth Musters.

becoming a (wealthy) widower. Thereafter *his* address was given as 'Oxford Street', London, although he died in Hampstead in 1876 at the age of 89.

Fanny, the Dutiful Daughter

Frances (Fanny) Heywood was born in 1765, the fifth surviving child of James and Catherine Modyford Heywood and, like all her siblings, appears to have spent her childhood in the Devon countryside at Maristow. In the absence of family papers concerning the Heywoods, very little is known of her education or early life but there is little doubt that she came to play an important role in the household, if for no other reason than because by the standards of the time she married late. There is perhaps a hint of this in a letter of October 1796, the year that Fanny was married, when Anne Robinson, a friend of the family from Saltram House, writes that she must visit Maristow 'since it must be very dull for them to be quite alone since Miss Heywood married' (12 October 1796, PWDRO1259/2/300). As with his other three daughters, Fanny's father had no doubt looked assiduously to find a young man of breeding and wealth, regardless from which part of England his family hailed, but it was not until 26 September 1796 at St Mary's Church, Tamerton, that the event occurred, when she was 31 years old. Immediately thereafter, Fanny left home as a married women, this time for the distant Fenlands. Given the speed with which this was arranged, it is impossible to believe that it was not a reaction on her father's part to the entreaties of love made by William Dyott the year before. The latter was swiftly promoted to general and became the main aide-de-camp to George III but he was clearly not perceived as an adequate catch. It would have been in keeping if this inference was on grounds of family wealth. Dyott was Irish by birth and by all accounts had to work for a living.

Fanny's new husband, who was ten years her junior, was Thomas Orby Hunter of Crowland Abbey, Lincolnshire, the great-grandson of Major-General Robert Hunter, one time Governor of New York and New Jersey (1710–9), after which he was elevated to become the governor of the wealthier colony of Jamaica (1728–March 1734). Thomas, who was 21 at the time of the wedding, had already inherited an estate said to be worth £10,000 per annum (*Hampshire Chronicle* 5 November 1796). Thomas Orby Hunter the elder, his grandfather, was MP for Winchelsea in East Sussex, two miles south-west of Rye and seven miles north-east of Hastings. He was first returned on the Treasury interest in May 1741 and again in June 1747. Winchelsea at that time had a tiny electorate and in 1747 he came in second place in the two-member constituency with a vote of only 12 electors. He was re-elected in 1754 and served more or less continuously until his death in 1769. Orby Hunter held numerous minor posts in various administrations including becoming a treasury lord between April 1763 and July 1765. He was generally regarded as competent, hardworking and honest in an era when that could have seldom been said. He also owned significant slave plantations in Jamaica, inherited from his father, Robert (1666–1734). The Rent Books from Jamaica in 1754 indicated a large holding of 1,800 acres in Westmoreland near the high lands around Negril in his name. Thomas' will of 1769 mentions messuages and estates in Jamaica and passes them to his eldest son, Charles, father of Fanny's husband. The surname 'Orby' derived from his mother, Elizabeth's, side as the heir of Sir Thomas Orby of Crowland Abbey.

The estates in Lincolnshire passed to Thomas' father, Charles, who died in September 1791, and then to him as the only child. Crowland or Croyland Abbey, seven miles north-east of Peterborough, was of great antiquity but did not come into the family until Charles II granted the manor and site of the old monastery to Sir Thomas Orby, who had attended him during the exile that followed the execution of his father.[32] The house was originally held for a term of 60 years, coming eventually to his youngest son, also Sir Thomas. It was then passed by the marriage of this man's only daughter to Robert Hunter and was inherited in turn in 1734 by his son Thomas Orby Hunter. The abbey was once a Benedictine monastery founded

32 The terms 'Crowland' and 'Croyland' tend now to be used interchangeably but the latter is the correct ecclesiastical usage from medieval times.

in 714, destroyed by the Danes in 870 and rebuilt in 947. At the dissolution in 1539 parts of the building were pulled down and another section was rebuilt as a parish church that is still in use. The manor house remains in East Street, Crowland, just to the west of the abbey site and is a property with ten bedrooms consisting of an original house of 1690 and a Georgian extension of the mid-eighteenth century built after George II granted the inheritance of the building to Thomas' grandfather in 1751 (TNA HL/PO/PB/1/1751/25G2n81).

The couple had three daughters, the first of whom died very young. Fanny Hunter was born five years after the marriage but died by the time she was six on 27 November 1807.[33] The second daughter, Charlotte Catherine (born 11 July 1802) enjoyed a normal life span. The third daughter (Georgiana Mary, born 24 May 1807) was the first to marry. Her husband was George Wombwell, son and heir of the first-class cricketer and member of the Marylebone Cricket Club (MCC), Sir George Wombwell. He was 30 years old when they married on 23 June 1824, whereas his wife was only just 18. The marriage took place by special licence at the family's London home in Grosvenor Place, Mayfair, officiated by the Dean of St Paul's (the Very Rev Gerard Wellesley). For reasons which are not clear, the bride was not given away by her father but by HRH the Duke of York instead.[34] Eventually on the death of his father in October 1846, George inherited the baronetcy and Newburgh Priory at Coxwold, North Yorkshire, and associated estates which had come into the family through his mother, formerly Lady Anne Belayse, the daughter of the 2nd Earl of Fauconberg.

Following her mother's precept for late marriages, Charlotte also married a Wombwell on 21 May 1836, when she was 33 years old. Charles Wombwell was the son of Sir George Wombwell's (2nd Bart) second marriage and he, like his father-in-law, was a lot younger than his wife at the time of his marriage, being only just 23. This meant

33 She was buried on 1 December 1807 at Rottingdean in Sussex.

34 HRH Duke of York was a friend of Thomas Orby Hunter and visited him when in that part of the country (see *Ipswich Journal*, 9 January 1819).

that the surviving daughters of Fanny Orby Hunter married half-brothers but she herself did not live to see the second marriage, dying at the age of 69 on 23 January 1834.

Like her slightly older sister, Maria Henrietta, Fanny Heywood was painted by John Hoppner. In 1779, he sent seven pictures to the annual exhibition of the Royal Academy including one of her commissioned by her father when she was just 14 years old. The description of the work in a volume on the artist published in 1909 describes it these words: 'Whole length, standing, directed towards, facing and looking to front, cap and high feathers; dark dress cut low on bosom; right hand on head of Newfoundland dog to left, left hand holding dress; landscape in distance. Canvas about 90 x 60 inches' (McKay and Roberts, 1909: 131) (Plate 37).

The portrait is listed at about the same time as belonging to Sir George Orby Wombwell and located at Newburgh Priory.[35] It was exhibited at the annual exhibition of the Society of British Artists in 1833 where its ownership then is given as T. Orby Hunter Esq. A coloured mezzotint of the painting was produced by John Young and published on 1 December 1800. It shows a well-developed girl with an innocent expression dressed in silk adorned with bows and feathers in a sylvan setting stroking an adoring Newfoundland dog.

As with her older sister, Sophia, dogs seem to have played an important role in Fanny's life. A later painting by Ben Marshall featured her two spaniels 'Diver' and 'Shuttleback' against a beach backdrop, presumably on the East Coast.[36]

Charlotte and Charles Wombwell produced only one child, a

35 See Skipton, HPK (1905) *John Hoppner*, London, Methuen: 103. The abbey has a notable art collection which includes the portrait by Gainsborough of Catherine Heywood, Fanny's mother and wife of James Modyford Heywood. The abbey is also well known for possibly containing the body of Oliver Cromwell. Legend has it that Cromwell's daughter, Lady Fauconberg, whose husband in the seventeenth century owned the abbey, bribed the guards at Westminster Abbey to substitute another corpse when Charles II after the Restoration ordered the body of Cromwell to be exhumed and then hung, decapitated and quartered at Tyburn. The real corpse, it is claimed, was then taken to Newburgh and entombed on the top storey behind an appropriate inscription.

36 This painting was sold by Christies in 2011 for £51,000.

daughter (Frances Charlotte) born in Hanover Square, London, in 1841. She survived to a considerable age, dying on 6 March 1920 and outliving her husband Clifton Gascoyne by 17 years. Georgiana being so much younger when she married produced four surviving sons, all of whom followed their father by becoming military men. Her husband, Sir George Wombwell (1792–1855), 3rd Baronet, served in the 10th Hussars and fought in the Battle of Waterloo. Thomas Orby Hunter in his day had been an arbiter of fashion and his son-in-law appears to have pursued the same path after his military career. During the early part of Victoria's reign he became a close friend of Lord Adolphus Fitzclarence, the illegitimate son of William IV by the actress and courtesan Dorothea Bland, as one of the 'dandies' of fashionable London.[37] As Thomas Escott (1897) put it,

> Next to the representatives of the reigning family and to the statesmen who were the props of the young queen's throne, the attention of the Hyde Park crowd was fixed upon a little group of gentlemen, remarkable for the perfection of their toilettes, and for the special attention manifestly bestowed upon their hair ... falling gracefully over the white collar (1897: 6).

He goes on to say that these included 'the two inseparables' Sir George Wombwell and Lord Adolphus 'Dolly' Fitzclarence.[38]

Among the four sons, the first (Sir George Orby Wombwell, 4th Bart) had a distinguished military career becoming a lieutenant in the 17th Lancers during the Crimean War, taking part and managing to survive in the Charge of the Light Brigade at the Battle of Balaclava on 25 October 1854. When he died in October 1913, he was the last surviving officer from that ill-fated adventure. At

37 Dorothea Bland, sometimes referred to as 'Mrs Jordan', was by any standards a larger than life figure. Of Irish parentage, she eventually made her way via a number of relationships (and children) to the London stage where she caught the eye of the Duke of Clarence (the future William IV) bearing him at least ten children. It is also claimed by some that her descendants include one David Cameron (http://en.wikipedia.org/wiki/Dorothea_Jordan).

38 He died on a visit to Newburgh Priory on 17 May 1856, the year after Sir George Wombwell passed away.

this point, having lost his two sons on military service, the title and estate, then 12,000 acres at Newburgh and surrounding areas, passed to his brother, Henry Herbert Wombwell, who died in 1926. Another brother, Adolphus Ulick, named after his father's close friend, would have inherited the title had he lived, but he died in 1886 as a lieutenant-colonel at the age of 52.[39]

Despite the large estates in Lincolnshire, the Orby Hunters appear, as was so common at the time among wealthy elites, to have spent most of their time in the more fashionable parts of central London. Fanny is known to have accompanied Sophia on some of her many visits to the royal circle in Brighton. During these years, the family home was in Bruton Street, Berkeley Square. It was to here that Catherine Heywood, Fanny's mother, moved from the Mayfair home in Grafton Street she shared with her late husband in the early 1800s. Her will dated 14 May 1805 is from her daughter's address, indicating again that Fanny was perhaps the closest daughter to her parents. Sometime between 1822 and 1824, Fanny and Thomas moved to the marginally less fashionable address of Grosvenor Place in Pimlico and it is here that she died on 23 January 1834 aged 69. Her body was, however, interred in St James' Piccadilly – a stone's throw from Bruton Street.

In 1829, at the age of 54, Thomas Orby Hunter, who was still regarded as a leader of London's fashionable circles, sold the Lincolnshire estates at Crowland to Sir John Paul for the not inconsiderable sum of 332,000 guineas in order, it was said, to concentrate entirely on London life (*Sun* 26 June 1829). He was, however, as an obituarist was later to write, 'prominent in the annals of the turf' and it is perfectly possible that this sale was forced upon him by his creditors.[40] The likelihood of this eventuality is supported by the sale of household goods and effects very soon after the loss of his wife from a rented property called Newsells Park near Royston in Hertfordshire reported in the local newspapers at that time (*Hertford Mercury and Reformer* 16 June 1835). He died on 13 December 1847 at home in Grosvenor Place. His will provides mostly

39 The last brother, Frederick Charles, died even earlier at the age of 44 in 1889.
40 *Gentleman's Magazine* April 1848: 441.

for his elder daughter Charlotte Orby Wombwell, who inherited his house, personal possessions and assets, other than a sum of £5,000 to his younger daughter, Georgiana. His estate was valued in total at £45,000 (*Morning Post* 5 February 1848).

Conclusion

The four daughters of James and Catherine Modyford Heywood were paradoxically both obedient and independent at the same time. All married as they were commanded to do by their father to men with no knowledge or interest in rural life in West Devon and whose desire was that they should be fecund and well supported financially. He did not concern himself with their emotional attachments to the candidates he selected and the result in at least three out of the four cases was considerable unhappiness that blighted as least part of their lives. Their responses were by no means the same. One outplayed her family at engaging in 'high society' without even the handle of prestige bestowed by a title. Another suffered a loveless marriage to a usually absent naval officer until boredom and neglect generated – or possibly revisited – an illicit affair that unluckily led her to be cast adrift to die prematurely alone. A third took to the pen to express her emotions in barely concealed stanzas purporting to be the secret lives of plants but entitled, inter alia, 'ambition', 'scandal', 'folly', 'envy' 'temptation', 'despair', 'cruelty', 'vanity', 'adversity' and 'jealousy', and ended up being exploited by a scoundrel. Finally, Fanny, diverted at the last moment from being whisked away by a doting young officer, became chatelaine in a gloomy medieval mansion in a family not unlike her own except with more money, but married to a younger man whose life appeared to revolve around gambling and fashionable clothing.

Each in her own way tried to develop a creative streak inherited from her mother, and possibly nourished by her early life in rural Devon. It is certainly true that the eighteenth century, particularly in the second half, was for a small elite a world of fashion, taste and discernment. But this was made possible by a tsunami of artistic talent. It was the age of Bach and Handel, and later of Mozart and

Haydn. Arguably too it was the fulfilment in Britain of centuries of promise in fine art; not just the great names of Reynolds and Gainsborough but also Romney, Hoppner and the Cornish hero John Opie. This comprised one world but as important, and of arguably greater significance was the renaissance in science, engineering and their application to industry and everyday life. For many the Age of Enlightenment meant learning from Priestley or considering what Lavoisier had to say on the emerging science of chemistry. The works of Joseph Banks, Adam Smith and Rousseau were read and debated and, as important as formal religion observance was during this period, it lost its power to stifle scientific understanding. This was also a world where people took pride in the new application of steam power by James Watt or in the manufacturing potential of the 'spinning jenny' advocated by James Hargreaves and benefited hugely from Edward Jenner's thinking on the place of vaccination in controlling disease. This second revolutionary world was not one that penetrated the *beau monde* at Maristow House, and even less in Bath or those parts of the capital where the Season mattered more than science.

The question arises as to whether the failure to engage with this intellectual ferment, aside from attending the opera or commissioning a yet-to-be famous artist to assuage one's vanity, was simply a product of idleness induced by sanitised wealth from the Caribbean. It is impossible to deny that this may be partly true but two other factors played a part. The Heywoods were ill-educated, partly because of a lack of application and partly because the most significant players were women, for whom a serious education was thought inappropriate and liable to harm their prospects as mothers and compliant partners of wealthy men. It took the following owners of the Devon estate to demonstrate that individuals can and do make a real difference. In this case, Jamaican wealth, when allied with a total disregard for fashionable diversions and at the same time a culture of entrepreneurialism, produced a century or more of unrivalled activism.

Chapter 8

The Struggle for Legitimacy

The accession of the Lopes family to the Maristow Estate almost coincides with a new century. The story opens with the arrival of one of the most colourful, complex and interesting figures not just in the life of rural Devon but nationally. There is, however, a tendency to paint Manasseh Lopes as an unsophisticated simpleton of no education, fresh off the boat from a Jamaican rural background and whose only claim to pre-eminence was the fortune he inherited from his sugar baron father, Mordecai 'Mordet' Lopes. With more than a hint of antisemitism, this background is thought to explain why he opportunistically swapped his religion, why he bought his way into Parliament and why, later on, he fell foul of the law, ending up in Exeter jail. Whereas the Heywood family had been Anglo-Jamaicans of some class, here was an *arriviste* who had used his Caribbean connections to connive his way into the life of a landed gentleman.

These assumptions and this depiction are wrong on almost all counts. He was in fact far more knowing and sophisticated than this image suggests; he was well versed in the ways of elite English aristocratic society and came not from a sugar plantation in rural Jamaica but from a family owning a transnational company operating on at least three continents. He was based in London for a quarter of a century before he bought Maristow House and during that time he became one of the most successful bankers, financiers and brokers within a community that was itself famed for its expertise in these fields. His sins, if that is how they could be described, were those commonplace in the culture in which he found himself. Being Jewish and economically highly successful was enough to elicit numerous attempts to undermine him. Perhaps the first task, however, is to examine the culture from which he came.

The Sephardim of Jamaica

The Sephardim are one of the great diasporic peoples of the globe, whose persecution and subsequent flight stretches back for more than two thousand years. The expansion of the Roman Empire into the Eastern Mediterranean in the sixth decade BCE led to colonial rule over Judaea and a century later to an uprising between 66–70 CE that produced the destruction of Jerusalem, the burning of the Temple and the establishment of a people in permanent exile. By the Middle Ages, this dispersal had led to two distinctive regional groups, albeit with a common underlying identity, the Ashkenazim of eastern and northern Europe and the Sephardim of the Iberian Peninsula, North Africa and the Middle East.

During the period of rule by Moorish peoples of North Africa, the Jews in Spain, who were a substantial community, enjoyed a period of relative calm and prosperity. By the thirteenth century Moorish influence was weakening, culminating in the *Reconquista* and thereafter domination from Rome. After a period of relative peace the Christian elite became more assertive and less tolerant, leading eventually to increased violence against both Jews and Muslims. At the end of the fourteenth century, the only alternative for many Jews was to convert to Catholicism, and after that time the *Conversos* or 'New Christians' became a recognised social grouping. That was by no means the end of the repression. The Inquisition was an attempt in part to root out Crypto-Jews or *Marranos* who professed adherence to Catholicism in public but reverted to Judaism in private and all those who had converted were subject to suspicion. Indeed, *Conversos* were initially the prime targets of the Inquisition whose only choice other than a martyr's death at the stake was one of flight and exile.[1] Some Spanish *Conversos* fled to Portugal but that country's own inquisition, starting in 1536, meant that flight further afield was the only option for many. While Catholic

1 The Inquisition reached its zenith in the late fifteenth century under the infamous Dominican friar Tomás de Torquemada, whose cruelty and bigotry led directly to approximately 2,000 executions primarily among Jews, *Marranos*, *Moriscos* (Islamic converts) and Moors. The edict of 31 March 1492 prompted more than 40,000 Jews to leave Spain.

repression, which lasted for centuries, led to many thousands of deaths, exile was the alternative and as a result tens of thousands of Jews fled to other countries, some of them to Portuguese and Spanish possessions in the Americas. Even today the Jewish communities of Spain and Portugal are tiny both numerically and as a proportion of the overall population, but the descendants of those who left have maintained both an inner strength based on family loyalty and external community ties to other families with parallel histories all over the world. It is impossible to understand the commitment to trade, and entrepreneurialism in general, without an appreciation of the shared experience of persecution. It is no exaggeration to claim that it was the experience of repression that turned a shared religion into a sense of a common *ethnic* identity.

Portuguese-speaking Sephardim found life relatively congenial in Brazil and many became involved in the nascent sugar industry, as well as in trade. The fall of Brazil to the Dutch in 1624 and increasing anti-Jewish sentiment found some willing to become more focused on Dutch possessions in the New World, just as other family members had found Amsterdam a more or less safe haven. The repossession of Brazil by the Portuguese in 1654 enhanced this process; for example, when Recife in northern Brazil fell a number of Jewish families left for Cayenne and Surinam (Merrill, 1964: 37). Shifting allegiances between European powers in the Caribbean basin soon meant that the Sephardim were ideally placed to exploit the two great trade links in the region, that between Dutch Curaçao and Amsterdam on the one hand and Barbados and London on the other. It was a small step then to take advantage of the new opportunities that opened up when the English routed the Spanish garrisons in Jamaica and took over the island in 1655. While some Jews must have been long-term residents under the Spanish occupation, and some families undoubtedly moved with governor-designate Thomas Modyford, it would seem that others were specifically recruited from Surinam. Gordon Merrill writes, for example,

Negotiations were drawn out over seven years on behalf of

> ten Portuguese Jewish planters with 322 slaves who desired to emigrate to Jamaica from Surinam under the terms of the Treaty of Breda.[2] No fewer than four of these planters had the name of Pereira, and the remaining six were named Prada, Mesa, de Silva, Gouia, Antonijs, and Baruch (Merrill, 1964: 41).

As we shall see, both Pereira and Baruch are names associated with the Lopes family so it is possible that expertise in sugar cultivation was an initial factor in relocation to Jamaica. This did not necessarily remain their preferred activity. Merrill points out that by the end of the seventeenth century there were 80 Jewish families in Jamaica, approximately the same number as in Barbados, but in the former the Jews mixed planting with trading. In time, the latter quickly became their economic activity of choice (1964: 47).

While Jews were tolerated in most of the West Indies at this time, their acceptance was based on a realisation of their economic importance. Antisemitism was never far beneath the surface and this, together with their recent experience of persecution by the Catholic Church, generated a community that was culturally inward-looking, even though economically it was the opposite. Cultural endogamy served to preserve newly energised religious freedoms but, when combined with a widely distributed population globally, it was also readily adapted to establishing trading ties. Family loyalties were readily mobilised to create networks of moral trust (Trivellato, 2012; cf. Hancock, 1995, Kaplan, 2000 and Snyder, 2006). Geographical propinquity may have played a part in this process. Originally concentrated in the old capital St Jago de la Vega (later Spanish Town) and Port Royal (the major port), by the first quarter of the eighteenth century, after the great earthquake of 1692 had devastated the latter, the Jewish population was still overwhelmingly urban with more than 40 per cent by then in the new capital, Kingston (August 1989: 28).

2 This is a reference to the second Treaty of Breda signed on 31 July 1667 between England, the Netherlands, France and Denmark that brought a short-lived end to the second Anglo-Dutch War (1665–7).

The importance of Jews in Jamaica's economic fortunes has gone through phases of academic opinion. Early authors such as Andrade (1941), Friedenwald (1897), Gardner (1971 [1873]) and Kohler (1902) all argued for the significance of this role. Other authors such as Schlesinger (1967) and Merrill (1964) supported this view, but a few years later opinion shifted and writers such as Claypole, (1970), Pawson and Buisseret (1975) and Bridenbaugh and Bridenbaugh (1972) all tended to underplay their significance, partly because of the relatively small size of the Jewish population, particularly in the early period immediately after the English occupation of the island. In the Census of 1680 only 17 of 507 households were Jewish. This rose to 80 by 1700 and by 1735 the Jewish population numbered 700–800 or approximately one-tenth of the white population overall (Meyers, 1998: 56). Just before the American War of Independence, there were as many Jews in Jamaica as in Canada and all 13 of the English colonies in North America put together (August, 1989: 27). There was, however, a higher proportion in urban areas. By 1720 Jews were 18 per cent of the population of Kingston (Arbell, 2000: 37).

The fact that the Jewish population was small compared with the white population did not mean that they were less prosperous than the new arrivals from England and elsewhere. An interesting study of probate court inventories for the period 1685–1716 by Allan Meyers (1998) showed convincing evidence that Sephardim traders were wealthier than their Anglo-Jamaican counterparts. This wealth was not simply accumulated or spent but recycled through money lending and the provision of credit lines that were used by Anglo settlers to create plantations (Meyers, 1998: 49). His examination of inventories for the period 1685–1716 showed that Jewish merchants had a median estate value of £1,369 compared with Anglo merchants who had only a median of £406 (1998: 68). Moreover the Jewish merchants held a higher proportion of their wealth as creditor assets, underlining their role in money lending and extending credit (Meyers, 1998: 70). A study of wills carried out by Thomas August (1989) revealed that those with sufficient resources to leave assets were overwhelmingly merchants (55 per cent) or shopkeepers (16 per cent). Only one in eight listed their occupations as 'planters' (1989: 28; cf. Fortune, 1984).

It seems very probable that a small number of Jamaican Jews were slave traders often through the facilities of the South Sea Company (Fortune, 1984). Interestingly too the inventories studied by Meyers showed that Jews were more likely than Anglo merchants to be slave owners (72 per cent against 57 per cent) but this did not necessarily mean field labourers (1998: 72). A particularly strong feature of Sephardic skills was the ability to communicate with and exploit the Spanish trade, made illicit by colonial administrations, but thereby more lucrative, particularly when it came to the provision of slaves for sale since the Spanish had no regular trade links with the West African coast (Zahediah, 1986a and 1986b). On the other hand, unless they were planters, Jews were denied the ownership of more than two slaves and these would have been domestic workers (Arbell, 2000: 50). As Marcus (1970: 51) comments, 'though Jamaica was one of the world's great slave markets, there is very little evidence that Jamaican Jewry was engaged in that traffic except in the purchase and sale for servants for use in their own homes and shops'.

It would be false, however, to conclude that life in Jamaica was altogether rosy. Rediscovered religious identity and economic success brought in their wake renewed types of discrimination and repression. These took a number of forms but included some that were officially sanctioned. For example, a motion for 'regulating elections' was passed in the Assembly on 12 February 1707–8 which included the clause that 'no Jew, mulatto, Negro or Indian shall have any vote at any election of members to serve in any Assembly in this island'. This discriminatory treatment carried an economic burden also in the form of the 'Jewish Tribute', a special tax levied on the 'Jewish Nation' as a whole. Unusually, the tax was set at a global figure and communicated to those considered the leading lights of the community, who then had the thankless task of gathering back as much as they could from other Jewish families.[3] Interestingly, this

3 For example, in June 1669, the separate tax was set at £4,000.

provoked special pleas from those who did not consider the 'Jewish Nation' as homogeneous. For example, on 10 December 1706, Jewish planters laid before the Assembly a plea for exemption from the levy (Judah, 1909: 152). They repeated this petition, which had fallen on deaf ears, some years later:

> A petition of some of the Jews of this island setting forth, that being natives of and planters in the same for many years past and not dealing in trade and having paid their deficiency and other taxes usually paid by the planters thereof, they might be eased in respect to the general tax intended on the rest of their nation (National Assembly, 9 April 1728).

The Assembly, which they were precluded from joining, repeatedly turned down this plea, along with any attempt to waive the discriminatory tax itself, on the grounds that 'by reason of their religion' the Jews are 'exempted from expensive offices and services' incurred by others. It went on to claim that among their number were those who 'by indirect or under-hand dealings or correspondence with the Spaniards, and spreading false accounts, hinder the sale of goods carried thither, to the great loss and damage of the English inhabitants of the island' (Judah, 1909: 157). Clearly 'the Jews could be first class merchants, but were second class citizens' (Arbell, 2000: 41).

This attempt to curtail the success of Jewish merchants by imposing upon them additional costs did not go unanswered. The Jewish traders responded with a plea direct to the king (George II) in which they rejected these claims and pointed out that discriminatory legislation of this sort would simply result in Jewish-owned businesses relocating to other territories. They also stressed that these restrictions did not apply to foreigners or to Jews living in Great Britain. The plaintiffs clearly won this argument because the king replied via the island's Council that he was against such 'partial proceedings' but tempered his comments by saying that since the tax had been levied for some years, it could not be abandoned until the following financial year, 'it being his Majesty's determined resolution, that, after the expiration of the present year, you do not, upon any pretence whatsoever, give your assent to any act or acts whereby such additional tax shall be imposed upon the Jews' (22 March,1738–9; Judah, 1909: 164). This response, channelled through the island's Council, generated a furious burst of antisemitism. On 7 May 1741, the chief justice justified the discriminatory tax on the grounds that

> The Jews in this island are a very wealthy body, their gains considerable, and acquired with great ease and indolence and with little risk, and their fortunes so disposed, that the usual methods of laying taxes will not affect them; they are generally concerned in, nay have almost entirely engrossed, the whole retail trade of this island, furnish our people with materials of luxury, tempt them to live and dress above their circumstances, carry on a traffic with our slaves greatly prejudicial to the planter and fair trader, encouraging the negroes to steal commodities from their masters, which they sell to or barter with the Jews, at inconsiderable and under values; and, when by such means they have amassed great wealth, they lay out their money at interest, by which the public stock is in no way increased; and it must ever be against the interest and policy of every country, to encourage the heaping up of such riches among them: That it is in this light the Jews are taxed separately, and not on account of religion or country (Judah, 1909: 170–1).

This diatribe continues by arguing that because they are 'exempt' (banned) from civil and military offices, juries and other burdensome services which others perform, these apparent freedoms 'amply make up for this taxation' (Judah, 1909: 172). In May 1741, the governor, acting on the royal instruction, rejected this legislation but eventually was forced to prorogue the legislature in the face of a continued refusal by the planter class to water down their antisemitic stance. Jamaican Jews cannot have been under any illusions concerning their white overlords; their solution was to remain separate with clear cultural boundaries, and to use their economic skills as a defensive weapon as well as an avenue to a better life.

Despite all of this there is truth in the proposition that the struggles of West Indian Jewry in general occurred earlier than elsewhere and in an important sense could be regarded as pioneering:

> It was not only economically and culturally that eighteenth century West Indian Jewry enjoyed a centrality which North American Jewry would not achieve for a long time to come. Politically, too, the Jews of the islands were in the van. There can be ... no question that the struggles of the West Indian Jewish communities for civil and economic rights hastened the grant of further liberties and immunities to Christian Dissenters and to Jews in England herself and in other British colonies (Marcus, 1970: 138).

This was particularly true of the Dutch Jews because of their experience of greater rights in Surinam and Curaçao.

The Lopes Family in Jamaica

Manasseh Lopes came from a long line of Sephardic Jews whose origins lay in Portugal. The community in Jamaica was remarkably endogamous, as elsewhere in the Caribbean, and it is hard to find any non-Jewish members in his family tree.[4] His great-grandfather on his mother's side was an early member of a family whose name figures prominently in the story of Jews in the Caribbean. Jacob Baruh Lousada was born in Bridgetown, Barbados, in 1681 but lived in Jamaica by the time of his marriage to Abigail Lamego. It is here that he was buried in Hunt's Bay in June 1722.[5] Sometime after, Abigail must have moved to London where she died on 10 March

4 I am indebted for what follows to the remarkable genealogy drawn up by recent descendants of these families (see http://www.barrow-lousada.org/genealogies/).

5 The Hunt's Bay cemetery lies on a spit of sand on the western side of what is now Kingston Harbour. It is one of the earliest known Jewish cemeteries in the New World founded in the mid-seventeenth century when Port Royal on the other side of the bay was the major port. Jews were not allowed to be buried in Port Royal and the deceased were rowed across the bay for burial.

1736 and was buried at the Jewish cemetery in Mile End. They had five children, one boy and four girls. The oldest, Aaron, also died in London, in Bury Street, St James', Piccadilly in 1768. He appears, however, to have first married his cousin Grace Lousada, who died at the age of 19 in Kingston, Jamaica, and was buried in Spanish Town. The oldest of the girls was Rachel Lamego Lousada and it was she who brought the Lopes name into the family.

The Lopes family in Jamaica were traders, merchants and small-scale financiers, one of the most notable of whom was Manasseh's grandfather on his father's side, Abraham Rodrigues Lopes, who appears to have spent all his life in St Jago de la Vega. Abraham, who was born in the first few years of the eighteenth century, married Rachel Lamego Lousada, probably around 1728. Their first born son was Mordecai Rodrigues Lopes, Manasseh's father.[6] While his wife had a short life, dying sometime between 1 May and 30 June 1741, possibly as a result of a further pregnancy, Abraham lived into his late seventies or early eighties. On this side of the family too there was a strong London presence, particularly in Bury Street. In addition to Manasseh's great uncle Aaron who had died in Bury Street in July 1768, this was also true for his great aunt Leah in 1764 and his great aunt Sarah in 1788. The *Gentleman's Magazine* says he died on 13 March 1788 in St Jago de la Vega and described him as 'merchant of the Jewish nation and formerly one of the readers of the synagogue in that town; a man of most respectable character'.[7]

6 Abraham's will, which does not at the time it was composed suggest great wealth, left his 'lands, tenements, negro slaves and hereditaments' to his wife and three children, Mordecai and his two sisters Abigail and Esther. Mordecai was named after Abraham's father who was married to Rebecca Lamego and died in 1758 (American Jewish Archives, Liber of Wills 23 Folio 195, 14 April 1743). The will was signed on 1 May 1741 but not witnessed, and presumably countersigned, until nearly two years later (14 April 1743). The witnesses included his brother-in-law, Aaron Lamera (Lamego) and his cousin by marriage, Jacob B(aruh) Lonsada (Lousada).

7 *Gentlemen's Magazine* 1788 Vol. 63: 933). It is possible that this Abraham Rodrigues Lopes married again after his wife's early death. A grave in the Spanish Town cemetery records the passing on 3 November 1784 of Esther, daughter of Abraham and Esther Rodrigues Lopes at the age of 21 years and 9 months.

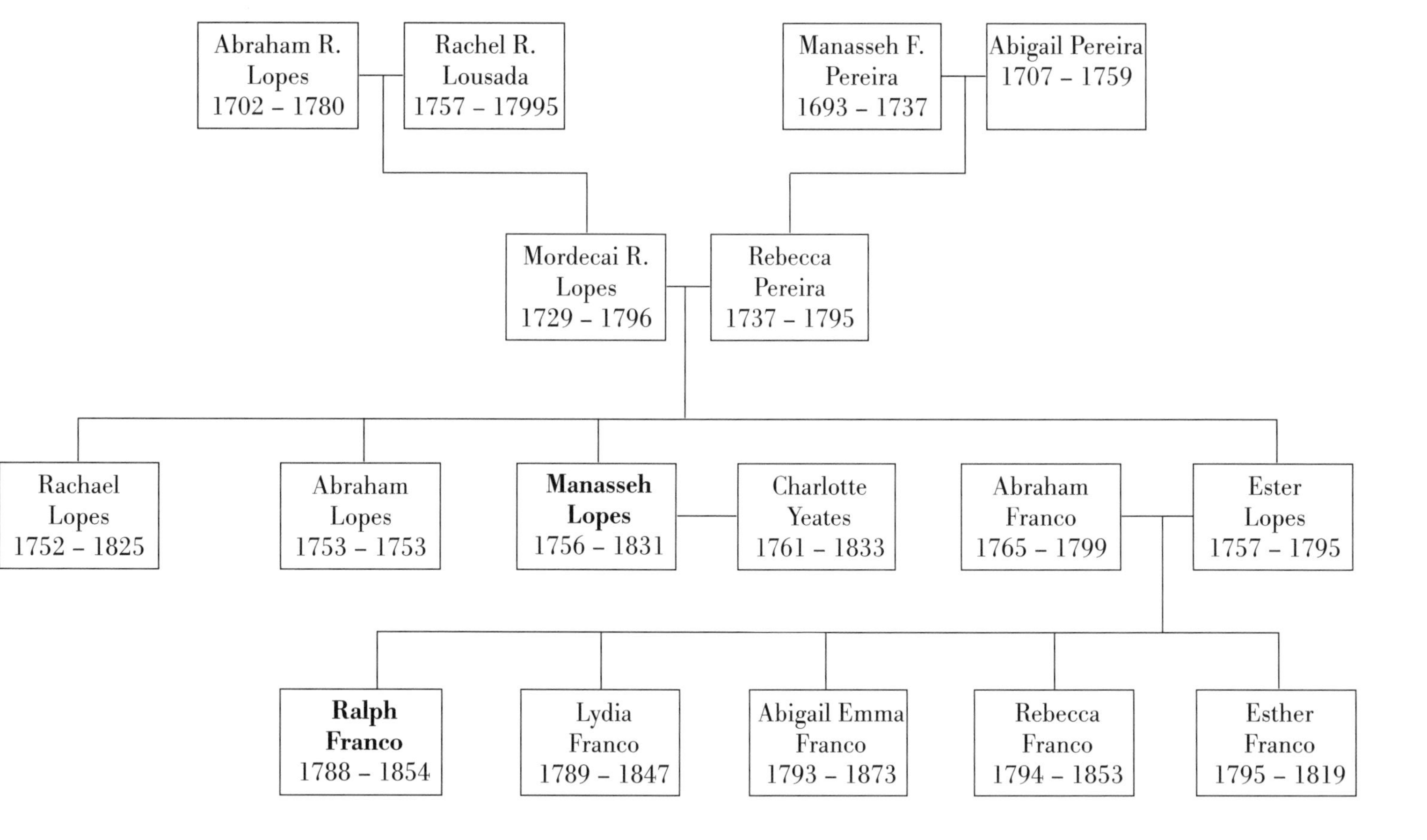

Lopes Line of Descent (1st – 2nd Baronet)

Mordecai Rodrigues Lopes, sometimes known as 'Mordet', was born in 1729 and like his father became a merchant and trader during his early adult years in Jamaica. He had a younger sister, Abigail, born in the 1730s. Both offspring introduced the third great Sephardi name into the family tree when they each married someone from the Pereira lineage; Mordecai marrying Rebecca, daughter of Menasseh Pereira, in October 1752 in Jamaica, and Abigail marrying Benjamin, son of Joseph Pereira, probably at about the same time or a little later. Mordecai and Rebecca Rodrigues Lopes had four children starting with Rachael born in late 1752, followed by Abraham born on 24 November 1753, then Manasseh born on 27 January 1756, and finally Esther born in 1757.[8] Rachael Rodrigues Lopes lived in Jamaica until the death of her husband, her cousin, Isaac Pereira, in 1788; thereafter moving to London until her own death in 1825. As we shall discuss below, Manasseh and Esther moved with their mother and father to London in 1773.

There is no doubt that Manasseh Lopes' grandfather was Abraham Rodrigues Lopes who married Rachel Lousada, the daughter of Jacob Baruch Lousada. A difficulty arises, however, in that Jacob Lousada had a brother, Emanuel, and both brothers married into the Lamego family, Abigail in the former case and Esther in the latter. To add to the potential confusion Emanuel and Esther also had a daughter called Rachel and she too married an Abraham Rodrigues Lopes, but in this second case he died in Jamaica in 1741.[9] Manasseh's grandfather, Abraham, is always listed as being a 'Portugese Jewish Merchant', a similar trade to his wife's family, and he was known to be economically active until later in the century. This point is important because it was mostly the other side of the family, that which descended from Emanuel Lousada,

8 There is some confusion as to Abraham's age at death. This is because sources misread the year of his death as 1758 instead of 1753. The latter is much more probable because the inscription on his tomb in the Old Kingston Cemetery mentions that he died on 18 December and lived only 24 days (Barnett and Wright, 1997). Manasseh's birth date is often given in the old style calendar as 1755.

9 I am very indebted to Julian Land and Alan Pereira for making this clearer (see www.barrow-lousada.org).

which was involved in sugar plantations. For example, from 1792 (or possibly before) Emanuel Baruch Lousada – who was the grandson of the original Emanuel mentioned above – is listed as the owner of 760 acres in the Parish of St Ann in the County of Middlesex known as the Banks Estate with 117 slaves in that year. The estate passed to his son Jacob in 1797 and three years later to his grandson, Isaac. In 1816, this estate had an inventory of 113 slaves and 45 livestock. Isaac also owned from 1821 until his death in London in 1831, the Carlisle Estate (906 acres) in the Parish of Vere in the County of Middlesex with more than 220 slaves. In other words, some members of one side of the family did become sugar planters, but not the side from which Manasseh Lopes was descended.[10] Indeed, the Lopes family who came to own the Maristow Estate had greater wealth than was likely through sugar plantations, whose fortunes during the relevant period of development were in relative decline.[11]

Because Mordecai Lopes and his father Abraham were so clearly traders and merchants, it is tempting to posit a connection with yet another Abraham Lopez who was born in Portugal in 1711 and who

---

10 There is one exception to this generalisation. Manasseh's brother-in-law, Isaac Pereira, through his older sister, Rachael, was a plantation owner and when he died in 1788 his wealth passed to his oldest son, Benjamin Lopes/Lopez Pereira, who appears to have lived in London in some style from the age of approximately 20. His addresses in the city include Fitzroy Square, Jubilee Place, Chelsea and Great Marlborough Street, but there is some reason to think that he squandered his fortune, since in May 1813 he was committed to Fleet Prison on account of non-payment of debts. His assets at that time were recorded as 'nil'. Manasseh Lopes' will mentions a legacy to the wife of Benjamin Pereira 'his lately deceased nephew' (PRO 11/1785/283).

11 Scholarly debates concerning the profitability and economic viability of the late eighteenth-century Jamaican sugar industry and the plantation society that sustained it have passed through a number of phases. Central to the arguments has been the abolition of the slave trade itself in 1807. Was it the case that this achievement was a victory for moral principle over avaricious profit or, alternatively, were profits so meagre that a system based upon coerced labour no longer appeared – as it once undoubtedly had – as a high road to riches? Eric William, who famously went on to become Prime Minister of Trinidad and Tobago in the first years of its independence after 1962, wrote the first major critique of the high moral principle argument in his Oxford DPhil thesis (originally published in 1944 as *Capitalism and Slavery*) but since then many other contributions have argued the opposite.

became a significant trader in Jamaica.[12] This one was the half-brother of Aaron Lopez who migrated to Newport, Rhode Island, in 1766. Aaron became one of the wealthiest settlers in pre-Independence North America and founded a business that included Abraham as an important partner. Aaron Lopez is reported to have arrived in Newport from Portugal at the age of 21 on 13 October 1752, with his younger brother David, to join an older half-brother Moses who had been there since the mid-1740s (Bigelow, 1931: 757–8). After failing in trade with the English port of Bristol, Lopez determined to try two other routes, one with the slave coast of Guinea and one with Jamaica. In 1767, Lopez sent out nine ships to the West Indies, delivering livestock, provisions and timber on the outward leg from Rhode Island and returning with sugar and molasses. He was able to call on the family support of his half-brother, Abraham Lopez (full brother to Moses), living in Savanna-la-Mar, a newly developed port town and capital of the Westmoreland Parish at the western end of Jamaica (Bigelow, 1931: 762). Abraham arranged for Aaron to have the services of one of the best sea captains available who not only knew ships but 'had an extraordinary knowledge of the needs of planters, the packing of cargoes, their sale in Jamaica, collecting

12 This Abraham Lopes was the second son of Diego José Lopez by his first marriage, 'a man much respected and esteemed in Portugal'. As a *Marrano*, he was christened 'Michael' (Miguel in Portuguese) (Kohler, 1894: 103). His older brother Moses, christened 'José' after his father, migrated first to London, then to New York and finally to Newport, Rhode Island, in the early 1740s. Diego Lopez' second wife was also a Lopez, possibly a cousin, and with her he had three more sons, all of them also 'christened' in Portugal. Edward (or Duarte in Portuguese) the oldest and Gabriel the youngest migrated to Newport, being renamed after being circumcised by Benjamin Gomez of New York as Aaron and David. Aaron was only 21 when he arrived in Rhode Island but he had a wife and daughter (Anna and Catherine in Portugal; Abigail and Sarah in Newport) (Kohler, 1894: 104). Abigail died in 1762 and he was married again a year later to Sarah, daughter of his business partner Jacob Rodriguez Rivera, and produced ten more children. Miguel/Abraham Lopez was the last one to migrate from Portugal to America being rescued by Aaron in 1766 when he sent his ship *America* to Lisbon to fetch him and his family, having with him his first wife Joana and three sons, Duarte (Edward), José (Joseph) and João (John) (the mother became Abigail and the children respectively Moses, Samuel and Jacob). At some time thereafter he moved from Newport to Jamaica where he remarried a woman called Sarah who bore him six more children before dying on 26 March 1767 aged 35 immediately after the last one was born.

debts, and the best means of getting a load of sugar, molasses, and rum for the return voyage' (Bigelow, 1931: 765). These cargoes undoubtedly included slaves.

Between the years 1764 and 1768, Lopez sent six vessels to the slave coast and each of them returned via the West Indies before returning to Newport. The brig *Africa*, for example, contained 45 slaves for sale at Kingston in 1766 and another 69 on her next voyage in 1768 (Platt, 1975: 603). She provided a further 49 slaves in Jamaica in 1774, while other vessels owned by Lopez sold a further 293 in Jamaica and 383 in Barbados in the years from 1771 to 1775 (Platt, 1975: 608). This Abraham Lopez played a key role in accepting slave cargoes and arranging for their sale at a commission of 5 per cent of the revenues raised (Platt, 1975: 611). Shipping slaves was, however, only a modest part of Aaron Lopez' business. By 1775, he either owned or had an interest in more than 30 ships trading in the Americas, Europe and the Mediterranean, and in the years leading up to the War of Independence (1775–83) was famed as one of the most eminent merchants in all 13 colonies. He has been called 'a Colonial American Merchant Prince' and was described by Ezra Styles, Christian pastor and president of Yale, as 'a merchant of first eminence; for honour and extent of commerce probably surpassed by no merchant in America' (Chyet, 1970; Gutstein 1939; Schappes, 1976). Unfortunately, given the richness of this story and its connection with what was to become the United States of America, there seems to have been no family or business links with the traders of the same name in Spanish Town and Kingston.

The conclusion that can be drawn therefore is that Mordecai Rodrigues Lopes, his son and his father, were never planters. This is not to say that they would not have possessed domestic slaves, nor that the slave trade or providing funding for plantation owners was never part of their portfolio of economic activities.[13] They came from an urban background and in all probability their initial trade

13 For example, the will of Abigail Pereira dated 15 January 1791, Mannaseh's aunt and brother of his father Mordecai, left to her nephew her house in Balham, £5,000 and her 'negro slave' Betty who was awarded £5 and her freedom.

involved importing the goods and materials upon which plantation life depended. In this they conformed very closely to the majority of Jewish families on the island. How wealthy the family was when they left Jamaica in 1773 is hard to judge, but certainly once in London both Mordecai and his son Manasseh clearly found an environment in which they could prosper. Further evidence concerning the degree to which Mordecai Lopes was integrated into London life, rather than being an absentee Jamaican landowner, can be derived from his will (PRO 11/1272). The will is dated 23 April 1795, which was under a week before his wife Rebecca's death, and was proved just under a year later on 16 March 1796 following the testator's death aged about 66 on 29 February. He was buried a week later in the Spanish and Portuguese Jewish Cemetery in Mile End. Three points stand out from the will.

The first is the lack of any mention of Jamaican possessions of any description; in particular, it is clear that he did not own at his death any plantations or estates. This, of course, does not mean that he never did but it does suggest that, after he arrived in London at the age of 44, some at least of his wealth derived from his London-based career. This is also not to say that he had no attachment to the island as he specifically left £100 (Jamaican money) to the Wardens and Elders of the Synagogue of Kingston and a small sum to the island's poor Jews, but all remaining legacies were held in the form of 3 per cent Consolidated Bank Annuities.[14] The second point is that his will identifies legacies amounting to more than £87,000 (approximately

14 These investments, often referred to as 'consols', were issued by the Bank of England to assist in financing its activities. They were 'consolidated' because they replaced a range of other investment vehicles with varying interest rates issued in the period after 1751. Later they were known as government bonds or 'gilts'. In the late nineteenth century they comprised more than half of government debt and were often used by creditors as a way of providing a regular income during later life, particularly because they paid interest quarterly rather than less frequently as became common later. Sephardi Jews played a particularly important role in both founding the Bank of England and in providing a disproportionate amount of the finance used to establish its operations. As early as 1701, investors with Sephardi Jewish names held nearly one-tenth of those with the minimum investment necessary to stand as the governor of the bank (£4,000) (Guiseppi, 1955–9: 53).

£10 million in 2020) which means that he was a very wealthy man when he died. The lion's share of this sum was inherited by Manasseh (£50,000 plus the inheritance intended initially for Mordecai's wife, his house in Clapham and the residual estate after other legacies were paid) but all in the form of 3 per cent consols. The sum of £30,000 was divided equally between his daughter, Rachael, and her children and his other six grandchildren, the offspring of his late daughter Esther and her husband Abraham Franco.

The final point of note is that the administration of Mordecai's will was entirely dependent upon three trustees, all of them relatives but also stalwart members of London's Sephardim community and wealthy men in their own right. The first was his son Manasseh who was 41 years old at the time of his father's death and had been living with or near his father in England for the previous 23 years. The second was Moses Isaac Levy, who in 1795 was listed as living in Piccadilly, London. Moses Isaac Levy was the son of Isaac Levy who had married Mordecai's niece, Abigail, daughter of his aunt Esther Abigail Lamego (Esther, Mordecai's mother's sister, had married Moses Lamego in 1736). The *Gentleman's Magazine* of 1759 records the marriage of Moses Isaac Levy to 'Miss Lamego' on 22 December of that year. By this date, Levy had made a great deal of money fulfilling contracts to supply the British Army during the Seven Years War, which was by then entering its second and final phase. In public life he had risen to become vice president of the Board of Deputies of British Jews, an organisation that he was to lead as president from 1789 to 1801.[15] A few years after his marriage Moses Isaac Levy bought 'Prospect House' in Wimbledon, South London, a fine 60-acre estate adjacent to what became the Atkinson Morley Hospital.[16] He was clearly a man of great wealth and influence.

15 The Board of Deputies was originally set up in 1760 by the London-based Sephardim to support the new king (George III). By the early years of the nineteenth century it had merged with a parallel body established by the Ashkenazim but retained its original name, which it does to this day.

16 The hospital, which was established in the second half of the nineteenth century, became famous for its innovative use of brain scanning technology. It closed in 2003.

The final trustee identified in the will was Emanuel Baruh Lousada. Since there were a number of members of the extended family with this name, it is important to be aware which one this was. Mordecai Lopes was the grandson of Jacob Baruh Lousada who had a brother with this name. This Emanuel had a son called Jacob in honour of his uncle who married another Abigail Lamego, daughter of Isaac Lamego, and came to London in late 1741. Their first son, born in 1744, was the Emanuel Baruh Lousada in question. He married Rebecca Ximenes, daughter of David Ximenes and Rebecca da Costa Athias, on 2 May 1770 in Bevis Marks, London. Some confusion can occur with this man's cousin of the same name who remained in Jamaica becoming a very successful merchant (*Anglo-Jewish Notabilities*: 127). Burke's *Landed Gentry* states that this Emanuel Baruh Lousada 'lived in great splendour, on his West India estates' (Burke, 1863: 900).[17]

The London-born Emanuel Baruh Lousada became highly respected among the city's Sephardim. His ancestor Moses Baruh Louzada had been one of the founders of the London's Spanish and Portuguese Synagogue (Bevis Marks) and in 1663, before the present building was constructed, had served as its first *gabay* or treasurer. Emanuel Baruh Lousada is listed as living at 4 Adam Street, St Martin-in-the-Fields, between 1772 and 1780 and during this period he applied to the College of Arms for armorial recognition for his family which was granted to 'Emanuel Baruh Lousada of St Martin-in-the-Fields, Westminster' on 28 January 1777.[18] Emanuel was among the 'modernisers' of the synagogue, signing along with

17 The estates included Richmond Old Works, a sugar plantation, but which he was unlikely ever to have worked personally since it came to him as a creditor of the previous owner.

18 The text of his application claims that he and his family have 'used Armorial Ensigns but on examining the Records of the College of Arms he does not find the same duly registered and unwilling to use any Ensigns of Honour without lawful authority requested the favour of his Lordship's warrant for our devising granting and assigning to him, to the Descendants and Sisters of Jacob Baruh Lousada his father and the descendants of his uncle Aaaron Baruh Lousada of Jamaica such Arms and Crest as they may lawfully bear and use...' suggesting perhaps that he had resided in London for a long period, probably all his life until this date.

Manasseh Lopez the *Escamoth* in 1784 (year 5544) or plea for the language of the synagogue to be English.[19] Later, he was appointed a member of the *Mahamad* (sometimes *Ma'amad)* or council of the elders of the London synagogue. Although the elders or *Yehidim* consisted of all those who enjoyed the full rights of membership, the *Mahamad*, whose policies tended to be conservative and strictly imposed, comprised only five people, four wardens of the synagogue plus the treasurer. By the time of Mordecai's will, Emanuel's London address is listed as 'Percy Street' and since he was not registered as the owner of a lease in that street it is a reasonable surmise that later in life he stayed when in London with Mordecai and Rebecca Lopes at No. 14, the house that the Lopez family occupied from 1794.

In addition to his role in the synagogue, Emanuel Baruh Lousada was also very well known as a man of wealth, property and influence. He was listed as a proprietor of the Royal Institution in the early years of the nineteenth century from very soon after its creation in 1799. The list of supporters reads like a 'who's who' of Georgian society, including among many others the leading architect, John Soane. Baruh Lousada was called in and examined by a parliamentary select committee and asked whether he was a subscriber to a loan to the Bank of England in January 1796. He replied that he was a contributor of £50,000, thereby making it amply clear that his wealth was very considerable (*Parliamentary Register* 2, para 619–20: 199). He was best known, however, as a land owner and property developer in East Devon. In 1793, when very well established in London, Emanuel bought 125 acres of land on Peak Hill above the then small and inaccessible fishing village of Sidmouth in East Devon that had become recognised as a place of some refinement after George III visited in 1791. On the land he had bought Lousada built a fine mansion, thereby demonstrating that Jews could use their wealth to become landed gentry and also to differentiate themselves from the then much poorer Ashkenazim pouring into the East End of London from Europe's eastern fringes

19 Hitherto it had been in Portuguese with translations into Spanish and was to remain this way for a further four decades (Moses, 1901: 156).

(Plate 38). Peak House was described as on the 'western declivity' at Sidmouth: 'From the grounds of Peak House, the spectator has a fine reach of the ocean, the white cliffs of Charmouth and Bridport, and the bold promontory of Portland' (Butcher, 1805: 453).

The house, originally built in 1796, soon became the centre for many family visits and Lousada can also be credited with helping to establish Sidmouth as a fine Regency town for the aristocracy and royalty.[20] His contribution was recognised locally and a committee of the local citizenry presented him with a watercolour of the shore at Sidmouth inscribed to Emanuel Baruh Lousada 'to whose active exertions and liberality of spirit' the town of Sidmouth and its surrounding areas were indebted. While it is very probable that Mordecai Lopes never saw Peak House, it is inconceivable that Manasseh Lopes was not a visitor. Indeed, it is not entirely fanciful to suppose that this first gave him the idea of buying into the life of a landed aristocrat in Devon, that most blue-blooded of counties.

Emanuel and Rebecca had no children and after Rebecca died in 1820, Emanuel, on his own death at 88 on 29 February 1832, left Peak House to his nephew, son of Isaac Baruh Lousada (1748–1831) and Judith D'Aguiler (1747–1821), who was also called Emanuel (PROB 11/1797). He too was a merchant owning an important West Indian-London trading company in partnership with another relative, Simon Barrow. Like his uncle, this nephew made significant contributions to life by the sea and became so well-known and established locally that he was made High Sheriff of Devon for the year 1842–43, probably the first Jewish person to receive this honour. As was true of his forebears, however, there was a darker side to his trading operations. During the period of abolition, Barrow and Lousada made a number of claims for losses incurred by the freedom granted to slaves owned by them. For example, they received £2,536 18s for 120 slaves on the Banks Plantation at St Ann's in Jamaica (1 February 1836/T71/857/Jamaica 447), £4,194 18s for 208 slaves on the Vere Plantation once owned by Emanuel's deceased father, Isaac (1 February 1836/T71/858/Jamaica

20 Peak House was rebuilt in 1904 for the then owner, Sir Thomas Dewey. It was then converted in 1981 into four apartments.

Vere 36) and £65 for part-ownership of six slaves in Barbados (26 November 1838/T71/897; Barbados 274). This amounted to a little under £6,800 or £542,000 in 2020 money (https://www.ucl.ac.uk/lbs/person/view/12241).[21] This Emanuel left £100,000 on his death in 1854 but much of this would have been inherited from his father and uncle.

Manasseh Lopes in London

Unlike the second period of Manasseh Lopes' period in England, after he bought the Maristow Estate, the first is characterised by a seeming reticence to be identified or reported upon in public discourse. For the last quarter of the eighteenth century, his appears to have been a world of discretion hidden behind the impressive cultural fortifications of London's Sephardi community. Even among such talented men, however, his reputation appears to have become one of outstanding success in terms of financial acumen.[22] The Lopes family was specifically mentioned as 'among the chief Jewish financiers of northern Europe' (*Jewish Encyclopedia*, 1906) and Manasseh Lopes is specifically mentioned in the *Jewish Virtual Library* as a 'leading banker'.[23] Inevitably, this reputation leaked out in some quarters and as with all men whose activities became the stuff of legend, fact and fiction became inextricably combined. For example, Cecil Roth, the compiler and first editor of the famous *Encyclopaedia Judaica*, published in 26 volumes between 1973–91, in writing about Sephardi banking was in no doubt that 'Manasseh Lopes was a leading banker during the 18th century' (Volume 13: 189). He had picked up, however, on an apocryphal report that Manasseh, in addition to banking, was a stockbroker who 'made a fortune by speculation on false reports of Queen Anne's death'. This report arose from John Ashton's book *The History of*

21 The references above are to the catalogue of payments made by the 'Legacies of British Slave Ownership' project run by University College, London.

22 This may well have been true of the womenfolk but they were clearly confined to domestic duties.

23 An American-Israeli Project (http://www.jewishvirtuallibrary.org/jsource/History/history.html).

Gambling in England, originally published in 1898. In this work, Ashton discusses the spreading of false news as a way of rigging financial markets by undermining investor confidence, thereby creating buying opportunities as stock prices fall. In an age where communication could take weeks to be confirmed, it was relatively straightforward to announce that the Spanish or French had invaded, or that ships crucial to the fortunes of the East India Company had been lost at sea. The results could be dramatic and Ashton writes that one such occasion was during the reign of Queen Anne when 'a man appeared, galloping from Kensington to the City, ordering the turnpikes to be thrown open for him, and shouting loudly that he bore the news of the Queen's death' (1898: 247). The effect on stock prices was dramatic and Ashton continues by saying that 'Manasseh Lopes and the Jews bought all they could, and reaped the benefit when the fraud was discovered' (1898: 247–8). The only problem with this story is that Queen Anne died on 1 August 1714 or more than 40 years before Manasseh Lopes was born (cf. Dale, 2004: 18).

What is intriguing is that the story has been endlessly repeated and Manasseh Lopes has been linked thereby to international finance. In those years, the leading financial centre in northern Europe was undoubtedly Amsterdam, where Sephardim played a prominent role. In Werner Sombart's (1951) rebuttal of Max Weber's theories on the links between ascetic Protestantism and the rise of capitalism, he writes:

> The effects of the Jewish *haute finance* in Holland made themselves felt beyond the borders of the Netherlands, because that country in the 17th and 18th centuries was the reservoir from which all the needy princes of Europe drew their money. Men like the Pintos, Delmontes, Bueno de Mesquitta, Francis Mels and many others may in truth be regarded as the leading financiers of Northern Europe during that period (1982: 54).

He goes on to argue, 'Under Queen Anne one of the most prominent financiers in England was Menasseh Lopez, and by the time the

South Sea Bubble burst, the Jews as a body were the greatest financial power in the country' (1982: 55).[24] Commentators would often draw connections between the dependency of London on Amsterdam as a by-product not only of family connections amongst the Sephardim, but also the important link at the level of the royal family following William of Orange's elevation as William III in 1689. Possible links between members of the Sephardim and the royal family may be part of the reason for the elision of the life of Manasseh Lopes and Queen Anne.[25]

Inevitably, such activities aroused that form of prejudice based upon the loathing of those achieving greater success than oneself. One example was the English-born populist Labour politician in Australia, Francis George (Frank) Anstey (1865–1940), who went on to become a minister in the pre-Second World War Labour administration. Anstey wrote a number of books, most identifying the City of London as a constraint upon the fortunes of Australia. In one, *The Kingdom of Shylock* (1915), he identified those who manipulated capitalism from the shadows and, in his judgment generated the conditions that led to the Great War. As his title suggests, he considered that chief among them were the Jews, particularly those based in the City of London. Looking back on the history of this phenomenon he wrote:

> After Medina came the Jew, Manasseh Lopes. Then came Samson Gideon and the Goldsmids – Abraham and Benjamin. They were succeeded by the Rothschilds.[26]

This tract was repressed during the Great War and reissued as *The Money Power* afterwards with some of its antisemitism redacted, but it serves to show that even those without much knowledge of

---

24 It is, of course, possible that another Menasseh/Manasseh Lopes existed during the early years of the eighteenth century but, if so, no other trace of him has been left to posterity.

25 LV Birck (1926; reprinted 2014) *The Scourge of Europe: The Public Debt Described*, Explained and Historically Depicted Abingdon, Routledge, p. 199.

26 This sentence also places Lopes earlier than is correct. 'Medina' was Sir Solomon Medina (c.1650–1720), the first Jew in England to be knighted (1700) and Sampson Gideon was born in 1699, dying in 1762.

eighteenth-century London could identify Manasseh Lopes as a significant financial player well before he embarked on the career for which he is most famous; namely, his bid to become a member of the English landed aristocracy.

It is also worth recalling that subscribers to the 'Queen Anne rumour story' were not all hostile. More recent works, in particular, with the horrors of the holocaust imprinted on their memories, have tended to be much kinder. Paul Johnson, for example, in his recent history of the Jews tells us that 'the Menasseh Lopes family under Queen Anne, the Gideons and the Salvadors under the first three Georges, played notable roles in maintaining the stability of London financial markets' (Johnson, 1987: 282). Also, in an era when antisemitism was highly prevalent, literary opinion at a much lower level of social class could sometimes be insightful and sympathetic towards Jewish financiers. One excellent example is provided by Henry Franks who read a paper to the Manchester Literary Club in 1879 entitled 'The Waste of Intellect as Exhibited by the Jews'.[27] Franks faced head on the 'popular prejudice that Jews have more covetousness and greed for gold than other people'. He then regaled his audience with the story of the 'great financier' Manasseh Lopes and the fictitious story of Queen Anne's death saying that this was not the result of his greed but rather evidence of his 'sagacity and courage'. Noting that 'enormous fortunes were realized in a day' he goes on to say: 'Yet afterwards, when the simple-minded citizens took a walk abroad and passed the magnificent country residence of old Lopez (*sic*), I have no doubt that they said: "That house belongs to a rapacious and swindling old Jew".'

With great insight Franks concludes that 'the bare fact that [the Jews] succeed better in amassing gold is only evidence that they have in a larger measure the faculties which favour its acquisition, such as industry and perseverance, and the forethought and insight which in literature we call imagination' (Franks, 2013; original 1879: 149).

27 The Manchester Literary Club was established in 1862 to provide entertainment and education to its members from the city and environs by reading aloud papers on literary and other topics.

This picture of Manasseh Lopes is suggestive of someone who was widely known and highly respected for his financial acumen. He was, in other words, the George Soros of his day and would have agreed with the latter's aphorism that 'markets are constantly in a state of uncertainty and flux and money is made by discounting the obvious and betting on the unexpected.' What precisely those bets were is not known but, along with the normal returns on financing debt, they appear to have made both he and his father exceptionally wealthy.

Move to the Countryside

The transition of Manasseh Lopes from West Indian merchant to country landowner and aspirant member of the aristocracy appears on the surface to present a number of puzzles. How was it that someone, even with considerable financial resources, could locate a suitable estate for sale, proceed to buy it and within the space of a few short years become an MP, a baronet and someone close to the centre of power, a goal that had eluded the previous owner of the Maristow estate even though he had been assiduous in cultivating members of high society and had the education and sophistication to do so with ease? It is tempting to speculate that Manasseh Lopes and his father Mordecai had known of and interacted with members of the Heywood dynasty in Jamaica. This is most improbable because the Sephardim suffered a miserable degree of exclusion in Jamaica and there is no evidence that James Modyford Heywood ever visited the island. His father, who had been born in Jamaica, had died when Manasseh's father was only eight years old. Moreover, as has been argued above, there is no evidence that Mordecai Lopes or his son were ever planters in Jamaica. The answer to the puzzle may lie, rather unexpectedly, with the dissolute and spendthrift ways of the Prince of Wales, the future Prince Regent and ultimately George IV, who was 11 years old when the Lopes family arrived in London and who may have facilitated the purchase of the Maristow estate.

Manasseh Lopes moved to London with his parents and younger sister Esther in 1773 when he was 18. In 1786, at the age of 31, he acquired the lease of 119 Charlotte Street, just to the west of Tottenham Court Road, and remained there until 1795 when he moved a short distance to the north and west to 2 Fitzroy Square, a more expensive address. His father meanwhile had acquired the lease of 14 Percy Street in the same part of London at about the same time (1794) having previously owned outright a house on Clapham Common, then a more or less rural location, since just after the family arrived in London. Thus both father and son, with the experience of the rich pickings that were to be had by advancing loans to their sometimes less than careful Anglo rulers, were well placed to seek out those who could provide both a financial return and, even more important, an entrée to polite society.

Where better to start than at the top? George III's eldest son (and his two brothers) were ploughing through money at precisely this time without a care for the morrow, and were in constant need of funds to bolster their extravagant lifestyle. Although the evidence for this familiarity with the royal circle is not conclusive it was widely believed. For example, in 1896, in an article on the Prince of Wales (later Edward VII), the *San Francisco Chronicle* accused him of following the example of his great uncle when also heir-apparent who 'frequently dined and supped in the company of old Manasseh Lopes the West Indian money lender' (5 April 1896). Again, in an obituary of Sir Massey Lopes, the son of Ralph Franco Lopes, Manasseh's nephew, in 1908, the *Chicago Tribune* included the following sentence: 'Menasseh Lopez attached himself to the fortunes of the prince regent, afterwards George IV, was always to be found in his entourage, and invariably had rolls of £100 Bank of England notes in his pocket at the disposal of his royal patron' (14 February 1908).

We should remember that the eighteenth century was a period in which Jewish traders and financiers were largely welcomed in London. In 1740 an Act was passed permitting Jews who had been resident in the colonies for more than seven years to become naturalised. Proponents of the 'Jew Bill' of 1753 pointed out that, despite their small number, Jews were responsible for a twelfth of the nation's profits and one twentieth of foreign trade. Although this bill when passed was almost instantly repealed in the face of mounting antisemitism, it led to higher levels of conversion to Anglicanism and some softening in prejudiced views.

Plausibility is added to the reports on Manasseh's involvement in money lending at the highest level by the well-known fact that the Prince of Wales prior to becoming Prince Regent in 1811 made extensive use of money lenders, mostly Jewish. Even before reaching his age of majority in 1783, the prince appears to have indulged an unbridled enthusiasm for expenditure.[28] Aside from gambling and the normal pursuits of young male aristocrats in wine, women and song, he felt it incumbent upon himself to spend voraciously on art work and on decorating his new London base at Carlton House. As early as 1784, the caricaturist Thomas Rowlandson had portrayed the young prince handing over a sealed title-deed to Jewish money lenders and he and others often returned to this theme (Plate 39).

By 1787, the House of Commons felt compelled to offer £161,000 towards the prince's debts and a further £60,000 for the work on Carlton House.[29] This did not come close to covering his obligations and writing of the year 1787, Fitzgerald (1881) comments:

> Like other gentlemen of the town, our Prince had recourse in his necessities to the usurers. One of the most notorious money-lenders who came to his aid was a personage known as 'Jew Travis,' or 'Treves,' with whom the Prince had transactions. Later came 'Jew Solomon' and 'Jew King' (1881: 112–3).

The last named was a reference to John King, born Jacob Rey, who became one of the most notorious 'unconventional Jews' of

28 His preceptor (tutor responsible for his education) from 1776, later Bishop Richard Hurd, a favourite of George III, said of him that he would become 'either the most polished gentleman or the most accomplished blackguard in Europe – possibly both'.

29 This proved totally inadequate and eight years later in 1797 he owed a staggering £630,000 (the equivalent to more than £55 million in income terms in 2020), a significant proportion of which was comprised of unsettled accounts with artists and craftsmen (Millar, 1986: 586).

Georgian London, a place where 'there were fortunes to be made, social heights to be scaled, sexual favours to be won' (Edelman, 1982–3: 71). Even by the standards of Jewish aspirants to higher social levels, King was an exceptional example, changing his name very early in his life. As Todd Edelman writes, 'Even wealthy Sephardim who had severed their ties with the Jewish community, such as Samson Gideon, David Ricardo, and Manasseh Masseh Lopes, did not trouble to anglicize their names' (1982–3: 73). What King did do, however, was to emulate the lifestyle of his creditors, even to the point of being famed for the excellence of his table. He also sank to the level of their morality. Edelman makes the perceptive observation that 'in embracing fraudulence to secure his fortune "Jew" King was doing no more than giving expression to the spirit of the age, or to be more precise, to the standards of those circles with whom he did business' (1982–3: 78). Manasseh Lopes was almost the same age as King and, newly arrived in London, would have had no difficulty in adapting the lessons from the colonies to life in the city. Desperately indebted members of the ruling elite were quite prepared to cast aside social conventions and contemporary prejudices in order to avail themselves of short-term solace, and were prepared to offer extraordinary rewards in both money terms and social advancement. At one point, George, Prince of Wales, is reputed to have offered a promissory payment of £10,000 plus an Irish peerage after the king's death for a £5,000 loan (Fitzgerald, 1881: 229).[30]

The lessons of this era were plain. If you used your money to good effect without worrying too greatly about adhering to the morality which the need for it highlighted, your wealth and social standing could be greatly enhanced. If Manasseh Lopes was a money lender or financial middle-man to the young royal brothers, then there is an obvious explanation for how a new landowner from a foreign land could avail himself of an honour which has

30 George also sought money in Paris and often refused to honour the interest payments due on these loans. Numerous creditors were thereby revealed or in some cases returned to revolutionary Paris and ended up being guillotined (Fitzgerald, 1881: 232–3).

been described as 'a status symbol for country gentlemen and social climbers'.[31] Some commentators were clearly not in doubt: 'The prince regent availed himself of his power as such to confer a baronetcy upon Menasseh (Lopes) by way of part payment of his obligations' (*Chicago Tribune* 14 February 1908).[32] There is also an obvious explanation of how someone who had probably never strayed far from London could find himself the owner of an estate in what must have seemed a far-flung corner of the realm. The prince and his two brothers, Frederick Duke of York and William Henry Duke of Clarence, attended an endless sequence of balls and masquerades, many organised by 'Prinny' himself at Carlton House, to which Sophia Musters, the most senior of the Heywood sisters, would have been invited. As Fitzgerald wrote in the more repressive years of Victoria's reign, 'at these entertainments the fairest and most aristocratic dames were not ashamed to mix with courtesans who enjoyed the royal patronage; indeed, there was a general obsequious acceptance of public scandal which now seems incredible' (Fitzgerald, 1881: 27). How easy it would have been for the prince himself to have known of James Modyford Heywood's wish to dispose of the Maristow estate and to have passed this information on to his wealthy associate whose interest in Devon had been stimulated by his visits to Peak House.[33]

There is other evidence that Manasseh Lopes had a direct line of communication with the future George IV; this time later

31 RG Thorne in HC 1790–1820 (https://www.historyofparliamentonline.org/research/parliaments/parliaments-1790-1820)

32 An alternative explanation, advanced by David Nicolson (later 4th Baron Carnock and a Lopes family member) was that Manasseh may have been sufficiently financially powerful to have used his wealth to stabilise the stock market prior to Trafalgar, implying that the prime minister (Pitt the Younger) was the primary cause of this elevation. He wrote to George Lopes, 'if he did that, that would surely have been a sufficient reason for the grant of his baronetcy; and, with the victory over the French, have enabled him to make a profit at the same time' (Nicolson to Lopes, 9 September 1998). Profiting from the country's indebtedness was very probable later but unpersuasive at this time when Manasseh had apparently struggled to buy Maristow House only a few years before.

33 The estate was formally on the market from 1791 but known to be available for some time before this.

when he was Prince Regent. In 1810, Sir Manasseh Massey Lopes, as he was by then, bought the parliamentary seat of Westbury in Wiltshire reputedly for the sum of £75,000 from the Earl of Abingdon. This rotten borough returned two members to the Commons between 1640 and the Great Reform Act of 1832 and at the byelection of 1814 he offered one of the two seats to his nephew Ralph Franco, while the other remained with Benjamin Shaw, who had occupied the seat since 1812. In 1818, however, he removed Shaw and replaced him with Lord Francis Conyngham, the 21-year-old second son of Henry, the 1st Marquis Conyngham, and his wife Elizabeth. Lord Conyngham, who had been elevated to a marquis in 1816, was 'a courtier married to an attractive wife' (Smith, 1999: 184) and it seems very probable that the request to Lopes came from the Prince Regent, since at the time he was freeing himself from the rather cool clutches of Lady Hertford in order to court, if that is the appropriate word, Lady Conyngham, who was to become by the time he ascended the throne as George IV in 1820 one of his most enthusiastically retained mistresses and his companion for the whole decade of his reign.[34] In other words, the prince – possibly remembering the favours Lopes had granted in the past – made the request in order to enhance his prospects with Lady Conyngham.[35]

34 Lady Conyngham, whose ample frame matched that of the increasingly corpulent king, spent much time with him at Marlborough Row, her London residence near Carlton House, and at Brighton. She is said to have gratefully received many baubles and jewels for her friendship, including gemstones from the Crown jewels. She retained her position until the king's death in 1830 when she disappeared into wealthy obscurity in Paris, where she survived another 30 years. Although the second son lasted barely a year as a parliamentarian, Francis Conyngham went on to receive many other royal favours becoming first groom of the bed-chamber and master of the robes for the whole decade of George IV's reign, during which time he also served as under-secretary of state for foreign affairs and as a lord of the Treasury. Although not regarded as a man of great talent, he retained high office after George's death becoming lord chamberlain 1835–9 and was reputedly the first to break the news to Victoria of her new role in 1837.

35 It is unlikely that money would have changed hands since the Prince Regent was still mired in debt and Manasseh Lopes and Ralph Franco went on to each represent Westbury in later years.

The Purchase of the Maristow Estate

Manasseh Lopes married Charlotte Yeates, only daughter of John Yeates of Monmouthshire, on 19 October 1795 at St Michael's Anglican Church at Horton, then in Buckinghamshire. Horton was a small village just over a mile to the south and west of Colnbrook and not far from Windsor. It is now sandwiched between the reservoirs on the glide path to the west of Heathrow, but would then have been a peaceful hamlet, perhaps most famous for being the village where John Milton (1608–74) lived between 1636 and 1638. Charlotte was 34 years old and Manasseh 40. Very little is known about how they met, but clearly marrying a gentile was a major step in shedding the outward trappings of his Jewish identity (Plate 40). It is often claimed that the couple had one daughter, Esther, who died aged 24 in 1819. In fact they unofficially adopted Esther when her mother, Manasseh's younger sister, died immediately after giving birth to her in February 1795.[36] It is certainly true that the couple brought her up as their daughter just as they acted as surrogate parents to Esther's older brother Ralph, who went on to inherit both the baronetcy conferred on Manasseh in October 1805 and, indeed, his whole estate when he died in 1831.[37]

After Mordecai Lopes' death in 1796, Manesseh Lopes acted swiftly to apply his inheritance to the purchase of the Maristow estate. He agreed to buy it in 1798 after the death of James Modyford Heywood, but the transfer deed itself is dated 13 March 1799. This massive document bears the signatures of Catherine Heywood of Grafton Street, Richard Earl Howe, Sir Abraham Elton of Clevedon Court, Thomas Dunn of Lincolns Inn, John Musters of Colwick Hall, Sophia Musters, Albermarle Bertie of Hazely Hill,[38] Emma Bertie, Lewis Montolieu of Putney, Maria H Montolieu, Frances Hunter, Thomas Orby Hunter of Crowland Abbey, and John Keysall of Temple Bar

36 In some sources, it is asserted correctly that she and Manesseh had no children (e.g. Burke, 1833: 102; *Gentleman's Magazine*, 1833, 153: 379).

37 For whatever reason, Manasseh and Charlotte must have known they would have no children of their own by 1805 when Ralph Franco was named as the inheritor of the title.

38 Near Farnham in Surrey

(PWDRO/3872). The purchaser is given as Manasseh Lopes of Fitzroy Square in the parish of Mary le Bone. The comprehensive indenture lists all the properties contained in the sale. It details everything in the 1704 agreement, with the exception of the Cornish properties sold earlier, and adds some acquired during James Modyford Heywood's lifetime. There is no mention of the Jamaican properties so all these had either been sold or they were separately inherited.

The Maristow estate was first placed upon the market in 1791, five years before the youngest surviving daughter, Fanny, married and left home. It clearly had not sold by the time James Modyford Heywood died in April 1798 and was therefore remarketed. It was described in the sale particulars as a 'Capital Mansion' with five very extensive manors containing 8,300 acres of enclosed lands and a further 10,000 acres of common land with a combined rental value of £5,290 net per annum.[39]

These were Maristow (1,229 acres with a gross value of £970 per annum), Buckland Monichorum (*sic*) (261 acres with a gross value of £535 per annum), Bickleigh (3,833 acres with a gross value of £2,383 per annum), Shaugh Prior (488 acres with a gross value of £490 per annum) and Walkhampton (2,557 acres with a gross value of £1,858 per annum). Landlord costs reduced these gross rents to the net value above. The five manors contained 250 dwellings, almost all let on the customary 'three lives' system.[40] Potential buyers were assured that the mansion house was 'elegantly fitted up, and fit for the immediate reception of a large and genteel family, with all convenient offices, standing in a beautiful lawn of about 40 acres, well wooded on the banks of the River Tavy, commanding the most delightful and agreeable prospects'.

The description of the layout of the house included a drawing room (31 feet by 21), a library (27½ by 19 feet), a hall floored with Portland Stone (28 by 19 feet) and three smaller rooms all with

39 In 'historic standard of living' terms or purchasing power of rental income this is equivalent to approximately £460,000 in 2020 terms (see http://www.measuringworth.com/m/calculators/ukcompare/relativevalue.php).

40 These 'lives' were named at the time the lease was signed so inevitably at a later date some would have one, two or three lives remaining.

fourteen-foot ceilings. The details describe a 'handsome staircase' leading to the first floor with three bed-chambers, each with a dressing room, and seven other bedrooms, above which there were attic rooms for staff. The particulars mention the 'well arranged' offices (kitchen, scullery, laundry, larder, washhouse, brew house and dairy) as well as the stabling for 24 horses and standing for four carriages. The walled gardens were clearly a feature, extending to two acres with a hothouse stocked with 'pine plants and vines' while the estate also included the 'most desirable appendage' of a salmon fishery let with the associated Barton (tenanted farmhouse) but buyers would be comforted to know that 'a proper quantity of fish is reserved for the occupier of the mansion'. Manasseh Lopes took advantage of the final sentence which declared that 'a considerable part of the purchase money may remain at interest on security of the estate'. The deed of sale shows that only £35,000 was paid upfront from the sale of securities (with values of £5,000; £17,000; £5,000; £5,000 and £3,000). The balance of £30,000 was 'secured to be paid' at a later date. It was not until 13 March 1801 that the final tranche of money (£15,750) was handed over with interest, by which time Earl Howe was dead.

This may suggest that Manasseh was still using his wealth to generate a return elsewhere. In addition to the substantial inheritance he received following his father's death two years before, he had also just come into a significant sum from the death of his aunt, Abigail Pereira. Her will was proved on 23 March 1798 or just before James Modyford's death in April of the same year. Written in 1791, it left him her house in Balham plus all her possessions (except for a pair of diamond rings). He also received a cash inheritance of £5,000 and all the 'future issue and increase' of her Jamaican slave Betty, even though she herself had been granted freedom. More important, he also inherited all the residue of her estate after modest legacies so this could have made a major contribution to the purchase price.

As later chapters will confirm, there is no gainsaying the fact that Manasseh Lopes was a remarkable man. Interestingly, his early

Plate 26. Mrs Musters and Child by Sir Joshua Reynolds n.d. (c. 1788)

Plate 27. Mrs C J Fox by Sir Joshua Reynolds, n.d.

Plate 28. Mrs Musters by George Romney 1779-80 (76.2cm x 63.5cm)

Plate 29. Miss Sophia Musters by George Romney (after) c.1780. Oil on canvas (75.2cm x 62.5cm)

Plate 30. Sophia Musters' painted window originally at the east end of the chancel in St John the Baptist Church, Colwick, 1817

Plate 31. John Musters Esq on his grey horse 'Baronet' by Richard Barrett Davis 1845

Plate 32. Memorial to Sophia Catherine Musters by Richard Westmacott, 1819

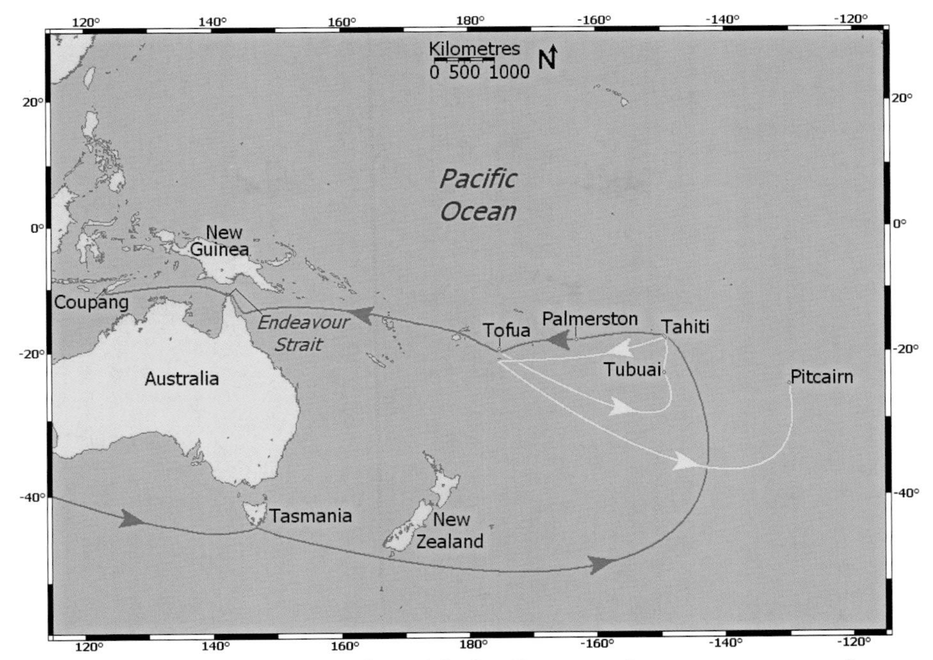

Plate 33. Route of the Bounty (red – original; yellow – mutineers; green- return by Captain Bligh)

Plate 34. William Bligh aged 59 by Alexander Huey (1814)

Plate 35. Captain Peter Heywood 1773-1831 by John Simpson (© Royal Museum, Greenwich)

Plate 36. Maria Henrietta Montolieu by Richard Cosway c. 1787 (Miniature 71mm x 57mm)

Plate 37. Frances ('Fanny') Heywood (Mrs Orby Hunter) (Coloured mezzotint by John Young, 1800)

Plate 38. Peak House, Sidmouth 1826

Plate 39. The 'Money Lenders' by Thomas Rowlandson (London), November 8, 1784. (Public domain)

Plate 40. Manasseh Massey Lopes and Charlotte Lopes (née Yeates) c. 1800 (English School)

Plate 41. 'The Late Elections' by Henry Heath, 1829 published by Thomas McLean (© BM No.15683)

Plate 42. 'The Vision' by Isaac Robert Cruikshank published by Gabriel Shire Tregear, 1829 (© BM No. 15767)

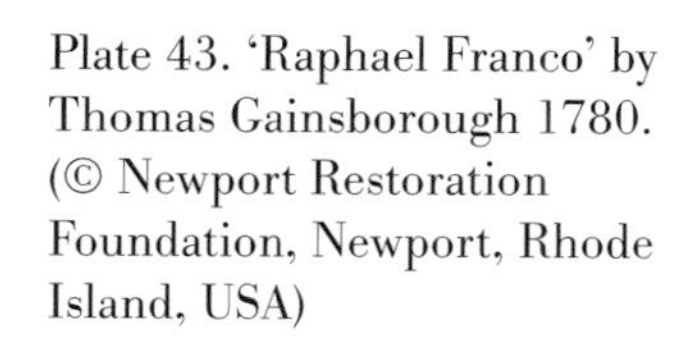

Plate 43. 'Raphael Franco' by Thomas Gainsborough 1780. (© Newport Restoration Foundation, Newport, Rhode Island, USA)

Plate 44. Engraving of the procession of Sir Ralph Lopes following his election in February 1849 (*Illustrated London News*, 17th February 1849)

Plate 45. 'R. Franco – became Lopes' by James Gillray (© Jewish Museum, London)

Plate 46. 'Local Taxation' Sir Massey Lopes by 'Ape' (Carlo Pellegrini), *Vanity Fair*, 1875)

Plate 47. Maristow House (South elevation, c. 1875)

Plate 48. Sir Lopes Massey Lopes, 3rd Bt. c. 1870 by Maull & Polyblank (© NPG Ax8570)

Plate 49. Heywood House, Heywood, Nr Westbury

Plate 50. Lopes Mausoleum, Bratton Road Cemetery, Westbury

Plate 51. Ludlow Mausoleum, Bratton Road Cemetery, Westbury

Plate 52. Rudolph Ackerman 'Maristow House' (Aquatint published in 1828)

Plate 53. Remodelling of Maristow House by George and Yeates, 1907-1909

Plate 54. Sir Henry Lopes (1st Earl Roborough) by Frank Eastman (© Exeter University).

life appears to confirm the proposition that the harsh crucible of plantation Jamaica produced sharper financial sensibilities than had hitherto been found elsewhere, whether in Jewry or not. This is not to say that early nineteenth-century England was an easy terrain. Far from it, as Lopes was shortly to find out. His chosen path most certainly had bumps along the way. The direction he chose to go was not unusual but his reason for gravitating to politics was. Quite unlike the usual motivation for men of wealth cleaving to political elites, it was not for personal aggrandisement.

Chapter 9

Politics and Persecution

With the failure of the Jewish Naturalisation Act in 1754, it was still illegal for Jews to stand for parliament or to participate in English public life in any but charitable roles for all the years that Manasseh Lopes and his father, Mordecai, had lived in London. Indeed, it was not until 1839 that practising Jews could gain citizen rights and thereby enter a national election. It is perhaps indicative of his intentions that Manasseh should court and marry a gentile in 1795 so that by the closing years of the eighteenth century it became clear that if the trappings of status that Maristow represented were to be followed by an ascent into the institutions of civic society, then the religion had to be seen to be abandoned. Picciotto (1875), considering conversions from a Jewish perspective, makes the point that neither Manasseh nor his father had been close followers of the synagogue in these years and argues that 'indifference to form leads to indifference to principle, and convenience points to a change which can do no world harm, and may conduce to a great many material advantages' (1875: 306). While it is true that political advantage may have triggered his departure from the synagogue, it is probable that this was but one strand of causation in a transformation of his identity from financier to landed gentleman.

The first point to note was that he had been married to a gentile for seven years before the apparent break with Judaism occurred. We do not know whether or not this was with the blessing of his father. It is possible that it was not, since his wife's name does not appear in a codicil to his will and neither is she mentioned in the will of Manasseh's aunt Abigail, who lived for three years after the wedding and made generous provision for her nephew. While it is true that the former will was drawn up six months before his son's wedding while the latter will predates it by four years, nonetheless there was plenty of time to add a clause recognising Manasseh's choice of spouse, if either had so wished. On the other hand, he stood to gain richly from both his father's and his aunt's wills, which may argue against the possibility that the marriage was seen at the time as a cultural break. It was true, however, that some economically integrated Jews did appear to show a preference for adherents to the established Church.[1]

A second factor was the shifting composition of London's Jewish population and the wish on the part of some Sephardim to separate themselves from their Eastern European cousins by indicating their greater integration into mainstream culture. This was the age in which the Ashkenazim, hitherto largely comprised of door-to-door salespeople, peddlers and petty traders, suddenly began to compete as money-men and brokers. Nathan Mayer Rothschild, for example, set up a textile trading business in Manchester in 1798 before moving to London and rapidly becoming a highly successful dealer in government securities and foreign bills of exchange. It is also significant that other notable Sephardim followed in Manasseh Lopes' footsteps. Among the most interesting was the political economist David Ricardo, who at the age of 21 in 1793 had eloped with Priscilla Anne Wilkinson and went on to be baptised in the Church of England. In some ways Ricardo, although considerably younger than Manasseh Lopes, followed closely the same career trajectory. In addition to his economic theories of trade, he made a substantial fortune in the City of London, became an MP and went on to become a country squire of some significance.[2]

There is no doubt, however, that these factors aside, the most powerful motivation for conversion was to avoid, or attempt to avoid,

1 Picciotto waxes lyrical on this point: 'Many a Samson became an easy prey to many a Delilah. The golden tresses, the sapphire eyes, the soft voices of the fair daughters of Albion did more to draw followers from the Synagogue to the Church than is usually imagined' (1875: 200).

2 Although disinherited and estranged from his family, Ricardo bought Gatcombe Park in Gloucestershire in 1814 and subsequently died there in 1823 at the age of 51.

the systematic discrimination against Jews that had gradually risen in intensity throughout the second half of the eighteenth century. As Picciotto put it:

> A university education was as unattainable as if they had been Hottentots; the army would disdain to admit Israelites within its ranks; the bar carefully excluded them; and a father could not even with safety settle upon his children landed estates. The only liberal profession they were permitted to follow was that of medicine. When a proficiency in that art had been acquired at great disadvantage, the usual difficulty stared the Jewish physician in the face. The hospitals would not open their wards to him; Christian patients would not consult him; public offices were out of the question; and Jewish young men were driven to tender their services gratuitously, or at a paltry pittance, to the authorities of their own community, merely to practice (*sic*) their profession (1875: 198).

Although focused primarily on migration from across the Channel, the passing into law of Lord Granville's Alien Bill of 1792 added to the uncertainty of Jews in England by making it unclear whether they would be allowed to remain, or at the very least whether they would be permitted to move freely around the country, since clauses in the Act gave new powers to the king and his government to control the movements of foreign nationals.

It seems quite obvious, however, that the prospect of buying his way into the House of Commons was the immediate consideration that gave rise to Manasseh's decision to become baptised into the Anglican faith.[3] He said as much in a letter dated 11 July 1802 to the *Mahamad* of the Bevis Marks synagogue in London's East End:

> A recent circumstance in regard to my future situation, which will very soon appear, makes it incompatible to my

3 Manasseh Lopes was baptised into the Church of England on 30 June 1802 at St Pancras Old Church, Camden.

> remaining any longer a *yahid* or member of the congregation, and I have desired my friend, Mr. Moses Lindo, junr., to apprise you of my intention and to pay my account with the Synagogue.

The letter concludes with an expression of good wishes for the welfare of his late brethren and indicates that he had instructed Lindo to present the Synagogue on his behalf with £150 for the *zedaka* or charitable fund (Picciotto, 1875: 304–5).[4] The 'recent circumstance' to which the letter alludes was his election two days before to the parliamentary seat of New Romney on the Kent coast. This borough had a charter of incorporation from Edward III as one of the eight Cinque Ports. It was supposed to have voters consisting of a mayor, 12 jurats (i.e. magistrates, members of a permanent jury or other legal officials), 26 common-councilmen and an indefinite number of freemen, but as they fell away and were not replaced 'eight are deemed sufficient to exercise the same constitutional powers...' (Oldfield, 1792: 69). The borough was controlled by Sir Edward Dering (6th Bart), who used a simple method of securing support:

> His property in the neighbourhood is tenanted out, *without lease*, at *very easy* rents, to the electors; who, feeling that gratitude, which never fails to inspire those immediately interested in the present possession of a good thing, could not be so ungenerous as to oppose the inclination of a passive landlord, in so *trifling* a concern as that of the election of a member of parliament (Oldfield, 1792: 69; emphasis in original).

This did not mean that he necessarily returned himself in one of the two seats that were available. In the mid-1790s, Dering is reported to have received financial offers to return Whig candidates

4 Picciotto wrongly asserts that this letter came from Mordecai Rodrigues Lopes on behalf of himself and his son. Mordecai Lopes had been dead for six years when the letter was written. There is no evidence that Mordecai ever lost his religion.

at the time of the Regency Crisis, but had preferred instead those recommended by the Tory prime minister, William Pitt, for which he had received from the Treasury payment of £11,000.[5] His son, also Edward, controlled the borough from 1798 to 1811 and, given that Manasseh Lopes was at that time politically and culturally an outsider, it has to be assumed that he paid Dering for the seat which he held from 9 July 1802 until 4 November 1806.

It is important, therefore, to be aware that parliamentary seats prior to the Great Reform Act of 1832, were more concerned with influence than representation. This instrumental approach to politics was endemic to the system. Moreover, it was supported by government ministers themselves and had been common practice for many years. This is not to say that it was never opposed. William Maddocks, for example, who entered parliament for Boston in Lincolnshire at the same time as Manasseh Lopes, became well known for putting down motions against this form of corruption. In one such, in May 1809, he argued that Hastings, Rye, Cambridge, Queenborough, Westbury, New Romney and Cashel were well known to be corrupt boroughs (HP, HC 1790–1820).[6] Lopes may well have heard of this tirade for the following year he bought the borough of Westbury, so cementing an unlikely family association with Wiltshire that was to last well beyond his lifetime.[7] One thing is for sure and that is that the views of the electors would have been irrelevant in the case of New Romney where the *History of Parliament* comments, 'it is difficult to determine whether the seats were disposed of by private sale or by negotiation with the Treasury'. In the latter case the person who controlled the

5 In excess of £1 million in 2020 terms.

6 The *History of Parliament* records a private observation by Lord Grey at the time on the attacks by Maddox on the 'Treasury boroughs' in which he said 'These are no more than have been practised for the last hundred years, I believe, by every Treasury, nor would they have been brought forward in other times or by men of liberal spirit. But now a new code of political morality and honour has been adopted and everything seems to be greedily taken up that can tend to throw discredit on the general system of government.'

7 It is claimed that Sir Manasseh paid the enormous sum of £75,000 to Lord Abingdon's trustees for the patronage of Westbury.

borough would benefit from public funds; in the former, he would benefit from the private wealth of the person to whom the seat was sold. There is no evidence that Lopes ever visited the marshlands of Kent.

The most likely scenario is that Manasseh Lopes pledged his support for the Tory administration of Henry Addington after having paid Dering for one of the two seats returned from New Romney. Addington, whose family home was at Up-Ottery, five miles north-east of Honiton, was later made Viscount Sidmouth, and it is tempting to suppose that Lopes was aware of this Devon connection. Speculation of this kind is further enhanced by the choice of New Romney as his seat, for William Pitt, prime minister for the whole of the period from 1783 to 1801, had retreated to Walmer Castle in Kent after resigning following a disagreement with George III over the issue of Catholic Emancipation. Once there he could exercise his enthusiasm of defender of the realm against French ambitions in his role as Lord Warden of the Cinque Ports, including New Romney. Indeed, Pitt, whose family had deep roots in Kent, was active at precisely this time in promoting the defence of Romney Marsh against it being used as a bridgehead in the event of a French invasion.[8] These were days in which the French threat was ever present and Pitt employed his remarkable energies and administrative talents while out of office in organising a volunteer force, becoming colonel of the Royal Trinity House Volunteer Artillery and Cinque Ports Volunteer Corps. Lopes followed suit in becoming lieutenant-colonel of the Roborough Volunteers at precisely this time.

Conscious that his place in parliament would only last a little longer, and aware that Pitt had returned as prime minister in May 1804, Lopes had been searching for an alternative to New Romney. It appears that Plymouth, a local borough with a freeman franchise of only about 200, caught his eye. In July 1805, he made a further move

8 For example, the Royal Military Canal, on which work commenced in 1804, ran for 28 miles and followed the old cliff line abutting Romney Marsh and was completed with the enthusiastic support of William Pitt.

to distance himself from his Jewish past by successfully requesting from the king permission to add the name 'Massey' before 'Lopes' (with an 's' in place of the 'z'), a name which was to be passed on through later generations.

In the same month he lobbied Pitt to provide his 'friendly assistance to promote my success' in contesting Plymouth at the next election. He reminded the prime minister of his 'attachment and regard to your interest', which was presumably a reference to the support he had offered when representing New Romney, and confessed that this ambition made him 'more anxious of retaining a seat in Parliament' (PRO 30/8/153, f. 65, quoted in Thorne, 1986). The fact that he also reminded Pitt in the same letter of an earlier promise to reward his support with a title might suggest a more disingenuous purpose. In any event, Pitt, struggling to revive his former political supremacy, duly obliged and Lopes was rewarded with a baronetcy on 1 November of the same year.[9] Interestingly, knowing for whatever reason that he would not have a son of his own, the honour was bestowed with the remainder, or line of succession, transferring to his orphaned nephew, Ralph Franco, then a pupil at Winchester College coming to the end of his formal schooling before transferring to Brasenose College, Oxford.[10] Even as early as this, before Lopes became infamous for 'borough mongering', there were those close to Pitt who regarded him as an outsider. Lord Ellenborough, then a Cabinet member, in writing to the newly elevated Lord Sidmouth (Henry Addington) commented that the 'game of late seems to have been to pick up stragglers, and the new batch of baronets seems to have caught one at least in the

9 The relative weight attaching to the promise of political support versus the debt obligation owed by the Prince of Wales is difficult to determine.

10 Raphael Franco, baptised in 1802 as 'Ralph', was the son of Manasseh Lopes' younger sister, Esther, who died immediately after the birth of a daughter in 1795. His father was Abraham de Raphael Franco, a coral merchant who remarried after the loss of his first wife but died in Lucknow, India, in 1798. Both Raphael and his sister were raised by Manasseh Lopes and his wife Charlotte as their own children, which is presumably the reason for the choice of Ralph as their heir as, even if they had produced a male offspring, he would have been younger than Ralph Franco.

person of Sir Manasseh Lopes' (Sidmouth MSS, 23 October 1805). There seems little doubt that the inference here was that Lopes was struggling to catch up with his non-semitic peers. The awareness of a supposed Jewish phenotype was never far beneath the surface. For example, Sir William Elford, MP for Plymouth and Lopes' neighbour at Bickham, thought him 'good natured and civil' but described young Franco to the diarist Joseph Farington as looking 'the very essence of Judaism distilled from a thousand Jews', while Farington on a visit with Elford to Maristow felt that Esther Franco, living at the house as the baronet's daughter, had a 'Jew look' (Farington Diaries 5, 1801–3: 292). As with all racial stereotypes, this caricature did not depend only upon the outward trappings of religion or cultural preference. As Todd Edelman (2015: 314) points out, the *Annual Register* of 1806, noting the baronetcy of Sir Manasseh Lopes and his standing as the first person of Jewish descent to sit in the House of Commons, referred to him as 'a Jew Baronet'.

With the complex struggles at Plymouth turning out to be beyond him, Lopes' next foray after New Romney into the shark-filled waters of English parliamentary democracy was at Evesham. The constituency for most of the previous century had been the bailiwick of two Whig families: the Rushouts of Northwick Park and the Rudges, who owned the manor and whose interest went back to the last quarter of the seventeenth century. It was a borough where by 1800 approximately 700 freemen comprised the voters but despite these family interests there was no overwhelming elite, particularly on the Tory side, which made the two seats more appealing for outside wealthy participation.[11] Unlike New Romney,

11 During this period, there were 245 English constituencies (40 counties, 203 boroughs and the two universities of Oxford and Cambridge) returning 489 members. The franchise for counties was based on freeholders with a minimum land tax value of 40 shillings per annum, an electorate that amounted to approximately 190,000. The vast majority of the boroughs returned two members but the franchise varied significantly between them. In a few (13), voters were simply male householders (unless they received alms or were classified as paupers) but the number of these could be tiny. A large proportion of the boroughs (45 per cent) adhered to a 'freeman' franchise, although some allowed these men to be non-resident while others did not. The third category, comprising a further 18 per cent, were those where the franchise was 'scot and

Evesham was not a borough with ties to political leaders on the national stage and it is at first puzzling to understand why it should have attracted Manasseh Lopes. The answer probably lay in the close friendship that existed between Manasseh's father, Mordecai, and Moses Levi, his executor, fellow financier and leading figure in the fortunes of Bevis Marks. Levi had an illegitimate son, christened Thomas Thompson born in 1767, whose first class education and upbringing paid for by his father led him to enter the fray on the Whig side for this constituency in 1790. After winning the seat he successfully defended it in 1796, but after a relatively short political career, in which he steadfastly supported liberal causes, particularly parliamentary reform, Thompson left the country for Southern France, possibly because of gaming debts but ostensibly for health reasons, and did not return to contest the 1802 general election. He was detained by Napoleon Bonaparte's administration at Orléans in 1803 and did not return to England until 1815. Lopes meanwhile had maintained a close friendship with this young fellow *Converso* as is evident when upon Thompson's return he wrote recommending him to the home secretary:

> I trust your lordship will pardon my zeal to serve a particular friend for whom I feel most warmly interested, Mr. Thomas Thompson, lately returned from France after having been

lot' (householders paying rates to the borough); these returned 73 members during the period 1790–1820. The next were corporation boroughs (those with municipal bodies granted some degree of self-government) of which there were 25 returning 49 members to the House during this period. A further 30 boroughs were classified as possessing a 'burgage' franchise where the right to vote rested in the tenancy of a property previously designated as one with this right. These were easy prey for wealthy patrons who could simply buy up the freeholds of the properties concerned. This was also true of the final category, the 'freeholder' boroughs of which there were only seven, simply because the freeholds could form part of a wealthy patron's property portfolio. Further complexity was added by the fact that some boroughs adopted combinations of these systems and some changed from one to another. Moreover, with no *national* system of elections, some boroughs and counties undertook very infrequent elections while in others they were much more common. In all, however, money and status counted for much and local landed interests played a highly significant role in determining the profile of parliament.

> detained by Bonaparte (*sic*) during the whole of the last war. His conduct to his countrymen who passed as prisoners from Spain thro' Orléans (where he resided) is the subject of general admiration ... his knowledge of the language, character and intrigues of that nation fully qualifies him for the office of superintendent of aliens ... [he is] a perfect man of business ... it was with the passport of Mr. Thompson that Col. Jenkinson was enabled to quit Paris with dispatches (announcing Bonaparte's arrival) when orders were given to refuse leave to all attached to the Embassy.

Whether these representations were successful is unknown but unlikely since Thompson died in July 1818. Lopes, however, would surely have been aware that outside moneyed interests could be effectively deployed in this borough.

As things turned out his involvement was anything but trouble-free. After Thompson's departure, the vacant seat had been fought over in 1802 by Patrick Crawford Bruce, an East India merchant in London and a partner in the bank Vere, Bruce & Co., and Humphry Howarth, an ambitious fellow Whig. Howarth, who was descended from a Herefordshire family and had formerly practised as a physician in India, had unsuccessfully contested the same seat in 1796.[12] Bruce, a Tory, had garnered the support of both the aristocracy and local gentry and easily took the seat, but the disgruntled Howarth immediately petitioned parliament alleging bribery and intimidation on the grounds that 64 freeholders had been admitted to vote in what was a freeman borough. This petition was dismissed but Howarth was returned unopposed in 1806 after convincing Patrick Bruce to withdraw, presumably for a financial consideration. Unhappily for him, however, another election was called on 13 May 1807, not long after Manasseh Lopes' seat at New Romney had expired. Lopes is reported to have spent £10,000 at Evesham, which was enough to see him returned, but only with a narrow lead over Howarth (334

12 His surname is sometimes spelt 'Howorth' on the grounds that he may have been the illegitimate son of Robert Howorth, Sword-bearer to the Corporation of Worcester.

to 320 votes). The latter promptly petitioned again on the same grounds as before but adding the charge of bribery and treating by Lopes, as well as the wrongful admission of freeholders to the vote.[13] The controversial freeholder issue was not something that Lopes could have arranged but it was on these grounds and not for bribery or treating that he was unseated on 22 February 1808.[14] Unseating members on petition 'remained a regular recourse of Evesham's defeated candidates until it lost its remaining Member in 1885', but despite this Howarth went on to hold the seat for many more years.[15]

The following year attention again turned to Lopes' negotiations with the borough of Plymouth but these once more came to nought and the next chapter in Sir Manasseh's political saga drew him into the world of patronage after the deal he stuck with the Earl of Abingdon in 1810 for the borough of Westbury in Wiltshire. In an era before political parties had much of a presence locally, the role of patrons, usually the heads of wealthy local families, was often very significant in determining who could stand or sometimes indeed when elections would be fought. In the period 1790–1820, half of the English boroughs returned members sponsored by a patron and in the vast majority of the remainder they played some part, perhaps controlling one of the two members returned. Most patrons would have expected, and many would have received, some form of preferment (e.g. a baronetcy or a peerage) for their support of those in power, and this must be regarded as a major reason for their political engagement, but others may have been simply content with reflected social glory. Whatever objectives patrons had in mind, once achieved one or both borough seats could be sold to the highest bidder provided that he was prepared to toe the political line of the patron, which was most frequently to support the 'ministerial interest' (i.e. the government of

13 On this occasion, it was claimed that 122 freeholders had been allowed to vote out of a total electorate of 695.

14 See *A Report of the Proceedings before a Committee of the House of Commons on the Petition of H. Howarth, Esq. against Sir Manasseh M. Lopes, Bart. unduly returned by the Borough of Evesham at the General Election, 1807* by Edward Rudge Esq. FRS.

15 www.historyofparliamentonline.org/research/constituencies

the day). In this sense, therefore, they could be a form of investment, but the most tangible reward in the majority of cases was that of social elevation. As Edwin Jaggard, writing about Cornish political life in this period, argues, the rewards could be far greater than a mere seat in the House of Lords or Commons: 'The ownership of boroughs could lead to a baronetcy or a peerage if the patron could deliver his members' votes on critical issues to the government of the day, or if he permitted the government to return known supporters in his seats' (Jaggard, 1999: 22).

It has often been claimed that Lopes paid £75,000 or slightly more to Lord Abingdon to become the patron of Westbury, but this was an extraordinary amount of money and substantially more than he paid for the Maristow estate only a dozen years before.[16] On the other hand, this price was not totally out of line with prices realised elsewhere. The local patronage of Callington fetched £30,000 in 1824 when sold to the banker Alexander Baring. and very wealthy patrons hardly in need of more titles sometimes paid equivalent figures, as when the Duke of Grosvenor paid £70,000 and £81,000 respectively for Shaftesbury and Stockbridge.

If indeed Lopes did pay this sum, then the obvious question to ask is where the money came from? The most probable answer is that he benefited financially from supporting the massive build-up of contractors supplying the military forces engaged in the Peninsular War. The struggle with the French under Bonaparte had reached crisis point in 1808–9 when Lt.-General Arthur Wellesley, later the Duke of Wellington, was successfully struggling against the French to secure Portugal and use this as a springboard to advance into occupied Spain. All of this depended on complex supply chains that supported both the British Army in Portugal but also the reformulated and retrained Portuguese Army with which in April 1809 it was formally united. In 1810, 234 ships were operating between Britain

16 Add. 38255, f. 362; *Farington*, v. 292; NMM, WYN/107, Pole Carew to Pole, 20 November 1809, 24 Sept. 1810; R Harris and RC Hoare, *Wilts*. Westbury, 6. Lord Abingdon, who was a member of the Bertie family, was both eccentric and impecunious; the later on account of frequently placing bets on insufficiently fast horses.

and Portugal, 86 along the Spanish coast, 120 to Gibraltar and the Mediterranean (McLauchlan, 1997: 40). Many of these vessels left from Plymouth. For example in May 1810, the Treasury was asked to supply 90 days of provisions for 12,000 men and 1,000 horses together with another 30 days of reserve supplies in order to establish a new base at Cadiz. By 20 June five large merchant ships were loaded at Plymouth ready to depart, escorted by the Royal Navy (Hall, 1992: 33). The shipments were the responsibility of the Victualling Board, which had one of its three main offices in the Royal William Yard in Devonport. The Board was responsible for issuing contracts for the necessary supplies and for coordinating extensive networks of suppliers. These would in turn have required a steady availability of appropriate finance, particularly because the Board's requirements were stringent, not just in terms of quality but also in packaging to ensure that fresh food could survive the rigours of long sea passages. Christine Haynes, summarising a recent book on the impact of the Napoleonic Wars on those left behind, puts it well when she writes that the support network at this time included a large number of other actors including army contractors, 'who provided massive quantities of tents, knapsacks, canteens, uniforms, shoes, muskets, gunpowder, ships, maps, fortifications, meat, and biscuit; bankers and speculators, who funded the supplies as well as subsidies to Britain's allies' (2016: 544; cf. Uglow, 2015).

Manasseh Lopes, despite now appearing as a country gentleman, was essentially a financier and with his role in the local voluntary militia, his knowledge of the naval personnel in Plymouth and his proximity to Devonport (7.5 miles), it is inconceivable that he would not have been moved to help in this astonishing effort, as well as to recoup handsome profits for himself.[17] It is possible too that as a Sephardi *Converso*, the fact that the British were allied with Portugal, and were seeking also to free Spain from French incursions,

17 Although archive sources relating to naval contractors exist, they do not reveal how the massive outlays were financed. That evidence, if it ever existed, would lie in in family archives. It has been suggested that after Manasseh Lopes' death in 1831, his heir, Ralph Franco, destroyed many of his uncle's financial records. I am grateful to the Hon George Lopes for this information.

might have provided a further incentive for involvement (cf. Pereira, 1996). Commentators later in the century certainly believed that these opportunities were fully exploited by the then owner of Maristow House. For example, in 1891 the London correspondent of the *Nottingham Evening Post* writing on the contemporary family says of Sir Manasseh that he 'made a colossal fortune as an army contractor in Plymouth during the Peninsular War' (7 September 1891).

A more direct way of funding the war effort, and one which was arguably less risky, would have been to buy government debt and this he may have done in addition to supporting contractors. This was a period when public debt was rapidly increasing; by 1819–20, it had reached the unprecedented level of 2.6 times national income. Although in 1799 income tax had been introduced and doubled to 2s in the pound seven years later, much of this debt was 'funded' or transferable, non-redeemable long-term debt known as 'consols' (consolidated annuities) that were issued during this period at 3 per cent. This debt also doubled in size, increasing from just over £27 per capita in 1792 to £50 per capita in 1817.[18] The rate of return on consols, or on East India Company six-month bonds, which were not subject to usury law controls, was higher when demand was greatest. In other words, anyone lending to the government during the first decade of the nineteenth century stood to gain considerably more when compared with earlier decades, provided they were sophisticated in selecting appropriate vehicles for their investments, as was certainly true of Manasseh Lopes. In addition to government stock, Lopes was also a significant holder of investments in the East India Company. The system there, after the last change of the law in 1773, was that those with investments in India stock of £10,000 or above were entitled to four votes in General Court of Proprietors, who in turn elected the Court of Directors. Lopes was later to write that he felt great pride in his 'four stars in the India house' (East

18 There are those who have argued that such was the burden of the war effort that this impacted on investment and therefore growth in manufacturing and transport infrastructure (Williamson, 1987).

India House in Leadenhall Street was the London headquarters of the East India Company). At this time, the company was paying a dividend of 10.5 per cent.

It was also a period when speculators could accrue very significant returns. When reports of the war effort were positive, investors concluded that new bond issues would decline in favour of using reserves to buy in old debt. This meant that rates would fall and their traded value would rise. When the battles were lost, traders anticipated the reverse process; that is, the issuance of new debt at higher interest with subsequent falls in prices. Manasseh Lopes was well placed to take advantage of these fluctuations because of his technical sophistication and closeness to the port of Plymouth where tens of thousands of soldiers embarked and disembarked, along with a similar number of prisoners of war. The local indications as to how the war effort was going would have been unambiguous.

It is perhaps also relevant to observe that Jewish financiers were critical to sustaining the war effort. The name of Nathan Mayer Rothschild is often cited in this regard, but in the first decade of the century the real running was made by the Goldsmid brothers, Benjamin and Abraham. As Paul Emden says of them, along with the Barings they were '*the* loan contractors of their day' and critical to government strategy in paying for the war effort (Emden, 1935–39: 228). Although the Goldsmid family came originally from the border area of Germany, France and Flanders, they were joined in a number of enterprises by Abraham Mocatta and Emanuel B. Lousada, whom Lopes would have identified as Sephardi extended kin, the latter marrying Abraham Goldsmid's eldest daughter. Moreover, when well established, Abraham Goldsmid bought Morden Hall in South London from Isaac Mendes Pereira, to whom Lopes was also related. In 1809, the Goldsmid brothers advanced the astonishing sum of £14,600,000 in government debt that greatly assisted Lt.-General Arthur Wellesley in his first major victory in Spain at Talavera against the forces of the Spanish king, Joseph Bonaparte, at the end of July that year.[19] As Emden writes, this was 'from every point of view a marvelous achievement and by no means an unprofitable one, as in those far off days competition had not yet ruined conditions, and bankers charged a commission which amounted to as much per cent then as to-day per thousand' (Emden, 1935–9: 241).The period just before 1810 was one in which the return on consols significantly outweighed that on houses or land.

Possibly the most historically astute member of the Lopes family in the recent past also makes a very similar point. The solicitor David Nicolson, grandson on his mother's side of Sir Henry Lopes, includes in a letter to his cousin, Hon George Lopes, brother of the 3rd Earl, the view that the absence of an international banking system together with the fear of social disorder arising from the revolutionary age that was so evident within living memory in France and whose murmurings were clearly evident across the Channel, made covert financing of serious public debt far more attractive than it might otherwise have been. In other words, in the absence of arbitrage systems the close trading and family links of international Jewry were the next best thing. Interestingly, he cites the Lopes family motto (*Quod tibi Id alii*/do to another what thou wouldst have done to thee) as suggestive of the importance of moving money based on bonds of loyalty rather than legality (Nicolson to Lopes, 21 December 1998).

Before the Great Reform Act of 1832, Westbury was a burgage borough in which the right to vote lay with the owner-occupiers of freehold properties. There were 29 burgage boroughs in the land and in Westbury's case there were 61 properties to which the right to vote lay with the owner-occupiers. In theory, this would have given Lopes very little control except for the fact that the vast majority of the properties had been bought by Lord Abingdon and these passed to Massey Lopes after the settlement. As it turned out many of the houses were in a poor state and Lopes had to rebuild them, thereby guaranteeing the loyalty of his tenants. The alternative was to let

19 Joseph Bonaparte was imposed on Spain as monarch in 1808 by Napoleon, his younger brother.

them fall into such a ruinous state that no one would live there, thereby reducing the number of electors. He also made himself recorder of the borough, despite his lack of legal qualifications, which in effect guaranteed that he determined who the parliamentary representatives would be. The ownership problem was overcome by the legal manoeuvre at election time of making the existing tenants freeholders for an hour during which they were expected to cast their vote along the lines that the patron expected. Certainty was seldom guaranteed, however, not least because Westbury was well known as a borough that welcomed 'paying guests'. Sir Manasseh might have received £10,000 for each of the two seats since he chose not to sit himself at the election in October 1812. His two successful candidates, however, were men with political sentiments close to his own; Benjamin Shaw, a merchant and insurance director who held the seat until June 1818, and Benjamin Hall, a wealthy lawyer and industrialist, who also loyally supported the Tory administration of Lord Liverpool until the election of December 1814, when the second seat passed to Sir Manasseh's 26-year-old heir, Ralph Franco who, presumably not paying for the privilege, turned out to be less politically reliable.

During these years, Manasseh Lopes had not been idle in extending the Maristow estate and appeared to have ample resources to do so. He acquired the manor of Meavy from Hugh Malet in 1808 and, as the contemporary social commentator Cyrus Redding put it, 'he purchased land all round Maristow, his seat, as fast as he could obtain it, in order to extend his domains.' By 1820 he claimed to own 'about 32,000 acres belonging to me altogether in a ring fence', including common land (Redding, 1858, v: 159). He also invested heavily in East India Company stock to a level that entitled him to four votes in the elections for the directorate and this was also a period of major refurbishment for the house itself. For example, he retained the services of the architect Richard Brown known as the 'professor of perspective' around 1806–7 to design the redecoration of the mansion and commissioned cabinet makers of the highest quality to construct appropriate furniture often in the French manner incorporating 'Egyptian revival' designs issued by George Smith, 'upholder extraordinary' to George, Prince of Wales (1805).[20]

Writing about the time he began editing the *Plymouth Chronicle* as a 23-year-old (1808), Redding's gossipy memoirs provide an interesting insight into Lopes' character. Aside from the frequent references to his Semitic origins, Redding subscribes to stories that illustrated his money lending past and lack of a classical education, but also his community-oriented spirit.[21] One story relates to Lopes paying a substantial sum to help an uninsured shopkeeper rebuild his fire-damaged property and another tells how he went to extraordinary lengths to fulfil an obligation to cast his votes in favour of a director of the East India Company whom he did not know, but whose parlous financial situation had been relayed to him (1858, v: 159–62). These stories abound and almost always contain three elements. First, Lopes, who was described in an official Jewish history as a 'leading banker', is seen as someone with a generous spirit, particularly where someone of humble origins has fallen on hard times due to no fault of their own.[22] But, second, Jewish stereotypes always reappear, particularly in relation to how Lopes spoke, even though he spent the first 40 years of his life in Jamaica which, whilst cosmopolitan, would have used Hebrew only for religious services. The third feature, also a stereotype, is that financial instincts were so ingrained that they would be employed even when they made little sense. The best example, although it appears in a different guise elsewhere, is where the baronet was visiting the house of one of his tenant farmers who had fallen behind on his rent. The man of the house was away from home and the conversation addressed to his wife is supposed to have run as follows:

20 Fine Regency furniture from the refurbishment of Maristow House during this period occasionally comes to market. Examples would include a pair of ebonised mahogany caned library Bergere chairs, one sold by Sotheby's in June 2002 for £31,070 and another by Christies in May 2015 for £17,925.

21 For example, referring to him as 'little Sir M.M. Lopez (with) his Hebrew face' (Redding, 1858, v: 120).

22 See, for example, Jewish Virtual Library, 'Ancient Jewish History: Banking and Bankers' (www.jewishvirtuallibrary.org/banking-and-bankers.)

> 'Vat is de reason dat your husband does not pay me de rent?' 'Why, sir,' replied the woman 'the times are so hard that we can't get the money to pay it. Things fetch nothing and God knows what will become of us. I am afraid Thomas must go to gaol for he's behind with another or two besides you sir.' 'Ah dat is bad, dat is bad' said Sir Manasseh 'people should not get into debt? Vy do you get into debt? I thought you were industrious.' 'And so we are sir' answered the woman 'but we have both been very ill and we have now three children bad in bed with the typhus fever' and bursting into tears she led him into the room where the children were lying. 'Vell vell' he exclaimed 'do not cry do not cry. It is bad, it is bad I am sorry and I will do something for you. Let me see you can raise four or five shillings to buy one stamp?' (The stamp was procured). 'Ah dat will do.' Here is one bill for you at two months for sixty pounds on de bank. I will give it you – I will make you a present of it. 'But stop; you want de moneys – I will discount it and only charge you four per cent interest! There dat will pay your debts. Good morning: pay my rent in future and don't let de young ones have de fever again'[23] [*The Spirit of the Times* (1825) 1 (8): 127].

The 'bill' referred to is a bill of exchange, similar to a transferable cheque, which promises payment for a designated amount at a set date. The point of the story is that Lopes is so used to making money from taking over such bills for a price that he discounts it even when it is intended as a gift.[24]

With the money lost at Evesham and the enormous sum expended at Westbury, it is perhaps surprising that Lopes' quest for political influence appeared undiminished. Acting on an invitation in late 1811, Lopes stood in a byelection in Barnstable on 16 January 1812

23 This publication, which had a rather short life, abstracted 'all that is worthy of being preserved from the whole of our periodical literature, newspapers, magazines, relating to sciences, arts, public affairs, amusements etc.'.

24 The caricature of how Lopes spoke is more suggestive of Yiddish than Hebrew but the former is a Germanic language spoken by Ashkenazi Jews and it is hard to believe this is other than an ethnic stereotype.

caused by the sudden death of George Thellusson, a Pittite Tory with a reputation for underhand electoral practices.[25] Lopes spent quite heavily but had very little time to appeal to the 400 voters of the borough and he lost to the Whig candidate William Busk by 168 votes to 191. Later that year, however, on 8 October, he was returned in a three-way contest in the general election, topping the poll with 296 votes along with Sir Eyre Coote, a former Governor of Jamaica, with 218.[26] William Busk came a poor third but immediately complained against Coote on the grounds of 'the most open bribery'.

Nothing illustrates the tension between the quest for political influence and the costs created by being subject to discriminatory exclusion better than the saga generated by Sir Manasseh's entanglement with the electors of Grampound, a tiny borough on the Truro road into Cornwall. The context in which this arose is important. As the struggle for power between the monarch and the House of Commons became more salient in the sixteenth century and through to the Civil War, it became more important for the former to contain the ambitions of the latter, and what better way to do so than to fill the house with members whose position depended on being the 'King's men'? This happened throughout the land but nowhere more so than in the far-flung boroughs of Cornwall, a county itself whose lands were largely owned or controlled by the crown. Thus it was that Cornwall in the early years of the nineteenth century sent 44 members to the Commons, often sustained by only a handful of electors.[27]

---

25 Thellusson had successfully contested Southwark but been unseated on a petition alleging 'treating' or buying votes through illegally rewarding voters with presents, money or favours.

26 Coote, who was an army officer of Irish descent, was immensely rich and heir to his famous uncle of the same name but greater military glory. He was regarded as 'eccentric' for his penchant for paying to enjoy the flogging of public school boys (*History of Parliament online*, entry Sir Eyre Coote, 1759–1823).

27 For example in the late eighteenth century, Bossiney a tiny hamlet on the road to Tintagel in north Cornwall sent two members to Westminster while for a time having only one person qualified to vote, a feat that was matched by Helston in the south (Courtney, 1889: 183–205). During this period and right up to the Great Reform Act of 1832, Cornwall sent approximately the same number of MPs to Westminster as Durham, Northumberland and Yorkshire combined.

Grampound possessed a population in 1801 of 525 souls but only 60 of these were adult males possessing properties on which they paid 'scot and lot' and were therefore entitled to vote.[28] For the second half of the eighteenth century, the borough's patron had been Edward Eliot from St Germans, who used his position to sell seats to friends of the Conservative government. By the 1790s, Eliot's star had waned and his liberal-minded son, James Edward Eliot, had met with opposition as support rose for a new local patron, Sir Christopher Hawkins of the local estate at Trewithen. Hawkins himself sat as one member for the borough from 1800 to 1807, eventually falling foul of corruption allegations as rival interests vied to offer electors a greater return for their votes. Although deeply involved in subsequent plotting, Hawkins' role as patron was now progressively undermined and in November 1815 the local mayor, Alderman William Hoare, was sent to London to find a new patron who would be prepared to put up £8,000 to guarantee success.[29] The only one of a number of likely candidates seen by Hoare who showed any interest was Sir Manasseh, who in February of the following year sent down his agent George Hunt to negotiate a reduced 'loan' of £35 for each elector to support Lopes' nominees at the next election. It seems unlikely that Lopes intended to seat himself at Grampound, since he was already returned for Barnstable and the £2,000 in total that he offered appears only to have been designed to gain influence since an election was not due and Hunt was instructed to make clear to the electors that they were free to switch their allegiance to anyone offering more as the next election drew closer.

A critical person in what subsequently transpired was John Teed, a Plymouth merchant and ship agent who had been returned on

28 'Scot' is a corruption of *sceat*, an Anglo-Saxon unit of currency, while 'lot' refers to a portion or part, as in *allotment*. The phrase is therefore used to refer to those who paid a local property tax. Others would have got off 'scot-free'.

29 Hawkins was very active in developing and expanding the lands of Trewithen and it was said he 'could ride from one side of Cornwall to the other without setting hoof on another man's soil'. He is also credited with agricultural innovation and in opening new tin and copper mines and in supporting the clay mining industry of St Austell.

Hawkins' interest at Grampound in March 1808 only to be unseated on petition, but who on 9 October 1812 was again returned, this time with the support of another faction. Teed was always on the lookout for new interests in the borough, particularly if they could assist him in any way in securing lucrative Admiralty contracts. He was apprised of Lopes' involvement by one of the beneficiaries of his largesse, one Isaac Watts, and approached the baronet with a coalition in mind. Lopes turned him down opting instead for Benjamin Shaw, a London merchant whom he had entertained, probably as a paying guest, at Westbury in the 1812 election. As it turned out, in the election of June 1818 both Teed and Shaw tied in a poor third place to John Innes and Alexander Robertson, two wealthy Scots who reputedly paid £7,000 to representatives of the avaricious electors, including the duplicitous Isaac Watts.

In the normal course of events that would have been the end of the matter, except that clearly machinations at Grampound had got out of hand.[30] Although Teed and Shaw only managed 11 votes each as against more than three times that number for the two winners, Teed clearly believed that Lopes' arrangement would count for more because as soon as the first elector on the latter's list presented himself before the mayor, Teed's agent spoke up revealing to the returning officer the two year-old plan and who precisely it benefitted. The man's vote was nonetheless accepted but Teed himself then called for the bribery oath to be sworn for all subsequent electors, thereby forcing an admission or perjury on all those in receipt of the 'loan' of £35 from Lopes. Turmoil in the hall then ensued and Teed backed off after personal threats of violence were issued against him. In fact, it is very clear from the testimony of the former mayor (William Hoare who had originally approached Lopes) that Teed had known of the arrangement before the election and had chosen to indict many of the freeholders for corruption before it took place, along with Lopes and his agent; a strategy which was designed 'that himself and

30 The *History of Parliament* records that 'swindling was the order of the day: one Harvie raised £1,500 from two Cornish banks on the pretense of being a candidate for Grampound, but proceeded instead to Falmouth, where he embarked for France'.

another gentleman should have a sufficient majority in their favour so as to seat Mr Teed'.[31] Although Teed's strategy turned out to be hopelessly misguided, he was himself guilty of corruption although never indicted, since he admitted under oath that his actions were paid for by a 'sitting member'. This is unlikely to have been the impecunious John Innes and much more likely to have come from the more successful and very active Alexander Robertson, who hung on to his Grampound seat until 1826 when the borough was finally disenfranchised. Teed confessed to having received 'expenses' of £5,000 from this MP.[32]

The action against Lopes was, however, extraordinary by any standard. As his agent Hunt made clear at one of the official enquiries that Teed's indictment triggered, there was no question that 'the money was certainly lent with a view to gaining an interest in the Borough of Grampound', but there are three reasons why the charge of 'bribery and corruption' was an overstatement of Lopes' intentions (*Journal of the House of Lords* 12 April 1819: 329). First of all, at the time the payments were made no election was due and Lopes was careful to stress through his agent that no one elector receiving payment should feel obliged to support him when indeed one was called. Second, while it was clear that the electors of the borough expected to be paid for their votes, what Lopes offered could never have satisfied them because the 'going rate' was £150 per man, and both Lopes and his agent were well aware of this. The payments made by the successful candidates at the election of 1818 provide confirmation. Finally, the admission that the payments of £35 were intended as loans to achieve little more than currying favour is borne out by the fact that Lopes gave instructions to Hunt in 1817 to seek repayment of the loans when the beneficiaries were in a position to comply. Hunt testified that out of the 50 electors who were lent money, 22

31 *Speech of Lord John Russell in the House of Commons on December 14th 1819 on moving resolutions relative to Corrupt Boroughs with extracts from the Evidence on the Grampound Bribery Indictments* London, Longman, Hurst, Rees, Orme and Brown, 1820: 29.

32 *Ibid*: 36.

returned the loan to him with interest, some before the election of June 1818, but mostly just after the vote when they would have received a much larger sum from the successful candidates. The former mayor, William Hoare, received £306 but did not repay it. At no time during the initial indictment heard at Exeter Assizes or in subsequent hearings in both the Lords and Commons was Lopes himself called to give evidence.[33]

The election took place on 22 June 1818 and by 18 March the following year Lopes and 23 of the electors of Grampound were arraigned before Mr Justice Holroyd and a Special Jury. It transpired during the evidence presented that Mr Teed, when denied a coalition with Lopes, threatened him and the electors on the list he had obtained with prosecution unless he complied with his demands. Lopes is reported to have replied that he would protect the electors if it cost him £100,000 and suggested that the legal opinion he had received was that there was no case of bribery to answer because of the two-year time period between these events and the election itself. After a very cursory hearing the following day Judge Holroyd summed up indicating that if the witnesses were telling the truth the case was clear-cut. The jury returned a verdict of guilty without leaving the box (*The Times* 20 March, 1819).

It is not easy to discern from the transcripts of evidence presented what role, if any, antisemitism played in these summary proceedings. On the one hand, in a similar case Henry Swann, a gentile, was unseated on petition from the neighboring borough of Penryn for alleged bribery in February 1819 having been returned at all three of the preceding elections. Swann was found guilty of this offence at Bodmin Assizes on 11 August 1819. On the other hand, antisemitic remarks were clearly employed by the prosecution at trials where Lopes was cited. For example, a few days after the latter's trial a parallel indictment was heard against the parish clerk at Grampound, one Devonshire. The same prosecutor, Sergeant Pell,

33 See, for example *Minutes of Evidence taken in a Committee of the whole House, on indictments against Sir Manasseh Masseh Lopes, baronet, and others, for Bribery* 1819 (388) vol. 4.

opened the case against the clerk by declaring that Lopes was the cause of the defendant's undoing. On Lopes' wish to fund the voters he is reported as saying:

> 'This liberality was most extraordinary from one of Sir M. Lopes's character. But though the Baronet was said to be as rich as a Jew, it was most surprising that he never thought of relieving the distresses of any of the inhabitants, but of the electors only' (*The Times* 25 March 1819).

Because both houses of parliament became involved with these proceedings, sentencing was deferred until the autumn of 1819 at the King's Bench in London before Mr Justice Bayley. The court heard a report from Mr Justice Holroyd for the offences committed in Cornwall and, because some discussions had taken place in Plymouth or at Maristow House, Mr Justice Best summarised the conclusions of an almost identical indictment for offences committed in Devonshire. A plea of mitigation was entered by Mr Scarlett, Lopes' counsel, but it appears to have fallen on deaf ears. The attorney general, presenting the state's case, 'called upon the court to award such punishment as would prevent the recurrence of this public evil, and deter others from pursuing similar courses'. The presiding judge, in a statement that must have brought some amusement mixed with disquiet among MPs, declared that 'it was of the highest importance to the public that the purity of elections should be preserved'. He pronounced for the offence in Cornwall that Lopes should pay to the king a fine of £8,000 and be imprisoned in Exeter Gaol for 21 months and for his second offence in Devonshire he should pay to the king a fine of £2,000 and be further imprisoned in the same gaol for three months (*Times* 14 November 1819).[34]

With all the obvious disadvantages that the electoral system in the Regency period clearly possessed, it is not that easy to see how a newcomer or an outsider could gain electoral preferment without resorting to 'treating', the payment of expenses or other subventions.

34 The parish clerk Devonshire received six months in Bodmin Gaol and all the other defendants were given three months in the same place.

Jaggard makes the point that this was particularly so where the number of qualified electors was very small. As a result, payments in one form or the other were widespread:

> At Oxford in 1818 the Duke of Marlborough gave £20 for plumpers and £10 for split votes. At Malmesbury the small electorate were credited with £30 a vote until 1804 when a new patron offered £50. In 1802, votes at East Retford were supposed to have fetched 150 guineas each. When James Kibblewhite wrested Wootton Bassett from its co-patrons in 1807 he was supposed to have raised their 20 guineas a voter to 45 guineas. At Ilchester the contractor Alexander Davison gave £30 a man in 1802; at Tregony £20 a vote was usual (Jaggard, 1999: 58).[35]

This appeared to be the case regardless of the social standing of MPs concerned so when Mr Justice Bayley summing up against Lopes concluded that his 'rank and consideration ... greatly aggravated his offence, and called for additional severity' he was identifying him as an outsider to the English class system and not one of its regular pre-eminent members.[36]

This was by no means the end of Lopes' woes during 1819, his *annus horribilis*. During the main part of the proceedings in Cornwall, Lopes had sat for the North Devon constituency of Barnstable, which, like Grampound, had a long history of vote buying usually under the guise of payments for 'expenses'. This was true in 1812 but six years later the electorate had grown due to changes to the local rules. At the election on 18 June 1818, Lopes was placed second with 270 votes while first place went to Francis Molyneux Ommanney, a successful London naval agent who received the support of 330 electors. A third candidate was Sir Henry Clements Thompson, a former naval lieutenant who had lost an arm during the French Revolutionary War

35 'Plumpers' were voters who cast their vote for one candidate only.

36 See 'Grampound' in *The Late Elections: An Impartial Statement of all Proceedings Connected with the Progress and Result of the Late Elections* London, Pinnock and Maunder, 1818: 128–30.

and, somewhat obscurely, had been awarded a Swedish knighthood for destroying a French vessel off the coast of Gravelines, south-west of Dunkirk in 1803. Thompson received 199 votes and became so incensed that he immediately lodged a petition against both winners alleging 'illegal treating and bribery'. There is some reason for believing that an element of hypocrisy may have tainted Thompson's charges since, as a result of participating in this and another unsuccessful attempt at finding a seat, he ended up in prison for debt where he died of apoplexy in 1824.

In any event, the pattern of selecting Lopes for scapegoat treatment was repeated when the case was considered on 5 March 1819 by the committee of the House of Lords established as a result of the petition. The evidence clearly showed that Mr Ommanney's staff had made payments of £4,000 during the campaign, but they argued that these disbursements only included sums to electors to cover their costs for travel and accommodation where necessary, together with a small sum for 'lost time'. The agent for Manasseh Lopes, one Gribble, gave evidence that the former had placed a ceiling of £2,200 for his campaign and had stressed to him that this sum must only be used for legitimate expenses and that 'he would not have a shilling spent illegally'. Moreover, there had been an agreement that where electors had used their right to vote for both Ommanney and Lopes, then the expenses payment would be split equally between both campaigns. Nonetheless, the committee found in favour of Ommanney and allowed him to keep his seat whereas Lopes was unseated and sent for prosecution for bribery to Devon Assizes. Lopes, already waiting for sentence for the supposed infringements of the law at Grampound, was duly tried on 4 August when the same evidence by his agent and staff was repeated and the case was thrown out 'from defect of proof' (*The Times* 9 April, 18 June, 1 July, 9 August 1819). Despite this, parliament did not reconsider its decision to declare his election invalid.[37]

37 *Minutes of Evidence taken in a Committee of the whole House, on indictments against Sir Manasseh Masseh Lopes, baronet, and others, for Bribery* 1819 (388) 4: 351.

On the face of it, when reflecting on how the cases again Lopes arose and how when they were heard, it would be true to say that the evidence was used selectively against him. It is hard not to conclude that he was targeted for what he was, rather than for what transgressions he had uniquely performed. It was not his wealth or his character that marked him out, but rather it was his origins and his ethnicity that explained how he was treated. He was perceived as a foreign Jew but, perhaps significantly, this was not identified by those who objected to his treatment at the time. Some felt he was simply unlucky. One such was the lawyer John Whishaw, the leader of the 'Holland House set', named after the home of the famous Fox family of leading Whigs, who declared that he and his associates were 'disgusted by the violent sentence of the King's Bench against the poor *detected* briber, Sir Manasseh Lopez' (Seymour, 1906: 209; emphasis in original). Whishaw goes on to comment negatively on a condemnation directed at Lopes in John Cam Hobhouse's pamphlet (*A Trifling Mistake*) of 'Borough mongers', pointing out that they included 'the Duke of Bedford, Lord Fitzwilliam and other true friends of their country' (Seymour, 1906: 210).

There were others who argued that Lopes was simply a victim of a corrupt system. For example, in John Wade's *The Black Book or Corruption Unmasked* (1823), he is described as 'ill-treated' and Wade makes the point that those who joined in his condemnation 'never lift(ed) their voices against the *System* of which these practices are the necessary and avoidable accompaniment' (1823: 173; emphasis in original). A similar point was made by those who were active in campaigning for reform to the voting system. A doughty campaigner, Richard Milnes, in a speech at a dinner in Nottingham in 1823, argued that there had never been exhibited 'a more odious act of injustice, heightened by hypocrisy' and suggested that the judge who tried him 'got his own seat in Parliament in the same way': 'Big wigs and long robes not only hid a man's face from his acquaintances, but also from himself' (Milnes, 1825: 119).

But rather than see this as explained by the selection of a scapegoat made vulnerable by his heritage, it was his relative innocence that was thought to determine the outcome since, unlike his colleagues, Lopes had not sought to 'bribe off the petitioners who complained of bribery' as others would have done. Cyrus Redding also felt that 'he was more sinned against than sinning' but that was because he did not understand electioneering and as a result was continually fleeced. Years later, the cases against Lopes would simply cause puzzlement. For example, when commenting on a conviction for bribery in the 1860s, a local paper commented, 'there has been nothing like this trial since in the good old boro'–mongering days, when, for some unexplained reason, the converted Jew, Sir Manasseh Lopez, was tried, convicted, and sentenced for buying a seat, a traffic which at that time was as regular as the sale of stock' (*Launceston Weekly News and Cornwall and Devon Advertiser* 27 July 1861). Others argued that the case was important for 'precipitating the old reform bill (1832)' (*Western Times* 24 December 1880).

In fact, there is no evidence that Lopes was an innocent abroad; rather he appears to have deliberately chosen to fight seats where his wealth might be used to greater advantage and where in the past payments had proved effective in eliciting support. It is possible, too, that he felt his outsider status would be less of an impediment in constituencies where cash ruled. Certainly, Barnstable was one such borough where during this period the electorate had increased not only in size but also 'in fickleness and avarice':

'Only about a quarter of the electors were resident in Barnstaple, and the London outvoters in particular became an increasingly important element, well placed to find wealthy and gullible carpet-bagger candidates and to extort financial rewards for their support' (Fisher, 'Barnstaple' *History of Parliament* online 1790–1820).

But that does not justify how Lopes was actually treated either in Barnstaple or in Grampound. In fact the penalties imposed on him in the latter case were exceptionally severe. The fine of £10,000 is worth £652,000 in terms of comparative purchasing power at today's values and the prison sentence must have imposed an enormous burden on someone with no previous record of illegality.

Of course, there will always be those who will argue that all, regardless of wealth or social standing, should face the same penalty. While true, the whole point in this case is that they did not; Lopes alone was singled out to be an example when the system itself was uniquely flawed and other candidates behaving in an even more unscrupulous way were not sanctioned in any way. Moreover, there is no evidence that others were dissuaded from similar behaviour; rather they would have been comforted by knowing that this outcome would only apply to someone like Lopes. In fact, the opposite to equality was affirmed by Mr Justice Bayley, the judge in question, when he declared 'the rank and consideration of the defendant were circumstances which, in the opinion of the Court, greatly aggravated his offence, and called for additional severity' (*The Times* 14 November 1818). In November 1819, Lopes was marched off to commence his sentence in Exeter Gaol.

It is very probable that Lopes found his incarceration very hard to bear. This would have been especially so after the death of his niece, Esther, on 25 June 1819 aged only 24 at his London address (3 Arlington Street), whom he and his wife had brought up as their daughter. It is not known whether she committed suicide or died of a physical cause exacerbated or not by her mental state, but in any event it would have occurred in the months immediately following Sir Manasseh's widely publicised fall from grace. There was an inquest into her sudden death but it failed to resolve this issue. In the report of proceedings (*The Times* 28 June 1819) Esther was described as 'a most amiable and accomplished young lady'. Her lady's maid declared that she went to bed about 11pm as usual in good 'health and spirits' although she had complained of a pain in her bowels a week before. She went into her room which she shared with her sister ('Miss Franco Lopez').[38] The

38 Esther had three older sisters. It could not have been Abby-Emma, who had married the Rev Walter Radcliffe in 1812, but might have been either Lydia (born 1787) or Rebecca (born 1791). Rebecca is the most probable since she married the following year and in all probability regarded Arlington Street and Maristow as her homes at this time. Where Lydia was living is unclear, but she never married and at some stage in her life was committed to an asylum (Laverstock House, near Salisbury, Wilts). She died in Laverstock, aged 60, in 1847.

maid described going into Esther's bedroom to draw the curtains as usual: 'In about 20 minutes after, Miss Franco Lopez who slept with her, ran into witness's room crying that something was the matter with her sister. The family were alarmed, and Mr Fuller, the family surgeon, was sent for, who came immediately and attempted to bleed the deceased, but she was quite dead. His opinion was that her death was caused "by a sudden fit of apoplexy".'

Unhelpfully, the Jury, without seeking further evidence, returned a verdict of 'died by the visitation of God'. While Manasseh would have been able to attend her funeral at St James' Piccadilly, where she was buried under her family name of Esther Franco, this loss, together with the humiliation his detention surely brought upon the family as a whole, would have played a major part in the unhappiness and despair that his incarceration caused. A little after a month into his confinement he wrote, 'I fear my imprisonment will impair my health greatly as the agitation of my mind continues as severe as ever and want of exercise I find deprives me of sleep at night' (Letter from Exeter Gaol, 16 December 1819).

Moreover, since he was charged with misusing significant funds for political gain, he also had to bear the demands for loans addressed to anyone whose wealth had been widely publicised. One such was a letter from one 'Delvalle' addressed to him in Exeter Gaol in December 1819.[39] Lopes' reply is quite revealing, even though clearly designed to resist such entreaties:

> I think I may venture to impart to an old friend some of my private concerns. I am not so rich as the world gives me credit for. I was unfortunately seized with a mania for purchasing of lands, and in consequence purchased at an improper time when land was high (being at the time of war) and the funds

39 This was probably written by Abraham Delvalle, wine merchant of York Street, Covent Garden. If the letter was written by Abraham Delvalle, he was the younger brother of Abigail Delvalle, who was the economist David Ricardo's mother. The letter was written to request a loan for a 'Mr Wright' purportedly a client of Delvalle but almost certainly for himself. In the following year, Abraham Delvalle was declared bankrupt (*London Gazette*, 1822, No. 17803: 525).

> very low (Letter from Exeter Gaol, 16 December 1819)

He goes on to explain that his greatest mistake was to expand greatly the size of the Maristow estate thereby paying him less than 2 per cent on his outlay compared with the 5 per cent he was getting before. He claims that all he succeeded in doing was to lock up his capital 'in this unprofitable concern which although raised my vanity for a time in being thought a large landholder, yet I confess to you that I often feel the inconvenience of my folly, in thus reducing my income and depriving myself of the comfort of having any money at command.'

In parliament too there were many who felt the sentence on Lopes was too severe, as in a speech by the great orator and campaigner, Henry Brougham, on 21 February 1820. Also William Peel, Robert's younger brother, 'supported the call for remission of the prison sentences imposed on the Members Masseh Lopes and Swann for electoral bribery', discounting the counter argument that any remission would undermine parliamentary prerogatives (*Hansard* 11 July 1820). It is probable, however, that lobbying by Ralph Franco, Manasseh's nephew and heir, played a more significant role behind the scenes. Immediately after the intervention on 11 July, Franco wrote to Prime Minister Lord Liverpool, explaining that

> from the advanced age and daily declining health of my uncle I can with truth assure your Lordship that the early consideration of his case by his Majesty's Government will be an act of great humanity and the objection of its being an interference with the privileges of the House of Commons having been so effectively removed, I do most devoutly hope and entreat that it may receive your Lordship's powerful recommendation and that an early and happy decision may be the consequence and prospects and if your Lordship will condescend to see me or to notice this appeal, I shall ever deem it an additional favor I honor conferred upon your Lordship (BM Add MS 38286: 29 June 1820–9 August 1820)

The following day (14 July), Franco succeeded in gaining an interview with the home secretary, Lord Sidmouth (Henry Addington), and one day after that he wrote again to the prime minister to apprise him of the outcome, attempting to ensure that the two most significant players in government were aware of the necessity to intervene in Sir Manasseh's case:

> ... his Lordship most kindly assured me that in consequence of what had passed in the House of Commons, he would bring my uncle, Sir M. Lopes's case and petition (which is in his hands) again under consideration at the earliest possible moment. Assured therefore as I feel of your Lordship's good disposition towards my uncle, I do not feel it to be right to endeavour to obtrude myself upon you or to trespass upon your valuable time. I beg only to be permitted to repeat to your Lordship that my uncle's is a case truly worthy of the most humane consideration and to assure your Lordship that I do it not to create an effect, when I state that the witness as I have been of all his sufferings, there has been no one part more truly hurtful to himself and more painful to those around him, than the unceasing agitation of mind to which a state of suspense and uncertainty has subjected him, so that next to an actual release, the earliest possible intimation of what he may venture to expect would be a greater relief and kindness than I can possibly describe (BM Add MS 38286: 29 Jun 1820–9 Aug 1820).

Even Lord John Russell, who had insisted that exemplary punishment was deserved and necessary and had played an important role in arguing for disenfranchising Grampound on the grounds of its blatant corruption, sought to reduce the sentence imposed on Lopes (*Parliamentary Debates,* 1 July 1820, vol. 2, 367–76). He made the important point that because Lopes had always supported the government, remitting his sentence was more difficult 'because it might be supposed, in such a case, that ministers acted from a desire to support an individual who had been in the habit of affording political support to them'. These efforts appeared to bear fruit for on

29 July 1820, only eight months into his two year sentence, Lopes was freed from Exeter Gaol.

The success of this impressive lobbying could not prevent the renewed rumour in some circles that this apparent *volte-face* was actually the product of the low cunning to be expected from one of Sir Manasseh's ethnic heritage. The story gained currency that Lopes had negotiated his way out by threatening to return two radicals for Westbury who would be instructed to vote against the governing interest. The rumour, propagated in John Wade's scurrilous *Black Book*, was that a civil servant, one Mr Fortune, was sent down to Exeter with a free pardon and remission of the remainder of the sentence, if Lopes would make over his two seats to solid government supporters. However, '... the cunning old Jew swore that he would not give up the [control of the] nomination, which was worth £10,000'. As a result, 'Fortune made a second trip, and it was agreed to split the difference, to give up one seat, and retain the other' (*Black Book* 1823: 177). It is true that at the general election on 29 November 1820, only a few months after his release, Lopes returned himself at Westbury along with a paying guest and steadfast government supporter, the wealthy West Indian merchant and banker, Philip John Miles. Lopes retained this seat until 23 February 1829.

Despite being seated at Westbury at this time, Lopes does appear also to have been interested in the affairs of the constituencies of East and West Looe. This only became known due to a case in December 1825 before the court of common pleas when a lawyer called Elworthy, sought to obtain from Lopes payments that he had been promised for work relating to establishing the rights to vote of those not normally supporting the families that had traditionally controlled the borough. Lopes argued that it was not he but another party who should bear the costs involved, but the court agreed that some part of the charges should fall to the baronet (*The Times* 12 December 1825).

The affairs of Westbury did not figure very prominently in Sir Manasseh's life during the decade after his release but the town did come to assume considerable importance for his extended family. Ralph Franco, Lopes' heir apparent, sat for his uncle's borough as a Tory in the byelection in 1812 and again at the general election two years later. Unlike his uncle, Franco did believe in being present in the relevant constituency, becoming the lord mayor in 1819. While there he also became acquainted with the Ludlow family of Heywood House, eponymously named after a small village a short distance north of Westbury, and on 8 May 1817 married Susanna Gaisford Gibbs Ludlow, the daughter of Abraham Ludlow when he was 29 and she only just as old as the century.

Heywood House, and the manor of Heywood, had an interesting history, entirely unrelated to the family of the same name that had owned Maristow House for most of the preceding century. The manor had medieval origins and the house before the current one was built by James Ley, later Earl of Marlborough, in the seventeenth century. After passing through the ownership of the Phipps family, the house was bought by the cloth manufacturer Gaisford Gibbs in 1789. His widow married, secondly, the Bristol-based physician Abraham Ludlow and in a further twist to the tale, her daughter with Gaisford Gibbs, to whom he left Heywood House, married Ludlow's son, also Abraham. Their elder son, Henry Gaisford Gibbs Ludlow, inherited the house in 1822 and it was his younger sister who married Ralph Franco five years earlier. Much later in the century, one of their sons inherited Heywood House, which had been substantially rebuilt in the meantime, thus cementing still further the link between the Lopes family, Westbury and the manor of Heywood.[40]

Motivation for the Political Path

The important point was that while Manasseh Massey Lopes did indeed steadfastly use his parliamentary presence to elicit favours, there is no evidence that these were for himself; rather what he wanted to achieve was preferment for members of his extended family.

40 The house was at one time the administrative headquarters of the National Trust but was eventually sold for office use.

Indeed, it would be fair to conclude, since Lopes never spoke in the House of Commons, that his main motive for pursuing so diligently the path of political influence lay less with helping to steer the affairs of state and more with personal favours. There are those who might conclude that these would entail his own elevation to a higher social rank and it is possible that he did indeed lobby for an earldom, but there is no known proof of this. Two things are certain. The first is that he was persistently ignored despite pressing for favours on many occasions. So much was this so that his letters frequently betrayed an irritation bordering on the very opposite of the supplicant's normal humble plea, as in this letter to the prime minister in 1813:

> I have so often addressed you on the subject of my claims without the least notice having been taken of them that I cannot flatter myself that this letter will be attended with more success than the many which have preceded it. There always remains however to the injured one Consolation, of which God be thanked, [that] no man in this country however great may his power, however high his Rank can deprive them; I mean the Consolation of making known their complaints.

In claiming he is only seeking 'compliance with the strict principles of distributive justice', he possibly undermines his cause by his forthright observation that 'were I to draw any conclusion from the indifference that you have shewn my various applications I should be led to believe that ... the noblest privilege of Rank and power was to injure and ruin not to aid and preserve those who are placed in less elevated stations.'[41] Perhaps unsurprisingly, this missive does not appear to have elicited a response.

Undaunted, Manasseh Lopes wrote again barely nine months later from Maristow House again opening his letter with a heartfelt complaint:

> It is far from being my wish to be troublesome to you, though

41 Letter to the Earl of Liverpool, 31 March 1813, from Bath, Stanhope (Street?) (Add MS 38252).

> I cannot any longer withhold a disclosure of my feelings upon the total neglect and disregard I have experienced from every department of the government for some time past, the causes of which I am wholly at a loss to account for, as I have uniformly and strenuously supported the present government at an expense of not less than thirty thousand pounds by standing forward in three severely contest elections...

He then proceeded to list the recent elections where he had successfully stood (Evesham and Barnstaple) or where he had used his 'influence' for two other seats in parliament, 'which I reserved in the last dissolution for two ministerial members' (i.e. Westbury). In a very clear indication of the manner in which the patronage system operated, Lopes wrote that in the Evesham case he was sent for by the Duke of Portland 'to oppose a hostile candidate, which I accomplished at a considerable expense and trouble to myself and was promised ... that I should be remunerated in any thing that I desired.'

The second conclusion is that the preferment he required was strictly limited to members of his extended family. On this occasion, it was 'to procure the promotion of a very deserving young man (a relation of mine) who has served many years as a lieutenant in the Navy and is now serving in America'. The relation was the brother-in-law of his niece, Abby (née Franco), married to the Rev Walter Radcliffe living in Warleigh House, barely half a mile south of Maristow on the River Tavy just above its confluence with the Tamar. Lieutenant Copleston Radcliffe was born at Warleigh House on 23 April 1785 to Copleston Radcliffe (1744–1805) and Sarah Peter (1748–1830). He died in action in a successful attack upon three American schooners in August 1814 while serving on HMS *Star* at Lake Erie, Canada.

Another example arose from an event very near the end of his life when Lopes used his control of Westbury to accommodate the home secretary, Robert Peel. Peel, a political prodigy not dissimilar in some respects from William Pitt, had first been appointed to this office at the age of 34 in 1822. Having once supported the Test Acts, which restricted public office to communicants of the Church of England, he changed his mind and subsequently supported in 1828 the repeal of these restrictions. Peel had been elected to parliament to represent Oxford University in 1817 on a platform of opposition to Catholic Emancipation and felt obliged to offer himself for re-election after his change of mind, particularly because the university at that time was a hotbed of Anglican conformity. It has to be borne in mind that Peel's decision concurred with that of the prime minister, the Duke of Wellington, that the time had come to move government policy on restrictions upon Catholics from an open question, in which the government did not take an official view, to one of support for their removal. The main reason for the change was the impossibility of envisaging a Protestant authority in Ireland when that territory was overwhelmingly Roman Catholic. It is clear from Peel's memoirs that in supporting relief from restrictions imposed on the Catholic population, particularly in Ireland, he saw his role as implementing the will of numerous previous parliaments to act on, rather than ignore, the Catholic question. In this he was strongly supported by the Duke of Wellington.

The result, as far as his retention of the Oxford seat was concerned, was that he lost it by 609 votes to 755, although this was mainly because of the preponderance of Protestant clerics on the electoral roll, many of whom had little day-to-day contact with the university.[42] The victor was a high church Anglican zealot and former MP for Ripon, Sir Robert Inglis. In addition to supporting the prime minister on securing the relief from restrictions on Catholics, this was precisely the period when Peel was completing

42 The general view was that Peel might have lost the election but achieved a majority among more senior academic staff. *The Times* was in no doubt that they had made a stupid choice. Calling Sir Robert Inglis a 'nobody', a leading article concluded that the academics would rue their decision 'when they begin to find that they have a representative who cannot reward them as all good ecclesiastics wish to be rewarded' (23 February 1829). Cf. Machin (1963: 207–8).

his proposals for the Metropolitan Police Force based at Scotland Yard in Central London. In other words, it was imperative to find an alternative way for Peel to retain his position in the Cabinet. This was why Manasseh Lopes was asked by the government to come to the rescue for a financial consideration (£7,000), and he did so by offering to give up his own seat at Westbury to provide a safe return for Peel. Douglas Hurd (2017) in his biography of Peel captures how and why a speedy solution might be found: 'Sir Manasseh had a nephew who was Mayor of Westbury, and another nephew who needed a job.'

Unfortunately, while Westbury was no more averse to Catholic or Nonconformist emancipation than rural areas in general, the borough was suffering hugely from a downturn in prosperity, and being represented in parliament by a Tory member of the Cabinet was an unpopular eventuality. Rightly anticipating the result of the Oxford election on 28 February 1829, Lopes had vacated his seat five days earlier and proposed the home secretary to replace him. A by-election was held on 2 March which was accompanied by violent protests. The candidate himself did not deign to show up; instead William Holmes, the government chief whip, was despatched to oversee proceedings. It has to be said that much of the anger of the local populace appears to have been directed at Lopes himself for the covert way in which the transfer took place.[43] Lopes signed the return, along with his nephew, the mayor and his neighbour and relative Rev Walter Radcliffe. As Holmes later wrote, 'every other member of the corporation, and voters, declined taking any part in the proceedings' which may have also been because some at least were aware that while all this was taking place a leading opponent of Peel's views (John Halcomb, Hon Secretary of the Protestant Club in London) was speeding in a chaise and four on the road from London determined to put up against the home secretary. As Holmes put it:

> If he could have succeeded in getting himself put in

43 Although a disinclination on Lopes' part to buy off dissent may have also been an important factor. Holmes, however, must have been quite at home since he had been returned for Grampound (1808–12) and Tregony (1812–8).

> nomination I have no doubt that something very unpleasant would have occurred, but his worship the mayor was punctual to his time (10 o'clock) and the election was over before Mr. Halcomb could force his way through the crowd.

In any event, such was the fury of some at least of the locals that when it became clear what had occurred threats were directed at Lopes who was forced to retreat from the town hall to his house nearby whereupon stones were thrown through some of the windows. Holmes, however, appears to have been less concerned for Lopes and more for his creature comforts. He reported to Peel that 'I am writing this at Sir M. Lopes's house where the windows have been broken, and am very cold. I must wait for dinner, which is a cursed bore' (quoted in Farrell, S). Lopes himself appeared more sanguine. He wrote to Peel's office on the same day announcing his 'great pleasure and satisfaction' that the home secretary had been unanimously elected but also averring, 'I have felt in an awkward situation to take the steps I have after what has occurred at Oxford as it has occasioned a prejudice amongst my friends here' (BM Add MS 40399, f. 27, 2 March 1829).[44]

Peel himself, while admitting that he had come close to faring no better than he had at Oxford, was somewhat disingenuous in admitting to the complex machinations that preceded his victory, as his memoirs recall:

> After my rejection by the University, there being a convenient vacancy at Westbury, I became a candidate (a very unpopular one I must admit) for that borough. The Protestant feeling was much excited, even among the quiet population of a small country town; and notwithstanding all the assistance which Sir Manasseh Lopez (the patron of the borough) could

44 It is by no means clear whether the locals felt cheated or were appalled by Peel's apparent pro-Catholic sentiments. One local paper reported that what had upset them was that Lopes had not adequately paid them off. On trying to leave the town hall, the report claimed that 'some able-bodied men in frock-smocks bore him back again to the entrance to the hall, that he might start afresh and give them a better proof of his *bounty*' (*Keenes' Bath Journal* 9 March 1829).

> render me, my return was not effected without considerable difficulty (Peel, 1856: 342).

He does at least recognise that for Lopes these events were uncomfortable by noting that he had 'suffered in his person from one of the many missiles with which the town hall was assailed' but it is hard not to agree with the Devonian historian, WG Hoskins, when he wrote of these events that 'the hard-faced, solid governing classes of England – the Peels, the Plantas, the Holmeses – had used the outsider for their own ends and then thought no more of it' (1952: 418).[45]

It is somewhat ironic that while the central issue was greater equality for Catholics, the choice of Manasseh Lopes as the one to sacrifice his seat was replete with the usual adoption of negative Jewish stereotypes. Steven Farrell's report on these events, for example, includes a quotation from a letter of 10 February by Lord Lowther (MP for Westmorland) explaining what the plan was to Lord Lonsdale: 'a gentleman is gone down into Devonshire to find the old Jew Sir Manasseh Lopes to tempt him with a large price to vacate'. The pejorative implication of this sentence was firmly matched by a popular verse directed at Peel that managed to bracket opposition to Catholic emancipation with antisemitism:

> Once Peel the Rat for Oxford sat
> Of Christian men the choice
> But now he sits for Westbury
> Without one Christian voice
> By Christians spurned
> Where'er he turned
> He bribed an old Hebrew
> He bought his vote
> For many a groat
> And represents a Jew.

The rhyme appeared in a number of newspapers in April 1829 and

45 Joseph Planta, MP for Hastings, was secretary to the Treasury and as such was responsible for patronage and in ensuring government support.

was widely circulated, particularly in high-Tory circles.[46] The message in a cartoon dated 7 March 1829 indulges in not dissimilar sentiments (Plate 41). In Robert Peel's anti-Catholic days he was sometimes referred to as 'Orange Peel', particularly in Ireland, and in the 'The Peel thrown away or One Man's Meat is Another Man's Poison' the artist plays on this label. It shows a high church Oxford don responding to a peasant's query throwing the peel of an orange into a cesspit or dirt pit in which Sir Manasseh is mired. Just to make what meaning is intended quite clear, Lopes is labelled 'impurity of election bribery', the mire is referred to as 'Westbury – close sink of iniquity', while the Oxford don explains that 'the *Peel* has *suddenly turn'd sour* and as sour things are not good for my *constitution I discard it* – the old gentleman in the dirt pool, being of a grosser habit is better able to stomach it – what might be the ruin of me can do him no harm.'[47]

The nephew whom Lopes wished to assist was Henry Cowper, born in 1788, who in 1811 had married Rebecca Lopes Pereira, the daughter of Manasseh Lopes' older sister, Rachael, born in Jamaica three years before her brother in 1752. Rachael had nine children with Isaac Pereira, a Jamaican planter, of whom Rebecca was the fifth, born in 1780. Cowper was at the time of his wedding paymaster in the 7th battalion German Legion based in Bexhill in Sussex.[48] Rebecca had followed her uncle's example and converted to Anglicanism being christened on 31 October 1808 in St Pancras Parish Church. By 1829, Cowper was unemployed and was anticipating that his wife's uncle would be of assistance in obtaining a foreign posting.

46 See Cahill (1975: 439) and Gaunt (2014: 31) that both reprint this verse and provide some context for its significance.

47 See George, MD (1952) *Catalogue of Political and Personal Satires Preserved in the Department of Prints and Drawings in the British Museum*, xi (1828–32) Nos. 15683, 15726, 15767.

48 The King's German Legion was established by George III when members of the royal family were nearly all German and when Napoleon's forces occupied their home state of Hanover. They fought at Copenhagen but notably made a major contribution to Wellington's forces on the Peninsular where they comprised 20 per cent of British fighting forces. Although most of the men were German a quarter were 'foreigners' and Henry Cowper was one of these, having been born in Harwich, Essex. The KGL consisted of 2,678 men in four battalions.

On 14 October, some seven months after the Westbury debacle, Lopes wrote to Peel in his usual no-nonsense manner:

> I have been in expectation (for the last six months) that his Lordship (Lord Aberdeen, Foreign Secretary) would have granted me the appointment long before for Mr C(owper) knowing that Madeira and Bahia have both been vacant for some time past. I must therefore entreat of you, my dear Sir, to use your kind interference with his Lordship to obtain the former Consularship if you can, if not the latter, and I shall consider myself particularly obliged to you, as I feel deeply interested to serve Mr Cowper from his connection with my niece and besides he has been long out of employment in consequence of his expectation of an early appointment to the situation.

A week later, he received a less than compliant reply from Peel intimating that there was no point in pursuing this matter since he had already raised the issue three or four times.[49] On 30 October, however, the home secretary wrote to Lopes confirming that Cowper had been appointed to the consulship at Pernambuco in north-eastern Brazil, a poor state on that part of Brazil jutting into the Atlantic whose capital, Recife, was surrounded by sugar plantations dependent at this time on slave labour. We now know that Peel's entreaties to the foreign secretary on Lopes' behalf were supportive but once again replete with references to his Jewish heritage:

> I had very little communication with Sir Manasseh Lopes on the subject of my return, but ... I really think the old Jew rendered essential service by consenting to vacate at the time he did ... I understand that his own estimate of the damage done and service rendered was an *English peerage*. I think a foreign consulship much nearer the mark.

49 It was reported that Peel's comment to Planta on receiving these requests was 'what a torment this Jew is!' (Add MS 40399, ff. 361,370, 371, 374).

This sentiment was, however, further spoiled by Peel's subsequent comment on the Pernambuco appointment: 'I wish I could prevail on Sir Masseh Lopes to accompany him there' (BM Add.MS 40312, ff. 65, 73, 74; 40320, f. 117; 40399, ff. 27, 361, 370, 371, 374. Farrell 'Westbury'). Unhappily, the appointment may not have been an overwhelming success since a little over a decade later Cowper appeared as a prisoner before the Court for Relief of Insolvent Debtors.[50] A few years later, when Dame Charlotte Lopes prepared her will in the months following her husband's death, she specifically left a legacy to Rebecca and to the three sons of the marriage, but not to Cowper himself even though he lived another 46 years, dying in 1877.

Despite Peel's allusion to a peerage for Lopes, there is no evidence that he did in fact lobby for this honour.[51] Public opinion if anything seemed to suggest that the sordid details of the Westbury affair prompted Peel himself to dream of an earldom as a cartoon from May 1829 suggests (Plate 42). The young home secretary is shown waking from such a dream after being lulled into slumber by the problems of police reform and paying off Lopes for the Westbury imbroglio (See Rubens, 1969–70). Instead, the following year Peel inherited a baronetcy from his father and a little later the seat in parliament for Tamworth in Staffordshire, the constituency that contained the family seat of Drayton Manor.

William Hoskins, the distinguished historian who did so much to revive a wider interest in local history, was one of very few to comment sympathetically on the life of Manasseh Lopes. Calling him a 'curious, almost fantastic, character', just after describing the dramatic turn of events at Westbury he speculated,

> One wonders what Sir Manasseh Lopes thought as he sat in his library at Maristow, an old man nearing 75, looking

50 The court existed from 1813 to 1861 to hear pleas for relief from prison for those unable to pay their debts. Bankruptcy is only one type of insolvency. The court existed to agree proposals for reparations to creditors.

51 The *Devizes Gazette* (26 March 1829), picking up on the apocryphal rumour that Lopes was to be created Lord Roborough, commented that 'we presume this is an abbreviation of Rottenborough'.

> across his sloping lawns down to the broadening reaches of the lovely Tavy; the Tavy shining in the soft western light of a March evening, with the dark hanging woods of Whittacliffe and Blindwell rising on the far side towards Bere Alston and the hills beyond; and the only sound in the intense quiet of that spring twilight the far-away whistle of the curlews coming up from the estuary flats by Gnatham Point, as the evening tide ebbed away to the sea (1952: 418).

One wonders indeed; there is no doubt that the events at Westbury marked a turning point. Lopes did not stand again for parliament even though he still possessed great influence in Westbury and ensured that two supporters of the government were returned at the General Election of 1830. One was Sir Alexander Grant (known as 'the Chin' because of his peculiar physiognomy) who was a wealthy West Indian plantation owner and a friend of Peel, his London neighbour. The other was Michael Prendergast, an Irishman from Galway, unsurprisingly a pro-Catholic emancipation supporter who was almost certainly a paying guest, but whose liberating principles did not extend to supporting moves in the late 1820s for removing similar restrictions on Jews.

An Assessment

Lopes himself was in declining health in 1830 and early in the following year he became seriously ill with symptoms of paralysis. He died on at the age of 76 on 26 March 1831 at Maristow House and was buried in Bickleigh Church where there is a memorial to him by Richard Westmacott. His will dated 21 November 1829, shortly after his success in extracting some preferment for his niece's husband, Henry Cowper, is a complex document that reveals two of his major strengths. It is replete with clauses that make sure that his beneficiaries are protected against the vagaries of the economy and, second, it is focused entirely on sustaining his extended family. The major beneficiary was, of course, his nephew Ralph Franco who inherited the baronetcy, the Maristow estate and the London residence, in all reputed to be worth at the time £800,000.[52] The only requirement was that he should change his name to Lopes, to which he readily complied.

It is perhaps unsurprising that Manasseh Lopes' will is complex. He had no children of his own and no brothers.[53] But he had two sisters and although one of them died in childbirth after only ten years of marriage, they produced 15 children between them. His older sister Rachael had married Isaac Pereira in Jamaica in 1771 and borne him nine children before he died at the young age of 38 in 1788. Two of these children pre-deceased Manasseh but all of the remaining seven were recognised in the will with, as was customary, nephews receiving more than nieces, but here careful discernment was exercised. For example, Manasseh Lopes Pereira received a legacy of £5,000 in 3 per cent consols whereas his older brother Mordecai Lopes Pereira, who had managed to marry four times, received only £200 and an annuity of £150. Manasseh Lopes was closer to the children of his younger sister Esther Franco, partially because she had died so young and partially because the four who survived were physically closer to him. Ralph, the only son, was his heir but of three nieces one was brought up until her early death in Manasseh's household and one married his neighbour at Warleigh (Abby Emma Radcliffe). The other, Rebecca Lopes Franco, was the widow of Robert Barton when Manasseh died in 1831. Robert Cutts Barton, the son of a vice-admiral of the same name, was a Royal Navy commander and a Devon man and this side of the family lived in Devon or in London.[54] Both Mrs Barton and Mrs Radcliffe were well recognised in the will (PROB 11/1785/283; IR26/1263/214; *Gentleman's. Magazine* (1831, i: 465–6).

When it comes to assessing the achievements of Manasseh Lopes,

52 In wealth terms in today's money that would be approximately worth £65 million.

53 He did have an older brother, Abraham, born in Jamaica in November 1753, but he died in 1758 when Manasseh was just three years old.

54 Robert Cutts Barton, who died on 23 October 1827, was a midshipman aboard HMS *Victory* at Trafalgar and, later, co-owner of a large sugar plantation in Antigua.

there are three aspects that stand out. The first is that he was an exceptionally competent banker and financier. Barred by prejudice from many conventional money lending institutions, he managed to utilise the training his father had bestowed to great effect. It is important to appreciate that this was not the product of attendance at advanced institutes of learning. Educational provision in Jamaica in the last quarter of the eighteenth century was rudimentary and later commentators have frequently alluded to his limited appreciation of what would have been regarded as a basic understanding of classical literature.[55] He did, of course, inherit considerable wealth from his father and while in Jamaica, and for the first period of his life in London, they no doubt acted together. It would have been a tough apprenticeship since plantation societies were not always noted for the adherence of their citizens to the rule of law, and slave societies brutalised both the oppressed and their oppressors. Lending large sums, often without collateral, while potentially highly profitable, was certainly not without considerable risk.

It is well known that the Prince of Wales was constantly in need of funds to sustain his extravagant and spendthrift habits. If, as is highly probable, Manasseh played a leading role in providing short-term support to the prince, then the fact that he does not seem to have incurred a loss is itself indicative of a high degree of financial acumen. For example, by the time the prince reluctantly agreed to marry, possibly bigamously, Princess Caroline of Brunswick he owed the extraordinary amount of £639,890, most of it in bonds or IOUs to a range of creditors. In order to bail him out a government commission contested many of the creditors' claims and a considerable number went bankrupt as a result. The dangers of being in any way engaged in advancing funds to the Prince of Wales or either of his two brothers, the Dukes of York and

55 The most common story, although possibly apocryphal, has Lopes responding to a request from one of the Modyford Heywood daughters for some valued volumes from the library in Maristow House after it had been sold. He had been told the books in question were 'the classics' but on being unable to locate them, he invited the women to come and help identify the books and when she did so he is reported to have said, 'Oh, I thought they would have had the title "classics" upon them.'

Clarence, have been well documented. They ranged from the probable outcome of non-repayment or refusal to meet interest obligations, to something much more sinister. The most egregious of these strategies arose in relation to the infamous 'French Loan' when the three princes, after having reneged on interest payments for a Dutch loan of 350,000 guilders, agreed to proceed with another bond for £100,000 arranged by a bankrupt named Jean-Jacques De Beaune.[56] The bond was divided into smaller portions and sold mostly to French aristocratic investors anxious to cleave more closely to the British monarchy to help stave off the growing revolutionary threat at home. Many came to England expecting to live in safety on the interest earned from their loan. The Prince of Wales complained bitterly to the government when approached for interest by these creditors and the government responded by utilising the provisions of the Alien Act of 1793 (33 Geo 3) and sent 26 of them back to France, whereupon at least fourteen were guillotined, a fate which also befell most of those involved in the arrangement of the bond, including De Beaune.

If there is any worthy outcome from this farrago it is that these events were documented in widely circulated pamphlets. Perhaps the most savage of these was published in 1814 under the title *Nobilitas Sola Atque Unica Virtus: The Royal Criterion or a Narrative of the transaction relative to the loans made in London by the Prince of Wales, Duke of York and Duke of Clarence*.[57] The jurist and historian, John Andrew Hamilton, summarised the prince well when he wrote, 'there was not in his character any of that staple of worth which tempts historians to revise and correct a somewhat too emphatic contemporary condemnation' although even his many detractors often pointed out that his incompetence and character

56 The Dutch loan was arranged by Abraham Goldsmid, who was promised a commission that was never paid.

57 The pamphlet, the title of which translates as 'virtue is the one and only nobility', concludes 'the British Princes, by their proceedings in the business (the foreign loans) appear as if the laws of England had no authority over them, as if they could at their pleasure contract debts, or commit their names to paper, to bind themselves with every legal solemnity, and then, in defiance of all law, and all justice, discharge them by a command to their own servant to destroy what they have so signed' (1814: 57).

served to constrain what had hitherto been the overweening power of the monarch (*Dictionary of National Biography* 21: 204). The manner in which Lopes was able to leverage advantage from this dangerous man even exceeded the example of Sophia Musters, who survived in his close circle longer than almost anyone else.[58] In her case sexual allure matured into the comforts of non-judgmental friendship, whereas Lopes pursued a more ambitious trajectory. Lopes was highly skilled in not just making money but in employing this capacity to enhance his political aims. As the foregoing has shown, he did so not for the purpose of wielding political power for its own sake but to sustain the fortunes of his extended family.

Of course, there will always be critics who will point out that Lopes and other merchant families of Sephardi origin owed their success to participating in the slave trade and in exploiting the institution of slavery itself. As far as the former is concerned, there is no doubt that Manasseh Lopes, his father Mordecai and grandfather Abraham would have all participated in financing plantation supplies, including West African slaves. They were, however, part of a small, closed-knit community that, while disproportionately focused on trading, made up a tiny minority of the sector overall. Moreover, there is no evidence that the family actually concentrated on the slave trade. On the contrary, with other professions closed to them, they made use of extended ethnic networks, the vast majority of which supplied foodstuffs, fabrics and equipment. There is also no evidence that members of the immediate family were ever plantation owners, but rather that they lived and worked in an urban environment (cf. Faber, 1998).[59]

58 It is tempting to speculate that contact between these two, albeit probably fleeting, may have been the avenue through which Lopes became aware of the opportunity to acquire the Maristow estate.

59 This is not to argue that there were no planters of Jewish descent in Jamaica in the eighteenth century. For example, the following were listed in the 1754 'Quit Rent Book' survey of 1754 and there would have been others but amounting to less than two per cent of the 1550 holdings listed: Aaron Barou Lousada 140 acres in St John, Abraham Israel 581 acres Clarendon and Vere, Moses Kellet 4,452 acres in Clarendon and St David, Solomon Mendes 320 acres in St John, Joseph Aguilar 269 acres in St Catherine, Moses Bravo 300 acres in St Andrew, Abraham Henriques De Sousa 100 acres in St Catherine,

This is not, of course, to deny that the family would have owned slaves, but these would have been small in number and used in domestic and business premises. For example, the will of Abraham Rodriques Lopez, Manasseh's grandfather, dated 14 April 1743, leaves all his worldly goods to his wife Rachel, his son Mordecai and his two daughters equally but in the event that all pre-decease his wife then she is empowered 'to sell and dispose of all or such part of my lands tenements negro slaves and hereditaments whatsoever as she thinks proper' (SC-7387, American Jewish Archives, Cincinnati, Ohio). It has been noted already that Manasseh himself brought one female house slave with him from Jamaica and as late as 1826 the slave register for Jamaica showed that Rachel Pereira, his sister, had three female slave registered. This was down from the four recorded in the previous registration period, the reason for which was given as 'manumission'. She died on 1 December 1825 in London (Covent Garden).

The second remarkable aspect of Manasseh Lopes' career was the extraordinary degree to which he managed to negotiate a rigid class system replete with antisemitism. He was a man for whom extended family was all, yet even when he was targeted with the most scurrilous social exclusion, as in the Grampound case and the imprisonment that followed, which very nearly destroyed him in mind and body, he bounced back when many lesser men would have succumbed. The context in which this occurred is as significant as the events themselves. It is not known, for example, how his niece, Esther, died but she did so in his house in Arlington Street after her uncle's conviction and weeks prior to his incarceration. When Manasseh Lopes' sister died just after giving birth in February 1795, she left behind a nine-year-old daughter (Rebecca), a seven-year-old son (Ralph), a three-year-old daughter (Abigail Emma) and possibly another daughter, in addition to the new baby given her mother's name. In the absence of their father, Manasseh looked after them all, possibly very early on with the assistance of his mother but she (the former Rebecca Pereira)

Isaac Mendes Gutteres 3,169 acres in St Dorothy, St John and St Thomas in the Vale, Isaac Gomez Silva 1,189 acres St James, Joshua Gomez Silva 300 acres St James, Isaac Lopes Torres 198 acres in St Andrew and Vere (CO 142/31. See http://www.jamaicanfamilysearch.com/Samples2/1754lead.htm)

died almost immediately on 29 April 1795 in London. His father, Mordecai, prepared a will just six days before his wife's death and by March the following year he too was dead.

In the meantime in October 1795 Manasseh was married by special licence issued by the Faculty Office of the Church of England on 15 October 1795 to 34-year-old Charlotte Yeates in the Anglican Church of St Michael, in Horton, Buckinghamshire. The family, who were always claimed to have come from Monmouthshire, were living at the time of this wedding in Penn, Buckinghamshire.[60] This marriage between a then practising Jew and an Anglican clearly breached the classical institution of Jewish marriage (*kiddushin*), and when taken with the decision of Lopes to ensure his baronetcy passed to his nephew, might suggest to some that this marriage was companionate rather than intended to produce heirs, but the latter might equally have been a side effect of his wife's age at the date the title was conferred (44). What it does mark, however, is a determination to create a conventional home for his late sister's family as well as signalling his determination to take a step in the direction of cultural assimilation into a rural elite.

As this chapter has shown, powerful influences were equally determined to brand him with what they saw as the incubus of a Jewish heritage. Esther Franco was baptised into the Church of England on 17 June 1812 and the entry in the register says, 'Esther Franco an adult born a dissenter in Charlotte Street Bloomsbury as alleged January 18th 1795' (Register of St Pancras Old Church Camden), and it is hard not to fear that when she died seven years later it may have been at her own hand. Whether this is true or not, there seems little reason to doubt that her loss was a major factor in

60 Either Charlotte's father, John Yeates, remarried or she had a brother, also called John, since a marriage is recorded of someone with that name on 24 September 1780 to Elizabeth Davies in Penn, Bucks. Somewhat curiously a Charlotte Yeates, probably a product of this marriage, is recorded as having been baptised in the same village on 11 November 1787 but as having died on 20 January the following year. A brother, James, died in Penn on 19 October 1789. The will of Charlotte Lopes, drawn up just after her husband's death, makes no mention of any beneficiary other than members of the Lopes or Franco families and their spouses and children.

the ill-health and misery that Lopes suffered in Exeter Gaol.

On a more positive note, Manasseh's powerful ambition earned him a string of 'firsts'. Almost immediately after converting to Christianity in 1802, he was appointed to the Commission of the Peace for Wiltshire and Devon, making him the first Justice of the Peace of Jewish heritage (Ebner, 2002: 50).[61] Even more striking is that he could also lay claim to being the first Jewish member of the Westminster parliament. All other claimants to this title in the early years of the nineteenth century were converts from Judaism to acceptable forms of Christianity, but none was earlier than Lopes.[62] Finally, he was the first Jew to become in 1810 the High Sheriff of Devon. It was not until 1842–43 that a practising Jew, Emanuel Lousada, nephew of Emanual Baruch Lousada who was a great friend of Manasseh Lopes and the first person he went to see in Peak House, Sidmouth on his release from prison, was honoured in the same way.[63]

These accolades of 'firsts' depend on what a 'Jew' is. Normally, it is taken as a combination of three properties – heritage (having at least one parent identifying as 'Jewish'), conviction (a believer in Judaism and the practising of its rituals) and identity, with the last

61 Another three decades were to pass before practising Jews were permitted to take a revised oath of office. Ebner points out the irony of Lopes' position in 1829 when he gave up his seat at Westbury to make way for Robert Peel: 'One wonders whether members of the Jewish community viewed a Jewish apostate who lost his seat for Catholic rights with pride or horror' (2002: 50).

62 William Jacob, MP for Westbury, elected in 1806, came close but more than 50 years were to pass before Lionel de Rothschild (first elected in 1847) was permitted in July 1858 to swear 'so help me Jehovah' instead of the Christian oath of adjuration. Lord George Gordon was MP for Ludgershall between 1774–80 but he only converted to Judaism in 1787 and another candidate, Sampson Eardley, first and last Baron Eardley of Spalding, was MP for Cambridgeshire between 1770 and 1780 but, while his father was a Jewish banker, his mother was English and he was baptised and brought up in the Church of England, which fact permitted him to be honoured with a baronetcy in 1759 whereas his father, with a much stronger claim, was denied. It was not until 1841 that Isaac Goldsmid was made a baronet without having to forsake his religion, 36 years later than Manasseh Lopes.

63 Manasseh Lopes' heir, Ralph Franco, did not receive this honour but his son, Sir Massey Lopes did (1857–8) as did his grandson Sir Henry Yarde-Buller Lopes.

being split between public recognition and self-definition. Fifteen per cent of modern Israeli citizens born as ethnically Jewish define themselves as 'atheist', whereas one in two define themselves as 'secular' (i.e. non-practising) Jews. 'Jewishness' is not therefore just a religion, so that one who rejects the faith is not thereby ceasing to be a Jew. Moreover, as we have seen, those in authority – from police officers to prime ministers – regarded Lopes as a Jew and made constant reference to this identity, usually in a disparaging context. It cannot be true both ways round. His achievements have to be accepted as Jewish 'firsts' because he was not permitted to be anything other and in all probability would not have wished to be.

A third remarkable achievement is that, while remaining childless, Manasseh Lopes managed to build a successful aristocratic dynasty that, as the following chapter reveals, was characterised by unstinting good works and public service. Indeed, while the founding of an aristocratic dynasty from humble beginnings in the West Indies was by no means unique, to achieve it in a relatively short period while belonging to a minority subject to systematic discrimination was impressive. In an insightful obituary for a fully accredited member of the family published in the early years of the twentieth century, the anonymous author writes that the life 'furnishes a striking illustration of the manner in which the descendants of a famous Jewish money lender can within the space of two or three generations be transformed into a Tory country family of the most exclusive and aristocratic description, allied to the oldest houses of the peerage' (*Chicago Tribune* 14 February 1908). What this chapter has sought to show is that not any 'Jewish money lender' could have made this transition.

Chapter 10
Legitimacy Gained

In the century that followed the death of Manasseh Lopes in 1831, the Maristow estate entered its post-West Indian phase, never again witnessing the buccaneering of the seventeenth century, the studied social engineering of the eighteenth or the explosive ambition that marked the end of the Georgian era. Now there was a period of calm; family life became normalised and the estate itself came to play a more central role, first through accommodating as far as was possible the drive for raw materials to fuel the industrial revolution and, second, through gradually applying the new principles of estate management to harnessing the land for efficient farming. Politics continued to play a role but more conventionally so; the clamour for acceptance was replaced by the gradual emergence of a Tory squirearchy, albeit one with an unusual passion for educational excellence and local munificence. But all that was to come later: the next period, through to the middle of the century, was one of transition.

The first point to note is that when Ralph Lopes inherited the Maristow estate from his uncle in 1831, he became overnight one of the largest landowners in Devon. Leaving aside properties in Wiltshire and Somerset, together with other local holdings in Plymouth, Modbury, Sampford Spiney, Beer Ferrers, and Whitchurch, the estate came to just over 24,000 acres in seven parishes in many of which he was the most significant landlord. This is shown in the following table which errs in one respect, namely that in a number of parishes (e.g. Buckland Monochorum, Shaugh Prior and Sheepstor) the remaining acreage was comprised largely of unproductive moorland, much of it common land. In other words the dominance of the Maristow estate was more pronounced than the figures suggest.

Maristow Estate Holdings (1839–42) (Tithe apportionments)

	Acres	*(per cent of total)*	*Tenancies*	*(per cent of total)*
Tamerton Folliot	1,318	(28.1)	38	(14.6)
Bickleigh	2,323	(100.0)	98	(100.0)[1]
Buckland Monochorum	4,157	(60.8)	88	(41.5)
Meavy	1,187	(36.1)	27	(30.0)
Shaugh Prior	2,651	(30.45)	67	(65.7)
Sheepstor	2,491	(69.3)	12	(28.6)
Walkhampton	10,055	(95.4)	99	(71.7)
Total	24,152		429	

Source: TNA: IR 29/6, 9, 10, 30

Owning a large estate is not the same as running it well. As the following assessment will reveal, Sir Ralph Lopes spent too much time in Wiltshire, in London and in generally enjoying the benefits of being an aristocratic landowner to be overly concerned with the state of the tenements he owned, or the farming methods of the tenants occupying his lands. Later in the century, when the estate passed to his eldest son, this neglect was conspicuously reversed.

Early Life

Raphael Franco was born on 10 September 1788 to Esther, Manasseh Lopes' youngest sister, and her husband, Abraham de Raphael Franco. It seems possible that the couple had met in Jamaica, where Esther was born, but much more likely that they met in London where Esther had lived with her parents from 1773. Abraham Franco, listed as a resident of America Square (a street and small square in the City of London built around 1760 and dedicated to the American colonies), was granted denizen status on 13 April 1776. In 1780, at the age of 15, he is included in Land Tax Records as a tenant of 'Mr Pitfield' in a house in Hounslow, Isleworth, where a 'Miss Franco' was also present as a tenant of the same person, most probably one

1 In about half the cases one or more other part-owners were involved.

of his four sisters. In 1785, Abraham is recorded as a business tenant at Fenchurch Street, Aldgate, and the following year at Portsoken, John Street, one of the wards of the City of London just outside the city walls and bounded on the east by Spitalfields and on the west by Aldgate. Esther and Abraham were married on 28 April 1785 in the Bevis Marks Synagogue, Mile End Road, when Esther was 27 and Abraham was 20.[2] It seems unlikely that they ever returned to Jamaica and Abraham's background had little or no Caribbean influence. He was descended from a distinguished line of coral and diamond merchants of Sephardi origin who settled in 'Leghorn' (Livorno) early in the eighteenth century (Trivellato, 2009). His father, Raphael Franco, was one of the founders of a company at 106 Fenchurch Street that had traded in coral and uncut diamonds between Livorno, India (Lucknow) and eventually Brazil when the diamond trade there opened up in the early eighteenth century.[3] Abraham Franco is listed in trade directories as providing financial and broking services at 77 Hatton Garden in 1789–90, although there is reason to suppose that he was less successful as a businessman than his forebears.

In November 1790, Abraham Franco was sued and lost a case in the Court of Common Pleas in connection with a bargain struck with one Judah Pariente to borrow money against goods at a high cost that he objected to repaying when the time came, presumably because he was out of funds (*The Times* 15 November 1790). Indeed, he is listed among bankrupts as a merchant and insurance broker of Bedford Square (Gower Street), London, in 1793 (*Edinburgh Advertiser* 30 August 1793), although on 6 May the following year he was able to pay his creditors an unstated dividend, presumably to try and settle his financial affairs (*Kentish Gazette* 18 April 1794). It is possible that these financial troubles affected his mental stability. The records reveal that Abraham Franco, late of the Parish of St Marylebone, was fined 17s 4d for assaulting Isaac Hyams on 26 September 1793. He was also fined £1 3s and 8d on 6 December 1793 for attacking

2 His birth year is usually recorded as 'about 1765' but it is possible he was a year or two older than this would suggest.

3 Raphael Franco was married to Leah D'Aguilar on 6 April 1761.

David de Silva and Benjamin Pereira when his address was given as Suffolk Street, Middlesex Hospital. Moreover, his financial troubles appear to have had even more serious consequences since his name appears on the Fleet Prison Discharge Book and Prisoner List on 10 July 1795, which provides details of a whole series of warrants dated June and July 1795.[4] Not only did he lose his wife in childbirth in early 1795 but he also lost his brother David, still living in Livorno, in the same year. Thereafter he appears to have fled to India, where he was remarried on 5 September 1796 to an Irish widow, Frances Chauvet (née Boileau) of Benares in Calcutta St John. This marriage produced two sons, George Fleming Franco born on 25 November 1798 at Benares, and Abraham Francis Franco born 29 November 1799 (d. 1821).[5] He died before 6 December 1799 for he appears as the 'late Abraham Franco' in his second son's baptism record.

This fall from grace certainly did not afflict Abraham's father who had a reputation for being a highly skilled and respected merchant. A portrait by Thomas Gainsborough, which identifies the sitter as a man of the City of London by its reference to a distant St Paul's (Plate 43), suggests someone of some wealth and commercial success, even though he died aged 35 the following year.[6]

After the death of his mother in 1795 and the absence and subsequent death of his father, it is almost certain that Raphael Franco the son was cared for by his uncle and aunt in Maristow House. It was they who would have arranged for his education at Tonbridge School in Kent, near to which he was baptised into the Anglican faith as Ralph Franco at Shipbourne Church on 17 May 1801. In 1803, he moved to Winchester and on 21 April 1807 at the age of 18 he successfully

4 There is, of course, no way of knowing whether this person was a namesake.

5 George Franco was married to Eliza Harriet Fagan on 7 January 1824 at Futteh Ghur (Agra). He was then a civil servant in the East India Company's Bengal office. He died in London on 22 September 1870 when he is recorded as living at 8 Eaton Place, although he died at 56 Brunswick Square, Brighton. He served as a JP in London after his retirement from India. His half-brother, Ralph Lopes, recognised him with a £100 legacy in his will. His brother was a writer in Bombay in 1819 but for whom and on what is not known.

6 This portrait was sold by Christie's on 8 July 1910 when it was bought by the heiress Doris Duke's father and is now owned by the foundation in her name. It hangs in her former residence at Rough Point, Newport, Rhode Island.

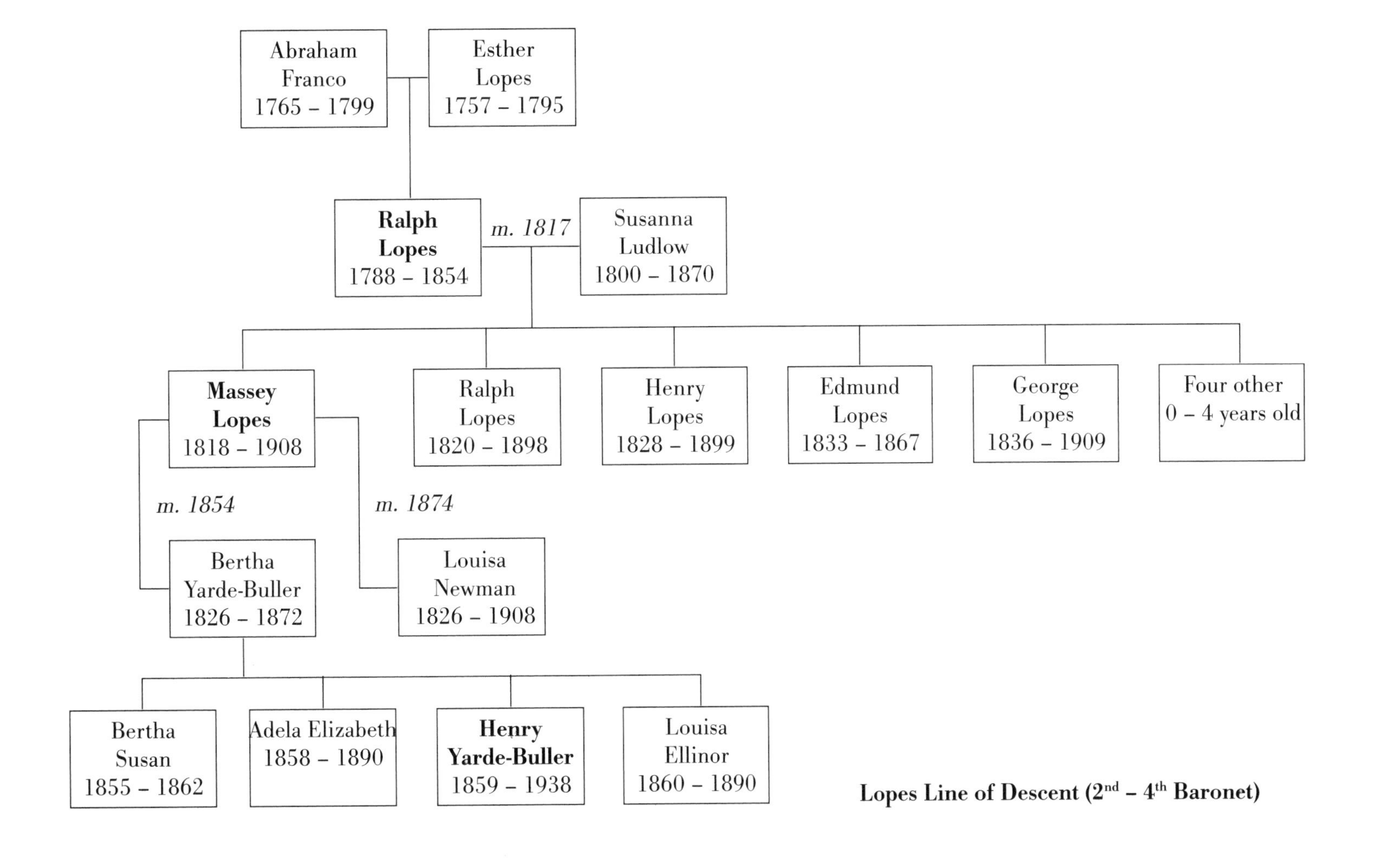

Lopes Line of Descent (2nd – 4th Baronet)

matriculated into Brasenose College, Oxford, where he went on to receive his BA in 1811. By this time his uncle was busily engaged in massaging his electoral fortunes in the House of Commons and had little time for the borough of Westbury on which the year before he had expended so many of his financial resources. Thus it was that Ralph, at only 25 years of age, was drafted in to serve as mayor of the borough in 1813, a role to which he was to return on three more occasions (1819, 1824 and 1828). Indeed, prior to his uncle's death in 1831, Ralph Franco spent a significant part of his time in the borough and it is reasonable to suppose that these experiences helped to formulate his early political opinions, which initially were less those of the Tory country squire and more supportive of liberal causes. For example, his uncle placed him in one of the two parliamentary seats he commanded in Westbury in the election on 5 December 1814 when, showing some independence of spirit that was later to leave him, he took the Whig whip.[7]

Ralph and Susanna Franco had nine children, seven sons and two daughters, but not all survived into adulthood. They lost their third son, born at Roborough House in 1822, after only a few months and likewise their first daughter, who died in infancy in 1826. Similarly their fourth son, who was the first to be born at Maristow House in October 1831, only lasted seven months while their second daughter and last child, named after her mother, was less than five when she died in 1847. With the exception of the first born son and heir, Massey Lopes Franco, the remaining four surviving sons were all more closely connected to Wiltshire than they were to West Devon. Ralph himself was listed as a freeholder in Westbury in 1818 and it is very probable that this refers to the manor house, which came to his uncle with the purchase of the borough in 1810. It is a handsome late Georgian house on the corner of Maristow Street and the Market

7 Westbury was a borough where the right to vote before 1832 was vested in 'burgage tenements' or rental properties owned by the crown or by a local lord of the manor. Occupiers of such properties could convey their voting rights as they chose (i.e. for the highest price). This was the principal means whereby a constituency became known as a 'pocket' or rotten borough. In practice, members were chosen by the corporation consisting of the mayor and up to 13 'capital burgesses', all of whom were under the direction of the proprietor, Manasseh Lopes.

Place. Manasseh Lopes also built, and presented to the town in 1815, a town hall bearing his crest, close by the Lopes Arms that had long been an inn but was renamed to honour the patron.

Westbury itself, despite being of Roman origin and sitting in a rich arable district on the edge of Salisbury Plain, owes much of its fortunes to the industrial revolution, particularly in relation to the textile industry where at one time eight factories employed more than a thousand workers. The fortunes of the workers were therefore heavily reliant on this industry and when it began to decline in the early nineteenth century, great poverty ensued and a militant streak emerged that undoubtedly influenced local political debate even though suffrage before 1832 was so heavily restricted.[8] In fact the mayor and a dozen 'capital burgesses' (tenants of properties owned by the lord of the manor incorporating a right to vote) were in practice the electorate and each of them received instructions from their landlord, who was also the recorder.

There was no election in 1814 but, as the foregoing suggests, Manasseh Lopes could remove or place whom he chose. Westbury was represented by two 'paying guests', Benjamin Hall and Benjamin Shaw. Lopes removed Hall in order to seat his nephew who mostly supported the Tory government under the Earl of Liverpool (PM 1812–27). As a sign of later convictions, Franco sided with the government in May 1816 against Catholic emancipation. Possibly wanting him to be closer to Maristow House, his uncle suggested another borough for the 1818 election and put him up for Newport near Launceston, where he fared badly receiving only 15 votes, admittedly out of an electorate numbering no more than 60. He stood again for Westbury in the election of June 1818 when the other position as MP was taken by Francis Conyngham.[9] He resigned in April 1819 when it became clear that his uncle was going to be sent to prison and he would have been available to comfort his aunt and Esther his younger sister before

8 William Cobbett (1912) on his rural adventures described the town memorably as a 'nasty odious rotten borough, a really rotten place' (ii: 78) and the local workers 'the worst used labouring people upon the face of the earth' (ii: 55).

9 Lord Francis Conyngham, referred to in Chapter 7, was an Anglo-Irish soldier and courtier to the Prince Regent and later when George IV.

her early death a few months later. From before the birth of his first son in June 1818, it is reasonable to suppose that both he and his wife were in west Devon. Massey Lopes Franco was born in Haxter Lodge on the Maristow estate close to Roborough House, as was his younger brother Ralph Ludlow Franco born in September 1820. Thereafter they must have moved into Roborough House where the following three confinements occurred.[10]

The Middle Years

In political terms, the years between 1819 and 1831 were a wilderness period for Ralph Franco. True he was Mayor of Westbury for a total of four years in the 1820s and he served as a major in the North Devon Militia in 1821. As far as Westbury was concerned, however, his uncle – on his early release from imprisonment mainly due to Ralph's initiatives – removed both of the representatives returned for the borough in the election of March 1820 in order to seat himself and a very wealthy personal friend (Philip John Miles, heir to a fortune from Jamaican plantations), presumably as a paying guest. His uncle, perhaps understandably wary of seeking to win over electors in another borough, returned himself again in the election of June 1826, alongside another wealthy Tory landowner.[11]

It was not until the general election on 2 May 1831 that Ralph Franco rejoined parliament, again for Westbury for which he had just become patron on the death of Manasseh Lopes. He now also became the 2nd baronet and five days after the election changed his name, and that of all his surviving children, to Lopes as demanded as a requirement of inheritance in his uncle's will. It was at this time, in the tumult prior to parliamentary reform, that Ralph Lopes could be said to have reached the high point of his parliamentary career. His experience

10 Although Massey Lopes Franco was also baptised (July 1818) in St George's Hanover Square in Mayfair London, when the family address is given as Princes Street right next door.

11 Sir George Warrender (1782–1849), a banker and landowner widely regarded as lacking in both intelligence and sophistication. Lady Morley is credited with the comment on news that he was to share the office of privy seal with another that 'Warrender [was] to be the privy' (*History of Parliament* online, *Members* 1820–32).

at Westbury both as an MP 12 years before and, more particularly, as the economic fortunes of the town declined in the period after, that he became a convert to the principle of electoral reform. After the debacle in 1829 when Robert Peel had used Westbury as a method of retaining his membership of the House, his uncle, then ailing, had installed two government supporters, one of whom, Sir Alexander Cray Grant (a very wealthy West Indian absentee planter), was adamantly anti-reform while the other, Michael Prendergast, was only lukewarm. Both were removed by Ralph Lopes, one to seat himself and one because of his political views. He chose instead for the other seat a man called Henry Hamner on the understanding that he was pro-reform. It appeared that this was not so, and Ralph acted decisively in removing him immediately in favour of a Whig like himself at this time, Henry Stephenson, a near neighbour of his uncle's London home and the illegitimate son of the eleventh Duke of Norfolk. This second choice was far more successful as Stephenson is credited with the comment:

> I have come into the House at my own request to support the present measure considering that the happiness, the welfare and the comfort of the country depend on the destruction of that detestable oligarchical power which has too long existed (*History of Parliament* online, *Members*, 1820–30).

Although Ralph Lopes cannot be regarded as an active participant in parliamentary debates, the issue of electoral reform was certainly one on which he had strong feelings as he expressed to the House:

> From his first entry into public life he had been the consistent and uncompromising advocate of Reform, though if he looked to motives of mere personal aggrandizement, he should be opposed to a measure which went to destroy his borough patronage. Without professing more patriotism than any other supporter of the present Bill, he would add, that he cheerfully sacrificed all rights of borough proprietorship, at what he conscientiously believed was the shrine of his country's good (*Hansard* 20 January 1831).

It must be said, however, that despite this seemingly liberal commitment, Lopes was not driven by an egalitarian impulse. For example, in the debates over reform he argued for agricultural interests to receive special privileges and was not in favour of the proposition in the draft reform bill, and indeed in its subsequent passage, that the criterion for voting should be the possession of property with a minimum assessed rental value of £10 per annum:

> Let the £10 man have his vote, but let another who is higher rented or rated have two or more votes, rising according to a graduated scale. You thus preserve your own consistency, you keep faith to the public and you obviate the pernicious and overwhelming tendency of the £10 tide of voting. You give to property that due and just influence it ought to have, and rely upon it by doing this you will satisfy all parties, *high* and *low*, those *for* as well as those *against* reform, and you will give a feeling of security to thousands who are friendly to reform, but have a *deep, a rooted, though a silent dread* and apprehension of the £10 city and borough franchise (*History of Parliament* online, *Members* 1820–1830; submission to the Lord Chancellor, 3 June 1831) (emphasis in original).

In the same representation, he argued further that ministers of the crown should have *ex officio* membership of parliament.[12]

As earlier analysis has suggested, there is little evidence that Manasseh Lopes ever actively lobbied for an earldom, but that cannot be said of Ralph Lopes. In a remarkable submission to the lord chancellor on 12 January 1832 he not only requests favourable consideration when it became clear that the passage of the Reform Bill would depend on packing the House of Lords with new members who would outvote objectors, but also links this claim to reforming a system under which his uncle unfairly suffered. It constitutes a submission that is as disingenuous as it is imaginative:

12 Ralph Lopes was one of three landowning reformers but others from the urban boroughs swelled that number. Eventually, Wiltshire as a whole lost 16 seats, leaving a total of 18 overall. Westbury went down from two to one member of parliament.

> [T]he much regarded relative whom I have succeeded, and to whom I am so deeply indebted, was persecuted, and with unreasonable severity punished, for the breach of those laws pronounced to be inherent in a system, now about to be abolished. It has been a source of pride to me to have had an opportunity to vindicate his memory, by the voluntary and cheerful sacrifice I came forward to make at the call and under the emergencies of the government, and the country. Surely then, I may, I trust, be pardoned in saying, that I should feel an honest exaltation, if any act of mine could obliterate the painful feelings his sufferings occasioned, and the record of circumstances connected with them. And may I not, without invidious comparison, but rather in honour of him advance, that if he was made bitterly to atone for the liabilities to which he unguardedly subjected himself, the part I have taken, in an equal degree, gives me some title to a share in the honours about to be advanced to those who have promoted the question of reform, or have in that cause made any sacrifices of a personal nature (Brougham MS).

In other words, months after inheriting a vast fortune, his claim to further social advancement would help right the wrongs of his uncle's treatment. Unsurprisingly, his submission was disregarded. Later commentators also spotted that his seeming commitment to a liberal measure might smack of opportunism in another sense, as in an article looking back some years later on the election of 1832, which argued 'had Sir Ralph Lopez presented himself in any other character than as a reformer it is by no means certain that he would have come in so easily' (*Wiltshire Independent* 13 September 1849).

In 1835 he was elected by acclamation unopposed for the borough of Westbury (*Exeter and Plymouth Gazette* 24 January 1835). In 1837, however, he ran up against serious opposition and lost by two votes (96 to 98 out of 201 electors) to John Briscoe whose views chimed closely with the increasingly impoverished textile workers in the borough. Briscoe was an ardent reformer and equally committed opponent of slavery who was a genuine independent liberal spirit with an enthusiasm for measures to combat rural poverty. He was a particularly strident proponent of educational opportunities for the poor (*Devizes and Wiltshire Gazette* 24 August 1837). This outcome occurred despite the fact that Lopes engaged in all kinds of schemes to boost his popularity including splitting tenancies to enhance voter numbers, improving the housing of labourers by moving them into cottages and adding land to their tenure.

Four years later in June 1841, now arguably revealing his true colours as a Tory, his commitment to these tactics did bring their reward for he was again returned unopposed, although his enthusiasm for maintaining the untrammelled hegemony of the Protestant Church served him well in an age when pressure was mounting to lessen discrimination against Roman Catholics, particularly in Ireland.[13] In 1847, however, he encountered twin obstacles that again led to his defeat. The first was the collapse of the last remaining large textile factory when Matravers and Overbury went into terminal decline. The second was that he was then up against even more serious opposition in the form of James Wilson a liberal politician but, more importantly, a highly successful Scottish businessman and founder of the *Economist* magazine whose principles then as now were to market freedoms and unfettered trade, arguments that contrasted severely with Lopes' pronouncements in support of the Corn Laws and protectionism more broadly.[14] Wilson served as MP for Westbury from 1847–57 and then for Devonport until 1859 and *Hansard* reports that he made more than 600 speeches or interventions in the House.

---

13 Ralph Lopes paid for the rebuilding of the parish church at Bickleigh in 1838. In replying to a speech at the relaying of the foundation stone he said he was ever grateful for being brought up in the Church of England (*Devizes and Wiltshire Gazette* 12 April 1838).

14 James Wilson was a man of humble origins but great abilities. He rose to be financial secretary to the Treasury and but for an early death would have achieved even more. It was said of him that 'complication did not lead to indecision – the result was always straightforward and intelligible. In an arguable case it was never left in doubt what he decided, and why he had come to that conclusion' (Thomson, 1870: 545). The same could be said of his magazine, which he edited for the first 16 years and which is now the most successful economic and financial publication in the Anglophone world with a circulation in excess of 1.6 million per week.

Later Years

Despite the fact that Sir Ralph was frequently credited with promoting the interest of the farming community and praised as a landlord, after his defeat at Westbury he in fact spent more and more time in Mayfair.[15] In 1845 he had taken over the lease of 46 Upper Grosvenor Street (South Side), part of the Grosvenor Estate, and it was from there on 23 November 1848 that he wrote to the chairman of the South Devon Division making it clear that he would like to return to parliament at the byelection caused by the retirement of Lord Courtenay on his appointment as poor-law inspector (*Western Times* 2 December 1848).[16] In this letter he commits himself to opposing two policies of Sir Robert Peel: first, the proposed enlarged endowment to the Catholic clergy (which became known as the 'Maynooth question') and second, 'the withdrawal of Protection from Native Industry' (i.e. freer trade consequent upon the repeal of the Navigation Acts).[17] This position greatly enhanced his appeal to the South Devon Tory party.

It is hard to overstate the importance of the Catholic question, even in the form of a very modest increase in a grant to one seminary. It is true that St Patrick's College at Maynooth, 15 miles to the west of Dublin in County Kildare, was the largest Roman Catholic seminary in Ireland, but the proposal was modest; namely to enhance a grant

15 See *Exeter and Plymouth Gazette* 16 October 1841. Very close to the election of 1848, it was claimed that since he inherited the estate (of Maristow) 'he [had] devoted himself with praiseworthy zeal and self-denial to those duties which many of the landlord gentry have only since then been thinking about' (*Exeter and Plymouth Gazette* 25 November 1848).

16 From 1832–85, the county of Devon was divided into two constituencies, North and South, each returning two members. Lord Courtenay had been returned at the General Election of 1841.

17 Peel's policy in respect of the former was to increase a grant to a Catholic seminary at Maynooth in order to ease tensions between Catholic Ireland and Protestant England. The Navigation Acts restricted trade with the colonial empire to the vessels of the mother country. They were repealed in 1849 and together with the repeal of the Corn Laws in 1846, that had favoured landed interests by keeping grain prices artificially high, lowered the costs of foodstuffs and thereby controlled demands for higher wages in a period when rural incomes were under great pressure, particularly in Ireland after the potato blight of 1845.

made on its foundation in 1795 from £8,000 per annum to one of £26,000 in order to help sustain the burgeoning demand for priests. It has been recorded that between 1790 and 1847 more than 2,000 Catholic churches were built in Ireland, often with the financial support of the Protestant Church of Ireland (Grimes, 2009: 147). High Tory opinion, however, was not so charitable. In the election of 1849 for South Devon, the leading candidate, prior to the letter from Sir Ralph Lopes, was Samuel Trehawke Kekewich (1796–1873), MP for Exeter 1826–30, who has been called 'the model of an English country squire'. Kekewich was also a Tory but one of a liberal persuasion and more inclined therefore to support Peel in granting this small measure of Catholic emancipation. Not so Ralph Lopes, who wrote an open letter to the press entitled 'letter to the Electors of the Southern Division of the County of Devon' on 28 November 1848 saying, inter alia, 'I could never be induced to consent to any proposal for that purpose (supporting the proposed increased endowment), and I now repeat to you my feelings and opinions on that subject, maturely considered and long and sincerely entertained and acted on by me' (*Western Times* 2 December 1848). The result was that Kekewich withdrew from the race and Lopes was elected unopposed at a meeting on 13 February 1849 outside the Sessions House in the Castle of Exeter with only five hands raised against him. Lopes was introduced as someone who had already served in parliament for 30 years and had a major qualification as 'one of the greatest land owners in the county'. Following his adoption, the successful candidate, in accord with tradition, then disappeared into the Sessions House and emerged in knight's armour and spurs in order to parade on horseback through the city (Plate 44).

The High Sheriff (Sir Trayton Drake) then said that on the subject of 'settling an endowment on the Roman Catholic clergy of Ireland' Lopes was 'an advocate of toleration in its most extended sense but would never consent to the endowment of the most intolerant sect of Christians on the inhabitable globe' (*Exeter Flying Post* 15 February 1849). This attitude stood in marked contrast to that of his uncle, Sir Manasseh Massey Lopes, who 20 years earlier had supported the ministry of the Duke of Wellington on Catholic emancipation (*Western Times* 17 January 1829).

It would also appear that this advocacy of toleration did not extend to those fellow citizens from the religious background into which Lopes was himself born 60 years before. Asked by a Mr Tucker at the same meeting 'whether he would vote in favour of the abolition of Jewish disabilities, in order that Baron Rothschild might take his seat in Parliament...', *The Times* reported (14 February 1849) that Sir Ralph 'considered Protestant Christianity to be an essential part of the constitution, and sooner than go to Parliament to break into that principle he would retire from the hustings'.[18] Moreover, his commitment to maintaining the exclusion of Jews from public life was made even clearer in an approving report in the local press soon after his successful lobbying to stand for South Devon:

> As the important question of the admission of Jews to Parliament will probably be again submitted to the House of Commons next session, it is a source of great gratification to be able to announce that Sir Ralph Lopes will give it his decided opposition. In a letter to a gentleman of this city the worthy baronet says: 'Should any friends be doubtful as to the course I should take on the subject to which you refer (the Jewish Disabilities Bill), you may quite satisfy their minds on that point; I never did approve of it, and should give a decided vote against it' (*Exeter and Plymouth Gazette* 2 December 1848).

The cartoonist James Gillray[19] (Plate 45) saw the Jewish connection, somewhat unfairly represented by porcine creatures frantically

18 Lionel de Rothschild had been elected to parliament in 1847 as a Liberal member for the City of London but was prevented from taking his seat due to his inability to swear the Christian oath. It was not until July 1858, after a number of attempts by the House of Lords to pass the Jewish Disabilities Bill had failed, even though supported by the Commons, that a non-Christian oath of allegiance was deemed acceptable.

19 Print of Sir Ralph Franco marked in pencil on reverse 'Mr F–co, a gentleman well known on the turf – a converted Jew indicated by the pigs running away. Generally called "The Great Boots"'. Signed J.B. 1845. Jewish Museum London.

leaving the scene, as highly relevant to who Lopes was and nothing could reveal more clearly his determination to disavow this past. Unlike his uncle, whose adoption of Anglicanism was shallow and mostly unobserved, Ralph Lopes was a regular churchgoer and even an enthusiastic congregant.

A not dissimilar outcome occurred in the following general election of June 1852, when Lopes was again elected unopposed and, as before, sat with Sir John Yarde-Buller.[20] What was different was perhaps the growing power of the Whigs, mostly representing the emerging urban middle class. The Tory party continued to be divided with the greater part, including Lopes, staunchly promoting the protectionist instincts of the landed aristocracy against the Whigs, free traders and the 'Peelites', the supporters of the former Tory prime minister Robert Peel opposed to the Corn Laws, which had by this time been firmly repealed. South Devon was a bastion of landed interests and a local paper reported that both Yarde-Buller and Lopes in sustaining the Conservative cause were setting themselves against 'the evils of democracy' (*Western Times* 17 July 1852). Although this was a turbulent time in British politics, it was not one in which Lopes played a significant part. In fact, *Hansard* records only one debate in which Ralph Lopes ever contributed and that was in 1849 when he spoke against what he considered an undue burden of taxation on proprietors of landed properties, such as himself.[21]

By 1853, Ralph Lopes was severely unwell but at various times in that year he seemed to rally. On 28 January the following year, however, he died at Maristow House with what a local paper described as 'disease of the heart and liver'. Since the same report, published on the day of his demise, declared that 'his mind has given way under the severity of the attack', it may have been that cirrhosis played a part (*Western Times* 28 January 1854).

Many of the obituaries that appeared immediately after Sir Ralph's death eulogised his contributions as an enlightened landlord

20 Yarde-Buller had first been returned for South Devon in 1835. His daughter, Bertha Yarde-Buller married Ralph Lopes' eldest son Massey Lopes.

21 As shown earlier, however, this was not the only occasion on which Lopes made an interjection in Parliament but his contributions were very rare.

and focused on his charitable commitments. For example, for the five years preceding his death, he had been president of the Plymouth Royal Eye Infirmary and also its largest benefactor. One exception was published very soon after his decease in a local paper that normally supported Whig causes. The anonymous obituarist summed up how Lopes had come into his property and title but continued,

> He had no very bright example before him in the senatorial career of his uncle, and we are not aware that Sir Ralph 'bettered the instructions' of Sir Massey in his parliamentary career. During the latter part of the late Baronet's life, illness incapacitated him from attending to public business, and when he had health neither his sympathies nor obligations permitted him to do much good to the general public.
>
> During the time that Sir Ralph sat in Parliament, whether as Mr Ralph Franco or Sir Ralph Lopes, we are not aware that his name stands connected with any one liberal measure, or that he showed any great trait either of intellect or feeling calculated to advance the progress of society (*Western Times* 4 February 1854).

Noting that he abandoned liberal principles on the death of his uncle, the obituary goes on to say that he was a 'zealous Protectionist' and condemns the rumour doing the rounds that the intention of the Tories was to replace the late baronet with his eldest son, Massey Lopes, in the South Devon seat:

> Can there be a greater mockery of the representative principle than thus to attempt to hand the seat over to the son of a man who, as a representative, leaves not one single act of public service to mark his tenancy of the proud distinction from which death has snatched him away?

It is not clear whether the rumour of a dynastic political succession had any truth in it and it could be argued that these comments, appearing only days after Ralph Lopes' death, were in poor taste and may have been unnecessarily hurtful to his widow but it is true that after the Great Reform that he had done his best to support, his contribution to parliament was weak and self-serving.

It is interesting to note that even after Sir Ralph's proclamations on maintaining antisemitic principles in relation to parliament, commentators were not so prepared to accept the transition from the supposed traits of inheritance. Even though Lopes had now been buried at Bickleigh Anglican Church, the commentator above still saw him as 'gathered to Abraham's bosom' and as scheming for his son's selection since 'these people have not abandoned the shrewdness of the ancient race in adopting the faith of their more modern brethren'. In fact, Ralph's heir, Massey Lopes, was not selected immediately for South Devon; rather in the first instance the light of preferment fell on the young Sir Stafford Northcote to be the replacement MP.[22] A report on the hustings in the same issue of the paper cited above quoted Northcote in a reply querying his views on letting Jews into parliament, as saying, 'Let them into Parliament – why I am now trying even to keep the grandson of one of them out.' The seat was eventually taken by Lawrence Palk (later Lord Haldon) until the election of 1868 when Massey Lopes did indeed take over.

The will of Sir Ralph Lopes was originally prepared in May 1850, nearly four years before his death. It reflects the wishes of a man who took great care with his family obligations as well as with his financial affairs. It is exceedingly long and detailed but offers few insights into his character other than the foregoing. Having rebuilt the church of St Mary the Virgin at Bickleigh, he clearly thought he deserved public recognition and commanded that a monument should be erected to his memory and one also to his daughter Susannah, perhaps fearing that otherwise none would be commissioned. This did, however, allow him to specify the maximum sum that could be

22 Sir Stafford Northcote, later the first Earl of Iddesleigh (1818–87), held various senior official positions including chancellor of the exchequer and foreign secretary.

expended (150 guineas in his case and £50 for his daughter). Apart from that the will is unexceptionable. Sir Massey, his eldest son, inherited the huge estate but generous provision was made for Lady Lopes and, in particular for his second son, Ralph Ludlow Lopes, who received substantial property in Somerset and in Wiltshire after his mother's death. The remaining three sons are recognised with a significant financial sum but only on their attaining the age of 25. It is clear that he hoped that one or other of his younger sons would wish to enter Holy Orders and should this come to pass, the will specifies that the advowsons owned by the family in both Bickleigh and Walkhampton should be mobilised to ensure an opening, even if this meant removing the existing incumbent. Interestingly there is a recognition that the properties on the estate require renewed investment and Sir Massey is commanded to reserve one-third of the estate's income for that purpose (PRO 11/2188; cf. *Morning Post* 14 March 1854).

There is one other unusual provision that stands out in the will. This is a clause that bequeaths his private papers to his widow and to his second son (Ralph Ludlow Lopes) on trust to examine these after his decease and to destroy those they consider private papers, passing the remainder to his executors as part of his residual estate.[23] As the solicitor David Nicolson (Lord Carnock) noted after examining this will as part of an exchange of letters on the family's history with his cousin Hon George Lopes, this is a most unusual provision, it being more common to ensure access for future historians by preserving this resource. Nicolson advances two interesting possibilities for these clauses (Nicolson to Lopes, 22 October 1998). The first was to shield from public scrutiny family conflicts. He identifies one 'Pereira', son of Ralph's older sister, but there was no such person and he must have been referring to a cousin, son of his aunt, Rachael, who had married Isaac Pereira in 1771 and produced four sons but none of these was living at the time the will was drafted, although it is perfectly possible that family correspondence existed that showed one or other of these seeking

23 Later codicils remove a role for his widow and insert the two older sons.

financial support from either Manasseh or Ralph Lopes. His second theory is more plausible. Noting that the same provision was found in the wills of the Rothschilds, he suggests that some of the papers may have related to financial dealings in the years before 1815 when his uncle was enjoying the fruits derived from helping to sustain the Napoleonic Wars:

> I feel sure that many of the papers of Sir Ralph would have related to transactions of the kind that I have suggested; not necessarily his own transactions, but also those of his predecessors. The destruction of such papers would have been imperative for the protection of others than his own family. Our predecessors were no strangers to political corruption; if there were any papers of this kind, they would have had to be destroyed (Nicolson to Lopes, 21 December 1998).

Although very alive to the family dilemma posed by the Jewish heritage, Nicolson does not include this as another possible reason for the censoring of the private papers.

Dame Susanna Gibbs Lopes died tragically at the age of 69 when visiting her third son Henry Charles Lopes at his residence, East Hill House in Frome.[24] She had been out riding and changed into a muslin dress on returning home. Standing with her back to the fire on Friday 26 March, it is thought that it ignited and before anyone could reach her, the room was on fire and she had received severe burns from which she died the following morning (*Western Times* 29 March 1870). Her body was interred at Bickleigh on 2 April 1870. Her death underlined the division of the family between the West Devon seat and the properties in Somerset and Wiltshire. Lady Lopes clearly felt more at home in the latter than she did at Maristow, being closer to her family roots and, indeed, to the families of three of her four surviving sons. Earlier in the year of her demise, her address was often given at 46 Upper Grosvenor Street or at The Grange near Bradford,

24 Frome at that time was the largest cloth manufacturing town in either Somerset or Wiltshire.

Wiltshire, the home of her youngest son George Ludlow Lopes (1836–1909).

Sir Massey Lopes

If Manasseh Massey Lopes made an instrumental and largely tokenistic rejection of his religion and past, then his nephew and heir, Ralph Lopes, spent his career pursuing what he conceived to be the life of an English country gentleman, largely untroubled by the massive political and economic currents swirling around him. At best, this served as a platform for his heirs to pursue a more active stance, both politically and in career terms.

Massey Lopes Franco, the eldest of the five sons of Ralph and Susanna Gibbs Lopes who survived infancy, was born on 14 June 1818. He was educated at Winchester College and Oriel College, Oxford, graduating in 1842 with a 4th class degree in Classics (MA 1845) by when he had changed his full name to Lopes Massey Lopes. Very soon afterwards he spent a year in Scotland as an apprentice farmer and agricultural concerns were very close to his heart for the rest of his life.

Sir Lopes Massey Lopes, 3rd baronet, was married in the year of his father's death (1854) to the Hon Bertha Yarde-Buller only daughter of Sir John Buller-Yarde-Buller and his wife Elizabeth; in 1858 on his retirement Sir John was raised to the peerage as Baron Churston of Churston Ferrers and Lupton between Paignton and Brixham in East Devon. He was 35 years old and she was almost ten years his junior. They married at St George's, Hanover Square, Mayfair subsequently producing two daughters, then a son and two more daughters, the last of whom died soon after birth. The first daughter, Bertha Susan, was born on 12 March 1855 and is listed in the 1861 Census as aged five when all the family were in Maristow House. She died aged six in 1862 but, confusingly for genealogists, Sir Massey's younger brother, Henry Charles Lopes (see below) married in the same year as his older brother, also had a daughter named Bertha Susan, born on 16 January 1870 who died in 1926.[25]

25 This Bertha Susan Lopes married Charles Bathurst, 1st Viscount Bledisloe

The death of daughters was to haunt Sir Massey since in 1890 he lost both his remaining daughters, Adela (Ada) Elizabeth born on 29 January 1858, and Louisa Ellinor, born on 9 August 1860. Happily, his son and heir, born on 24 March 1859, thrived and lived to a grand old age, dying in 1938. What must have seemed like the 'Maristow curse' took Sir Massey's first wife on 13 January 1872.[26] Two years later on 25 August 1874, Sir Massey married again to Louisa Newman the fourth daughter of Sir Robert Newman and his wife Mary Denne of Mamhead House, near Dawlish.[27] Again, they were married in London, this time at St Peter's Eaton Square.

Precisely how much time the family lived in London is difficult to calculate but it was probably substantial. Early in his career (1857), he became Sheriff of Devonshire but this would not have required a full-time presence in the county. According to the *St James's Gazette* (10 May 1902) Maristow was visited by Queen Victoria and the Prince Consort and there is no doubt that he invested heavily in the estate and put considerable energy into defending its interests. One example is the battle he had with the Plymouth Corporation over the latter's extraction of increasing amounts of water from the Meavy and other streams, thereby affecting fishing on Maristow estate land (*Western Morning News* 8 January 1870). However, the court case that ensued revealed that his cousin Copleston Lopes Radcliffe of Warleigh (1818–83), who had been engaged by his father Ralph to be responsible for part of the estate, was actually in day-to-day management of all of it during Massey's tenure (*Western Morning News* 17 May 1870).[28] Moreover, on the 1871 Census Sir Massey Lopes is listed as at 28 Grosvenor Gardens Mayfair aged 53 with his first wife Bertha, aged 45, and three children Ada Lopes (13),

later, after his wife's death, to become Governor-General of New Zealand.

26 She was interred in the chapel at Maristow House (*Western Times* 23 January 1872).

27 In this he was following his father-in-law from his first marriage who in 1861 had taken the second daughter of the same family as his second wife.

28 In 1876, Coplestone Radcliffe bought the magnificent Plympton House and estate at Plympton St Maurice with the intention of developing its lands on modern farming principles so it is reasonable to suppose that he was well rewarded for his management at Maristow.

Henry Yarde-Buller Lopes (12), and Louisa (ten), together with a governess, lady's maid, housekeeper, housemaid, under lady's maid, scullery maid, kitchen maid, upper housemaid, butler and footman. A decade later, they were also there at the same address with the second Lady Lopes, two daughters (23 and 21), Henry (22), and ten servants. In 1885, Massey Lopes retired from parliament and to some degree also from public life so it is perhaps no surprise that by 1901 he was living at Maristow House with Louisa his wife aged 74, and 13 staff (five housemaids, a scullery maid, housekeeper and lady's maid, a butler, two footmen, and two grooms).[29]

By and large it would appear that the land of the Maristow estate had been preserved during Sir Massey's long tenure. It is true that the official return for *Owners of Land in 1873* listed Maristow as possessing only 126 acres with a rental value of £1,348 per annum but this referred only to the house and its immediate grounds and not the estate as a whole.[30] A more reliable guide is Bateman's overview of great landowners, surveyed in 1879 and published in 1883. It becomes clear that a major divide existed between those, like Massey Lopes, whose principal holdings were in Devon and Cornwall and those who simply held part of their land in one or both of these counties.

Name	Acreage	Gross rentable value (£)	Devon/ Cornwall (%)
Duke of Bedford	86,335	141,793	27.6
William Henry Carew-Pole	4,328	6,401	100.0
Lord Churston	10,903	11,464	92.7
Lord Clinton	34,776	32,613	52.1
Augustus Coryton	9,385	9,944	100.0
Earl of Devon	53,075	45,520	37.8
Viscount Falmouth	30,606	42,904	84.6

29 In 1890 and again in 1895, the London City Directory lists Sir Massey at his London home, followed by Maristow and the Manor House Westbury, Wilts.

30 His younger brothers, Henry Charles Lopes in Frome (Somerset) and Ralph Ludlow Lopes in Melksham (Wiltshire) were listed as 434 acres with a rental value of £581 and 909 acres with a rental value of £1,320 respectively.

Cyril Fortescue	22,985	18,093	87.6
Trehawke Kekewich	4,734	5,942	100.0
Sir Massey Lopes	12,103	10,668	98.9
Earl of Morley	4,238	8,209	100.0
Earl of Mt. Edgcumbe	18,223	24,181	100.0
Lord Robartes	22,234	30,730	100.0
Earl of St Germans	12,791	17,191	47.1

Source: Bateman, J (1883) *The Great Landowners of Great Britain and Ireland*, 4th edition, London, Harrison

The former tended to have smaller acreages and to live at least part of the time on their estates. There were exceptions such as the Earl of St Germans, who held more than half his land in Wiltshire, Gloucestershire and Kent while residing at Port Eliot in St Germans, but by and large the generalisation holds true. Where local holdings predominated the rental value per acre usually comfortably exceeded one pound sterling per annum but for Maristow it was considerably less (88p), which may be because of the proportion of poor land at high elevations. Lord Robartes, for example, at Lanhydrock managed £1.38 per acre, while Trehawke Kekewich, a close friend of the family, managed something similar at £1.25 per acre from his estate at Peamore, Exminster, probably because of its proximity to Exeter city. Landholdings near or in urban centres may have boosted the returns for Carew-Pole (£1.48) (Anthony, near Torpoint), the Earl of Morley (£1.94) (Saltram, near Plymouth) and the Earl of Mt. Edgcumbe (£1.33) (holdings in Stoke Damerel, Plymouth).

What is striking, however, is that the total acreage for the Maristow estate is approximately half what it was 40 years earlier. This figure is deceptive for although some outlying lands had undoubtedly been sold, these figures relate to land that could be let for agricultural purposes. In other words, the land holdings themselves may not equate to all land; the Maristow estate, for example, included unproductive common land and parts of Dartmoor that would have been unusable for arable or even in some cases for sheep. Importantly also, the financial returns indicated do not equate to total income; they are returns on land used largely for agricultural purposes and while some include, for example, mining leases, others do not. They do not include wealth held as cash or loans, nor indeed rental income from houses.

Encouraged by his father, then ailing, Massey Lopes stood for the family constituency of Westbury in 1852 against the incumbent Whig, James Wilson, his father's *bête noire*. Once again, Wilson was too strong but only just so since the 34-year-old Lopes received support from nearly 49 per cent of the turnout, losing by only seven votes. He had his revenge in 1857 and in 1859 and 1865 when on all three occasions he was returned unopposed. In the General Election of 1868, Lopes was invited to follow his father again by standing for South Devon. In the interim, Lawrence Palk had joined John Yarde-Buller in the second seat but on the latter's elevation to the peerage as the 1st Baron Churston in 1858, the second seat was taken by the old Tory favourite, Samuel Trehawke Kekewich. Palk then moved on, creating the vacancy for Lopes to fill. Unusually, since in all cases since 1841 no contest had occurred, by the time Massey Lopes arrived on the scene in 1868 an opponent had materialised in the form of the philosopher Bertrand Russell's father John (Lord Amberley). South Devon, however, stuck to its Tory guns and Lopes and Kekewich put paid to Liberal hopes.

At the adoption meeting in Plymouth on 27 August 1868 the proposer from the local Conservative Party was careful to underline Sir Massey's credentials by referring to his father as 'one of the few conservatives who had acumen enough to see the wisdom of the great Reform Bill of 1832, and he left his party to vote for that measure'. Sir Massey emphasised his commitment to the liberal wing of the party by responding, 'there is no private or public act he ever did for which I honour him more than that'. Even his dedication to landed interests is cast in a liberal cloak for he is reported as declaring:

> I am not a man for class interests – I am as much interested in manufactures as I am in agriculture, and I am quite satisfied that one cannot endure without the other, but I still positively assert that the legislation of the past twenty-five years has been to the detriment of agriculture rather than for the benefit of it.

He then continues with the dubious proposition that while land and property produce only one-seventh of national income, they bear the total burden of taxation. Nonetheless, the seconder of the motion to adopt Sir Massey for one of the South Devon seats was in no doubt that they had the right man for 'whether it with reference to the Royal Agricultural Show, the fat cattle show, the hospital, or the orphan asylum, they always found Sir Massey Lopes ready to come forward, with hand and purse ready to assist them' (report of the meeting at the Mechanics Institute in Plymouth 27 August 1868, *Exeter and Plymouth Gazette* 28 August 1868). Lopes was firmly lodged in this constituency until he retired from active politics in 1885.

Massey Lopes is widely credited with an enthusiasm for modernising agricultural production, and certainly there is evidence of considerable investment in the Maristow estate during his lifetime. He also championed agricultural interests more generally, particularly through his leadership of voluntary associations. For example, he was elected president of the Bath and West of England Agricultural Society in June 1873 and served as president of the Royal Agricultural Society in 1884, afterwards succeeded by the then Prince of Wales. If there is one enthusiasm, however, for which he was identified, it was his relentless campaign for relief from the burden of local taxation on land and property, rather than on incomes more generally. The second half of the nineteenth century was actually one where taxation as a proportion of national income had been on a downward trajectory since rising to the giddy heights of 20 per cent immediately after the Napoleonic Wars (Hartwell, 1981: 137). While it was true that by 1851 total tax take was increasing, it was still the case that customs dues and excise duties contributed 65 per cent of all government revenues, while land taxes comprised well under 10 per cent (Hartwell, 1981: Table 4). In fact, even during the early years of the century and certainly later it was borrowing that funded wars and customs and excise imposts that paid the interest and for peace time services. Given this, it has to be said that Lopes was remarkably successful in pressing the case for large landowners, such as himself, to be relieved from some of that which they did contribute.

Interestingly, his main argument against the taxes imposed on land and houses was historical. This was a period long before the welfare state but minimal provision was made for financial distress through the 'poor rate'. Lopes argued that the taxing of real property (land and houses) made sense originally when employment on the land was basically the only work available. The industrial revolution, however meant that other forms of employment were now growing apace, yet were not required to contribute. Moreover, by no means all the funds generated by the 'poor rate' were spent on the poor; rather the fund appeared now to be used for a variety of additional purposes, including the police, highways and even educational provision. Lopes managed to include in his argument that evergreen complaint of country landowners, the advent of free trade. If agriculturalists had lost out through greater competition, how doubly unjust it was to expect them to contribute so highly to local revenues. What was needed, he argued, was a Royal Commission to examine this question and propose a strategy of alleviation. He concluded with this plea: 'All must admit that taxation was an evil – it was a necessary one; but any undue proportion of taxation thrown upon any particular class or interest was not only an evil, it was an unmitigated curse – a national disaster, for it tended to blight and paralyze that interest' (*Hansard* 23 February 1869).

For his pains, Lopes did not receive the promise of a Royal Commission but only a commitment to investigate the matter further. It is hard to see what else could have been achieved, given the modest level of the poor rate (10–12.5 per cent) and the fact that as a major landowner Lopes would have been a major beneficiary of any policy of alleviation. He did, however, receive a great deal of support from others in a similar position. Albert Pell, for example, member for the Southern Division of Leicestershire, refers to Lopes as 'our local taxation chief in Parliament' (1908: 267).[31] Others of the same persuasion included Henry Chaplin and Clare Sewell Read.[32] Gladstone himself also agreed that this was an urgent matter and would be examined as soon as the Irish question was settled. *The Times*, however, was in no doubt 'it cannot be denied that the weight of argument last night was entirely on the side of Sir Massey Lopes' (*The Times* 24 February 1869).

Lopes eventually triumphed when in April 1872 he and his supporters defeated Gladstone's government on a similar motion by 259 to 159, leading eventually to the Agricultural Ratings Act of 1879, passed with the more sympathetic support of Disraeli's second Conservative administration, although the prime minister himself appears to have regarded Lopes with some suspicion. Writing to Lady Bradford about his strategy when forming his government, he noted that Clare Read and Massey Lopes had 'enchanted the farmers' and that his strategy had been to 'include every "representative" man, that is to say everyone who might be troublesome...' (Disraeli to Lady Bradford, 27 February 1874 cited in Monypenny and Buckle, 1920: 295–6). Improbably, Disraeli's policy of parking Lopes where he could be less troublesome was to appoint him as Civil Lord of the Admiralty where his energies were displaced as far as possible from land issues to something on which, as far as is known, he had no prior interest or competence. Nonetheless he is credited with

31 Pell was a Council member of the Royal Agricultural Society but was better known for being credited with having invented rugby union while a pupil at the eponymous school.

32 Henry Chaplin, first Viscount Chaplin (1841–1923) was a landed aristocrat from Lincolnshire improbably known for an infamous love triangle having been jilted at the last moment but who bettered his opponent by owning the winner of the Derby in 1867 when the latter had bet his shirt on any but Chaplin's horse. He went on to become the first minister for agriculture in 1889. Clare Sewell Read (1806–1905) was another landed aristocrat and member of parliament for a number of Norfolk constituencies. He became a well-known judge at agricultural shows and author on land-related topics.

reforming the administration of the Admiralty office and placing the Royal Naval College at Greenwich on a surer financial footing (Plate 46).

Massey Lopes remained in this position until 1880 but even after that made a number of speeches in debates on Admiralty issues. On all subjects he made a total of 157 contributions to proceedings in the house but it was seven years after he was first elected that he was aroused to contribute on the two great national issues that preoccupied him; first the allocation of taxation between landed and other interests and, second, the financial support for the nation's fighting forces. He kept up his campaign for many years, objecting, for example, to the merging of agriculture with commerce when it came to government administration and pointing out that there were five different departments of government dealing with agriculture (*The Times* 22 December 1882).

Unsurprisingly, the second issue was widely supported and newspaper reports appeared that proposed his elevation to the peerage (e.g. *Western Morning News* 3 April 1880). Two other concerns, however, marked out his later years: first, engagement with local political debates, and second, a concern to support charitable causes that were close to his heart. As far as the first was concerned, he had been High Sheriff of Devon in 1857 but between 1888 and 1904 he served as an alderman of Devonshire County Council. He was also a major benefactor of numerous good causes, especially the South Devon and East Cornwall Hospital that received over £16,000 in donations from him.[33] To this day, its successor institution still sustains buildings and wards that carry the Lopes and Maristow labels. Later, he could claim the record for the number of years he was a JP – a total of 65 years from 1842 until 1907 (*Warminster and Westbury Journal* 4 May 1907). Also following his father's lead some years before, he paid for repair of Bickleigh Church in 1861 and 1882 and he erected almshouses in 1873 in memory of his first wife. This was also the reason for the commissioning in 1871

33 His portrait by Mr AS Cope, RA, painted in 1900, was in the committee-room of the South Devon and East Cornwall Hospital, Plymouth.

of the present chapel, integrated on the eastern side of Maristow House. It was built in the Gothic style very close to the site of the ancient chapel of St Martin dating from the thirteenth century, which originally belonged together with the manor to the canons of Plympton. Opened in October 1879, the design and rebuilding was the work of Piers St Aubyn. It is constructed of dressed random rubble with yellow freestone dressings under a roof of local slate. It is a handsome building with a fine spire in Bath stone and finely wrought marbled interior. As photographs taken a little later show, a magnificent conservatory, was also added at about the same time (1871) (Plate 47).

While it took some time to materialise, towards the end of his life Sir Massey Lopes appears to have concluded that the family had permanently divided as far as landed estates were concerned between West Devon and Wiltshire. In July 1904 he put up for sale 22 lots in Westbury consisting of just under 70 acres (30 acres of which was suitable for housing) plus existing houses, 13 cottages, a builder's yard and orchards. A little later he added another 45 cottages comprising together all his Westbury holdings (*Wiltshire Times and Trowbridge Advertiser* 2 July 1904). Even the town hall, built by Sir Manasseh Lopes, was included but in that case it was withdrawn from auction after the town council expressed an interest and it was eventually sold to them for £325 plus an additional £52 for the market tolls and weighbridge. The council deliberated at length whether to make this investment but eventually decided that the need for more office space was persuasive (*Wiltshire Times and Trowbridge Advertiser* 6 August 1904).[34]

Sir Massey Lopes died at Maristow in his 89th year on 20 January 1908 after a few days' illness. *The Times* obituary (21 January) noted his contribution to the interests of agriculture but also refers to his efforts to 'rebuild almost every farmhouse and cottage' on his estate that had become worn out due to long leases and leases for lives. It did not refer to his father's neglect of these issues nor to the

34 The town hall, although barely 50 years old, was described at the time as in 'poor condition'.

requirement in his will that required something similar, but it did praise his son's farming methods and the breeding of good stock. In particular it commended his practice of giving prizes for the best crops grown on the estate and went on to say that 'the Maristow estate under his management became a model of administration'. Probate was granted in London on 24 March 1908 to Sir Henry Yarde-Buller Lopes, Robert Lydston Newman and Thomas Rowle (solicitor) with the estate valued at £655,988 9s 6d.[35]

The will (Prob 11/430) is interesting for two main reasons. The first is that the residual estate after £140,000 was reserved in a trust to pay various annuities, was divided into three equal parts. One-third went unencumbered to Henry, his only son and sole surviving child, but the next third made use of the Settled Lands Act 1882 (revised 1890) to ensure that the estate was retained within the family, even if – for whatever reason – it was not profitable or of no great interest to subsequent generations.[36] The second point of interest is that the final third was for charitable works chosen by his wife or failing her by his son Henry. This was in addition to specific legacies identified by the testator. For example, he left £5,000 to the South Devon and East Cornwall Hospital (Lopes Endowment Fund) for the Lopes and Maristow Wards (*Western Times* 28 March 1908). A thousand pounds was left to the Devon and Cornwall Eye Infirmary in Plymouth and the same to the Plymouth Dispensary. Other beneficiaries included the Royal Hospital for Incurables at Putney, again for the Lopes Ward and similarly for the Lopes Ward in the Cancer Hospital in Fulham Road, London. Smaller charitable beneficiaries included other local institutions such as the British Orphan Asylum and the Blind Asylum, both in Plymouth (Prob 11/430) (Plate 48).

His second wife, Louisa, died a short time later on 27 April 1908 aged 80. Her widowed sister, Mrs Harriet Massingberd (Harriet Anne Langford) from Gunby Hall Lincolnshire, had visited Maristow

35 In excess of £40 million in 2020 terms.

36 Under s.10(2) of the 1890 Act a 'principal mansion house' and its grounds cannot be sold, exchanged or leased by the tenant for life without the consent of the estate's trustees or by an order of a court.

after Sir Massey's death to provide some comfort and support, but tragically died herself of heart failure a few days before her sister's demise (*Scotsman* 28 April 1908). Lady Louisa is reported never to have got over her husband's death and that of her sister. She died of influenza followed by bronchial pneumonia (*Clifton Society* 14 May 1908). She was buried with Sir Massey in the chapel at Maristow (*Western Morning News* 2 May 1908). Probate on her estate valued at £44,650. 9s. 7d was granted on 27 June to Robert Lydston Newman, Rt Hon Gerard James Noel and Sir Henry Yarde-Buller Lopes. In addition to family bequests she gave more money to the South Devon and East Cornwall Hospital to which her husband had given 'upwards of £16,000' and the balance to her nephews, Sir Robert Newman and RL Newman (*Morning Post* 1 July 1908).

With the perspective granted by the passage of time, it is possible to see Sir Massey's life and interests as a major transition. His father's interregnum was confused by comparison; he was uncertain of his own identity, his status as a major landowner and his potential for swaying events from the privileged vantage point of parliament. Sir Massey, an altogether more talented man, had no such doubts. Maristow offered a wonderful opportunity to show how the land should be used and parliament offered a golden way to argue for the benefits of life when lived upon it. Of course, inherited wealth provided almost total freedom from the constraints of disciplined labour but this could be balanced by a ready willingness to support good and worthy causes. Above all, he was in no doubt about his identity. He was not a colonial, let alone someone, in what was still an antisemitic age, burdened by any such stigma.

The Wiltshire Branch

Nothing underlines the last point more than the fortunes of his younger siblings, as the same could be said for all who survived into adulthood. The one major difference for the four other sons of Ralph Lopes was that they followed their mother's place of birth and early residence, although this is not to imply a major fissure in the family for they must have continued to meet on frequent occasions, not least through each maintaining a London residence very close to one another. The second son, Ralph Ludlow Lopes (1820–98) was educated at Winchester College and matriculated into Christ Church, Oxford, on 3 June 1840 aged 19 and left with a BA in 1844, converted two years later in to an MA. He attended the Inner Temple and was called to the Bar in 1847. Exactly paralleling his elder brother he linked another political dynasty with his own; in this case by marrying Elizabeth Kekewich, the third daughter of Samuel Trehawke Kekewich and Agatha Maria Sophia Langston, on 4 September 1851. After his father died three years later, he invested a significant proportion of his bequest into buying the Sandridge Park Estate to the east of Melksham, eight miles north of Westbury. This large estate of 900 acres contained a house formerly owned by Lord Audley (Sandridge Hill House), but between 1856 and 1859 Lopes constructed a new mansion, where he was to remain for the rest of his life.[37] The 1861 Census shows Sandridge Hill House still existing but containing only a couple and their ten-year-old daughter. Ralph Ludlow Lopes (40) and his wife Elizabeth were joined in the new house by their four children (Ralph Kekewich Lopes (eight), Henry Ludlow Lopes (seven), George Lopes (three) and Elizabeth Julia (two), and 11 staff.

Ralph Ludlow Lopes did not enter parliament and nor did he practise as a barrister but he led an extremely active public and business life nonetheless. In 1869 he was High Sheriff of Wiltshire and he was Recorder of Devizes from 1877–87. He was Deputy Lieutenant of the County and a JP for 11 years.[38] He is credited with the revival of the Melksham Agricultural Society and the Melksham Rifle Corps was also largely created by him (*Devizes Gazette* 3 March 1898). On the business front he was equally active, particularly in

37 Sandridge Park has commanding views to the south across the Vale of White Horse to Salisbury Plain and the Mendip Hills. In the recent past it was used as a hotel but was sold as a private residence in 2018 for £2.8m.

38 Ralph Ludlow Lopes served from 1866 to 1874 as chairman of the second court at Devizes and Marlborough before being promoted to the chairmanship of the same sessions (1875–84). He was chairman of the Quarter Sessions for Devizes 1876–84 and for Warminster 1870–1, 1874 and 1876 and for Marlborough 1875–83.

relation to the emergent railway companies. He represented, for example, 2,204 shareholders of the London and South Western Railway Company. He was also a shareholder in the Brighton Railway Company holding £4,500 stock. He was also a director of numerous life assurance and utilities companies (e.g. Eagle Assurance, British and Foreign Water and Gas Works Company). Later in the 1880s he was a director of the Mortgage Company of England.

Ralph Ludlow Lopes had inherited from his father the properties in Somerset acquired by Sir Manasseh Massey Lopes in 1829. These consisted principally of agricultural holdings at Bratton Manor near Wincanton that were sold by him in 1862 (SRO, DD/BR/fc 9). Having spent heavily on the Sandridge estate, he was not as engaged as his older brother in charitable good works but he did donate land for a new church school in 1873, the same year that his father-in-law, Samuel Trehawke Kekewich, died, aged 77. In 1877, on his appointment as Recorder for Devizes, there was some local controversy over the fact that he was more of a businessman than a barrister: 'The custom has been to give these little plums of the profession to practising barristers, and I expect the appointment of Mr Lopes will stir up a lot of ill-feeling against the Government among the scions of many Wiltshire Houses' (*North Devon Journal* 27 September, 1877). The article continues: 'If the Liberals had done such a thing there would have been a great outcry.'

Ralph and Elizabeth lost their second son, Henry, to typhus while he was serving as a captain with the 74th Highlanders in Cairo during the Anglo-Egyptian War in December 1882, while their oldest son Ralph Kekewich Lopes, who was called to the Bar in 1877, also predeceased both his parents (*Wilts and Gloucestershire Standard* 24 November 1877).[39] Ralph himself died on 28 February 1898 aged 77, leaving an estate valued at £95,000. He was interred at the new church of St Andrew in Melksham where his wife donated to his memory a series of gold mosaic panels inserted on the carved

39 This son had a chequered career both professionally and financially. He was declared bankrupt in 1888 and died intestate with assets of only £2,938 (*Edinburgh Gazette* 1 June 1888).

marble and alabaster reredos or altar screen. She continued to live in Sandridge Park with her spinster daughter Elizabeth (Julia) Lopes until her death on 23 December 1904. Julia stayed on until her own demise aged 47 on 14 July 1906, leaving an estate valued at £32,192.

This left only the third son, George, who in November 1897 had married his cousin Ernestine Francis, fourth daughter of her husband's older brother Henry Charles Lopes when he was 40 and she 32. He had worked as an assistant engineer on the Croydon, Oxted and East Grinstead Railway and also the London, Brighton and South Coast Railway and in 1889 was enrolled as a full member of the Institution of Civil Engineers. He became a JP for Wiltshire and had earlier served as major in the Territorial Royal Engineers (Railway Staff Corps). He lived much of his life at Hove, near Brighton, but died on 28 June 1910 back at Sandridge.[40]

The third son of Sir Ralph Lopes, Henry Charles, born on 3 October 1828 at Maristow, was much more active on the political stage, but is perhaps best known for his distinguished legal career. He was educated at Winchester and Balliol College Oxford, after which he was called to the Bar, Inner Temple, in 1852. Two years later, in the year of his father's death, he married Cordelia Lucy, oldest daughter of Erving Clark of Efford Manor (Egg Buckland, Plymouth), whose grandparents on her mother's side were Trelawneys who lived and died in Spanish Town, Jamaica. This suggests that in his early adulthood he maintained a West Country connection. Indeed, in 1858 he was listed as a freemason at the Lodge of Sincerity, East Stonehouse. Henry was put up by the Conservative Party for the Launceston constituency at a byelection in 1868 and continued a long tradition of uncontested elections by being unopposed both then and at the General Election later the same year. The following year he became a QC after 12 years in practice on the Western Circuit. He had been made Recorder for Exeter in 1867 and continued in that role until 1876 when he was knighted and appointed a judge at the High Court. Meanwhile he

40 The estate of George Lopes was valued for probate at £68,271 9s 10d.

had changed parliamentary constituency by achieving an 8 per cent swing against the Liberals at the 1874 General Election for Frome, a seat which he had to abandon on being appointed a High Court judge. By 1885, he entered the Privy Council and was elevated to become a Lord Justice of Appeal, a position that he retained until 1897 when he was raised to the peerage as Baron Ludlow of Heywood in the Queen's Jubilee list (*The Times* 26 October 1897). He was highly regarded as a judge in civil cases, including divorce, although it has been said of him that a 'place among the great lawyers of the nineteenth century could not be claimed for him' (*Dictionary of National Biography*, 1901). Of his political career, *The Times*, although respectfully recording his undoubted achievements, said of his political career that he made 'no great mark in the House' and agreed with the assessment of the 1901 biographer that 'though a careful lawyer, he never attained a commanding position in the profession' (26 December 1899).

For some years Henry Charles Lopes and his family had lived in Eastleigh House Monkton Farleigh, east of Bath and some eight miles north of Bradford-on-Avon. This is where the couple's first three children are recorded at the Census of 1861. Eventually eight offspring were born but two did not survive infancy, although a male heir, also Henry, did together with five daughters. By the 1870s, the family were living in East Hill House, Frome, and it was here that the tragic fire occurred that led to the death of Susanna Gibbs Lopes, Sir Ralph's widow.[41] Her brother, Henry Gaisford Gibbs Ludlow, died on 28 August 1876 aged 68, and Heywood House passed by inheritance to Henry Charles Lopes and he moved there at approximately this time to make it his country seat.[42] He maintained a leasehold property in London (8 Cromwell Place) and that was where he could have been found on the night of the 1881 Census with his wife and no children. By 1891 the whole family were at

41 In 1873, the estate at Frome is listed as possessing 434 acres.
42 The inheritance was slightly complicated by a clause that left a life interest in the estate to Endymion Porter the son of Ludlow's younger sister. He appears to have ended up at the Frome property (East Hill House), which suggests a swap or two-way sale to buy out his interest in Heywood House.

Heywood House; Henry Charles Lopes and Cordelia his wife, aged 63 and Susan (32), Cordelia Lucy (30), Ethel M (27), Henry Ludlow Lopes (25) solicitor, Ernestine F (22) and Bertha Susan (21) plus ten staff. Lord Ludlow died at the age of 72 in London on Christmas Day 1899 of influenza but was buried in Heywood, Wilts. By that time he had been a widower for eight years (Plate 49).

Their only son, Henry Ludlow Lopes inherited the title and the house but he clearly wished to be associated even more closely with the neighbourhood for in 1904 he persuaded his uncle to part with the manor of Westbury. He retained it until 1920 when his London home in Portland Place became his primary residence. He died childless in a hunting accident in 1922 (*The Times* 9 November 1922).[43]

Edmund Francis Lopes was the fourth son of Ralph Lopes, born on 19 October 1833 so never had to change his surname from Franco. He attended Oriel College, Oxford, matriculating on 2 June 1853 aged 19, but very little is known about his subsequent life. He does not appear to have graduated nor is there any evidence that he married. He died at St James' Place London on 28 February 1867 aged just 33 after a short illness. He was buried at Bickleigh and his estate was valued for probate at under £25,000. Slightly more is known about the fifth and final son, George Ludlow Lopes, born in 1836. He attended Rugby School and Exeter College, Oxford, matriculating on 12 October 1855 aged 19, although there is also no evidence that he attained a degree. He served as a lieutenant in the 16th Lancers and later in life became a JP in Wiltshire and a Deputy Lieutenant of the county. In 1871 he married Georgina Emma De Arroyave (1836–1912) who produced two sons, George de Arroyave Lopes (1872–1929) and John Ludlow Lopes (1882–1961).

After a somewhat peripatetic early life, including a spell at Hardenhuish House in Chippenham, where he joined the

43 The 2nd Lord Ludlow, who was also a barrister, was Deputy Lieutenant of Wiltshire in 1900 and a member of the London County Council for Marylebone (1904–7). In 1902 he was promoted to lieutenant in the Royal Wiltshire Yeomanry (Prince of Wales' Own Royal Regiment) and fought in the First World War as a staff captain.

Lansdowne Lodge (1878–1909), George Ludlow Lopes finally settled at Northleigh House, Bradford-on-Avon, Wiltshire (Westbury Constituency) with his wife and sons George and second son, John Ludlow, together with eight staff. He is described in the Census return for 1891 as a JP, deputy lieutenant and 'formerly in the army'. By 1901 he was again at Northleigh House 'living on his own means' aged 64 with his 61-year-old wife and son John Ludlow, aged 18 and the same number of servants. George Ludlow Lopes died aged 73 on 3 October 1909 and left an estate valued at £123,210 11s 6d. His wife lived on at Northleigh House for a further three years dying on 17 April 1912. She had seven staff at her death and probate was granted on 17 June 1912 to her oldest son George with assets of £36,112.

An interesting feature of this couple's life in Wiltshire was that their point of reference as far as the extended family was concerned was wholly on his mother's side of the Lopes family. Nothing suggests this more than the fine mausoleum that George had built at the Bratton Road Cemetery in Westbury where he and Georgina his wife are interred (Plate 50). It is a Romanesque Revival construction built around the time of George's demise and is listed Grade II by Historic England. It is built as a miniature Norman-style chapel and the listing reads:

> Ashlar built with moulded cill and impost strings, latter carried over round headed windows. Moulded eaves cornice to stone tile roof. Coped verges with segmental capped footstones. Gable end to East. Oculus in gable. Arcaded band below. Round headed entrance of 3 orders, centre enriched with chevron ornament. Tudor arch doorway with 16 panel doors. 2 shields in tympanum.

A significant bequest was contained in George's will to ensure that the mausoleum was maintained.

It is hard not to conclude that this extravagant gesture was motivated in part at least by a desire to outshine in death the Ludlow Mausoleum built to accommodate George's older and more successful brother Henry Charles Lopes. This is only metres away and is an altogether more modest hexagonal edifice, although grand enough to have also earned a listing as worthy of preservation. Historic England's entry reads:

> Rough faced snecked rubble with parapet, angle finials, cupola and gabled lantern. Blind tracery to parapet, centre panel taller with light. Finials have poppy heads, gablets and shield-form corbels. Each face of main wall has a 4 centre arch window containing 2 trefoil headed lancets and centre lights. Chamfered plinth. Basement below further chamfered plinth, reached by dog leg stairs. The structure is enclosed by cast iron railings with fleur de lys headed stanchions on dwarf wall (Plate 51).

In three generations the Lopes family had passed through the same number of iterations. To borrow from Hegelian logic, if Manasseh Massey Lopes, with his ambitious but buccaneering mentality, was the thesis, then Sir Ralph, the careful, rather colourless, plodder was the antithesis. His sons, when considered together, were therefore the synthesis; energetic, successful and public spirited but overwhelmingly conventional.

Henry Yarde-Buller Lopes

In this regard Henry Lopes, who inherited the estate and title in January 1908, was the logical extension of this transition. Whereas his father had devoted a great deal of his energy to transforming the tenanted farms and the hereditaments upon them, Henry, the only son, was never so focused upon the land or the support of the landed interest. With Sir Massey there was always the tendency to conflate his enthusiasms, as energetic and determined as they were, with the enhanced prosperity of a class of person of which he was a leading representative. His only son, by contrast, was committed to public service to an unusual degree and, as a result, became admired as much as he was respected.

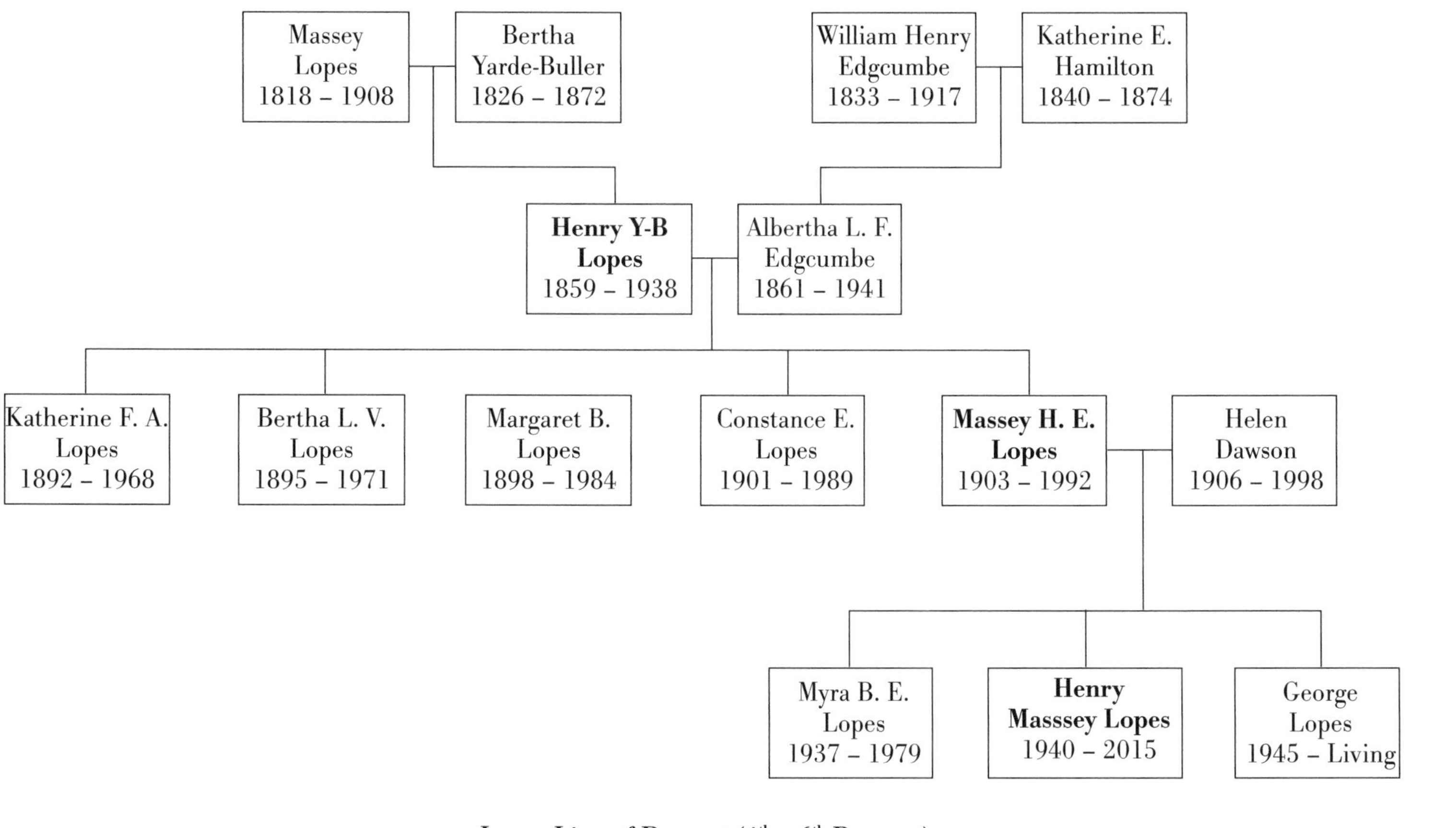

Lopes Line of Descent (4th – 6th Baronet)

Henry Yarde-Buller Lopes was the only son of his father's first wife, Bertha Yarde-Buller. He was born in 1859 and received a conventional education for someone of his social class, matriculating into Balliol College, Oxford, on 31 May 1879 and proceeding from there to the Inner Temple where he was called to the Bar in 1888. His military service was confined to volunteering first in the Devon Yeoman Cavalry and subsequently in the 3rd Devonshire regiment. In 1891 when he was 32 years old, he married Lady Albertha Louisa Florence Edgcumbe, second daughter of William Henry, 4th Earl of Mount Edgcumbe. The marriage produced four daughters and, eventually, an heir; Katherine Frederica Albertha born 25 September 1892, Bertha Louisa Victoria Yarde-Buller born 30 October 1895, Margaret Beatrix born 12 February 1898, Constance Elizabeth born October 1901 and finally Massey Henry Edgcumbe born 4 October 1903.

Naturally, Henry Lopes was a supporter of the Conservative Party and it looked at first as if he was going to emulate his father's longevity in the Commons. As a young man just short of his 30th birthday, he was put up against the Liberal Francis Mildmay, in the newly re-established seat of Totnes but came in with under 43 per cent of the vote despite being described by the *Western Morning News* (6 November 1885) as 'a thorough Lopes, faithful to the progressive Conservatism of his family'. He was selected as a candidate in July 1890 for Grantham and despite being rather unfamiliar with regional issues affecting the constituency squeezed home by 33 votes at the General Election of 1892 (*The Times* 11 July 1890). He increased his majority tenfold in the repeat General Election in 1895 but could not overcome the support for the popular Liberal cricketer Sir Arthur Alexander Priestley in the so called 'Khaki' election of 1900 which marked the end of his parliamentary career.[44] This outcome was not for want of

44 The term 'Khaki election' arose from the mistaken belief that the United Kingdom had emerged victorious in the Second Boer War. The election was notable for the large Conservative majority, the first showing of the Labour Representation Committee, later to be the Labour Party, and the first appearance of Winston Churchill as an MP.

trying since he stood for Torquay against Liberal anti-protectionist opposition in 1906; a view that did not go down well locally. In 1909 he invited 300 party workers from Torquay to Maristow House, fed and watered them well and made and received rousing speeches in the Conservative and Unionist cause, mainly opposing the budget of the Balfour government (*Torquay Times and South Devon Advertiser* 17 September 1909). His opponent Francis Layland-Barratt, who had taken the seat from the Conservatives in 1900, seemed to have had the upper hand. He was defeated by 460 votes but when he tried again in January 1910 he came a lot closer, losing to the same opposition by only eleven votes.[45] He is reported as trying to stand for Sir Reginald Pole-Carew's seat in Bodmin but when it was eventually contested in 1916 on the latter's resignation it was won by the Conservative, Charles Hanson (*Exeter and Plymouth Gazette* 7 February 1913). He was much more successful at the local government level, standing as county councillor for Compton Gifford in 1914 and after winning there was elected chairman of the council as a whole in December 1916.

Restyling Maristow House

After his marriage in 1891, Henry Lopes and his developing family lived in Roborough House but on the death of his father in 1908, he immediately commissioned the London-based architectural practice of Ernest George and Alfred Bowman Yeates to make major additions to Maristow House.[46] A print published by Rudolph Ackermann shows the house as it appeared in 1826, a few years before his grandfather took over the property. What we see is a substantial Georgian house in a sylvan setting with regular symmetrical projecting wings facing south towards the river. The roof line, in particular, is simple and uncluttered[47] (Plate 52).

45 He did not try again in the repeat election in December the same year when the Conservatives did not stand.

46 The speed with which these works were completed may suggest that they were commissioned in 1907 while Sir Massey was still alive. The family retained a London residence at 54 Cadogan Square (*Western Times* 13 July 1934).

47 Published in Ackerman (1828) *Repository of Arts, Literature, Commerce,*

The architects in the early twentieth century were clearly influenced by the Neo-Baroque preferences of the Victorian era. Each wing was substantially extended, the roof line now appeared more castellated with the addition of balustrading, heightened chimneys and pitched roof elevations to each of the two extensions.[48] The front porch was now massive, extending right through the roof line with giant pilasters and a segmental pediment. The whole edifice was made to feel grander by the lowering of the front lawn and the addition of formal steps breaking through a protective wall. In addition, eighteenth-century symmetry was lost through the addition of bow-front extensions to the east-facing wing and on the north-east corner (Plate 53). Internally, the dining room in the west wing was enlarged and oak-panelled, and the library in the east wing received similar treatment except that the elaborate fluted pilasters and fittings were in mahogany. A letter of 16 December 1909 from the architects states that estimates of about £16,000 had been accepted for the building work, including £1,000 for 'deeper foundations – new basements, extra floors, division walls, raising roof, rebuilding bays etc', £103 19s 1d for 'walnut in lieu of deal finishings to the business room', £1,349 for library panelling, £648 for dining room furnishings from Haywood and Wooster, £925 for electric light plant and £503 for electric light wiring (cited in Binney, 1990).

Whether the 'Edwardian Grand Style', as Grainger (1985) calls it, is an improvement is a matter of taste but it was certainly intended to impress and was completed in an astonishingly short time after Sir Massey's death. By the end of 1908 the contractors, Messrs Lapthorn and Co of Plymouth, had finished their work and Sir Henry Lopes and his wife gave a celebratory dinner for all concerned (*Torquay Times and South Devon Advertiser* 1 January 1909).

As would be conventional for an aristocratic family with four daughters, a great deal of attention must have been expended on marrying them off to appropriate partners. In this the couple did

Manufactures, Fashions and Politics.

48 Perspective and block plan prepared by architects George and Yeates 1907–09 (see Grainger, 1985, Vol 4: 833).

rather well, particularly given the grievous loss of young male officers in the Great War. Marrying in the order of their birth, the first, Katherine, married Commander the Hon EA Nicolson RN DSO, second son of Lord and Lady Carnock, on 9 October 1919 (*Western Morning News* 10 October 1919). His younger brother was the famous diplomat Sir Harold Nicolson, husband of Vita Sackville-West (*The Times* 10 October 1919).[49] The second daughter, Bertha Louisa, married Captain James Murray Pipon RN on 29 December 1921. He was appointed commodore of the Royal Naval Barracks at Keyham in January 1932 (*Western Morning News* 16 January 1932). By the following year he was listed as Rear-Admiral JM Pipon and three years later promoted again to vice-admiral (*Western Morning News* 5 August 1933). The third daughter, Margaret, married Captain Henry Archibald Graham (*Western Morning News* 27 January 1927). He was the younger brother of the distinguished army officer Major-General Sir Miles William Arthur Peel Graham, KBE, CB, MC, DL (14 August 1895–8 February 1976). Their mother Ellen was the great-niece of Sir Robert Peel and her second marriage was to George Asquith. Lady Asquith was a noted writer and editor. Finally, Constance, born in 1901, married at the age of 38 Marcus Cheke, who was press attaché in Lisbon at the time and later in the 1950s Minister to the Holy See (*Western Morning News* 31 October 1939).

This only left the one son and therefore heir, Massey Henry Edgcumbe Lopes, who was born on 4 October 1903. Educated at Eton and Oxford, at the age of 22 he joined the Royal Scots Greys rising to captain and from 1936–37 he served as aide-de-camp to George Villiers, the 6th Earl of Clarendon, during the last two years of his tenure as Governor-General of South Africa. At his coming of age in 1924 his father Sir Henry announced that he had passed half the Maristow estate to his son (Buckland, Meavy, Walkampton and Sheepstor). Massey Lopes married Helen Dawson, the daughter

49 The title of Lord Carnock eventually descended through this branch of the Nicolson clan so that the present baron is the author Adam Nicolson, husband of the writer and horticulturalist, Sarah Raven.

of Lieutenant-General Edward Finch Dawson of Launde Abbey in Leicestershire, on 15 October 1936.[50] He left the army on the death of his father in 1938, but rejoined at the outbreak of the Second World War.[51] Thereafter he held honorary posts (e.g. Vice-Lieutenant of Devon in 1951 and lord lieutenant for over 20 years, 16 July 1958–5 October 1978). He was also a JP and governor of Exeter University but could not be said to equal his father in contributions to public life. It is true that he frequently opened events, awarded prizes and chaired meetings but no more than other lords of the manor with inherited titles (Plate 54).

In addition to passing half the land of the Maristow estate to his son, Sir Henry Lopes sold off part of his 'outlying estates' by auction on 12 February 1919. The auction was held at the Bedford Hotel in Tavistock and conducted by Messrs Ward and Chowen. The land was described as 'situate close to Horrabridge Station and Roborough Down and in and around the villages of Horrabridge, Meavy, and Buckland Monochorum initially comprising five good farm and other residences with suitable outbuildings and land attached'. The lots consisted of 185 acres, eight cottages in Buckland, three in Meavy and two at Huckworthy Bridge (*Western Morning News* 11 January 1919). Other properties were added a little later in Walkhampton, and Samford Spiney so that there were 30 lots in Horrabridge, including the Manor Hotel, two other houses, two farms and the rest in pasture parcels including 26 acres for building in Samford Spiney. There were another four lots added comprising 13 cottages (*Western Morning News* 11 February 1919). In 1927, more properties went under the hammer comprising Torr Farm (36 acres) and Ludbrook Woods (16 acres) in the Denham bridge area (*Western Morning News* 26 July 1927).

50 David Nicolson (4th Baron Carnock) offered a typically trenchant but nonetheless acute observation on this marriage to the Hon George Lopes, the second son: 'the Dawson family would not have been regarded as belonging to the top aristocracy at the time of your father's marriage. I think that Sir Henry and Lady Albertha would have regarded the marriage as disappointing' (Nicolson to Lopes, 9 September 1998).

51 Lord Roborough rose to become lieutenant-colonel during the latter part of the war.

Perhaps because the family were particularly conscious of their need to adopt the social norms of aristocracy, even when after the First World War these had become less formal elsewhere, there were strict conventions governing family gatherings in the 1920s. One of Sir Henry and Lady Albertha's grandsons recalled many years later that the house was presided over with great precision by Eddy, the butler:

> My mother and father used to have Sunday dinner at Maristow every week, when the family were in residence; dinner jackets, black ties and boiled shirts were always worn. When we were older my brother and I sometimes used to go. I remember being greeted by Eddy and his two footmen; our coats would be taken and placed on the two sofas which flanked the entrance to the hall, there being no pegs for hats and coats; when we were ready, Eddy would conduct us into the drawing room. He never looked round; I never knew how he knew that were following him, but we always were; he walked bolt up-right; he entered the drawing room without knocking, walked halfway along the breadth of the room, turned right and proceeded halfway up the room; and announced us, with impeccable formality. He then withdrew (Nicolson to Lopes, 3 August 1998).

There is little suggestion here of the fun-loving lifestyle of the 'bright young things' of the period, nor of the romanticism of the author's aunt, Vita Sackville-West.

In the New Year's honours list in January 1938, Sir Henry Lopes at last received recognition for his many years of public service when he was elevated to the upper house as Lord Roborough. On 24 March that year he celebrated his 79th birthday but died of heart failure at Maristow House on 15 April. In a local newspaper obituary published a few days after his death he was described as 'one of Devon's outstanding personalities' whose appointment as Baron Roborough 'was received with much gratification throughout the county and was regarded by all as a distinction richly deserved for practically a lifetime's work on behalf of the community of which he was such an illustrious member' (*Devon and Exeter Gazette* 22 April 1938).

There is little doubt that Sir Henry Lopes, as he was until towards the very end of his life, was committed to high standards of public service. Another local paper summarised his life well when a report of his death announced: 'there have been few men who have given greater service to public welfare' (*The Western Morning News and Daily Gazette* 16 April 1938) while the obituary in *The Times* said on the same day that he was an 'outstanding figure in the public life of Devon'. It went to draw parallels between Henry Lopes and his father, seeing both as standing for

> Equitable local and Imperial taxation, the welfare of the agricultural labourers, the cheap transfer of land, county boards, labourers' cottages and allotments, no taxes on the food of the people, a firm foreign policy in order to protect the commerce of an Empire on which the sun never sets, national prestige, the union of Church and State, religious though not sectarian education – not free for those who are willing to pay for it; and an utter detestation of wild, sham and impossible schemes for the injury of existing institutions, and the unsettling of the minds of the people (*The Times* 16 April 1938).

While this summary is not without some truth, father and son were actually quite different. Whereas the former was indeed quintessentially an agriculturalist, always committed to upgrading and improving the land and all who depended upon it, his heir had an entirely different focus. Sir Massey was a man who fought ferociously against those whom he considered under-appreciated or were ignorant of the noble craft of husbandry. He appointed a young man called Adam Douglas Fenton as the agent for the Maristow estates and inculcated into him these values and standards. Fenton lasted in this role for more than 50 years and died aged 76 in June 1946 and any continuation of this tradition owes much to him. Henry Lopes depended entirely upon him since his passions lay elsewhere (see *Western Morning News* 15 June 1946).[52]

52 This is not to say that he was uninterested in agricultural advancement. For example A few years before he died, he had entertained Prince George (Prince of Wales) at Maristow and accompanied him to the Devon County Agricultural Show at Tavistock (*The Times* 19 May 1932).

Henry Lopes chose to make his undoubted contribution in three main ways. First he played a very active role in the administration of local government, his most obvious role in this regard being the 21 years he served as chairman of Devon County Council. Second, he supported with his own funds, and with his time on relevant committees, those activities that he considered bettered people's lives. Chief among them was the support he lent to the University College of the South-West at Exeter where he followed the Prince of Wales in becoming president of the Court of Governors and made personal endowments in excess of £20,000. The obituary in *The Times* (16 April 1938) argued that 'his work for the college since 1922 was perhaps the climax of his crusading'. Even though he never saw the college transformed into a university it 'remains his memorial'.

It is worth recalling how the upgrading of higher education in the South-West stimulated significant opposition, particularly in Whitehall, which on numerous occasions declined to grant university college status to the fledgling institution. In the early 1920s, however, there was a change of sentiment:

> Suddenly the wheel of fortune moved. The Devon County Council allied itself to Exeter City Council as a working partner in the College Scheme. Sir Henry Lopes, Bart., the Chairman of Devon County Council, is primarily anxious to promote a University for the South West, but he recognises that the first practical steps towards that goal is to make Exeter University College strong. Sir Henry has been a tower of strength in the negotiations that have been in progress (*Western Times* 20 March, 1920).

This meant firstly applying for a Charter of Incorporation. Lopes succeeded in getting the Prince of Wales to agree to be the first president of the University College when granted its incorporated status. The *Western Times* remarks that this marked a turning point for now it looked as though the college was not just an Exeter issue but one for the whole South-West. Lopes was initially deputy president of the Council of the University College of the South West but was appointed president in 1937 (*Western Times* 31 March 1933). Little wonder therefore that when he died Dr John Murray, principal of the College, added a glowing supplement to the *Times* obituary writing that 'he radiated warmth, and he gave with a free hand; Devon mourns a prince of men and thousands a friend'. The contribution of Sir Henry Lopes to the aspirations of the university college was recognised long after his death. For example, in 1940 at the opening of the Roborough Library on the Streatham campus, the deputy president described him as 'a great west countryman whose services to the college can hardly be exaggerated and whose honoured name is not only attached to the library, but is imperishably associated with the college and the university movement in the South-West' (*Western Morning News* 9 May 1940).

For 15 years he was also president of the 'Three Towns Nursing Association' and on many occasions made available the house and grounds at Maristow for fundraising events. Carrying on from his father, he was treasurer of the Royal Hospital for Incurables at Putney for over 30 years and, closer to home, served as vice-president of the Crownhill Convalescent Home and chairman of the Board of Management of the South Devon and South East Cornwall Hospital in Plymouth at Greenbank.[53] He also did much for the Devon Nursing Association and, rather astonishingly, in September 1936 opened the gardens for delegates to the Trades Union Congress meeting in Plymouth. The local paper reported that 'interest was shown by some of the delegates in the row of cottages at Roborough where George Odger, a trade union pioneer and the first working man to stand as a candidate for Parliament, was born 133 years ago' (*Western Morning News* 10 September 1936). He was also Sheriff for Devonshire in 1913 and for many years a trustee of Kelly College in Tavistock. In other words, he went out of his way to focus his attention on health and education and often made significant financial contributions to both spheres during an era when they depended to a large extent on voluntary contributions.

53 At Putney, Sir Massey Lopes endowed a ward named after his first wife, Lady Bertha Lopes (*Western Morning News and Daily Gazette* 20 April 1938).

Finally, and perhaps more controversially, he chose to join and support organisations that promoted public service in a Christian context, such as the freemasons. He had become installed as a member of the Maristow Lodge in 1901 (*Totnes Weekly Times* 19 January 1901) and later was made Provincial Grand Master for Devon (*Exeter and Plymouth Gazette* 23 November 1928). It is clear that masonry captured for him a laudable spirit of public service. He declared in 1930 in a speech that 'Freemasonry today is perhaps one of the greatest bulwarks against Atheism and that materialism which is creeping in and paralysing the civilised world at the present time' (*Western Morning News* 16 January 1930). At a meeting at Maristow Lodge to celebrate his elevation to the peerage, he is reported as saying,

> Nothing I have done in my life's work has given me greater pleasure and satisfaction than to have been the head of the Province of Devonshire, and to feel that from the east to the west I have been held in that affectionate regard that I know is mine from the numerous letters I have received from all the lodges of this province.

Just a few days before he died he spoke at a meeting of Lodge Sincerity in Plymouth to launch what became the Roborough Lodge in which he described freemasonry as 'professing the highest ideals' in trying to accomplish work in the country as a whole 'of the greatest possible value' (*The Western Morning News and Daily Gazette* 16 April 1938).

Whereas his father 30 years before had left an estate valued at £653,000, probate was granted on the wealth of the first Lord Roborough at less than a quarter of that sum: £154,729 with estate duty of £21,722 (*Western Morning News* 14 June and 21 November 1938). A combination of factors played a part in this apparent decline in fortune. First, he had already granted his son half the estate some years before; second, he had sold a considerable proportion when prices were low; third, he had given money to charitable causes and, finally, there was the rapid decline in valuations of country estates as death duties and increased income taxes ate away at property values. It would appear, however, that the estate included the property formerly owned by the earl's brother, Ralph, at Sandridge Park, Melksham, which after the war was turned into a country house hotel (*Wiltshire Times and Trowbridge Advertiser* 23 February 1952.)

Largely unheralded and unseen, these years were tolling the end of the English country house as it had hitherto existed. It is very striking that when the succession occurred, Captain the Hon Massey Henry Edgcumbe Lopes, of the Scots Guards, 5th baronet and 2nd baron, did not move into Maristow House but stayed at Roborough House and later moved to Bickham House, a small country house dating from 1876 that adjoins the Maristow estate to the north-east.[54] This appears to have been the strong preference of the new Lord Roborough's wife as she immediately started to furnish Bickham House, having hitherto lived in the Dower house at Roborough (Roborough House). She is quoted very soon after the succession as saying, 'there will be no breaking away from the tradition at Maristow and the estate will be carried on as the late Lord Roborough would have wished' (*Western Morning News* 23 April 1938). The message was clear, however: the new Lord Roborough had no intention of using the estate to sustain either of the larger houses, which were increasingly difficult to staff and which would be subject to death duties at rapidly increasing rates.[55] It is true, though, that the family stayed in Roborough House during the war years and all three of

54 A little later there was a more widespread recognition of the plight facing large country houses. For example, Maristow was one of a number included in an article appearing in the *Western Morning News* entitled 'West Country Mansions standing empty and forlorn' due to declining incomes and increasing taxation (5 June 1950). Maristow was described as 'one of the seats of Lord Roborough'. In December 1949, the *Tatler* reported that the new earl and wife were moving into Bickham House from Roborough House.

55 Although Estate Duty rates were initially rather low (8 per cent) they were clearly on an upwards trajectory. Moreover, the 1911 Parliament Act had precluded the nobility from using their domination of the House of Lords to defeat motions of the lower house. The second baron was to some extent prescient as during the coming war death duties that had reached 50 per cent of valuations were raised to 65 per cent thus sounding the death knell for many fine country houses. Those that could not find an institutional use were frequently demolished.

their children were born there. The first (Myra Bertha Ernestine) was born on 22 July 1937 and died at the early age of 42 on 2 August 1979. The older son, Henry Massey Lopes, who acceded to the title on the death of his father in 1992, was born very early in the war years (2 February 1940) while the second son (Hon George Lopes) was born near the end of hostilities in February 1945 (*Western Morning News* 23 February 1945). Lady Roborough, the first earl's wife, died in Plymouth in March 1941.

Maristow House was shielded from demolition by its relative proximity to Plymouth docks. Soon after the war broke out, it was requisitioned by the Royal Navy as an auxiliary hospital. Most of the furnishings from the house were removed before the Navy moved in and placed in storage. Just after the unconditional surrender of Axis powers on 8 May 1945, the young earl and his wife made a major decision that more or less sealed Maristow's fate, disposing of the greater part of the furnishings from the house, many of which dated from Sir Manasseh's refurbishment in the early years of the preceding century. As perhaps an indication of the distaste with which this 'old' furniture was perceived, it was decided to use a local auctioneer rather than one of the famous London houses (BHJ Wood of Tavistock Road, Plymouth). Two sales were envisaged, and because of the quantity of furnishings involved, each took place over two days. The first was held on 25 and 26 July 1945 at Bickham House. Just to give an indication of the material that was sold off, the items included a Sheraton satinwood secretaire bookcase, a pair of lacquer cabinets, carved gilt console tables, Chippendale-design carved mahogany writing desk, sets of mahogany dining chairs and tables, many mirrors and other writing desks and tables, carved and gilt torcheres, barometers, longcase and mantle clocks, mahogany wardrobes, bow-front chests and much else besides. Also included were curtains, table covers, blankets, linen and copper ware. English, Oriental and Continental chinaware, glass and many oil and water colour paintings were also cleared (*Western Morning News* 24, 25 and 26 July 1945). Unsurprisingly, given the quality and condition of the items and the presence only of local bidders, all the items found ready buyers. The event was repeated on 20 and 21 November the same year after local buyers had caught their breath.[56]

When the house itself was released from naval use in May 1947, Lord Roborough offered it to the Church of England on a 'loan-lease' as a home for retired clergy and their wives. The house was described then as having 45 bedrooms and its own chapel but this included additional accommodation added by the former tenants (*Western Morning News* 15 November 1947). This use of Maristow (and, as was initially proposed, Cotehele) attracted a grant of £7,500 from the National Corporation for the Care of Old People with the balance of conversion costs (total £20,000 estimated but eventually £28,000) came from the Church (*Western Morning News* 8 March 1948). The house was intended to provide accommodation for up to 60 retired clergymen and their wives, while nursing care could be offered for a maximum of 20 people. The first occupant, Rev H Leigh Murray, moved in in April 1948 but he must have had the house more or less to himself for this ill-fated plan did not really get off the ground for more than two further years (*Western Morning News* 14 April 1948). It was not until October 1950 that advertisements appeared for housemaids and waitresses (52s 6d per week) and a little afterwards that more residents arrived. In early November five married couples, eight single women and four single men moved in (*Western Morning News* 4 October 1950; 2 November 1950). Unfortunately, in early 1952 a fire broke out in the roof and the damage was such that all the residents had to be permanently rehoused, and by the following year the house was closed up.

The next use of Maristow House was in 1954 when Devon County Council arranged to take over the semi-derelict building in order to create a residential school for educationally challenged girls of junior school chronological age. The council appointed as head teacher the redoubtable Mimi Hatton, a 40-year-old lady with experience of teaching the children of occupying British forces in post-war Germany (British Families Education Service) as well as

56 The house cannot have been completely denuded of furniture since the Dartmoor hunt ball was held there on 4 January 1949.

running a similar school for girls in Kent for the preceding two years. She supervised the restoration process and appointed the staff. The school ran until 1976 when Ms Hatton retired and the building was taken over by Plymouth City Council. After two years of lying empty, it was leased to a company to be used as a field study centre and base for outward bound courses for young people. In 1981, over a hundred young people were staying at the house when another fire destroyed more of the house, followed by a third three months later.

At this point the Lopes family applied for permission to the Planning Inspectorate to demolish the house. A public inquiry was held and – unsurprisingly given its setting and history – the application aroused strong opposition and was refused. The building was placed in the hands of trustees who again applied for permission to demolish, which, partly due to informed pleading by the Ancient Monuments Society at another public inquiry, was also turned down. Then an architect, Dr WPJ Smith, put forward proposals to convert the house into 32 self-contained flats and houses with shared use of the extensive grounds. In planning terms this proposal was accepted but after extensive negotiations and, despite being supported by the Buildings at Risk Trust, it proved impossible to raise sufficient historic buildings grants and the proposal was eventually withdrawn.

Thereafter the fortunes of the old house took a turn for the better. Reputedly heading for Plymouth airport in a light aircraft piloted by his wife, the architect Kit Martin spotted the corrugated iron-draped roof of the house as they followed the course of the River Tavy. Martin, the founder of Historic Houses Rescue Ltd, had at that time (1995) at least eight country house projects to his credit, including the first, Gunton Hall, Gunton Park, Norfolk, that he had converted into 20 separate dwellings in 1980 and which subsequently went on to win *Country Life*'s 'Genius of the Place' Award. The principles of Martin's approach were basically threefold. First to convert country houses into smaller units while maintaining as far as feasible the old wall divides so that each has some aspects remaining of their previous grandeur (e.g. high ceilings, original mouldings, fire pieces etc.). The second ambition was to ensure that all conversions did not impede the relationship between the house, outbuildings and the parkland in which they were originally set. The third was to complete all the work using traditional techniques carried out by craftsmen and women with requisite skills and without recourse to grant funding. The evidence would certainly suggest that this was a winning formula.[57]

The challenges that this approach entails are substantial. In the Maristow case, despite Kit Martin's success in obtaining the freehold and subsequent planning approvals, the house had been subject to sustained vandalism and theft in addition to probable arson attacks. Binney (2000) includes a depressing quote from the new owner: 'We were faced with the theft of a large number of fireplaces, much of the 18th century stair balustrading, the bookshelves in the library and all the Edwardian oak paneling in the dining room.'

By 2000 all 12 properties had been quickly sold but even then these problems persisted. For example, the first occupants of the newly converted East Wing accosted thieves as they struggled to get away with the centrepiece of a fine eighteenth-century garden fountain adjacent to the chapel, fortunately preventing its departure. Roborough House did not fare as well, despite being in rather better condition. In October 1982, it was bought by a coach company from Yelverton as a base from which coach trips could commence while patrons' cars were safely stowed in the 12 acres of grounds. Lord Roborough, together with the Lord Mayor and Lady Mayoress of Plymouth and 500 guests, were on hand to celebrate this new beginning.

While Maristow House in its new incarnation may have been offloaded to a new category of owners, mostly retired professionals (military, medicine, academic etc.), the family itself, although much transformed by the tide of events, continued apace. The 2nd earl, Massey Henry Edgcumbe, died on 30 June 1992 aged 88 in Tavistock, while his wife, the former Helen Dawson, passed away in 1998 at the age of 92. His first-born son (Henry Massey Lopes born

57 In the Maristow case, it is recorded that the trustees 'made a substantial contribution to repairs' (Binney, 2000).

on 2 February 1940) married twice, producing two sons and two daughters by the first marriage and two further daughters by the second. He died in London on 8 February 2015 at the age of 75, and his son, Massey John Henry Lopes (born 22 December 1969), thus became the 4th Baron Roborough. While the 3rd baron followed precedent in serving in the military, becoming a lieutenant in the Coldstream Guards, he also acquired professional qualifications as a professional associate of the Royal Institution of Chartered Surveyors (ARICS), a trend that was continued by his successor, who works in London in the finance industry.

This transformation of economic fortunes reflects a profound change in the possibilities of depending entirely on land to maintain a wealthy lifestyle. While there are contradicting examples, the historian David Cannadine is surely right to conclude that by 'the late 1930s, the British landed establishment was less British, less landed, and less of an establishment than it had been at any time since its marked disintegration first began during the 1880s' (1990: 606). Increasingly, fame and fortune did not now reside with a traditional ruling class, and land became seen as more of an encumbrance than a comforting embrace for one's family. Trade, once sneered at, became the preferred avenue of accumulation, and a growing class of professionals, whose fees were formerly kept in check by the weight of deference, could now roam free to feast upon the minutest needs of their clients. The Lopes dynasty was also part of this massive social change; having spent the whole of the nineteenth century clambering into the ranks of English landed gentry, they then faded from it along with so many other families with more established pedigrees.

It is interesting to recall that Manasseh Massey Lopes more than a century before had chided himself for his 'mania for purchasing of lands' on the grounds that 'it don't pay me 2 per cent besides locking up all my ready money in this unprofitable concern which altho' raised my vanity for a time, in being thought a large landowner, yet I confess to you that often feel the inconvenience of my folly in thus reducing my income and depriving myself of the comfort of having ready money at command' (Letter from Exeter Gaol, 16 December 1819, cited in Chapter 9). His heir's eldest son, Massey Lopes, in two letters written on the same day to *his* son, at a time when he clearly thought he had not long to live, shows a similar ambivalence to the virtues of landed estates. In the first, he reflects on his work to improve the land and continues,

> I affectionately entrust you to take a *personal* interest, yourself, in its management and further improvement, and not only to use it for your own benefit and enjoyment, but to consider the interest and welfare of those who will be dependent upon you (Sir Massey Lopes to Henry Lopes, 14 June 1904).[58]

On the other hand, in the second letter, after reflecting on the strength of the securities that his son will inherit, he adds, 'I would strongly advise you not to invest in land, there is no future in poor land, and it only brings worry and anxieties.' As this family history clearly suggests, on acceding to the title and land, Henry took both messages to heart, upholding and enhancing the opportunities for public service and charitable giving on the one hand while disposing of unprofitable land holdings on the other.

In one very important respect, however, Maristow House and the huge estate around it performed a vital function. David Nicolson, second son of Sir Henry and Lady Albertha's eldest daughter, noting the sensitivity of both the first Sir Massey Lopes and his son Sir Henry to maintaining their social position, stressed that this 'depended entirely on Maristow and, most important, the chapel' (Nicolson to Lopes, 9 September 1998). Again, with great perspicacity, he points out that using Piers St Aubyn as the architect for the restoration of the chapel was itself significant because he was 'a very well established Anglican ecclesiastical architect'. In other words it underlined their faith in and support for the established Church, shown again in Sir Henry's case with his commitment to the Masonic order. Nicolson

58 I am most grateful to the Hon George Lopes for providing access to this correspondence.

put it even more starkly: 'why is the chapel at Maristow so important in your family's *weltanschauung*? Because it represents, and was intended to effect, the distancing of your family from its Jewish pedigree' (Nicolson to Lopes, 9 September 1998). To this day, as if to underline this point, the chapel is retained by the Lopes family, even after the rest of the house and outbuildings were restored, converted and sold on.

Few others could be said to have reinvented themselves so successfully as the Lopes dynasty. By the time the two great houses on the estate were abandoned, the family showed no trace of a West Indian past and no longer bore what they once conceived as the incubus of a Jewish identity. Ironically, they were only able to achieve this feat because of the remarkable financial acumen, family loyalty and capacity to surmount blatant discrimination, which some might consider quintessentially Jewish attributes, that Manasseh Massey Lopes had demonstrated more than a century before.

Afterword

The case study comprising the focus of this study is unusual for three reasons. First, the separable dynasties whose fortunes are described here did not owe their origins to the inheritance of wealth, social standing or political position. They were in an important sense self-made. None were aristocratic; indeed, none could point to a lineage further back than a few generations. The key figures were all outsiders. As a result they lacked titles and influence and chose to generate them where possible. This is the creation of social mobility despite the prevailing rigid system rather than because of it. Certainly none started out poor and inheritance did play an important role in the middle period, inducing as it so frequently does, passivity and the diversions of pleasure seeking, but even this was not 'old money' but money recently minted elsewhere.

Second, they adopted all three of Weber's pathways to power at various times with one or other being predominant when prevailing conditions favoured it. The seventeenth and early eighteenth centuries were the mercantilist era when Britain struggled to maintain the financial rewards of a diverse empire while paying for vast forces to defend it. The Modyfords sought to exploit the opportunities that this era presented. The later eighteenth century, by contrast, appeared more stable, at least on the home front. While struggles with the Spanish, Dutch and French continued apace, this was an age of science and the arts, but gentility mattered, albeit sustained by the great awakening of religious conformity that lasted for more than a subsequent century. As always where morality appears unchallenged, religion offers only the carapace of conformity; beneath the surface a toxic brew of infidelity and intrigue bubbled, feeding the gossip of those with no serious work to divert them. The first 'age of celebrity' extended to buildings and certainly to contacts. The question addressed by the Heywood dynasty was how to position family members to take advantage of the potential for social esteem this offered. In the early nineteenth century political change was in the air as the old system crumbled in the face of newly emerging urban classes unprepared to accept exclusion from all decision-making. Rural life on long established estates felt very different, even as old fissures such as the Catholic question became even more central. The big issue for the landed gentry was how to make industrial society work for them by being able to control food prices in their favour and learning how to exploit growing demands for better transport links and the raw materials on which industrialisation depended. Politics became a serious business as new interests became enfranchised. The fortunes of the Lopes family showed one direction of travel, although not one without potholes along the way.

Despite all the diversity revealed in this story, the one great uniting influence was slavery and the trade that sustained it. All the families of Maristow House were West Indian either by birth, by adoption or by heritage. All may or may not have possessed African blood in their veins, but unfree African labour certainly coursed through their lives. It did not do so in the same way, however, because how each family was linked to the sugar plantations, in this case those of Jamaica, differed so markedly. There were, in other words, diverse *modes of engagement* with the world of plantation slavery from one dynasty to the next.

Modes of Engagement

Writing at a time in the late nineteenth century when transformation was in the air but before the conflagrations to come, historians and the emerging disciplines of the social sciences were trying to grasp how social and economic change occurred. Was it the result of periodic ruptures between those able to corner productive resources and those excluded from so doing? Alternatively, perhaps change was slower, more of an adaptive process analogous to Darwinian thinking from the natural world, but mediated by the human capacity for ideas, beliefs and ways of seeing that shaped how opportunities were explored and exploited. Max Weber's importance lay in appreciating that both were true and that the resultant complexities had to be addressed by a prior stage of classification. The types of power relationship were one such but human motivation cannot be reduced to this one dimension however important it may turn out to be.

The Caribbean encounter was characterised above all by a gulf of power between coloniser and colonised, and nowhere more so than in the case of slave owner and slave. Slavery clearly links one part of the globe with another and that link may be reflected in temporary or permanent transfers of people and property in either direction. This case study has focused on trying to unpick the relationship between one West Indian island and one country house in West Devon over time. At the outset, it was clear that commonalities existed, in the sense that all three families were concerned to use their West Indian connections gained by residence or birth to achieve greater wealth, social standing and influence. That they did so in different ways has been demonstrated. In fact, underlying these processes were different kinds of relationship between the metropolitan power and its emerging colony. Drawing back from the particulars, it is possible now to see more clearly what these patterns were, although it will take further research to assess fully their implications for either side. The first phase was motivated by a desire to expand trading horizons, even if this involved a temporary sojourn in the colonial environment to achieve the desired rewards. The second was a passive phase of never leaving the mother country but nonetheless, even as an absentee, managing to sustain productive capacity. The third phase was the diametric opposite of the first; equally activist but moving permanently from the colony to invest in the potential rewards of the colonial power. Couched in terms of Weber's 'ideal types' or one-sided accentuations that he proposed as an aid to comparison, we can see a distinctive set of characteristics associated with the 'sojourning', 'absenteeing' and 'investing' modes of encounter.

It is important to emphasise that this focus by no means includes all relationships between Britain and the West Indies, and some actors have been referred to whose experience cannot be captured by such a typology. For example, any school level history text book will tell students about the 'triangular trade' in which manufactured goods were shipped to West Africa, sold on and the proceeds used to buy slaves for transit to the West Indies, often under the most appalling conditions. Ships were then loaded with sugar, coffee or tobacco and sailed back to British ports. The Elton dynasty of Clevedon and Bristol, whose fortunes were forever linked to the Heywoods through Mary Elton, daughter of Abraham II, had an important role to play in the preceding story. They were not merely practitioners of the triangular trade; they very nearly invented it. Indeed, the Eltons were among the most active manufacturers, merchants, land owners and local dignitaries in the whole South-West. In her fine record of her family's fortunes, Margaret Elton wrote of the first Abraham,

> His profits from copper and brass, from wine wool and tobacco, from privateering and from making up shipments of those goods most attractive on the Gold Coast in return for slaves, and in Jamaica for sugar and rum, were ... enormous (1994: 38).

Although the family suffered many reverses (including the bankruptcy of Mary Heywood's brother) their encounter with Jamaica was certainly profitable but it was not a 'Caribbean encounter' as defined above. Although it is certainly true that members of the family owned plantations in Jamaica, they never lived there and would have as cheerfully traded slaves with, say, Virginia as with Jamaica. What made the family unusual was their ownership of important manufacturing capacity, particularly in brass wares and window glass, but as their property empire and local office holding underline, they were firmly based in Britain.

Sojourning

The Modyford brothers were typical of the seventeenth-century adventurers who went to make their fortune in the English-speaking

Caribbean. Starting in Barbados, where sugar was rapidly taking over from cacao cultivation, Thomas Modyford was the archetypal merchant opportunist but with the additional twist of a quick-witted realisation that more wealth could be harnessed by those who not merely owned plantations but who were also in a position to exploit trading links through being politically powerful. His younger brother was partially in his shadow but was even more dedicated to trade and less seduced by political office. Neither intended to stay longer than was necessary to accrue their desired fortunes, but both died in Jamaica. In that sense their mission was a failure, but financial success certainly came their way. Who is to say why they did not make it back to Britain? They both had ample opportunity and in Thomas' case he was forced back at His Majesty's pleasure, but the seductions of the tropics proved too strong and he, like James, returned to Jamaica. The attractions were more than making money. Despite the Restoration in 1660, puritan culture was widespread in the seventeenth century and it is possible that the appeal of rural Devon, largely on the losing side in the civil wars, was not as great as the opportunities for sexual exploitation and libidinous living in Port Royal. Yellow fever, the scourge of venereal disease and cirrhotic livers aside, lives may have been foreshortened but were perhaps more engaging, particularly for unaccompanied or single men.

If riches were to be extracted from enterprises overseas, someone had to build them. Jamaica in the seventeenth century was a frontier society where immense fortunes, like that of the Beckford family, could eventually be made. But it was also the cockpit of Europe where nothing could be achieved without the connivance of monarchs and parliaments. If planters simply went off on their own, where would their markets have been? Plantation society existed for the benefit of a wealthy few, but it was an intensely political project mainly because kings and courtiers expected their slice of the action. One moment piracy was condoned or encouraged; at another it was condemned and outlawed. Thomas and James Modyford understood all of that, but at great cost. Their progeny gained far more than they did, mainly because it was so easy to fall foul of powers elsewhere.

They lived no doubt licentious lives but had also to bear the neuroses of fickle masters.

The career of Peter Heywood also follows this pattern closely, even though his origins were different. He represented a new era but would not have known it. Like the Modyford brothers he died in Jamaica although, like them, would not have expected to do so. In his case the seductions of wealth generated by others but available through his wife's family sealed his fate. His son, a first generation West Indian, carried the torch back to England and attempted to apply his activist mentality to the rustic backwater that Maristow had become. There followed a disastrous period of family feuds, early deaths and internecine conflicts. Eventually, West Indian money oiled the way for a major transition to the next mode of engagement.

Absenteeism

Of the three types of encounter described here, this has been the one of most interest to previous authors. Perhaps the attraction is precisely its lack of authenticity as a strictly Caribbean encounter. In the variant considered here, its very passivity and preoccupation with consumption heightens still further the perception of exploitation in the use of slave labour. Wealth was accessed as and when needed but without the inconvenience of engaging first-hand. None of the Heywood family after their accession to the Maristow estate in 1751 ever went to Jamaica, yet their elaborate lifestyle, and the rebuilding of the house itself, depended intimately upon it. James Heywood senior was born in Jamaica and it was his retention of his estates, followed by his decision to relocate to Maristow in the early years of the eighteenth century, which established this instance of absenteeism. Early on, his was an activist stance based upon attempting to use his wealth to modernise the estate, but after the great fire of 1736 and his death soon after, these ambitions inevitably dissipated. This was a less than a happy period both early on when Creole perceptions clashed with old fashioned rigid rules of social hierarchy, and later when the estate was largely forgotten in favour of marrying off daughters to non-titled but wealthy squires wherever and whenever they could be found.

The extraction of wealth from the West Indies, and in particular from the forced labour of Africans kidnapped from their villages and torn from their kin, is not a new story. Neither was it unusual for the riches extracted from their labour to be funnelled into enhancing a privileged lifestyle of comparative ease back in the home country. Inevitably that is part of the story of Maristow House. In the eighteenth century, in particular, the lifestyle was one of fashionable amusements and distractions; the estate, just like the plantations of the New World, was out of sight and mind and run by others paid for that service. The Modyford Heywoods thought nothing of being away from the Devon countryside for months on end if the distractions of social intercourse in the salons of Bath or the Season's diversions in Belgravia called for their attention. It never occurred to them to visit Jamaica.

Although the Maristow example had very special properties it was by no means unique. William Thomas Beckford had a walk-on role in the story of Sophia Musters' early married life and later through the family of her long-term lover, but William Beckford senior is an excellent example of someone who, having cornered the Jamaican family's very considerable wealth, invested both his time and his money in the metropolis. In Perry Gauci's illuminating portrayal of his life (2013), we see someone determined to use this platform to launch a major political career in Britain. Beckford is seen by Gauci as an absentee and in one sense this is true. Born in 1709 in Jamaica as the second son of Peter Beckford, speaker of the Jamaican Legislative Assembly, he moved to Britain permanently in 1735 with the clear intention of making his mark on the political life of the metropolis. In this he was remarkably successful. He was returned to the Commons in December 1747 for Shaftesbury, but chose to sit for Dorset. He subsequently built a career in the City of London, mainly through his involvement with the Ironmongers' Company, becoming an alderman in 1752, sheriff in 1755–6 and lord mayor on two occasions (1762–3 and 1769–70). Throughout his colourful career in politics he steadfastly defended the West India planter interest and it is this, together with the huge investment of his fortune in property in London and Wiltshire, none of which he inherited, that makes it difficult to classify his engagement as that of an 'absentee'. He died in 1770 and left almost all his considerable wealth to his only legitimate son, William Thomas Beckford, for whom the classification as 'absentee' is wholly appropriate. William is not known to have ever visited Jamaica, from where his fortune derived, but was most certainly a gifted consumer of the wealth it generated.

It has to be said that William (1760–1844) was a truly extraordinary figure. His life inspires research and commentary to this day. The Beckford Society, for example, promotes the study of his multi-faceted life and works. He was a man with a profound knowledge of the decorative arts; he was a passionate collector, an art critic, travel writer and man of letters. He was an author, politician and someone for whom architectural imagination was given full rein in the application of his huge wealth to create astonishing buildings, most famously Fonthill Abbey in Wiltshire, featuring a tower of dizzying proportions and unstable foundations. A biography of published works on this remarkable man, published in 2006, runs to 6,000 references and the association mentioned above, one of several devoted to his works, publishes an academic journal and the society has sustained an annual lecture since 1996. The degree to which Creole preoccupations were present in him has been less researched than the extent of his absentee fortune.

Investing

The third mode of engagement reversed the first although there were some similarities. If the Modyfords saw their role as enabling plantations to come into being, so too did the Lopes family a century later. The early years were dominated by the need to allocate land and build a system for providing labour to work it. Sugar production is unlike most other agricultural enterprises because the product is not the cane but what can be extracted from it, in the same way that vineyards do more than grow grapes. In both cases they create a product from what they grow and that requires buildings, equipment and skilled techniques of production. It then has to be packaged, shipped and marketed. That requires investment capital, again opening a niche for Jewish financiers. While a few were indeed planters, most created money by lending it. They would have owned slaves for domestic work and they would have financed the importation of many thousands more and provided funds that enabled them to be bought and put to work. They cannot therefore be excused the stigma of slavery even though few would have personally engaged in sustaining the notorious violence that sustained it.

Like Beckford père, the Lopes dynasty was founded on a man born to experience a Jamaican childhood. Manasseh Lopes fits perfectly into the investor mould, using his resources to create a British dynasty that systematically shed its Caribbean heritage as quickly as it could, but he struggled with one special feature of it: namely its Semitic origins. He must have been unpleasantly surprised when on being taught by example from his British peers how to buy his way into the House of Commons, he ended up being thrown into jail and deprived of a significant part his fortune for following their precepts. This would have broken lesser men but one thing managed to keep him sane and that was an extraordinary commitment to his extended family. His investment path included attempting to achieve the life of an English country gentleman and in this he was successful, but his abiding achievement was to sustain his extended kin. Antisemitism in Jamaica and in Britain was turned on its head. Attempts to put him down simply strengthened his resolve, just as exclusion from other professions sharpened his brilliance as a financier. It is a Jewish story through and through, as is the determination to bring his wider family, be they Jewish or gentile, with him on this journey.

Manasseh Lopes was a hard act to follow and his nephew and heir did not excel. His late sister's grandchildren, however, showed a greater spark of aptitude but at the cost of ever recognising their roots. Massey Lopes and his siblings were orthodox Anglicans to the letter; they achieved the integrationist's dream of melding into the society around them, albeit without any perceptible recognition of either cultural strand that they brought to the table. The masonic lodge, the professional association or the political interest group was all that remained of their founding father's undoubted charisma.

As for the house itself, it stands today in its idyllic setting having so nearly followed its peers elsewhere by being torn down and used for building aggregate after the more saleable bits of craftsmanship were sent off to antique dealers and shippers to adorn the houses of the *nouveau riche*. But the house paid a price. Henry Lopes, who turned out to possess in full the virtues of a spirited contributor to the public good, was sufficiently deluded when young to believe that Gothic embellishments were an improvement on simple Georgian proportions. Much later still, after arsonists, vandals, the Church and city council had done their best to undermine the structure, the *coup de grâce* was the decision by the house's deservedly heralded saviour, Kit Martin, in favour of decapitation. Even now, with its absurdly tall stacks protruding from a flat roof unsupported by M Mansart's elegant design, it is still impressive.

References

Agnew, D.C. (1871) *Protestant Exiles from France in the Reign of Louis XIV: Or the Huguenot Refugees and their Descendants in Great Britain and Ireland*, Vol II, London and Edinburgh, Reeves and Turner.

Alexander, C. (2003) *The Bounty: True Story of the Mutiny on the Bounty*, London, Harper Perennial.

Allen, D. (1979) 'From George Monck to the Duke of Albemarle: His Contribution to Charles II's Government, 1660–1670' *Biography*, 2, 2: 95–124.

Amussen, S.D. (2007) *Caribbean Exchanges: Slavery and the Transformation of English Society, 1640–1700*, Chapel Hill, NC, University of North Carolina Press.

Andrade, J.A. (1941) *A Record of the Jews in Jamaica from the English Conquest to the Present Time*, Kingston, *Jamaica Times*.

Antunes, C. and Ribeiro da Silva, F. (2012) 'Amsterdam merchants in the slave trade and African commerce, 1580s–1670s', *Tijdschrift voor Sociale en Economische Geschiedenis* 9: 3–30.

Arbell, M (2000) *The Portuguese Jews of Jamaica*, Jamaica, Canoe Press.

Arbell, M. (2002) *The Jewish Nation of the Caribbean*, New York, Gefen Books.

Ashton, J. (1898) *The History of Gambling in England*, London, Duckworth and Co.

August, T.G. (1987) 'An Historical Profile of the Jewish Community of Jamaica', *Jewish Social Studies*, 49, 3–4: 303–316.

August, T. G. (1989) 'Family Structure and Jewish Continuity in Jamaica since 1655', *American Jewish Archives* 41: 27–42.

Austen, J. (2011) *Jane Austen's Letters* (ed D. Le Faye), Oxford, Oxford University Press.

Barbour, V. (1911) 'Privateers and Pirates of the West Indies', *American Historical Review*: 529–66.

Barczewski, S. (2014) *Country Houses and the British Empire, 1700–1930*, Studies in Imperialism, Manchester, Manchester University Press.

Baring-Gould, S. (1908) *Devonshire Characters and Strange Events*, London, John Lane.

Barnett, R.D. and Wright, P. (1997) *Jews of Jamaica: Tombstone Inscriptions 1663–1880*, Jerusalem, Ben Zvi Institute.

Barth, J. (2016) 'Reconstructing Mercantilism: Consensus and Conflict in British Imperial Economy in the Seventeenth and Eighteenth Centuries', *The William and Mary Quarterly* 73: 257–290.

Bateman, J. (1883) *The Great Landowners of Great Britain and Ireland*, 4th edition, London, Harrison.

Beaglehole, J.C. (1992) *The Life of Captain James Cook*, Stanford, Stanford University Press.

Belfield, G. (2014) 'Major-General George Dean-Pitt: from Plumber and Glazier to Knight of Hanover', *Journal of the Society for Army Historical Research* 92: 177–88.

Beckett, J. (2005) 'The Nottingham Reform Riots of 183', *Parliamentary History* 24 Supplement S1: 114–38.

Bennett, J.H. (1964) 'Carl Helyar, Merchant and Planter of Seventeenth-Century Jamaica', *William and Mary Quarterly* 21: 53–76.

Bigelow, B.M. (1931) 'Aaron Lopez: Colonial Merchant of Newport', *The New England Quarterly* IV (4): 757–76.

Binney, M. (2000) 'Maristow House', *Country Life*, 6 April: 112–15.

Bodian, M. (2014) 'The Formation of the Portuguese Jewish Diaspora' in Gerber, J.S. (ed) *The Jews in the Caribbean*, Portland, Littman Library of Jewish Civilization.

Borrow, G. (1825) *Celebrated Trials and Remarkable Cases of Criminal Jurisprudence from the earliest records to the year 1825*, London, Knight and Lacy.

Boyes, M. (1986) *Queen of a Fantastic Realm: Biography of Mary Chaworth*, Notts, self-published.

Boyes, M. (1987) 'Sophia Musters – friend of the Prince Regent', *Nottinghamshire Countryside*, Notts. Rural Community Council.

Bridenbaugh, C. and Bridenbaugh, R. (1972) *No Peace beyond the Line: The English in the Caribbean, 1624–1690*, New York, Oxford University Press.

Brockman, H.A.N. (1956) *The Caliph of Fonthill*, London, T. Werner Laurie.

Brooke, C. (2006) *The Rise and Fall of the Medieval Monastery*, London, Folio Society.

Brown, M. (1984) 'Anglo-Jewish Country Houses from the Resettlement to 1800', *Transactions of the Jewish Historical Society of England* 28: 20–38.

Brushfield T.N. (1883) 'Notes on the Ralegh Family', *Report and Transactions of the Devonshire Association* 15: 163–179.

Bryant, J. (2003) *Kenwood: Paintings in the Iveagh Bequest*, New Haven and London, Yale University Press.

Burke, B.A (1863) *Genealogical and Heraldic Dictionary of the Landed Gentry*.

Burke, J. (1833) *A General and Heraldic Dictionary of the Peerage and Baronetage of the British Empire*, London, Richard Bentley.

Burnard, T. (1996) 'European Migration to Jamaica, 1655–1780', *The William and Mary Quarterly*, 53: 769–96.

Butcher, E. (1805) *An Excursion from Sidmouth to Chester in the summer of 1803*, London, H.W. Symonds.

Cadbury, Henry J. (1959) 'Conditions in Jamaica in 1687', *Jamaican Historical Review* 3: 52–57.

Cahill, A. (1975) 'The Popular Movement for Parliamentary Reform, 1829–1832: Some Further Thoughts', *The Historian*, 37 (3): 436–52.

Chapman, G. (1952) (2nd edition; first published 1937) *Beckford*, London, Hart-Davies.

Chyet, Stanley F. (1970) *Lopez of Newport: Colonial American Merchant Prince*, Detroit, Wayne State University Press.

Claypole, William A. (1970) 'The merchants of Port Royal, 1655 to 1700' unpublished Ph.D. diss., University of the West Indies.

Cobbett, W. (1912) *Rural Rides*, London, J. M. Dent & Sons; Everyman's Library, reprinted 1924 and 1953, Penguin, 2001.

Cotton, W. (1856) ed John Burnet *Sir Joshua Reynolds and his works: gleanings from his diary, unpublished manuscripts, and from other sources*, London, Longman, Brown, Green, Longmans and Roberts.

Cotton, W. (1959) *Sir Joshua Reynolds Notes and Observations of Pictures*, London, John Russell Smith.

Cundall, F., N. Darnell Davis, and Albert M. Friedenberg (1915) 'Documents relating to the history of the Jews in Jamaica and Barbados in the time of William III', *Publications of the American Jewish Historical Society* 2 3: 25–29.

Dale, R. (2004) *The First Crash: Lessons from the South Sea Bubble*, New Jersey, Princeton University Press.

Dening, G. (1992) *Mr Bligh's Bad Language: Passion, Power and Theater on H.M. Armed Vessel Bounty*, Cambridge, Cambridge University Press.

Devine, T.M. (1978) 'An Eighteenth-Century Business élite: Glasgow-West India Merchants, c. 1750–1815', *The Scottish Historical Review* 57, 163, Part 1: 40–67.

Dick-Cleland, A. (1997) *Elton House History Album*, Maidenhead, the Landmark Trust.

Dresser, M. and A. Hann (eds) (2013) *Slavery and the British Country House*, Swindon, English Heritage.

Dunn, Richard S. (1972) *Sugar and Slaves: The Rise of the Planter Class in the English West Indies*, 1624–1713, New York, W.W. Norton.

Ebner, A (2002) 'The First Jewish Magistrates', *Jewish Historical Studies* 38: 45–73.

Egerton, J. (2007) *George Stubbs, Painter*, New Haven and London, Yale University Press.

Elton, M (1974) *Annals of the Elton Family: Bristol Merchants and Somerset Landowners*, Stroud, Allan Sutton Publishing.

Emden, P.H. (1935–39) 'The Brothers Goldsmid and the Financing of the Napoleonic Wars', *Transactions of the Jewish Historical Society of England* 14: 225–46.

Endelman, T.M. (1982–83) 'The Checkered Career of "Jew" King: A Study in Anglo-Jewish Social History', *Association for Jewish Studies Review*, 7/8: 69–100.

Endelman, T.M. (2015) *Leaving the Jewish Fold: Conversion and Radical Assimilation in Modern Jewish History*, New Jersey, Princeton University Press.

Escott, T.H.S. (1897) *Social Transformations of the Victorian Age*, London, Seeley and Co.

Ezratty, H.A. (1997) *500 Years in the Jewish Caribbean*, Baltimore, Omni Arts.

Faber, E. (1998) *Jews, Slaves and the Slave Trade: Setting the Record Straight*, New York and London, New York University Press.

Farrell, S., M. Unwin, and J. Walvin, (eds) (2007) *The British Slave Trade: Abolition, Parliament and People*, Edinburgh, Edinburgh University Press.

Fitzgerald, P. (1881) *The Life of George the Fourth including his Letters and Opinions with a View of the Men, Manners and Politics of his Reign*, Vol I, London, Tinsley Brothers.

Fizzard, A.D. (2002) 'Lay Benefactors of Plympton Priory in the Twelfth Century', *Transactions of the Devonshire Association* 134: 35–56.

Fizzard, A.D. (2007) *Plympton Priory: A House of Augustinian Canons in South-Western England*, Leiden, Brill.

Fortune. S.A. (1984) *Merchants and Jews: The Struggle for British West Indian Commerce, 1660–1750*, Gainesville, University Presses of Florida.

Franks, H. (2013 Original 1879) 'The Waste of Intellect as Exhibited by the Jews', *Papers of the Manchester Literary Club*, Vol. 5, London, Forgotten Books: 149.

Friedenwald, H. (1897) 'Material for the History of the Jews in the British West Indies', *Publications of the American Jewish Historical Society* 5: 45–101.

Friedman, S.S. (1998) *Jews and the American Slave Trade*, New Brunswick, Transaction Publishers.

Gardner, W.J. (1971) (1873) *A History of Jamaica from Its Discovery by Christopher Columbus to the Year 1872*, London, Cass.

Gaster, M. (1901) *History of the Ancient Synagogue of the Spanish and Portuguese Jews: the Cathedral Synagogue of the Jews in England Situate in Bevis Marks*, London.

Gauci, P. (2013) *William Beckford: First Prime Minister of the London Empire*, New Haven and London, Yale University Press.

Gaunt, R.A. (2014) *Sir Robert Peel: The Life and Legacy*, London, I.B. Taurus.

Gerber, J.S. (ed) (2014) *The Jews in the Caribbean*, Portland, Littman Library of Jewish Civilization.

Gilmour, R. (1983) 'Fletcher Christian's Last Days', I*sle of Man Family History Society Journal* 8 (2): 55–6.

Goldish, J.C. (2009) *Once Jews: Stories of the Caribbean Sephardim*, Princeton, Marcus Wiener.

Grainger, Hilary Joyce (1985) *The Architecture of Sir Ernest George and his partners, c. 1860–1922*, unpublished PhD thesis, University of Leeds.

Grimes, B. (2009) 'Funding a Roman Catholic Church in Nineteenth Century Ireland', *Architectural History* 52 147–68.

Guiseppi, J.A. (1955–59) 'Sephardi Jews and the early years of the Bank of England', *Transaction of the Jewish Historical Society of England* 19: 53–63.

Gutstein, M.A. (1939) *Aaron Lopez and Judah Touro: A Refugee and a Son of a Refugee*. New York: Behrman's Jewish Book House.

Habakkuk, H.J. (1950) 'Marriage Settlements in the Eighteenth Century', *Transactions of the Royal Historical Society* 32: 15–30.

Hamilton Jenkin, A.K. (1974) *Mines of Devon Volume 1: The Southern Area*, Newton Abbot, David and Charles

Hancock, D. (1995) *Citizens of the World: London Merchants and the Integration of the British Atlantic Community, 1735–1785*, Cambridge, Cambridge University Press.

Hanna, M. (2017) *Pirate Nests and the Rise of the British Empire, 1570–1740*, Chapel Hill, University of North Carolina Press.

Hartwell, R.M. (1981) 'Taxation in England during the Industrial Revolution', *Cato Journal* 1: 129–53.

Haynes, C. (2016) 'Remembering and Forgetting the First Modern Occupations of France', *Journal of Modern History* 88: 535–71.

Holzberg, C. (1987) *Minorities and Power in a Black Society: The Jewish Community of Jamaica*, Maryland, North-South Publishing Company.

Hoskins, W.G. and H.P.R. Finberg (1952) *Devonshire Studies* London, Cape.

Hunter, D. (2018) 'The Beckfords in England and Italy: a case study in the musical uses of the profits of slavery', *Early Music*, 46 (2): 285–98.

Hurd, D. (2017) *Robert Peel: A Biography*, London, Weidenfeld and Nicolson.

Hurwitz, S.J., and Edith Hurwitz (1965) 'The New World sets an example for the Old: The Jews of Jamaica and political rights, 1661–1831', *American Jewish Historical Quarterly* 55: 37–56.

Jaggard, E. (1999) *Cornwall Politics in the Age of Reform, 1790–1885*, Royal Historical Society, Suffolk, Boydell Press.

Jeffery, R.W. (ed) (1907) *Dyott's Diary, 1781–1845: A Selection from the Journal of William Dyott, Sometime General in the British Army and Aide de Camp to his Majesty King George III*, vol. 1, London, Archibald, Constable and Co.

Johnson, P. (1987) *A History of the Jews*, London, Weidenfeld and Nicholson.

Jones, R.E. (1980) 'Further Evidence on the Decline in Infant Mortality in Pre-industrial England: North Shropshire, 1561–1810', *Population Studies* 34: 239–50.

Jones, W. (1887) 'The Slannings of Leye, Bickleigh and Maristow', *Report and Transactions*, Devonshire Association for the Advancement of Science, Literature, and Art 19: 451–466

Joseph, A.P. (1975) 'Jewry of South-West England and some of its Australian Connections', *Transactions of the Jewish Historical Society of England* 24: 24–37.

Judah, G.F. (1909) 'Portions of a History of the Jews of Jamaica', *American Jewish Archives*, Cincinnati.

Kagan, R.L. and Philip D. Morgan (eds) (2009) *Atlantic Diasporas: Jews, Conversos, and Crypto-Jews in the Age of Mercantilism, 1500–1800*, Baltimore, Johns Hopkins University Press.

Kayserling, M. (1900) *The Jews in Jamaica and Daniel Lopez Laguna*, Publications of the American Jewish Historical Society, 12.

Kaplan, Yosef. 2000 *An Alternative Path to Modernity: The Sephardi Diaspora in Western Europe*, Leiden, Brill.

Kohler, M.J. (1894) 'Phases of Jewish Life in New York before 1800', *American Jewish Historical Quarterly* 2: 85–9.

Kohler, M.J. (1902) 'Jewish activity in American Colonial Commerce', *Publications of the American Jewish Historical Society*, 10: 47–64.

Landry, D. (2008) 'William Beckford's *Vathek* and the uses of Oriental re-enactment', in Makdisi, S. and F. Nussbaum, (eds) *The Arabian Nights in Historical Context: Between East and West*, Oxford, Oxford University Press.

Langford, V O. (1910–19) *Caribbeana being miscellaneous papers relating to the history, genealogy, topography, and antiquities of the British West Indies* (6 vols., London, Mitchell, Hughes and Clarke.

Lart, C.E. (1924) *Hugenot Pedigrees*, vol.1, London, Clearfield.

Le Faye, D. (2006) *A Chronology of Jane Austen and Her Family: 1700–2000*, Cambridge, Cambridge University Press.

Liedtke, W. (1989) *The Royal Horse and Rider: Painting, Sculpture, and Horsemanship1500–1800*, New York, Abaris.

Ligon, R. (1657) *True and Exact History of the Island of Barbados*.

Machin, G.I.T. (1963) 'The No-Popery Movement in Britain in 1828–9', *The Historical Journal*, 6 (2): 193–211.

McKay, W. and W. Roberts (1909) *The Works of John Hoppner R.A.*, London, P. & D. Colnaghi & co and George Bell & sons.,

Malthus, T.R. (1863; first published 1798) *An Essay on the Principle of Population, as it affects the Future Improvement of Society, with remarks on the Speculations of Mr Godwin, M. Condorcet, and Other Writers*, London, J. Johnson.

Manning D. and M. Postle (2000) *Sir Joshua Reynolds: A Complete Catalogue of His Paintings*, New Haven, Yale University Press.

Marcus, J.R. (1970) *The Colonial American Jew, 1492–1776: Volume I, II, and III*. Detroit, Wayne State University Press.

Maxton, D.A. and Du Rietz, R.E. (eds) (2013) *Innocent on the Bounty: The Court Martial and Pardon of Midshipman Peter Heywood, in Letters* North Carolina and London, McFarland and Co.

Melbourne, E.M.L. (1998) *Byron's 'Corbeau Blanc': The Life and Letters of Lady Melbourne*, Texas, A&M University Press.

Merrill, G. (1964) 'Role of Sephardic Jews in the British Caribbean Area during the 17th Century', *Caribbean Studies* 4, 3: 32–49.

Meyers, A.D. (1998) 'Ethnic Distinctions and Wealth among Colonial Jamaican Merchants, 1685–1716', *Social Science History*, 22: 47–81.

Millar, O. (1986) 'George IV when Prince of Wales: His Debts to Artists and Craftsmen', *Burlington Magazine* 128, 1001: 586–92.

Mintz, S.W. (1985) *Sweetness and Power: The Place of Sugar in Modern History*. New York: Viking.

Mirvis, S. (2013) 'Sephardic Family Life in the Eighteenth-Century British West Indies' Unpublished PhD dissertation, The Graduate Center of the City University of New York.

Mirvis, S. (2015) 'The Alvares Family Patriarchs and the Place of Pre-1692 Port Royal in the Western Sephardic Diaspora', *The American Jewish Archives Journal* 67: 1–46.

Mirvis, S. (2020) *The Jews of Eighteenth-Century Jamaica: A Testamentary History of a Diaspora in Transition*, New Haven and London, Yale University Press.

Monypenny, W.F. and G.E. Buckle (1920) *Life of Benjamin Disraeli*, vol. V, New York, Macmillan.

Morgan, K. (2007) *Slavery and the British Empire: From Africa to America*, Oxford, Oxford University Press.

Newman, B.N. (2018) *A Dark Inheritance: Blood, Race and Sex in Colonial Jamaica*, New Haven and London, Yale University Press.

Oldfield, T.H.B. (1792) *An Entire and Complete History, political and personal of the Boroughs of Great Britain; together with the Cinque Ports*, London, G. Riley.

Oliver, G. (1846) *Monasticum Diocesis Exoniensis*, Exeter, P.A. Hannaford.

Oostindie, G. and J.V. Roitman, (eds) (2014) *Dutch Atlantic Connections 1680–1800: Linking Empires, Bridging Border*, Leiden, Brill.

Parker, M (2012) *The Sugar Barons*, London, Windmill Books.

Pawson, M. and David Buisseret (1975) *Port Royal, Jamaica*. Oxford: Clarendon Press.

Peel, Robert (1856) *Memoirs by the Right Honourable Sir Robert Peel, Part I, The Roman Catholic Question 1828–9*, London, John Murray.

Pell, A. (1908) *The Reminiscences of Albert Pell sometime M.P. for South Leicestershire*, London, John Murray.

Penson, L.M. (1924) *The Colonial Agents of the British West Indies: a Study in Colonial Administration, mainly in the Eighteenth Century*, London, University of London Press.

Picciotto, J. (1875) *Sketches of Anglo-Jewish History*, London, Thübner and Co.

Platt, V.B. (1975) '"And Don't forget the Guinea Voyage": The Slave Trade of Aaron Lopez of Newport', *William and Mary Quarterly* 32: 601–18.

Polwhele, R. (1797) *History of Devonshire*, London, Cadell, Johnson, and Dilley.

Postle, M. (2005) *Joshua Reynolds: The Creation of Celebrity*, London, Tate Gallery.

Radford, G. H. (1895) 'Sydenham House in the parish of Maristow' *Transactions of the Devonshire Association* 27: 358–61.

Redding, C. (1858) *Fifty Years' Recollections, Literary and Personal, with observations on Men and Things*, London, C.J. Skeet.

Roth, C. (1932) *A History of the Marranos*, Philadelphia, The Jewish Publication Society of America.

Roth, C. (1941) *A History of the Jews in England*, Oxford, Oxford University Press.

Rubens, A. (1960) 'Portrait of Anglo-Jewry 1656–1836', *Transactions and Miscellanies* 19, Jewish Historical Society of England.

Rubens, A. (1969–70) 'Anglo-Jewry in Caricature 1780–1850', *Transactions & Miscellanies*, Jewish Historical Society of England 23: 96–101.

Rubinstein, W.D., M. Jolles H.L. and Rubinstein, (2011) *Palgrave Dictionary of Anglo–Jewish History*, Basingstoke, Palgrave Macmillan.

Samuel, E. (1992) 'The Portuguese Jewish Community of London', in the catalogue of the Exhibition of 1992, Jewish Museum, London.

Schappes, M.U. (1976) [1950] 'Merchant in Exile'. In M.U. Schappes (ed) *A Documentary History of the Jews of the United States 1654–1875*, New York, Schocken Books.

Schlesinger, B. (1967) 'The Jews of Jamaica: A historical view', *Caribbean Quarterly* 1 3:4 6–53.

Scott, B. (1997) 'The Rural Manor in South-West Devon in the Nineteenth Century', *Transaction of the Devonshire Association*, 129: 129–43.

Scott, W.R. (1912) *The Constitution and Finance of English, Scottish and Irish Joint-Stock Companies to 1720*, vol II Companies for Foreign Trade, Colonization, Fishing and Mining, Cambridge University Press:17–24.

Seymour, E. (1906) *The 'Pope' of Holland House; selections from the Correspondence of John Whishaw and his Friends, 1813–40*, London, T. Fisher Unwin.

Sheridan, R.B (1965) 'The wealth of Jamaica in the eighteenth century', *Economic History Review* 18: 292–311.

Sloman, S. (1997) 'Sitting to Gainsborough at Bath in 1760', *The Burlington Magazine*, 139, No. 1130: 325–8.

Sloman, S. (2002) *Gainsborough in Bath*, New Haven, Yale University Press.

Smith, A.E. (1934) 'The Transportation of Convicts to the American Colonies in the Seventeenth Century', *American Historical Review* 39, 2: 232–49.

Smith, E.A. (1999) *George IV*, New Haven, Yale University Press.

Snyder, H. (2006) 'Rules, Rights and Redemption: The Negotiation of Jewish Status in British Atlantic Port Towns, 1740–1831', *Jewish History*, 20:2: 147–70.

Sombart, W. (1951; reprinted 1982 and 2009) *The Jews and Modern Capitalism*, New Brunswick, Transaction Publishers.

Soyer, F. (2011) *The Persecution of the Jews and Muslims of Portugal*, Leiden, Brill.

Stuart, A. (2012) *Sugar in the Blood: A Family's Story of Slavery and Empire*, London, Portobello Books.

Summerson, J. (1959) 'The Classical Country House in 18th Century England', *Journal of the Royal Society of Arts*, 107: 539–87.

Tagart, E. (1832) *A Memoir of the Late Peter Heywood, R.N. with extracts from His Diaries and Correspondence*, London, Effingham Wilson.

Taylor, B. (1971) *Stubbs*, London, Phaidon Press.

Tewari, A. (2013) 'The Reform Bill (1832) and the Abolition of Slavery (1833): A Caribbean Link', *Proceedings of the Indian History Congress*, 73: 1140–47.

Thomas, H. (1985) *The Slave Trade: The Story of the Atlantic Slave Trade 1440–1870*, New York: Simon & Schuster.

Thomson, T. (1870) *A Biographical Dictionary of Eminent Scotsmen*, vol 3, London, Blackie and Son.

Thornton, A.P. (1955) *West India Policy under the Restoration*, Oxford, Oxford University Press.

Trivellato, F. (2009) *The Sephardic Diaspora and Cross-Cultural Trade in the Seventeenth and Eighteenth Centuries*, New Haven, Yale University Press.

Trivellato, F. (2012) *The Familiarity of Strangers: The Sephardic Diaspora, Livorno, and Cross-cultural Trade in the Early Modern Period* New Haven, Yale University Press.

Uglow, J. (2015) *In These Times: Living in Britain through Napoleon's Wars, 1793–1815*, London, Faber and Faber.

Wakeham, C. (2003) 'Maristow Estate Farmhouses 1800–1913: A Chronological Development', *Transactions of Devonshire Association for the Advancement of Science* 135: 111–72.

Walpole, H. (1910) *The last journals of Horace Walpole during the reign of George III, from 1771–1783*, with notes by Dr. Doran, London, J. Lane.

Waterhouse, E.K. (1953) 'Preliminary Checklist of Portraits by Thomas Gainsborough', *The Volume of the Walpole Society 1948–1950*, 33.

Waterhouse, E.K. (1958) *Gainsborough*, London, Spring Books.

Waterhouse, E.K. (1966–68) 'Reynolds' Sitter Book for 1775', *Walpole Society* 41: 165–67.

Watt-Carter, D.E. (1987) *Flete: a Historical Review*, London, Country Houses Association.

Watts (1987) *The West Indies: Patterns of Development, Culture and Environmental Change since 1492*, Cambridge, Cambridge University Press.

Williams, C.A. (ed) (2013) *Bridging the Early Modern Atlantic World: People, Products, and Practices on the Move*, London, Routledge.

Williamson, J. (1987), 'Debating the British Industrial Revolution', *Explorations in Economic History*, 24(3): 269–92.

Wilson, R.G. and A.L. Mackley (1999) 'How Much did the English Country House Cost to Build, 1660–1880?' *Economic History Review*, New Series, 52: 436–68.

Wolffe, M. (2004) 'Slanning, Sir Nicholas (1606–1643)', *Oxford Dictionary of National Biography*, Oxford University Press (online edn, Jan 2008 [http://www.oxforddnb.com/view/article/25714, accessed 14 March 2013]).

Worth, R.N. (1873) *A History of Devonshire, With Sketches of Leading Worthies*, London, Elliot Stock.

Worthy, C. (1887) *Devonshire Parishes or the Antiquities, Heraldry and Family History of the Twenty-Eight Parishes in the Archdeaconry of Totnes* (2 vols), London, George Redway.

Yogev, G. (1978) *Diamonds and Coral: Anglo-Dutch Jews and Eighteenth-century Trade*, Leicester, Leicester University Press.

Zahedieh, N. (1986a) 'The merchants of Port Royal, Jamaica, and the Spanish contraband trade, 1655–1692', *William and Mary Quarterly* 43: 570–93.

Zahedieh, N. (1986b) 'Trade, plunder, and economic development in early English Jamaica, 1655–1689', *Economic History Review*, 2nd series 39: 205–22.

Zahedieh, N. (2010) *Capital and the Colonies: London and the Atlantic Economy 1660–1700*, Cambridge, Cambridge University Press.

Zook, G.F. (1919) *The Company of Royal Adventurers Trading into Africa* PhD thesis, Cornell University (reprinted from the *Journal of Negro History* 4: 2, 1919).

List of Abbreviations

BM Add. - MS British Museum Additional Manuscripts

Bodleian – Bodleian Library, University of Oxford

CSP - Calendar of State Papers

DHC - Devon Heritage Centre

DNB - Oxford Dictionary of National Biography

NRO - Norfolk Record Office

LA - Linconshire Archive

Prob - Probate Office at Canterbury

PWDRO - Plymouth and West Devon Records Office

SRO - Somerset Records Office

TNA - The National Archives

WAM - Westminster Abbey Muniments

WSA – West Sussex Archives

Index